'Much more than a serial seducer, Casanova w~~ ~~eat European intellectual, a roman~~~~ of tremendous skill and energ~~~~ be the first to admit, the mo~~~~d, as this vivid and vibrant b~~~~ ~s Biography of the Year 2008

'In Ian Kelly [Casanova] has at last found his Boswell . . . An unexpected pleasure is the book's focus on food . . . a great blast of a book, packed with energy and information, marinated in sympathy and understanding, and rippling with enthusiasm right down to the final footnote.' *Sunday Telegraph*

'Superlative . . . a thoughtful, absorbing and hugely diverting book. Lushly illustrated, carefully researched and intelligently argued, this biography will entertain and enlighten.' *Daily Mail*

'Like Casanova, Mr. Kelly is something of a polymath, and his professional activities make him an apt guide to his subject. He is an actor . . . and the author convincingly represents Casanova's comic audacity, charm and brazen trickery as a *commedia dell'arte* played out on the stage of eighteenth century Europe . . . in this eloquent biography.' *Wall Street Journal*

'It becomes unimaginable that you would not buy this book . . . Like Kelly's previous biography of George "Beau" Brummell, *Casanova* is a treasure-house of life . . . the effect is as though we had gone around the back after the show. Here is Casanova himself, without the make-up and the trick lighting, talking through Kelly's subtle reticent voice . . . emerging, scaling the leads, opening the bedroom window, moving closer, smiling. It is Casanova. He's alive. He's alive!' *New Statesman*

'Kelly brilliantly communicates Venice's cultural importance and fashionability during Casanova's time.' *Mail on Sunday*

'Kelly's style is delightful . . . a great achievement, the fruit of meticulous and wide-ranging research.' *Irish Tribune*

'Kelly has a fine way with libertines and dandies . . . he approaches his subject with a healthy appetite for food and sex and provides a fresh angle on Casanova as a gastronome . . . as Kelly writes, Casanova's story asks us all "to live a little more fully."' *Independent*

'Kelly halts the action and talks directly to the audience about Casanova and travel, sex and, most interestingly, food . . . it is entirely to Kelly's credit specifically, his ability to re-imagine life on the hoof in eighteenth century Europe as a series of exhilarating mini-dramas that he has managed to make this story feel so fresh again.' *Guardian*

'He explores how Casanova revolutionised the way people view themselves as sexual and social creatures, and argues that he created "a modern sensibility of what it is to be a fully rounded man, alive to failures, fears and foibles, and very much attuned to a sexual motive force".' *Mail on Sunday*

'Enjoyable, illuminating, Kelly has written an adult book, or I should say one for grown-ups. There are no rippings of corsets here or purple passages (although there are salacious incidents) . . . He [Casanova] continues to seduce because he brought more to sex and sex writing, than the mere act; Ian Kelly captures this aspect of Casanova perfectly.' *Spectator*

'Incredibly impressive in every way and endlessly entertaining.' Clive Anderson

'Lots of sex then, but lots of everything else, too . . . crowded with incident. Rather than the shallow seducer of popular imagining, Casanova's appeal is as a man flawed, humorous, engagingly self-deprecating whose vast appetite for life still acts as a tonic on those who come to know him. Kelly conveys all this admirably, and his book makes an excellent introduction to a complex and surprisingly modern life.' *Financial Times*

'Captivating . . . in Kelly's hands the story makes for a thrilling read.' *Sunday Times*

'A moving testament . . . to the sheer power of the written word.' *New York Times*

Ian Kelly

Ian Kelly is an actor and TV presenter as well as the author of three internationally acclaimed biographies. His first, *Cooking for Kings* – the life of Antonin Carême, the first celebrity chef – became a New York stage play; his second *Beau Brummell*, was adapted by the BBC as a TV film and short listed for the Marsh Commonwealth Biography Prize. *Casanova* is his third book. He writes for various UK and US papers and periodicals on food and travel. He lives in London.

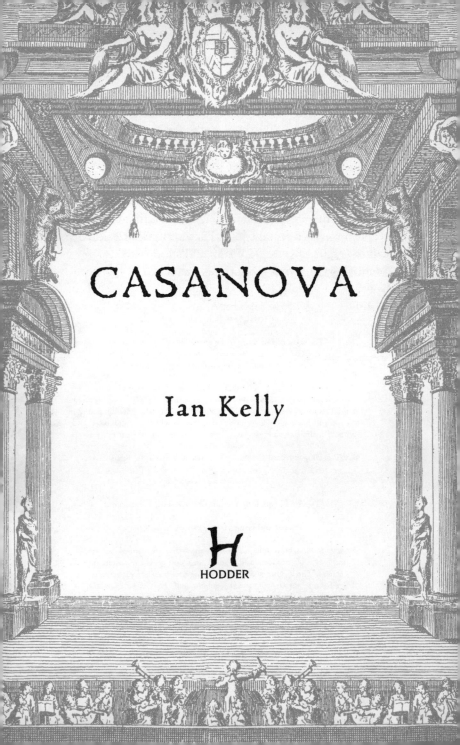

CASANOVA

Ian Kelly

HODDER

First published in Great Britain in 2008 by Hodder & Stoughton
An Hachette UK company

First published in paperback in 2009

1

Copyright © Ian Kelly 2008

The right of Ian Kelly to be identified as the Author of
the Work has been asserted by him in accordance with
the Copyright, Designs and Patents Act 1998.

A CIP catalogue record for this title is available from the British Library

ISBN 978 0 340 92215 6

Typeset in Sabon by Hewer Text UK Ltd, Edinburgh

Printed and bound by Clays Ltd, St Ives plc

Hodder & Stoughton policy is to use papers that are natural, renewable
and recyclable products and made from wood grown in sustainable
forests. The logging and manufacturing processes are expected to
conform to the environmental regulations of the country of origin.

Hodder & Stoughton Ltd
338 Euston Road
London NW1 3BH

www.hodder.co.uk

For C. K.

CONTENTS

CONTENTS

'One life is a world entire in miniature'

The cabbala of Rabbi Nathan
SECOND CENTURY AD

PRELUDE
the TEATRO DEL MUNDO

'In the first minute of my dream I see visions of dancing bodies, the form of which is all too familiar to me, illuminated in a mass of dazzling lights'

Casanova, dream-notes, 1791

12 September, 1791: gridlock on Prague's Rytířská and Harvířská streets. Horses jitter at the flares and fireworks. Food, being ferried in tumbrels from Příkopy monastery for the coronation ball, is escorted by troops in the face of a hungry crowd. And a sixty-six-year-old Venetian steps stiffly from his employer's coach into the lights of the Nostitz Theatre portico.

Only days earlier he had attended there the première of Mozart's new work, composed in honour of the newly crowned emperor. But *La Clemenza di Tito* had not pleased Giacomo Casanova any more than the royal party for whom it was written – the young empress had scoffed that Herr Mozart had written a '*porcheria tedesca*', a 'trashy German hotdog' of an opera. Casanova had preferred *Don Giovanni*. He had collaborated on the libretto and attended the première in the same theatre. '*Seen* it?' he was said to have responded to his old friend the Venetian librettist da Ponte. 'I've practically *lived* it.'

A transformation had taken place at the theatre since the opera première. As Casanova passed through to the parterre at the back of the Nostitz stalls, a view opened up to him straight out

1

of his Venetian childhood. Beyond the proscenium arch where just a week earlier there had been a stage, beyond the risen curtain, where Don Giovanni's history of conquests had first been catalogued, there was a cloth-decked stage set: a two-hundred-foot-long atrium built for the coronation ball that would take place that night. It stretched back beyond the orchestra pit, beyond the theatre's loading-dock and beyond even the rear wall of the stage-house, demolished by Prague's imperial professor of engineering so that the corridor ballroom might stretch beyond the disappearing-point of stage perspectives as if into infinity. Draped in eight thousand ells of Bohemian red linen, the stage-ballroom was filled with the entire Habsburg court, dancing to the music of Antonio Salieri's imperial orchestra cramped into the theatre boxes. The scene was reflected in a double phalanx of Venetian mirrors, the drapery and gold threads, the chandeliers and fake marbling, the *trompe l'œil* cornices and skies: a world entire – beyond art or reason – for one night only, riven in plaster and cloth, disappearing through the proscenium.

That night in 1791 at the Nostitz marked the end of an era. France was gripped by revolution and her queen, the new emperor's sister, was in prison. For many of the six thousand aristocrats on stage at the Nostitz under Giovanni Tartini's painted skies it would be the last dance of the world they had known – their final play-act at Venetian carnival – the last of many masquerades.

As a child, Casanova had seen similar spectacles. Every year in Venice at the Feast of the Ascension – when the doge ceremonially married the Venetian Republic to the sea and the whole city gave itself over to carnival – Venetians expected to enjoy their *teatri del mundo*, 'theatres of the world'. There were two types. One was a floating stage, owned by the Republic, that was moored off the Piazzetta San Marco and used for state-sponsored spectacles: grandiloquent enactments of mythical tales and celestial fables featuring gorgeously costumed aristocrats and fireworks. There were also, however, little street magic-lantern shows in the Piazza San Marco nearby: glimpses from the dark into a world both sublime and ridiculed, illuminations of rhinoceroses, freaks, 'Americans' and 'amorous views', re-created in the light of lantern-boxes for a brave new world of voyeuristic consumers. For this reason these little *teatri del mundo* were also known as *mondi nuovi* – new worlds. To judge from jottings Casanova made about his dreams, discovered in the Prague archive that now houses his unsorted notes (an inestimably exciting find for a biographer), Casanova's mind turned to these *teatri* after that night in 1791, and he dreamed of the Nostitz in surreal visions of naked dancing flesh; 'eyeballs and noses, the genitals of both sexes and other body parts the forms of which are all too familiar to me'. The century's great chronicler stood as witness finally to this last dance: the Habsburg court creating its own *teatro del mundo* in the form of cavorting human bodies, dazzled in theatre lights, mirrored in glass, dancing on stage sets.

From Prague Casanova returned to his desk at the library where he worked in a cold castle in Bohemia. His dreams were filled with disturbed memories, but his days were spent on a more structured narrative, one he would never see published: a record of the people and places, the smells and tastes, the sex and sensibility of the century before revolution. Casanova's eighteenth century had been in many senses a *teatro del mundo* itself – a world in thrall to the theatre. Shaped and mirrored in its lights and literature, revelling in theatrical artifice, Casanova's life – from his dream-notes and memoirs – was structured by this idea of performance, schooled as he was in the shifting, reflective perspectives of Venice and its *commedia del arte*. Born in Venice, then a theatre capital, into a family of actors, he had travelled his whole life and all over Europe in the long tradition of Venetian masqueraders. More than that, his success in life and love, as libertine and libertarian, had been bought by his ability to reinvent himself, play every card to his advantage and live entirely for a dazzling present. The irony would not have been lost on him that night in 1791 – able to feel alive only through memories and his writing – that his world seemed to understand most keenly the joys of living when faced with the drama of its artificial re-creation. His masterwork, *The History of My Life*, brings alive the century he lived in like no other document, but the singularly actorly joy with which he wrought his life remains also a testament to a new understanding of self. As every Venetian knows, there are masks, and there is substance behind the mask, and a revolutionary new dawn looked to understand personality with reference to both.

INTRODUZIONE
the OPERA BUFFA Called Venice

'Casanova's memoirs form the most complete picture of . . . the
century preceding the French Revolution [and] a mirror of life –
the innermost secrets of the life of man and an era'

F. W. Barthold, in 1846

Casanova would be bemused to discover that he is remembered
today almost exclusively for his sex life. He was a fiercely
proud intellectual and polymath, who worked at different
times as a violinist, soldier, alchemist, faith-healer and even
librarian, and originally trained to be a priest. Most of his life
was spent far from his native Venice, engaged at multiple
careers from Paris to St Petersburg, London to Prague to
Dresden, Amsterdam, Vienna and even Istanbul. He made
and lost a couple of fortunes, founded a state lottery, wrote
forty-two books, along with plays, philosophical and mathematical treatises, opera libretti, poetry and works on calendars,
canon law and cubic geometry. He translated Homer's *Iliad*
into modern Italian, helped introduced the oratorio into French
music, was a noted gourmet and practitioner of the cabbala
and wrote a five-volume science-fiction novel. Yet when he
died in 1798 the event was sufficiently unremarked for the site
of his burial to be soon forgotten. His international fame is
posthumous and is attributable to one work: his *Histoire de
ma vie* (*The History of My Life*), which lay unpublished in any
form for a generation after his death, and has not been
available in its entirety until recent years.

5

Casanova bequeathed to the world an unsurpassed record of living: 3800 folio pages covering his life from 1725 to 1774. He never wrote about the rest. Some days he meant to publish, on others to burn it all, every day to laugh at his past, and to travel, once he could barely walk, into the recesses of memory and an understanding of self. Himself. There is nothing quite like it of its period, and little to compare in the long history of lives. He wrote sometimes for thirteen hours a day, mainly from memory, but also from letters and notes he had kept intermittently and left around Europe with friends and lovers but now called in. He wrote to save his soul, or so he claimed, but it was a word he used as often as not to name his essential sexual self and even his penis. He died aged seventy-three in the expectation of an afterlife for a more orthodox concept of soul than that, however, and on another occasion he had said that he was writing to save his mind. It was an arrestingly modern idea. His doctor had suggested it as a cure for an old man's melancholia: 'the only remedy to keep [me] from going mad or dying from grief'. He wrote in a cold Palladian castle in Bohemia, far from his homeland and with few friends nearby, despised by the servants, a relic of a past age and the butt of jokes to many in the little town of Dux where he worked, notionally, as a librarian. And he wrote in French.

For a writer and historian Casanova is troubling. He lived most of his life for the impenitent pleasure of the moment, without reflection or forethought. He didn't write about most of it until old age cursed him with ill-health, penury and prolixity. He had been an artist of the immediate with a singular talent for happiness, which was part of what people found attractive in him. People fell for Giacomo Casanova, people who could offer him preferment, money or good times, complicity of soul, the delights of the table, or the simple clock-stopping, heart-burning, tumescent pleasures of the flesh. His life and his *History* of it, therefore, are not the usual stuff of history. They challenge us because *The History of My Life* begs us to live a little more fully, or at least more bravely, ourselves. It also challenges the historian because, though laced with the charm of the man himself, it is riddled with errors. He places Catherine the Great where we know she was not, but later he *did* meet her, and his *story* is the clearer for his reordering of events. Likewise the Prince de Monaco was not in Monaco when Casanova was: they had met in Paris. He places him in his principality on an otherwise dull journey. Casanova was not an historian, but neither was he trying to write a romance. The world he sought to understand was as much his internal landscape as Europe's on the cusp of a revolutionary age. The extent to which he was true to himself, to his experience of mankind and the men and women who made up his compelling century is the more interesting question and the greater concern to social historians, and to this book. It is vital not to suppose, because he erred on dates, that he lied about more intimate memories, but it has been generally supposed he did by those who are instinctively suspicious of romantic memoir. Yet despite its supposed meanders into fiction, Casanova's *History*, where it can be corroborated, turns out to be just that: history. Separate intimate witness is to be found as instances in the records of the Venetian Inquisition, in surviving passports, the testimony of the Prince de Ligne or Lorenzo da Ponte, or in legal documents even down to the records of Bow Street Magistrates' Court. One major concern of Casanova scholars and pioneering Casanovistes, who followed in the wake of the full publication of the memoirs in the 1960s, was to use all this corroborative evidence to untangle and, where possible, elucidate Casanova's text. It has taken a further few decades, until now indeed, for the essential truth to become accepted in the academic community: Casanova's works are simply *not* the 'notoriously unreliable' account of legend. He may well, indeed, have been an almost entirely honest chronicler, as he saw it. This is something that needs reiteration in the English-speaking world. If he erred on dates and places, writing decades after he was there, so might we all. If he conflated histories that took place over successive visits to particular cities, he can hardly have expected that he would be picked apart for it. But this does not excuse or explain entirely his willingness to claim to be where he could not have been, when he could not have been. Here, we must allow him his interest in keeping us or himself, entertained: his instincts as a writer and entertainer. This biography is, to some extent, a call to arms in his defence – as a social historian if not, necessarily, as chronicler of record or, indeed, as role model – and a companion and context to his monumental memoirs, the full twelve-volume edition of which too few of us have time to read but which educates, alarms, intrigues, amuses and arouses as much today as it would have done when it was written.

There are decisions, though, to be made as a biographer that are not forced upon a memoirist. One picks a path through the thousands of pages of memoirs, the hundreds of extant letters, the novels, plays, treatises and poetry Casanova wrote, via archives in Venice, St Petersburg, Moscow, London, Rome and Paris, and through his further nine thousand manuscript pages, which are now in Prague and in Dux Castle where he died. Through the scores of affairs – romantic, sexual, financial, intellectual – in which he was involved in the twenty cities in which he lived over a lifetime spent travelling some seventy thousand kilometres, through his own lies and those of others one finds a route and hopes it is true to the man and less error-strewn than the original. Casanova's genius was to eschew all such editing and write everything he could recall; indeed, as his friend the librettist da Ponte had it, 'perhaps he wrote too much'.

Casanova lived to see many unexpected and ultimately revolutionary consequences to the Age of Reason through which he had lived. The Enlightenment – an undirected movement of unparalleled intellectual exhilaration and drama – had shone new light upon all areas of human endeavour and natural law in the name of Reason. In French and English fiction, for instance, writers began to illuminate an inner, hidden or masked person, thus beginning a dialogue unthinkable in the Middle Ages. When Montaigne described an inner-self, an '*arrière boutique toute notre*' – a back room, if you will, of the mind – he planted an idea in the Western world-view that flowered as brightly in the new world of eighteenth-century portraiture as in the new art form of novels, but caused a revolution also in the memoir. Moreover, the Enlightenment, broadly, challenged the Catholic conception of self-denial and, indeed, 'self' as the wellspring of sin in the first place. Enlightened writers explored freely, and for the first time the concept of man as the acme of creation, and a proud, sometimes sensual ego, thus took centre stage in new genres, none more egocentric than Casanova's *History of My Life*. By dissecting the concerns of individual life as it is lived, in his love of food and sex as prime examples, Casanova was labouring in a radical new art form. As a writer he was a stylistic and sensuous revolutionary whose work can no longer be dismissed out of censure.

The literary work that had served as flagship for Casanova's *History of My Life*, as for the age in which he lived, had been the *Encyclopédie* edited by Diderot and d'Alembert. His *History of My Life*, is similarly emblematic of the Enlightenment in addressing the intimidating scale of human experience, applying a recognised literary form – one might call it in his case the picaresque memoir – and rendering a whole human world, without judgement, in the process. 'Have courage to free yourself', Diderot had enthused, and Casanova followed.

Casanova wrote mainly in French, and in his memoirs exclusively so. It was the language of the Age of Reason, of the Enlightenment *philosophes*, of courtly poetry and erotica. Casanova also believed it was a more refined language than his native Italian; and he was well placed to express the opinion. He was a gifted linguist – able to discourse in Latin in his early teens, even though he had not learned to read until just a few years before that. He spoke fluent French, Latin and Greek as well as having a smattering of German, English and Russian. And as a Venetian he spoke, in effect, two versions of Italian. French culture and literature was the model for Europeans, as far as lifestyle, art, fashion and mores were concerned, before during and after the French Revolution. But to write in French was to write not only in the language of fashion, diplomacy and love but also in the language of change. Yet he chose to do so in a style that was consciously ground-breaking. It has been argued that he knew slightly better, which is to say slightly more classical, French but repeatedly opted to write 'with an Italian accent', importing numerous Italianisms and reiterating for instance the construction '*laisser que*', following Italian practice, where '*permettre*' would be used then as now by a Frenchman. Even the French writer Crébillon had noted Casanova's style, and the freshness his Italian accent gave to much of what he said and wrote: 'You tell your story excellently . . . you make people listen to you, you arouse interest and the novelty of your language . . . and Italian constructions . . . renders your listeners doubly attentive . . . your idiom is just the thing to gain approval for it is odd and new and [this is a time when] everything odd and new is sought after.' It turned out to be sound advice.

The language of Rousseau served Casanova well in other ways. In French, the name of Eros, or Cupid, the central figure in eighteenth-century discourse on freedom and love, is the same: Amour. The god Amour is the personification of the feeling *amour*. The interplay enjoyed as a result of this double-entendre was well understood by Casanova as by artists of the period. Men and women of the Enlightenment, like Casanova, were – in Paris, Venice or Rome or St Petersburg – never more than feet away from the glinting, sexy, perplexing gaze of Amour, or Cupid; the bizarrely sexed-up wicked boy-child, who was at once prankster and god. This is a useful image in understanding Casanova and his times. During the Age of Reason, Amour embodied the irrepressible spirit of the age, a Lord of Misrule, who made wanton all the efforts of mankind to impose absolute order and sense on the world. He rightly decorated almost every theatre Casanova ever attended, as mascot to his journey through the central decades of the century that one later historian described as definable not so much for revolutionary philosophy as for sensuality: 'the very essence of the eighteenth century; its secret, its charm . . . its breath, its force, its inspiration, its life and its spirit'. The age of *amour* that produced Laclos's *Les liaisons dangereuses*, Diderot's *Les Bijoux indiscrets*, not to mention the sexually charged canvases of Watteau, Boucher and Fragonard, was beset by a particular ideological tension: what place did sex have in this new enlightened age? Casanova had an answer. The *game* of love and sex was what made sense of the chaos of his life and the world. It was a game personified by the destructive/ creative god Amour – a flash of irrationality and wicked fun in the modern world: an '*id*' before such an idea was forged. No one before had written about this as Casanova did: from the perspective of both combatant and victim. Going some way to demonstrating why Freud found in Casanova such an apt language for his *métier* and his mindset, the sex in *The History of My Life* holds a unique place in the history of our understanding of ourselves. It posited firmly, for the first time in the Western canon, the idea that an understanding of sex – with all its irrationality and destructive potential – is key to an understanding of self. *The History of My Life* is a revolutionary text that holds a fascination for much more than its catalogue song of conquests. It attempts a synthesis of the two dominant genres of the age, the libertine and the sentimental memoir, thus creating something much nearer a modern sensibility of what it is to be a fully rounded man, alive to failures, fears and foibles, and very much attuned to a sexual motive force. It attempts also a radical emotional honesty, a memoir unencumbered by guilt, addressing what it was to be alive in a revolutionary age, and pulsing still after two centuries with Casanova's life-spirit and testosterone, giving drama and human measure to the new freedoms that gave birth to the modern age.

This was the literary, artistic and philosophical backdrop to Casanova's self-involved drama; his intimate, salacious, rambling account of the life and times of an individual of questionable worth that would not have been possible without the cult of sensuality around the image of Amour and the Enlightenment belief in the universality of human goodness and worth and the Rights of Man. And if the Enlightenment connects to the modern age at all it is as a call to individuals to proclaim their rights and their unique value in the light of reason. The question may be to ask what sort of man could create an overarching narrative of his life based largely in the realm of the senses, and why.

At the ideological core of libertinism was the Enlightenment faith in a benign god, and the mandates of Nature. The extension of this was that sex was healthy, spiritual even, ordained by God, but was also a natural bedfellow to intellectual good health. Thus the libertine politician John Wilkes could write with pride that he produced his best work when in bed with the London prostitute, Betsy Green, after they had had sex, and Casanova could proclaim himself a sort of revolutionary by freely transgressing so many expectations of an older sexual morality. By using his knowledge of mathematics, chemistry, physics, alchemy and a babble of eighteenth-century sciences to make sense of his world and the fatalities that shaped his life, he shows his debt to the Age of Reason. By attempting to render reasonable sense of his adventures, in the form of a massive work of personal insight and social history, he proclaims himself a sort of Encyclopedist of humanity – himself the key object of dissection. And, last, as a natural humorist trained in stage cynicism and improvisation, his work stands as one of the great last-laughs at life; like Laurence Sterne, who wrote that 'my opinions will be the death of me', Casanova's humour became, as he once described his own condom, his 'prophylactic against melancholy', his way – as Sterne wrote – 'to fence against the infirmities of ill health, and other evils of life – by mirth.'

Casanova is unthinkable without Venice, though he spent surprisingly little of his long life there. Its style, its stones, its sexual sophistication, its supreme artistic confidence in the eighteenth century all closely informed his writing and his experience of living. It was also, fortunately for Casanova, the perfect century in which to be a travelling Venetian. Re-imagining Casanova's Venice is quite straightforward. Little has changed since the views inspired the great *vedutisti*, Canaletto, Guardi, Longhi and Tiepolo, to paint the tiny details of Venetian life known to Casanova. The bread, the tides, the church bells, the canals, *fondamente* (quaysides) and *calles* (alleys) remain intact, along with the grand and crumbling vistas of the *settecento*. Venice, where this book was in large part researched and written, is her old, improbable, alluring self: fecund or fetid, depending on your point of view or the prevailing wind, built to the rules of stagecraft and romantic drama, and not to those of nature or Reason. A city with water for paving stones, her own numbering of floors and houses, an indistinction between indoors and outdoors, between reality and reflection, between illusion and solidity makes its own impact on a writer, and on Casanova, 'in the middle of the sea on a great stone boat held at anchor, ineffectually' as one contemporary of Casanova's had it, 'by art alone'.

The Serene Republic of Venice was ruled in Casanova's day as an independent city-state by a doge, or duke, elected from a body of nobles, a patrician class, who had jealously guarded their rights and privileges for centuries. Although its inhabitants were widely considered to live better than almost any other city-dwellers in Europe, its reputation as a cultured and colourful imperial capital, enriched by its gateway position to the east and generations of successful maritime endeavour, was tempered by a separate reputation as a repressive and secretive society, ruled ruthlessly for the benefit of a close cabal of families with the collaboration of a corrupt church. The doge's government, while gorgeously costumed in Byzantine robes and abiding in a palace of unparalleled splendour next to the Piazza San Marco, relied on networks of informants, anonymous denunciations and the universally feared tool of state repression, the Venetian Inquisition.

Yet Venice was simultaneously becoming in Casanova's time a tourist city, as it is to this day – though in a slightly different style. It catered to differing expectations of glamour and of culture. It was the great age of the carnival, then the most protracted and wildly theatrical in Europe. There was mandatory mask-wearing, for an entire city, day and night, from October to Ash Wednesday, with a brief break for Christmas; a further fifteen days of carnival was added in the early eighteenth century, around Ascension Day. This exotic practice made many writers gasp. Masks lent the acceptable pretence of anonymity in a city that coupled intense drama with intense lack of personal privacy. Masking alters the codes of every human interaction, by corseting the usual signifiers of understanding, acceptance, disdain or distrust. Nothing is certain, so everything seems allowed. The strict caste rules of Venice were partially circumvented as a result of masking. To a boy growing up – even children wore masks – it allowed a half-year of make-believe when, in public, one could be anyone one wanted to be. Casanova lived his life in similar spirit.

Casanova's Venice was at peace through the eighteenth century, as was much of Europe. His travels were interrupted to an extent by the War of Austrian Succession (1741–8) and a further war of dynastic European power-shifting, the Seven Years' War (1756–63) that exported its strife as far as the Americas and Indies. But Venice was at peace for eighty years, from the Peace of Passarowitz in 1718 to the end of the Republic in 1797; this period saw the last great flourishing of the

Venetian *carnivale* until modern times, and with it all the Venetian arts. Antonio Canova was chipping marble on the Dorsodoro in Casanova's day, returning Venice to classical styles of purity and restraint even in the face of the exuberant rococo *palazzi* of the period. Canaletto was painting in a studio yards from where Casanova argued theatre politics on the Campo San Zulian and his canvases have left us an unforgettable image of the city of light and water. The red-haired priest Antonio Vivaldi was pouring his passion into the creation of four hundred concerti, besides church music and operas, and at the same time Baldassare Galuppi, less well regarded now, launched an internationally successful opera career while teaching at the Ospedale dei Mendicanti. His operas were often created in collaboration with the other great drama figure of the age, and lover of Casanova's mother, Carlo Goldoni. And though Venice was regarded by visitors and insiders alike as a ghost of its former self in political terms, its economy was not in decline, as has sometimes been written, and its inhabitants, from patricians to gondoliers, had much to feel happy about. Goldoni, like Guardi and Longhi on canvas and Casanova in prose, presented quotidian Venice as a happy comedy, an *opera buffa*, its everyday people going about their everyday lives. This, too, was revolutionary. Ordinary city people became the subject of art, just as they would for Casanova.

You could not have had in the eighteenth century a more urban childhood than Venice offered. It was Europe's most densely populated city, noisy and noisome. Market produce arrived from three to six a.m., and gondoliers began their early-warning calls at corners, at bridges and in mist between six and eight. The coffee shops were busy by seven. Perhaps only London, with its direct routes to the East Indies, took to the bustling coffee craze faster than Venice. Florian's, which opened in 1720, and Quadri's, in 1775, where Casanova drank on Piazza San Marco, were first and foremost cafés for *coffee*, for philosophising and gossiping, flirting and fleecing, exactly as they have remained.

But what becomes clear, from the testimony of Venice's many visitors as well as Casanova, is that the city's food and drink reflected its reality; it was cosmopolitan and ethnically diverse, perhaps more so than any other European city. 'The air was full of strange smells and tongues, and above all only by virtue of loudness rose the harmonious dialect of Venice . . . the Armenian in baggy breeches, the Jew in his long gabardine. The noble on his way to the council chamber replied by the wave of his hand and an *"adio caro vechio"* to the respectful salute of the *tabarro* [citizen] hurrying by about his business.' The city as a result of its many ethnic influences was alive always to the aromas of food. The ghetto, then as now, was famed for its small pastries that were 'exported' across the city. Vegetables and fritters were cooked and sold on the canal side, *venditore* of fish, vinegar, eggs, oil and bread plied their trade everywhere, manoeuvring baskets on their heads and *bigolante*, or water-carriers, crying their wares.

But what has been lost of Casanova's Venice are many of the theatres. Theatre was central to the experience of Venetians and to the culture of the Republic. There were comedy theatres in almost every parish, packed nightly from September to Lent and again from Easter to early summer. Only a few remain. To grow up in Venice, like Casanova, was to be born into an arts festival, specifically a musical-theatre one. 'By the eighteenth century,' wrote one visitor, 'Venice had parted with her old nobility of soul and enjoyment had become the only aim of life . . . she had become the city of pleasure . . . the convents boasted their salons, where nuns in low dresses with pearls in their hair received the advances of nobles and gallant *abbés*.' And everyone, from patricians to gondoliers, who were given free entry, was immersed in theatre. If theatre and theatricality made up one part of what it was to grow up in Venice, it was also Europe's primary experience of Venetians. Venice exported actors, singers, dancers and opera companies all over Europe and even to America. Casanova's mother, a comedy actress, spent most of her career outside Venice. So, too, would her son. Venetians were Europe's entertainers: its sought-after opera stars but also its favoured painters, fireworks technicians, masqueraders and makers of manners. Consequently Venetians exported their carnival disregard for reason and for rule, and the eighteenth century became *their* century outside Venice as well as within.

It is impossible to overestimate the fashionability of Venice and Venetians in Casanova's lifetime. Their attitude to life chimed easily with the morals and philosophy of the times: easy on piety, though indulgent of the festivals and rituals of Catholicism. Humanistic and unshockable, because old in experience. Questioning and sardonic; noting approvingly that a paradise in heaven did not preclude the cultivation of earthly paradises for as long or as little as we might be allowed to enjoy them, and alive to the realities of art and joy in artifice for those last generations before the Romantics told the world that truth was in Nature and feeling was more vital than style, sentiment or sex. To venture that one was a Venetian in eighteenth-century Europe, as Casanova did, was to wink at a reputation that was at once morally dubious, hedonistic, sophisticated and tawdry. This had a profound impact on his life and career. The background of the Venetian theatre into which Casanova was born sets the scene for the life of the great adventurer, as it places him within the theatre culture and economy of Venice and of eighteenth-century Europe, which was, in many senses, the centre of eighteenth-century city life. He was never an actor, though he worked as a dramatist, musician and, briefly, impresario but his life and his appreciation of it were shaped by the theatre.

If the Enlightenment memoir is one genre by which to understand Casanova's, the other is that of the actor or 'star'. In the eighteenth century, the scripts used to understand or even play at self ceased to be God's. Indeed, the whole distinction between being oneself and masquerading broke down, or was evaded, and, inspired by the novel wave of imaginative fiction and dramas of selfhood, the desire arose to play new parts, or even a multiplicity of them, through a lifetime. The role Casanova returned to over and over again, of Enlightened Libertine, was not the complete truth but was easy casting for him. His work fits less with the libertine memoir or contemporary erotica, with which it was originally classed, and more with the earliest performer memoirs – the works of London actors like Colley Cibber, David Garrick and the Kembles. These new-style memoirs, born of the same voyeuristic age that begat modern portraiture and the novel, are the origins themselves of 'celebrity' and 'star' biographies of today, addressing the duality of *being* and *performing*. It was something in which Casanova was well versed and well placed to explore – a performer's perspective on the world that he chose to take off the stage, into the bedroom, and on to the page.

Theatricality infused his writing as much as his life. He loved nothing more than to reverse expectations, to blur identities, poking fun at reality or rearranging it for his own pleasure and that of others. '*Faire semblant*' (to pretend, seem and make seem), '*jouer*' (player/gambler/actor also to play, play-act, gamble), '*comique*' (dramatic as much as comic), these are the turns of phrase that litter his writings about his escapades. 'What was required of me', he would later write of his travels and adventures, 'was the skill to play my role and not compromise myself . . . The thing,' he added, more pithily, 'is to *dazzle*.' The main purpose of a Venetian *commedia* troupe, such as formed Casanova's immediate family background, was to be as entertaining, in a faintly subversive manner, as the machinations of complex plots might allow. It was a style that necessitated fast thinking, fearless stagecraft and the appearance of spontaneity when, in fact, the forms, jokes and characters were often taken partly from stock and judged in the moment against the heat of an audience. Casanova wrote in a *commedia* tradition, but also took his world as a *commedia* set, with stock situations thrown at him against an ever-changing cyclorama. He acted in life, and later wrote with an instinct to amuse, entertain and keep the plot moving, casting himself as lead player – most often romantic lead – and master of devices. One of his earliest sexual experiments was to dress as a woman. One of his earliest great loves was a woman who passed herself off, on stage, as a man. As a lover he writes constantly of his 'role', and 'of drawing the curtain'. Dangerously and seductively schooled in the improvisational bear-pit tradition of Venice's world-famous *commedia del arte*, a dissembler and a pleaser, a narcissist but also an empathiser, practised in an assumption of confidence but in perpetual 'fear of being hissed', literate, sensitive, troubled, bullish: Casanova was nothing if not an actor. His life and his *History* were an attempt to find meaning in the interplay of internal and enacted self, and reconstruct reality in the realm of the senses, which was the essential dilemma of the city in which he was born. He came to embody an idea, a very Venetian and very eighteenth-century idea, that the most sophisticated pleasures feel elusive by the sham of their performance. Beside himself with the joy of being, he spoke to a new way of understanding human nature: through the artifice of its construction, its performance and its awareness that there was more behind the mask.

Casanova's Venice, however, like his life, was not an *opera seria*, not a tragic grand opera, but rather a comedy in the *commedia* tradition, an *opera buffa* of common folk as well as patricians, of love triumphing over reason, of fools duped and wrongs righted. For a Venetian there is always the understanding that life is performance, an expectation that each bridge will bring a new act, a new set of *commedia* characters, a new twist to the plot, a reinvention. We map out our lives in our mind's eye with a template based on our earliest impression of structure.

Casanova's was Venice. A map of the world and of life where nothing is straight – where no one knows for sure what is real and unreal, what is performed and what is not, what is stone or reflection – is a map of unfathomable complexity by no means inappropriate to the realities of living. Labyrinthine, reflective, and rhythmic, without the narrative architecture of *opera seria* or the linear construction of a novel. It was a dance to the music of the Venetian islands, without the pause of *intermezzi* when one might halt the story and reflect. Casanova's mind-map of Venice structured his *History of My Life* as a pattern based on that city of interlocking bridges, vistas and tides. It was an *opera buffa* learned there, but played out across the world and the geography of the human heart. A remembrance of past acts, a song to the rhythm of the lagoon and to the laughter of a Venetian theatre.

ACT ONE

THE CALLE DELLA COMMEDIA

1725–34

'A man born in Venice to poor parents, without worldly goods and without . . . titles . . . but brought up like one destined for something different . . . had the misfortune at the age of twenty-seven to fall foul of the Venetian government.'

Giacomo Casanova, *The Duel* (1780)

S o began Giacomo Casanova's first attempt at writerly reminiscence. In almost every point what he wrote was true. Except that the family into which he was born on 2 April 1725 in Venice was not merely untitled and poor, it was notorious.

Casanova was the son of actors, or at least of an actress, Zanetta Farussi, known as La Buranella because her family was from the northern lagoon island of Burano. The exact paternity of her first child, baptised Giacomo four days after Easter in 1725 was as open to speculation as that of all her later children. Her admirers included the playwright Carlo Goldoni and the Venetian theatre impresario Giuseppi Imer but also a string of aristocratic protectors, including eventually Britain's Prince of Wales – men who were taken to be the fathers of her children, all of whom bore the surname of her actor-dancer husband, Gaetano Casanova. Zanetta's second son, Francesco, later a landscape and military painter of international renown, was widely assumed to be the son of the heir to the British throne, who became besotted with La Buranella in 1727 when she played at the Italian Opera in London. Her eldest, Giacomo, later believed he was the son of the Venetian patrician and theatre owner Michele Grimani, and aspects of his early life support this, whereas others supposed him to be the son of the theatre manager, Guiseppi Imer.

Men, however, were to play only minor roles in Giacomo's early life. His grandfather and his father, or 'my mother's husband', as he sometimes tellingly referred to him, died when he was quite small. Women surrounded him in the tiny house in the Calle della Commedia, women who took centre stage and expected his attention and compliance, but who then, in the case of his mother most dramatically, abruptly left the stage, with Giacomo alone on it.

Zanetta Farussi – a small, fiery and unconventionally beautiful comedienne, according to contemporary critics – was a stage professional in an age when to be such implied, for a woman, a dual career. Though not all actresses were whores or courtesans, it was certainly assumed that women willing to subject themselves to voyeuristic regard onstage would favour their public in more intimate spaces, for the right terms and billing. This was especially true in Venice, which was one reason the city was a magnet for the younger male Grand Tourists. Admission to an actress's dressing-room suggested that an aristocrat or grandee could expect more delicate favours depending on his ability to support her person, purse, profession or family. Zanetta Farussi, a 'star', eventually, of the Venetian comic stage – and in Warsaw, Dresden, St Petersburg or London, where she went as leading lady of San Samuele Theatre Players – was not averse to using all her charms and skills to support her family and her career, and she had good reason to do so. At twenty-six she was a widow, in possession of famous good looks, a recognised and commercial stage talent in the exportable media of Venetian comedy and the sole wage-earner in an extended family of eight.

The house on the Calle della Commedia where Zanetta lodged her family was and is overshadowed on one side by tall apartment houses and on the other by the back of the Palazzo Malipiero, which blocked all light, and much noise from the Grand Canal, only yards away at the deepest point of its meander around the sestier San Marco. In 1725 the *calle* was also overshadowed at one end by the San Samuele theatre, but this playhouse, where his mother worked, built in 1655 and re-designed in 1747, is no more. His mother called her son Giacomo, the masculine version of her own name, Giacometta – Zanetta is the Venetian dialect version – rather than after her husband, which would have been more usual. This, too, may be a small clue that that Gaetano Casanova was not Giacomo's father. His maternal grandparents lived only a yelp away in the cramped Corte delle Muneghe, as they had since immigrating from Burano. His grandfather, a cobbler in an area still marked with the signs of its famous shoe-shops, had been called Gir-olamo, and this became Giacomo's middle name. Whether this helped mollify the old man, who considered the career of his daughter and son-in-law little more than an 'abomination' is unlikely: he died in any case around this time, reputedly of a broken heart at his daughter's ill-advised marriage into the theatre. Giacomo's grandmother, Marcia, was forgiving of her daughter now that Zanetta, too, was a mother and took over care of the baby who was sickly and troublesome.

It is unlikely that Giacomo Casanova was ever very far from the stage-door of the San Samuele theatre, not because his mother was always at work there – she spent several of his earliest years at engagements elsewhere in Europe – but because his grandparents lived in its shadow too. He was brought up in the squalid Corte della Muneghe – the family apartment in the Calle della Commedia seems to have been let when his mother was abroad – with three brothers and one sister: Francesco, born in 1727, Giovanni, born in 1730, Maria Maddalena Antonia Stella, born in 1732 and Gaetano Alviso, born in

1734 after their father's death. Standing shoulder to shoulder, the Casanova children could line the Corte della Muneghe from one end to the other.

First memories are often revealing. They begin the narrative we choose to construct for ourselves, and in a memoir of self-discovery and revelation such as Casanova's *History of My Life* his first memory is given suitable prominence. He claimed to be able to recall nothing from the first eight years of his life. This would be unusual enough, but the first memory that stuck, and which he could date to August 1733, four months after his eighth birthday, was of a catastrophic nosebleed, a trip to an occultist on the Venetian island of Murano, and a vision of the Queen of the Night.

Casanova credited himself with merely 'vegetating' before the age of eight, of having a soul incapable of thought or memory, but perhaps something more interesting was going on. As a small child he suffered recurrent heavy nosebleeds, and Marcia put her faith in a folk-medicine healer on Murano, famous then for its glass works as it is now. Murano, 'Venice in miniature', according to Goethe, was also nearer in every sense to the more primitive Venice that the Farussis knew well: Burano and Torcello where the earliest settlers of the lagoon had first optimistically plunged their larchwood pilings, and where ancient faiths still shared shorelines with Christianity and science.

On Murano a healer, most likely a Burano peasant known to Marcia, performed an elaborate ritual and incantation over Giacomo, some of it in the local dialect, gave him 'numberless caresses', undressed and dressed him and smeared unguents on his forehead. It made a deep impression on him. The 'witch', as Giacomo called her, also told him he would receive a visitor in the form of 'charming lady', who appeared that night at his bedside wearing the panniers and bejewelled headdress of a stage-goddess, a 'Queen of the Night'.

But it was Marcia's faith in him, and her love that seem to have made a more lasting impression on him than this bizarre 'vision'. His mother and father rarely, if ever, spoke to him, and everyone assumed not only that he was mentally deficient, but that the sickly silent boy would die young: his mouth gaped; he played, silently, with himself; he almost certainly caused the nosebleed, himself, exploring and over-exploring his physical self, an abnormally self-absorbed child.

After the visit to the healer the nosebleeds became less frequent. Marcia swore her grandson to secrecy, and he told no one. His grandmother's strong faith in the occult had a profound effect on him, as well as her disdain for the professional medical options open to her. Not only the nosebleeds were affected: from then on he was able to keep his mouth closed and talk more easily. He stored the event and its attendant mysteries 'in the most secret corner of a budding memory'. It was the first of many secrets he kept with a woman – an introduction to the feminine wisdom he often abused but held, undeniably, in deep respect.

The death of his 'father', Gaetano Casanova, from a brain tumour, followed soon after Giacomo's bizarre experience in Murano. Gaetano had been treated, to no avail, with an anti-spasmodic caestoreum, made expensively from the sebaceous glands of beavers. It was an early example for Giacomo of the credulousness of patients and eighteenth-century doctors' quackery. But before he died, Gaetano had secured for his children an oath of protection from the theatre-owning Grimani brothers, Alvise, Zuane and Michele, Giacomo's supposed natural father.

Under the guardianship of the Grimanis, the state of the eldest Casanova boy's health – he was still losing 'two pounds of blood a week' despite less frequent bleeding when he was thought to have 'only from sixteen to eighteen [in total]' – was deemed to warrant action. He was an embarrassment around San Samuele to his glamorous mother and his natural father. It was thought a change of air might help. Zanetta was later castigated, not least by Giacomo, for 'getting rid' of him, but sending him out of Venice to the cleaner air of Padua was thought at the time to be a life-saving move. Medical opinion had it that blood distempers such as Giacomo's were air-affected, and Venice was notoriously malodorous. Alvise Grimani, his uncle, was acting with good intentions when he intervened in the family conference to insist that Giacomo was sent away, especially as he also suggested that the apparent imbecile should be educated. He had noticed something no one else had: that the boy had a voracious and unusual mind. Alvise Grimani, an 'abate' or secular cleric himself, seems to have been the first to propose that the sickly boy might be fit for a career in the Church.

On 2 April 1734, his ninth birthday, Casanova left Venice for the first time. He sailed away from the Grand Canal in a *burchiello*, a sort of immense punt, which had cabins at either end and a long, low room at water level, 'like Noah's ark . . . beds spread on the floor where we all pigged together'. It was eight hours by boat to Padua. The nine-year-old was accompanied by his mother, his 'uncle' the Abate Grimani, and one Signor Baffo, a writer who lived nearby in the Campo San Maurizio. Baffo, a 'sublime genius and poet in the most lascivious manner', was a friend of Zanetta and this connection, along with Goldoni's known regard for her, may suggest that Casanova inherited, at least in part, his literary interest from his mother. Baffo was the one adult during that journey who applauded an unusual moment of observation and reasoning for which Casanova never forgot him.

Little Giacomo woke in the low punt to see the trees – possibly the first he had ever seen after a childhood in a Venice devoid of all parks. The trees were apparently moving on the bank. When his mother told him 'pityingly' that the boat was moving, not the trees, Casanova claims he hypothesised that therefore it was possible the Earth circled the sun, not the other way round. His mother scoffed, but Baffo was impressed: 'You are right, my child,' he said. 'Always reason logically, and let people laugh.' In constructing his narrative of himself, Giacomo the grown man gave undue prominence to this piece of advice and the occasion that gave rise to it.

Padua was not a city that Casanova remembered later with fondness. The small party from Venice left him in a lice-infested hostel run by a Slavonian woman. Zanetta paid her for six months' board – six sequins, or about two hundred pounds. The landlady said that was not enough, but Zanetta left anyway. And Casanova wrote – with the bitterness towards his mother that marked him all his life – she 'got rid of me'.

AT SCHOOL IN PADUA
1734–8

'It was applause . . . and literary glory that set me on the pinnacle of happiness'

Giacomo Casanova

A bate Antonio Maria Gozzi a teacher, violinist and priest, was twenty-six, 'plump, modest and ceremoniously polite', and living with his shoemaker parents when Giacomo Casanova came to Padua as his pupil. He was a doctor of civil and canon law, a lover of music and theology, a confirmed bachelor with an eclectic library whose shelves were open to his charge. They held volumes ranging from contemporary astrology to popular classical-erotic works, like Nicholas Chorier's *Satyra sotadica de Arcanis Amoris et Venus*, which Giacomo seems to have read. Gozzi also had a personable younger sister, Bettina, 'the prettiest girl on our street', according to Casanova.

Gozzi was the ideal tutor for the intellectually omnivorous nine-year-old. He was to be paid forty *soldi*, or the eleventh part of a sequin, each month, but he seems to have warmed fast to his work and his new pupil. Giacomo could not write properly, so he was put, to his shame, with a group of five-year-olds.

At first Giacomo was bitterly unhappy and homesick. But he progressed rapidly in his lessons, and in his relationship with Gozzi. The abate soon realised that his new pupil was sleeping badly as a result of his poor accommodation, and took the landlady to task. She blamed the maid for Giacomo's lice infestation, and beat him as soon as Gozzi had left. Nevertheless, she had to take better care of him once it was obvious that someone local was looking out for him, even if his family was not. Giacomo's health steadily improved.

Within six months of his arrival Gozzi had appointed him proctor – a sort of head-boy responsible for correcting home-work – and had suggested that he board with the Gozzi family. Together he and Giacomo wrote to Marcia Farussi, the Gri-manis and Signor Baffo, giving grim details of his life in the Padua boarding-house and intimating that he would die of neglect if left there. There was no immediate response from the Grimanis or Baffo but Marcia was on the next *burchiello* to Padua. The letter had been read to her; she was illiterate. She withdrew Giacomo from the boarding-house and delivered him, after a meal at the inn where she was spending the night, to the abate and his family. During the forty-eight hours she was in the city Marcia arranged Giacomo's immediate future: she paid in advance for his tuition, and had his lice-infested head shaved. The Gozzis gave him a blond wig, which hid his baldness but, with his thickening 'black eyebrows and dark eyes', exposed him to taunts of a different kind.

For the next two years, the Gozzis took Giacomo to the heart of their family. Vicenzo and Apollonia Gozzi were impressed to find themselves with a priest as a son, and that one of his pupils, touted as 'a prodigy' because he had learned Greek from Gozzi's books on his own, had come to board with them. Their only other surviving child, Elizabetta or Bettina, was, wrote Casa-nova, the first 'who little by little kindled in my heart the first sparks of a feeling which later became my ruling passion.' He was ten.

During the first year in Padua, Zanetta recalled Giacomo only once to Venice: she was due to take up an offer of a theatre contract in distant St Petersburg. His 1736 visit to his birthplace was afterwards branded on his memory for the juxtaposition of his old, Venetian family – theatrical, ribald, artistic – with his new 'family' in Padua, where he was already being considered for a career in the Church. The young Gozzi had never before been to Venice and Giacomo enjoyed showing him its cosmopolitan glamour, not to mention his mother, who was so 'marvellously beautiful my poor master found himself very uncomfortable'. He also became aware of the gap between an intellectual and a theatrical background: he was embarrassed by his mother, who couldn't resist flirting with the shy country priest, but also, for the first time, enjoyed her approval. Perhaps Marcia had persuaded her to look anew at the shy, sickly child she had sent away. In less than a year the boy once considered an idiot had become bright, inquisitive and febrile, able to sit at table and dazzle the company with his command of Latin. He went further. There was a dinner at Baffo's house on the corner of Campo San Maurizio by the church. In the shadow of the leaning campanile, a dinner guest from England, an admirer of Zanetta, decided to tease her clever son with a lascivious ancient riddle:

> *Discite grammatici cur mascula nomina cunnus*
> *Et cur femineum mentula nomen habet*

> Teach us, grammarians, why *cunnus* [vagina] is
>   a masculine noun
> And why *mentula* [penis] is feminine?

Giacomo rose to the occasion. Rather than merely translating, as his mother requested, he decided to answer the riddle in kind.

He wrote the Englishman a perfect pentameter in the form of a joke:

Disce quod a domino nomina servus habet.

It is because the slave takes his name
from the master.

The company roared, and the Englishman made Giacomo a
congratulatory gift of his watch.

Zanetta matched this by sending for *her* watch to give to
Gozzi, who was so overcome when she kissed him on both
cheeks that he withdrew, blushing, to the room in San Samuele
he shared with Giacomo. Later he told his pupil that his answer
had been 'magnificent', and Casanova dated from that moment,
at the small *palazzo* on the Campo San Maurizio, his desire for
literary glory, 'for the applause of the company set me on the
pinnacle of happiness.' For the first time he had been publicly
acknowledged by his mother and older men of letters, and all for
showing off his precocious wit. It was a heady evening.

After just four days Gozzi and Giacomo left Venice, but not
before Giacomo's 'uncle', the Abate Alvise Grimani, had given
them money for more books, and Zanetta, intriguingly, had
given them presents for Bettina: some Venetian silk, known as
lustring, and twelve pairs of gloves. She didn't want her son
entirely in the company of the gauche Gozzi, and had a mother's
instinct, perhaps, that he liked Bettina for reasons he barely
understood. More practically, it was Bettina who dressed Giacomo's hair, and his mother wanted him out of the unbecoming
wigs.

Bettina was several years Giacomo's senior and referred to
him as 'my child'. To begin with he was her doll. The tale is told
from Giacomo's point of view so we can never know if Bettina
really seduced him when he was only eleven, but in his account
this first romantic and sexual encounter was orchestrated more
by her than him. It has the ring of adolescent truth: simple and
far from pure. She washed him daily. She commented on his
changing body, touched and tickled him. She made fun of his

'timidity' while he was in paroxysms of self-doubt about how to handle the situation. He knew he wanted more. He knew she did too. He felt confused and inadequate.

She knitted him some stockings, and took them to him at their regular early-morning meeting in his bedroom to make sure they fitted. Her brother was celebrating mass.

Putting on the stockings she said that my thighs were dirty and at once began washing them without asking . . . I was ashamed to let her see me, ashamed though I never imagined that what happened next would happen. Seated on my bed, Bettina carried her zeal for cleanliness too far, and her curiosity aroused a voluptuous feeling in me which did not cease until it could not become greater . . . It seemed to me that I had dishonoured her.

Thus did Giacomo record his first sexual experience, in a style that, in action and rhetoric, became his signature. The climax – his first – might almost be missed in the detail of seduction and in the placing of intent and consequence on his partner as well as himself.

From the start he was as intrigued by the desire and responses in his partners as he was in his own – and as confused as any adolescent boy by the mixed signals of girls. He also suffered, or enjoyed, a hair-trigger response, not unusual in boys his age, well into adulthood and appears here to have ejaculated without anyone actually touching his penis.

With Bettina it was all over, physically, before it had begun and Giacomo was bewildered and distraught. With the ardour of a good Catholic schoolboy, he decided that the only way to make up for having dishonoured the sister of the abate was to marry her. Bettina seems to have taken it lightly: she promised him it would not happen again, but was soon plotting to take him to a dance as her escort, dressed as a girl. Later she gave him an elaborate explanation of what happened next: she allowed Candiani, an older boy, into her room, in circumstances

Casanova interpreted, perhaps rightly, as an insult to him and proof of her budding promiscuity. Candiani kicked him in the stomach when he found Giacomo eavesdropping outside Bettina's room – and Giacomo set about imagining his revenge. Later Bettina claimed Candiani was blackmailing her over her infatuation with Giacomo. The truth was impossible to uncover – then as now: over the next few days Bettina was gripped by a series of violent convulsions. In the confusion and alarm – Signora Gozzi was convinced she had been bewitched by a sorceress – Giacomo found a note from Candiani to Bettina that incriminated them both: 'When I leave the table I will go to your room; you will find me there . . . as you did the other times.' Gallantly Giacomo hid it, and, typically, laughed. Until Bettina was diagnosed with smallpox.

Such tragicomic domestic dramas seem not to have affected his studies – or, indeed, to have come to Gozzi's notice. Giacomo continued his work and Bettina recovered, although the disease left her scarred. She and Candiani barely spoke again, and two years later she married a local shoemaker. Casanova began the habit of a lifetime in remaining a close friend of the girl he called his 'first love'. In 1776 he was at her deathbed.

Meanwhile Zanetta had travelled to St Petersburg and returned to Italy. She had invitations to perform at the court of the King of Poland and in Dresden, and would never again live in Venice.

Giacomo was sanguine about her final departure from his childhood. He even dismissed the tears of little Giovanni – his eight-year-old brother and the only one of the Casanova children to be taken to Dresden with Zanetta – as sign 'that he was not particularly intelligent, for there was nothing tragic about her leaving.'

He returned to Padua and his studies. His boast that he had graduated as a doctor of law at only sixteen was long assumed to have been a lie, but it turns out to have been true. For his discourse on canon law he wrote a thesis on the rights of Jews to build synagogues – a controversial position at the time – and on civil judicature, he wrote about inheritance. The Paduan records make clear that he graduated in 1741, having enrolled at the university there in 1737, aged twelve, even though he was in Venice from 1739. During his later teens he moved back and forth between the two cities, reluctantly apprenticed to an advocate in Venice when in fact he wanted to become a doctor. The Grimani family were probably pushing him towards canon law and the greater respectability of the Church. Casanova wrote later that he told everyone repeatedly that his vocation was medicine 'but my wish was disregarded'. His legal training meanwhile imbued him with what proved a lifelong cynicism for law and lawyers, but he used his spare time well. With his instinctive and familial interest in folk medicine, he took extra-mural classes at the scientific institute of La Salute in medicine, physics and chemistry and developed a habit of self-diagnosis and treatment.

His family, though, were right to some extent in their choice of a church career for him. Had he pursued it, it would have moved him more securely away from the theatre and towards respectability, while offering a perfect stage for his rhetorical skills. But other of his talents and susceptibilities put an end to his progress towards officiating at that particular altar, or worshipping regularly at shrines of any orthodoxy but his own.

I BECOME A PREACHER

1739–41

'He was handsome, a connoisseur of wine and an epicure; his mind was keen with a vast knowledge of the world, he possessed the eloquence of the Venetians and . . . twenty mistresses.'

Casanova describes Malipiero,
his first aristocratic role-model

'He has just come from Padua where he had been studying at the University' were the words used to introduce the gangly, studious youth around the sestier San Marco, Venice's most fashionable district. Casanova was a changed young man from the quiet, sickly child who had been taken away on the *burchiello* five years earlier. He was tall for his age – nearing his mature height of six feet one and a fifth inches. He was thought to be highly intelligent and well educated, which was indeed the case, and in the little parish of San Samuele he was welcomed with enthusiasm by the parish priest. Father Tosello took him by gondola along the Grand Canal, from the *piazzetta* outside the presbytery to the Patriarch of Venice in St Mark's, to be tonsured and inducted in the first four minor holy orders. The ceremony took place on 17 January 1740.

These were the first four steps towards a church career, but did not imply full acceptance into the priesthood. Even so, Marcia Farussi received the news of her eldest grandson's elevation as her 'greatest comfort'. Giacomo's assumption of the title 'Abate' made him conspicuous locally – as if he wasn't already, with his etiolated frame, mop of curls and straight gaze. He became a fixture at mass and later in the pulpit. His position – especially after one useful introduction – gave him access to the salons of Venetian society, far above the expectations of an actress's son, and allowed him access to the many Venetian convents, where numerous schoolgirls and young women were reluctantly sequestered.

On his return to Venice Casanova lodged at first in the family apartment on the Calle della Commedia with his brother Francesco. His mother was still paying for its upkeep. The boys were left to their own devices because their grandmother was looking after the younger children in the cramped Corte delle Muneghe. In theory Giacomo was to be taken under the wing of his 'uncle' the Abate Grimani; in practice his entry into Venetian society took place as a result of his introduction, through Father Tosello, to the owner of the *palazzo* beside the church and the Grand Canal, a sprightly former senator who enjoyed nothing more than the company of the young.

In Casanova's account, the seventy-year-old Malipiero was rich in worldly goods and accomplishments, sociable and happy to surround himself with interesting young people, as well as a coterie of 'men of wit and intelligence and . . . ladies who had all gone the pace'. He was one of the foremost grandees of Venice, but he was also well placed to recognise Giacomo's talents and help him. Father Tosello would have been aware of this: his parish was worldly and lax in its attention to church practice and though Giacomo's later careers and reputation render it laughable that his friends and family thought him fit for the church, in the eyes of the parishioners and parish priest of San Samuele and Senator Malipiero, he passed for the perfect curate.

Abate Casanova became a regular dinner guest at the imposing Palazzo Malipiero. It had then, and has still, one of the
largest and widest *portego*s, or hallway-ballrooms, on the
Grand Canal, sweeping across four metres and opening five
windows on to one of Venice's finest views across the canal to
Ca'Rezzonico. Grasping a door knocker shaped from a writhing
Hercules and stepping on to the marbled chequerboard of the
palazzo's *portego*, Giacomo Casanova entered a new and elegant world he found greatly to his taste. Under the outstretched
bird's foot of the Malipiero crest, which claws at every corner of
the palace, and overlooked by naked gods and nymphs, the
teenage abate stepped on to a new stage. He met a great number
of 'ladies of fashion . . . as well as respectable ladies', who in
turn took the polite young newcomer to their hearts and
introduced him to their daughters – schoolgirls at local convents.

To the susurration of the tides, and the gossip on the marbled
stage of the *portego*, Malipiero 'inculcated the sound precept of
discretion' in Giacomo: he told him never to boast of his
friendships with women or the ease with which, as a churchman
and *protégé* of the senator, they welcomed him into their circles.

This lavish *portego* of the Palazzo Malipiero, all thirty-five
beams, uplit by the reflection of light from the canal outside,
gave dramatic footlights for the young actor, Casanova. The
largest interior in the parish – wider than the San Samuele
theatre, longer than the church – the *portego* represented a step
into real Venetian society. It was a stage that required presence
and poise – which Malipiero recognised and nurtured in Giacomo. The *palazzo*, steeped in the courtliness and romantic
cynicism of old Venice, became his world, spanning for him the
expectations of a church career and the enticing games of
Venetian salon society. He was less than ten yards from his
birthplace, but was being drawn into a dazzling new world of
opportunity. Venice, so often portrayed as a closed, decrepit
city, the most defined oligarchy of the *ancien régime*, was also,

ironically, one of the most democratic. Malipiero in his palace, Zanetta in her dressing room and Marcia in the Corte della Muneghe were within yards of each other, lapped by the same tides, oppressed by the same humidity and Tosello's long sermons. Giacomo was blessed, but not unusual, to have been spotted by the local grandee within a waterfront parish like San Samuele. The oligarchs of Venice guarded their rights and privileges – Casanova's story is on one level that of someone who dared to try to cross class barriers – but they also had access to the talents and youthful enthusiasms of those in their immediate locality.

To add to the muddied tides of interconnections and desires in this microcosm of Venice, the seventy-year-old senator was in love. The object of his voyeuristic desire was another close neighbour of the Casanovas and intimately tied to Giacomo's family. Teresa Imer was the seventeen-year-old daughter of Zanetta Farussi's former employer and lover at the San Samuele theatre, the impresario Giuseppi. The Malipiero *palazzo* garden overlooked the Imer household, which opened on the other side on to the busy Corte della Duca Sforza where theatregoers disembarked from their boats. Here, at her window, seventeen-year-old Teresa Imer displayed her ample charms while she practised singing. At seventeen, she was 'pretty, wilful and a flirt', very much in command of her audience from her bedroom window. Malipiero gained Casanova's affection by taking the boy into his confidence. He knew he was too old to be taken seriously as Teresa's lover but he was infuriated by her and her mother's professional soliciting. He complained to Casanova of the Imer women's behaviour and began to educate him in the wiles of professional courtesans.

The young abate's life revolved around trips to the church at one end of the Calle della Commedia, to the theatre at the other, and the *palazzo* that separated the *calle* from the Grand Canal. He ran errands for Father Tosello, and increasingly for Malipiero. He took to *palazzo* life and began to dress and behave to suit his new backdrop. He wore pomade and curled his naturally wavy hair. Malipiero, Father Tosello and Marcia warned him that his manner and appearance were being noted around San Marco as less than appropriate to an aspiring churchman. Malipiero, in particular, expected discretion. When Casanova argued that *other* abates were seen around town in wigs and perfume, Tosello persuaded Marcia to lend him the keys to the Calle della Commedia house. One night, while Casanova and his brother Francesco were asleep, he went in and cut off Casanova's fringe. It was a deliberate reining-in of the young blade, who responded with adolescent fury, 'so great that I shed tears'. He even threatened legal action against the priest. He was soothed only by his grandmother's contrition, and by Senator Malipiero's gift of an appointment with one of Venice's most sought-after hairdressers, who repaired the damage with curling tongs, smooth words and the fashionable new hairstyle, *en vergette* ('sprigged') and Giacomo was to some extent mollified.

The haircut caused a rift with Tosello. This might seem excessive, when Casanova had already been tonsured and was forced, by Venetian sumptuary laws, to adopt the sober clothes of an abate, but he vowed to Malipiero that he would never again set foot in the church of San Samuele. Malipiero told him he was quite right ('This was precisely the way to bring me to do what was wanted of me,' the older Casanova wrote), then issued him with a challenge. It was in Malipiero's gift as local seigneur to suggest a preacher for the pulpit of San Samuele on the day after Christmas. He put forward Abate Casanova. He had heard him hold forth among his elders in the canalside gardens at his *palazzo*, and had disputed with the young man himself on the manoeuvrings of the Imer women. 'What do you say? Does it please you?'

Casanova said it did. He was determined to 'say astonishing things'. Daringly, he took as his text for the feast of St Stephen not a biblical verse but, rather, one of the epistles of Horace, *Ploravere suis non responderer favorem speratum meritus*

('They lamented that their merits did not meet with the gratitude for which they had hoped'). The title proved prophetic. Casanova practised on his grandmother, who listened as she fingered her rosary and pronounced it 'beautiful'. He tried it out on Malipiero, who pointed out that it was not entirely Christian, but applauded the lack of Latin quotations, and sent him to see Father Tosello. Casanova dispatched a copy of his proposed text to Gozzi, in Padua, and had a letter straight back, exclaiming that he must be 'mad', while Father Tosello said he would never allow such an unbiblical sermon to be preached in San Samuele. He offered Casanova one of his own to read. But Casanova, filled with the bullish determination of youth, swore he would approach the Venetian censors and the Patriarch of Venice himself, if necessary, to prove there was nothing seditious in his sermon, and eventually Tosello relented.

Casanova delivered the sermon to some acclaim, and a collection plate that profited him 'nearly fifty zecchini . . . when I was greatly in need of money . . . together with some love letters all of which made me think seriously of becoming a preacher'.

It was his second seductive experience of public and intellectual approval. It marked, as had his repartee with his mother's English admirer, a nascent love of performing and extemporising. But the pleasure was shortlived: Father Tosello asked him to preach again, on St Joseph's Day, 19 March 1741, and Casanova's second sermon at San Samuele turned out to be his last.

On the appointed day he accepted also an invitation to dine with some aristocratic acquaintances: the Count of Montereale and his intended in-laws. Casanova was confident enough not to learn his sermon by heart, and to drink at lunch. He entered the pulpit, the site of his previous triumph and, in the theatrical term, 'dried'. There was, he wrote later, 'a low murmur from the restive audience' – he did not, one notes, refer to them as a congregation. 'I see people leave, I think I hear laughter . . . I can assure the reader,' he continued, 'that I have never known

whether I pretended to faint or fainted in good earnest.' Nonetheless he fell to the floor of the pulpit, gashed his head and was
carried out to the sacristy. Humiliated, he packed his bags and
went back to Padua to complete his law degree and 'completely
renounced the profession' of preaching. A churchman, however,
for the time being, he remained, and within a few months he was
back in Venice, hoping his failure as a preacher had been
forgotten.

ENTER LUCIA, NANETTA AND MARTA

1741–3

'They said, since I was intelligent, I could not fail to know what two girls who were good friends did when they were in bed together.'

Giacomo Casanova

Young Casanova did not lose his virginity to either of the obvious candidates: Father Tosello's niece with whom he became infatuated, or Lucia, a serving-girl he met in the Veneto who intimated to him she would happily have obliged. He was too scrupulous a young Catholic to accept Lucia's advances, and Angela Tosello held out for marriage over Casanova's choice of a church career. But Lucia and Angela became the 'twin rocks eminently shaped to . . . shipwreck [his virginity]', in that they guided him in a different and formative direction. In writing about his sexual initiation, he gave star billing to the two young women, who both inflamed and informed him. However, it was two others, friends of Angela, the Savorgnan sisters, Nanetta and Marta, who together took Casanova to their shared bed when he was seventeen.

Angela Tosello spent a great deal of time in the presbytery of San Samuele by the Grand Canal, though her family had a house nearby behind the theatre on the Calle Nani. She and Casanova first met when he was *en route* to Father Tosello's study to show the priest a copy of his Horace sermon. She was entirely at ease with the idea of accepting his advances, as long as they tended towards marriage. This 'perfect dragon of virtue', though only seventeen herself, insisted that he reject his career in the Church for her. His determination to adopt the Venetian veil of priestly promiscuity kept them apart.

The Savorgnan sisters acted as Angela's chaperones during the long embroidery hours when the three girls would listen to Casanova's effusive attempts to impress her. These sessions seem to have taken place at the presbytery and at the home of the Savorgnans' aunt, Signora Orio. The girls shared an embroidery teacher and, as an aspiring churchman, Casanova was able to attend their classes: by tradition girls might listen to improving texts and sermons while they stitched. At last, 'exasperated beyond measure', Angela granted him a small favour: she told him that 'abstinence made her suffer as much as it did' himself. But she had already consented to be his wife, she claimed, and that should be enough for him. If he was unwilling to give up the priesthood, she was unwilling to even to allow him a kiss.

Writing from the perspective of an aged *roué*, Casanova is clearly amused by his youthful ingenuousness and conflicted impulses. He wanted neither the partial sexual satisfaction Bettina had offered nor to consort with married women as their plaything. He wanted a torrid love affair, in the Venetian style, but would not contemplate marriage. He wanted to maintain his career in the Church, but play the game of love as it was played all round him: courtly, knowing, serially monogamous – and freely available to clerics. He wanted small favours, but was almost unsure, 'having a kind of virginity myself', on what terms he wanted the 'great prize'. Angela infuriated him, 'and I already found my love a torment'.

As the spring of 1741 sweated into summer, Casanova accepted an invitation to the country estate of the Count and new Countess of Montereale. It was and remains customary for wealthier Venetians to spend some of the sultry months far from the insect-plagued lagoon at country properties in the Veneto – that part of the old Venetian republic on the Italian mainland. Venetians with friends or patrons among the nobility – clergy, artists, actors and musicians – might expect to be included in these house-parties and escape the torpid heat and 'devouring gnats', described by one choked visitor as 'charged with all the venom of Africa'. For Casanova, the invitation to the Montereales' was the perfect escape from the twin torments of a steamy Venetian summer and Angela. But a slightly different torment awaited him at Pasiano, the Montereale country home near Friuli.

Lucia was the fourteen-year-daughter of Pasiano's caretaker. She was 'white-skinned, black-eyed . . . already formed as city girls are at seventeen', wrote Casanova, and 'she looked at me as frankly as if I had been an old acquaintance.' Like Bettina, Lucia seemed guileless and, also like Bettina, her affair with Casanova remained ill-consummated; though Casanova filled nine pages with his description of it. For the first time the writer has a woman leap fully formed from his memory on to the page. In narrating their encounters he falls instinctively into the language of the theatre: 'Re-enter Lucia, freshly washed.' She was the perfect stage *ingénue*: a country wench, pretty, unaffected, unspoilt; a child of nature who sat on his bed every morning to serve him coffee. Her parents merely asked him to try to broaden her mind.

Casanova revelled in the self-congratulatory satisfaction of winning a battle over temptation – one he rarely fought again – and eventually decided the most honourable path was to forbid Lucia his company. 'Unable to bear any more, yet growing more amorous every day precisely because of the schoolboy's remedy [a rare confession to masturbation]', he decided to ask her to leave him alone. Lucia laughed, and granted him all favours but 'the matter of essential importance' as they took to hours of adolescent snogging that left Giacomo feeling both ignoble and frustrated. 'What made us insatiable,' he wrote, 'through the eleven successive nights [that followed] was an abstinence which she did everything in her power to force me to renounce.' He decided he preferred the role of gallant and 'priest'. His 'gallantry' seems to have extended as far as oral sex but he was resolute in his determination not to take her virginity or, for that matter, lose his. He considered her too innocent and trusting for him to take full advantage of her.

In part this story stands as prelude to what happened on his return to Venice. But he saw it as a lesson in his responsibilities as both lover and rake. Soon after his visit, Lucia ran off with the Montereales' messenger, 'a famous scoundrel [who had] seduced her'. Casanova blamed himself: 'I [had been] proud,' he wrote, 'in my vanity that I had been virtuous enough to leave her a virgin, and now repented in shame of my stupid restraint. I promised myself that in future I would behave more wisely as far as restraint was concerned. What made me most unhappy was the thought that . . . she [would not] remember me without loathing . . . as the original cause of her misfortunes.' It was a sophisticated position. He wanted the joys of carnality but also to know that he had left his lovers with a positive memory of their encounter and an empowered position, as women. Even at seventeen, he rejected notching his bedpost, for his own as well as his 'conquests'' sake. Although he was piqued that someone he felt was less than his equal had succeeded where he had chosen not to, his main concern was for Lucia and his place in her heart. When he realised that she had run off, he was 'in anguish'. And years later, when he found Lucia, a lowly prostitute, in Amsterdam, he blamed himself for the trajectory of her life. 'A fear which I no longer find in my nature . . . a panic terror of consequences fatal to my future career, held me back from full enjoyment.' It would not retain him for long.

With this in mind, he returned to Venice in September 1741 and found himself in the unexpected but entirely welcome position as the object of a determined seduction. Nanetta and Marta Savorgnan were distant relatives and 'bosom friends' of Angela, the 'repositories of all her secrets'. Nanetta was sixteen, her sister a year younger. Their aunt, with whom they lived, Signora Orio, let some of her house on the Salidas San Samuele behind the church, keeping a fourth-floor room as a bedroom for her nieces, and, on occasion, Angela.

It was Nanetta who hatched a plot, communicated to the Abate Casanova, for him to befriend their aunt, through Malipiero, and arrange an invitation to visit the house. Once there, Nanetta would pretend to show him out towards the end of the evening, but would instead direct him to the fourth-floor room on a night when Angela was staying. It was quite risky, quite larky – and quite public between the girls.

The plan worked, in so far as they were locked in the fourth-floor bedroom, some time seemingly in September or October 1741, far away from their aunt or the lodgers, the girls giggling once the last candle guttered. 'There were four of us . . . and I was the hero of the play,' wrote Casanova, in typical style. But on that first night it turned farcical. The girls teased and laughed at him, Angela refused to come near him in the dark; he lost patience, and hurled abuse at her. The girls all cried, as did Casanova, who went home after Signora Orio had gone to morning mass. It was hardly the night of passion he had planned.

Then he went back to Padua to collect his final degree, a doctorate *utroque jure* and, after a two-month absence, received a second invitation to Signora Orio's. Nanetta was there, and claimed the girls were mortified by their behaviour, and that Angela wished to repeat the slumber-party. Casanova agreed, more out of the desire to wreak revenge on Angela somehow than in the hope that she would relent. On the appointed evening, however, only Nanetta and Marta appeared. They claimed they did not know where Angela was, but invited Casanova to sleep in their bed while they occupied the couch.

They made pledges of 'affection . . . and eternal fidelity', casting him as 'a true brother', then set about the two bottles of Cyprus wine and smoked meat he had brought with him for Angela and himself, extended with bread and Parmesan the girls had filched from their aunt's larder. For the first of many times, Casanova's rendering of events is given extra credence as well as extra human colour by telling details of what was eaten.

They started by playing a kissing game. They talked of Angela. The girls told him of a game they had played when she had stayed one night, when one of them had pretended to be Angela's 'dear Abate [Casanova]' and everyone was romping on the bed. They talked all the necessary nonsense and played all the necessary preamble of an adolescent sleepover, when sleep is the last and least concern. Eventually they resolved to go to bed together, as friends. Casanova complained he wouldn't be able to sleep unless he was naked. The girls said he could take off his clothes and they would not look. He told them they could hardly feel at risk in his presence as 'you are two and I am one'. Then they all feigned to sleep.

What happened next is one of the more famous and detailed narrations of a first sexual experience – and one of the more exotic. Given its particular mixture of fondly recalled detail, the extent to which the style of encounter remained fairly common for Casanova, and the disquieting intrusion of sexual knowing-ness, which must be more the writer's than the novitiate's, it is worth quoting in full:

They had their backs turned towards me and we were in darkness. I began with the one towards whom I was turned, not knowing whether it was Nanetta or Marta. I found her curled up and covered by her shift, but by doing nothing to startle her and proceeding step by step as gradually as possible I soon convinced her that her best course was to pretend to be asleep and let me go on. Little by little I straightened her out, little by little she uncurled, and little by little, with slow, successive, but wonderfully natural movements, she put herself in a position which was the most favourable she could offer me without betraying herself. I set to work, but to crown my labours it was necessary that she should join in them openly and undeniably, and nature finally forced her to do so. I found this first sister beyond suspicion [as a virgin] and suspecting the pain she must have endured, I was surprised [so] I let the victim alone and turned the other way to do the same things with her sister . . . I found her motionless, in the position often taken up by a person in deep untroubled sleep. With the greatest precautions, and every appearance of fearing to waken her, I began by delighting her soul [clitoris] at the same time assuring myself that she was as untouched as her sister; and I continued the same treatment until, affecting a most natural movement without which I could not have crowned my labours, she helped me to triumph; but at the moment of crisis she no longer had strength to keep up her pretence. Throwing off the mask [of affected sleep], she clasped me in her arms and pressed her mouth on mine.

Minutes later, the three got up, lit candles, washed 'in a bucket, which set us laughing and renewed all our desires', then sat 'in the costume of Golden Age', eating the last of the bread and drinking the wine. Replenished, they spent 'the rest of the night in ever varied skirmishes'.

Casanova's preferred style in revealing the first of his fully realised sexual encounters was at once uniquely his but also steeped in the literary conventions of his time. The lovers held masks over their true feelings, and played a game of understood but unspoken shared desires. They delighted in skirmishes where he acted the part of conquistador. As a man of his era – whether he felt this at the time or subsequently – he paid lip-service to the honour of virginity while seeking its ruin. There is also, undeniably, a colouring of coercion on the part of the young man that owes more to erotic literature than the likely reality of the moment – though it is also possible that the sisters felt coerced. Yet the lovers' 'triumphs' were to be mutual, their climaxes shared, the friendship long-standing, and Casanova remembered their lovemaking as a ridiculous roundelay. It enthralled him as a celebration of complicity, utterly without consequence or perceived danger, though for the girls especially it was laced with both. Casanova's first sexual love affair, with two sisters, echoes as a scenario throughout his life, featuring other sisters, mothers and daughters, and even cohabiting nuns.

As old Signora Orio left for mass, the parish's young abate slipped out of her house after the second of what would be many nights spent there. He, Marta and Nanetta remained sexual intimates for a number of years, and that first triangular sexual encounter imprinted on him deeply. It proved an academy at which he could study the *ars veneris*, as he would have termed them – the arts and craft of love and sex – to which he would dedicate himself for so long; the three once spent an entire night repeatedly making love – but also, he admitted, 'this love, which was the first of my life, taught me almost nothing of the ways of the world for it was perfectly happy, never disrupted by any discord, not tarnished by the slightest self-interest.'

It was also one from which Casanova profited rather more than the girls. It redoubled his burgeoning sexual confidence, convinced him that women could be as interested in uncomplicated sex as he was and gave him a comfortable venue in which to explore his and their physicality. Marta, more than Nanetta, may have remembered things differently. Nanetta married shortly after the all-night love-making while Marta entered a convent, Santa Maria degli Angeli on Murano, and went to some lengths to persuade some of her younger charges to ignore the attentions of one Giacomo Casanova. Eventually she took the name Mother Maria Concetta but said she forgave Casanova his part in their sexual experimentation: her eternal soul would be saved because she had spent the rest of her life in repentance. Her last words to

Casanova were that she would pray that he, too, could repent his libidinous ways.

But the young abate had other plans.

Casanova gives us three brief examples of the turn of his mind at this age, and his willingness to risk the censure of the Church and his elders in his headlong rush towards sexual opportunism. Two involve professional courtesans, the other a country bride. Teresa Imer had begun a professional flirtation from her bedroom window on the Corte del Duca Sforza and this had turned into fairly regular invitations to be part of the Malipiero salon. Here she would idle away the late afternoon overlooking the Grand Canal from the long balcony while the senator slept. One afternoon Casanova and she found themselves alone there together and someone, presumably Casanova, hatched the plot that they 'compared the differences in our shapes . . . in innocent gaiety'. It might have been just that – a childish lark – had not Malipiero woken unexpectedly, thrashed Giacomo with his walking-stick for his impudence and had him thrown out of the palace. It was a temporary end to Giacomo's relationship with his first aristocratic sponsor, but the beginning of his lifelong, somewhat fraternal regard for Teresa Imer.

Meanwhile he had met another professional flirt, Giulietta Preati, of that peculiarly Venetian species, actress-courtesan-musician. She was an accomplished and beautiful young woman who had been 'bought' from her father at the age of fourteen by a nobleman, Marco Muazzo. In exchange for her favours as his mistress, she was educated, schooled in music and a few years later found herself in Vienna playing the *castrato* role in an opera by Metastasio. She was a seasoned professional beauty of eighteen when Casanova and she met through Malipiero's circle of louche friends in 1741. They took an instant dislike to each other. A year later, however, after his encounters with Marta and Nanetta, either she sensed or he declared that she could no longer hold over him her worldliness, and she asked him to arrange a party for her. He agreed, defrayed some costs to her, and invited, among others, Signora Orio and her nieces. Most of the guests were Giulietta's friends and therefore, presumably, not drawn from Venice's more sedate circles.

At the party Giulietta hit on the idea that she and Casanova should swap clothes for one round of dances: she would wear his abate's cassock and breeches, he her dress and makeup. His tonsured hair was long enough at the back, he wrote, to be put in a chignon. But if she thought she could triumph in some Venetian masquerade and teasing of him she was mistaken. The increasingly assured young man took off his breeches to let her witness 'the too visible effect of her charms upon me'. They went downstairs together, although his shift was 'stained with the visible results of my incontinence', and although later Giulietta slapped him when he tried again to persuade her to feel his erection, she was clearly taken by surprise that the boyish abate should be behaving as a seasoned rake.

Similarly on a trip to back to the Montereale estate at Pasiano where Casanova had previously encountered Lucia, he met a young bride of somewhat rustic simplicity. In the course of a thunderstorm on a carriage ride out from the estate, he ruthlessly took advantage of her fear of lightning to persuade her on to his lap and under his cloak and eventually carried off 'the most complete victory that ever a skilful swordsman won'. He was seventeen. Although he takes the trouble in his memoirs to paint her as a somewhat silly and pretentious young woman, aware of his intentions from early in their flirtation, the episode hardly reflects on him as other than a sexual opportunist. The man who later claimed he wanted only to sleep with women with whom he was in love is exposed by his own pen. The young bride laughed it off, vowing never to share a carriage with any man but her husband. 'One learns the strangest things,' she said, 'from [Giacomo Casanova].' When she ran off, the postillion, their driver, was laughing. 'Why are you laughing?' asked Casanova, who had used the possibility of the driver looking around as his trump card in his coercive seduction of the bride.

'You *know* why,' Casanova records as the driver's smirking reply.

SEMINARIAN NO MORE

1743

'I eventually abandoned the Church in favour of the army on the principle that a uniform was far more flattering than a dog collar.'

Casanova

While Giacomo Casanova began the singular career as serial womaniser that would secure his later fame, his mother, on stage in Poland, was still plotting for him a future in the church. In the way of eighteenth-century church politics, Zanetta Farussi, a *commedia* star of no piety, was able nevertheless to convince the Queen of Poland, a fan, to write to her daughter the Queen of Naples, and suggest another admirer of the Italian stage, one Bernardo de Bernadis, vicar general of Poland, for a bishopric in Calabria which lay in the gift of the Neapolitan crown. In other words, Casanova's mother found herself able to help the career of a fellow Italian in Poland. Her price for so doing was that he should employ her son. 'He will set you on the road to the highest dignities in the Church,' she wrote excitedly to Casanova in early 1743, 'and imagine my happiness when, twenty or thirty years from now, I see you at last a bishop!'

Casanova wrote that his head was turned. He was to be sent away from Venice to work for a rising name in the Roman

Catholic Church, in Rome and the south of Italy. 'Goodbye, Venice . . . I told myself . . . I have done with trifling, in future I shall concern myself only with what is great and substantial.'

As a young man on the cusp of life – if we are to believe the older man who recalled him – Giacomo Casanova had the usual discomforting mixture of bridling self-confidence and barely suppressed fear. Doubtless he knew, even as an eighteen-year-old, that taking full priestly vows was in a clear Venetian tradition but hardly the action of an honest man; even the bride in Pasiano had won a confession from him that he was a sinning man of God. But ambition – and the challenge of rising to it – was already a drug for Casanova.

On 18 March 1743 Marcia Farussi, Casanova's beloved grandmother, died. He nursed her through her final illness. His bereavement had some immediate effects on his life. The Grimani brothers stepped in to handle the remaining Casanova estate and Giacomo was told that he would have to move out of the family home into cheaper rented accommodation. His mother remained in Poland. Despite, or perhaps because of, his imminent elevation to the priesthood and his first steps on the actual and metaphorical road to Rome, he set about selling off the furnishings of the apartment on the Calle della Commedia, first the wall hangings and bed linen, then furniture and Venetian mirrors. He pocketed the money without regard to his siblings (both Francesco and Giovanni were art students, Gaetano and Maria in the care of the Grimanis). It was a rash and angry act that set in motion a series of events that would have unforeseen consequences but which also spoke of an essential self-centredness, a man who believed the physical world – every last bit of it – was his own personal medium.

One effect of his sudden homelessness was that the Grimanis decided he should be sent to the seminary of San Cipriano, across the lagoon on Murano until Bishop de Bernardis summoned him to Rome. He entered the seminary in late March 1743, and although he thought it 'laughable' he should be placed there he seems to have accepted it with good grace, and was rowed across by Father Tosello, along with the bed and mattress seminarians were obliged to provide. He failed to confess to his parish priest that he was feeling weak and nauseous having spent his last night as a free Venetian in the arms of his 'two wives', making love, he claimed, until his penis bled for fear that it might be some time before he could break his new vow of celibacy. It was maybe a reasonable point, for while others laughed at the idea of Casanova in a seminary, he considered that he was now definitively 'on the road to the Papacy'.

Typical of the young Casanova, his predominant emotion on entering San Cipriano was to be feel slighted by the institution in which he found himself. He was 'insulted' by the need to sit an exam, insisting, correctly, that he was already a doctor, and decided to act the imbecile. He was placed in a class of nine-year-olds studying grammar, until his physics master from La Salute in Venice recognised him.

At San Cipriano he seems to have reverted in other ways too to more boyish behaviour. For one thing, he developed a crush on a 'handsome seminarian of fifteen' with whom he talked poetry and philosophy. They rapidly became inseparable. The seminarians occupied long dormitories and individual beds. Casanova goes into some detail to explain the tolerance of the priests towards the boys masturbating, but one prefect's task was 'to make very sure that no seminarian got into bed with another'. Unexpectedly, history's most famous heterosexual lover was expelled from his seminary for being caught in bed with another boy. Casanova's friend first unexpectedly got into his bed without invitation, and Casanova laughed at his risk-taking and told him to go away. A few nights later, though, Casanova took it into his head 'to return my friend's visit'. Again, he claims that they did no more than laugh, but when he stole back to his own bed he found it occupied. It was this second bedfellow who led to the expulsion. The prefect woke up and found Casanova's bed with two occupants.

The next day both seminarians were punished with eight lashes, which should have been an end to it but for Casanova's familiar raging against injustice and hypocrisy. Grandly, he asserted his right to complain to the Patriarch of Venice – and even persuaded his fellow students to swear that he and the other boy had never even been seen talking together.

Father Tosello was summoned and Casanova was put into solitary confinement. The rector of the seminary refused to believe that there had been other than 'scandalous complicity'. Casanova's intransigence and unwillingness to confess to wrong-doing escalated the scandal to the point at which the Grimanis were obliged to send their own gondola to collect him, and his bed, and bring them back to Venice in disgrace. The truth will never be known.

He was taken by Father Tosello to the Jesuit community, whence he absconded to Signora Orio's, to see his 'two angels'. There, he found himself unable to maintain an erection for 'worry . . . despite the two weeks [he claimed] spent in abstinence'. He was lost indeed. Penniless and feeling friendless, he spent his days in the library of San Marco, hoping to find a way to protest his innocence and rescue his reputation before the bishop arrived from Poland. For reasons he does not fully explain, but probably to do with the scandal at the seminary, he was arrested in the *piazzetta*, on the way home from the library, and taken in the Grimani gondola to the prison fortress of Sant' Andrea on the way to the Lido, 'where the Buccintoro stops on Ascension Day when the Doge goes to wed the sea'. He was a prisoner.

The ease with which men and women could lose their freedom in *ancien régime* Europe is one of the more striking motifs of Casanova's memoirs. In Venice in particular there was a facility with the arraignment of others that is chilling to the modern reader. Girls were taken forcibly to convents. Protesters, drunkards, debtors or those who **had simply** offended the powerful did not have the law on **their side**. Casanova seems to have been incarcerated on the orders of the powerful Grimanis – his own uncles and 'father' – in the hope that a short sharp shock might send the errant young man scuttling back on the churchly path to respectability.

Casanova spent his eighteenth birthday, 2 April 1743, as a prisoner, but a remarkably resilient one. He had found that a fellow inmate would dress his hair if he wrote letters for him and had sold his clerical garb to pay for the best prisoner privileges. He had a room with a view of the Lido island and had made friends with the small community of petty offenders. He had also befriended the young Greek wife of an aspiring lieutenant who needed someone to write petitions on her husband's behalf. She offered to repay Casanova with her 'heart' but offered no resistance when he requested a more accessible organ. An aspiring author, he even negotiated a three-part advance in payment for his writings over the course of the day – sex on contract, first draft and correction of proofs – and might have congratulated himself on any eighteen-year-old's ideal birthday, had three sessions with the Greek woman not also given him the unwelcome present of his first dose of venereal disease.

Understandably, Casanova became depressed, bored and resentful. The Savorgnan sisters were able to visit him on Ascension Day – the prison fort was a favoured place to watch the Doge's marriage to the sea – but he was unable to respond to their embraces as he was undergoing his six weeks of purging, abstinence and *medicina spagirica* – which ate into his meagre funds – in treatment of his gonorrhoea.

Casanova was released from Sant' Andrea on the order of the Grimanis when it was felt he had learned his lesson, and in the expectation of Bishop de Bernardis' arrival in Venice. He met the new bishop of Martorano, 'by the grace of God, of the Holy See and of my mother', a few days later. They spoke in Latin. It was agreed that they would travel separately to Rome, but meet there to go on to Naples and the new bishop's see at Martorano in Calabria. Casanova would journey via Ancona by sea from Venice, waving goodbye to his 'two angels' on the Piazzetta San Marco, with ten *zecchini* from the Grimanis and forty-five of his own and 'set off with a joyful heart, regretting nothing'.

END OF ACT I

CASANOVA AND TRAVEL IN THE EIGHTEENTH CENTURY

'I take pleasure simply in studying mankind, whilst travelling.'

Casanova to Voltaire, 1760

'It was the fourth sexual adventure that I had had of this kind which was not unusual, if one was a man travelling alone, and in a hired carriage.'

Casanova on the advantages of the eighteenth-century road

Casanova became adept at the art of travel. Scribbled notes survive in the Prague Archive of what he regularly packed, including, variously, a coffee and sugar tin, Italian seasoning, a compact stove and a pisspot. His memoirs are littered with references to the practicalities and harsh realities as well as the serendipitous pleasures of travelling in an age when anything might happen and time, in a sense, was suspended because no one knew how long any journey might take. This suited his improvisational spirit to the core such that he has left us a wealth of information on the first great age of leisure travel. And repeatedly one gets the impression he became addicted to travelling, and became one of its great artists, able to amuse himself, and those around him, for as little or as long as they might share the road in life.

In eighteenth-century Europe there were four ways of travelling overland. Those frequently on the road, like Casanova, could take their own carriage and horse, which few could afford.

They could take their own carriage and hire horses along the way – this was why journeys were divided into posts or stages. They could hire a vehicle and horses along the way, or face the rough trade of the public stage-coach.

Casanova seemed to relish rather than shun the close human contact travel afforded him. That said, of the estimated 64,060 kilometres he covered in his lifetime, a staggering distance when, broadly, it took a day to travel the distance we might now manage in an hour, he did nearly half in carriages he owned temporarily or had hired. Buying and selling of a carriage or coach at the destination was a recognised method of bringing assets across borders, and Casanova, who frequently based himself in cities for indeterminate lengths of time, did so on at least four occasions. He mentions more than twenty different types of vehicle – from folding-top calèches and open phaetons to *diables*, *diligences*, Italian *mantices* and racy *solitaires*. The coaches and chaises had various names across Europe, but all conformed – other than in the snows of Russia – to two basic types. There were two-wheeled cars, or chariots, and four-wheeled timber-framed wagons and coaches. The two-wheeled French *chaise de poste* was the most common, not the large four-wheeled coaches that survive in greater numbers.

These four-wheeled coaches, of which many public stage-coaches were older, heavier variants, were closed with hard tops, and suspended by braces and steel springs above the actual 'carriage', or lower frame, to which the wheels were attached. The form is familiar in that it is the clear antecedent of today's train compartments in some countries, but the dimensions were tighter in Casanova's time, which repeatedly brought him into close physical contact, for days at a time, with his travelling companions. 'The widths usual for the inside of bodies . . . was 3 feet five inches for two persons and 4 feet two inches for three persons on each seat [*vis-à-vis*]. The height of the seat from the floor was 14 inches and from the roof 3 feet six inches to 3 feet nine inches.' It was cramped, especially for a tall man.

French stage coaches were slightly more commodious. These *'diligences'*, sometimes referred to as gondolas, because they swayed so much on their springs, were fit only for the new post-roads constructed by Louis XV. They had three small windows on each side and were hung by leather braces on long carriages with immensely high back wheels and smaller ones in front. In 1770 Charles Burney, travelling in one, pointed out that though the seats were made for four, at weekends they often seated five a side. They also, uniquely, were oval, which made for a sociable encounter but also meant everyone's knees were crushed. The Paris–Lyon *diligence* was said to be the fastest in Europe. It travelled at a record-breaking and, at the time, reportedly dizzying five and a half miles an hour. Casanova did not enjoy his first experience of such speed, on the road to Paris in 1750. Such was his nausea that he felt his fellow travellers must have thought him bad company; a rare insult in Casanova's book.

Passengers made rapid and close acquaintance while travel arrangements were made. There was no opportunity to decline the close proximity of those whose trustworthiness, sobriety, moral standards or cleanliness was unknown. In a courtly age when the sexes were habitually segregated, travel pushed men and women close together. The elderly and infirm did not travel, and neither, by and large, did children. For a number of reasons, travel was considered a dangerous largely masculine sport, in which a woman's reputation was immediately suspect.

But more than the danger – of bedbugs, pickpocketing or highwaymen – there was the boredom. It took five or six days to travel from Rome to Naples, usually two to get from London to Dover, and many weeks to reach St Petersburg by land or sea. The long days and nights of close proximity to an unchanging cast, who were uncomfortable, sleep-deprived, irritable, rank with heat and dirty clothes were far from the romance of the road on which Casanova tends to concentrate. He often started his day's travelling in the middle of the night and 'played at cards, told stories etc. as is so usual in [this] situation that it is hardly worth mentioning.' The relief, therefore, with which new travelling companions might greet him, a charmer, actor, impressionist, raconteur and habitual 'pleaser' can hardly be guessed at. He even took to arranging meals based on what he had learned of his fellow-travellers' tastes.

There was no cult of the countryside in Casanova's Europe or, indeed, in Casanova's heart. He, like most travellers of the period, tended to speed at his vaunted five miles an hour through it with a barely disguised longing to get back to the city. Rivers were obstacles. Mountains were regarded with terror, before terror was fashionable. Casanova's descriptions of crossing the Pyrenees in 1768, Piedmont in 1769, and his opinion that the landscape was superior to that of the Alps, which he had traversed a number of times, are a rare exception in the travel writing of the time. In fact he tells us more about the countryside than almost any other writer of the period, although he concentrates on the inns and their inhabitants, the human landscape of country folk and rural food rather than the landscape itself.

Crossing the Alps was a hazard that added to the exotic allure of Italy. On this route, the traveller was obliged to dismount on to a mule or a mountain chair for the final summits. It was difficult – and expensive – to bring luggage, though some went to the expense of dismantling carriages to be carried over the Mont Cenis pass. The mule ride over the Pyrenees struck Casanova as a fine adventure, but the Alps were a vertiginous challenge. Charles Burney wrote of the squabbling of coach drivers and muleteers, as carriages were disassembled and packed on to mules. Like Casanova, he suggested that it was best not to look backwards 'like the Wife of Lot or Orpheus' on the ascent and considered the descent much more frightening for having to look down. Many preferred the sea route to Italy from the South of France, taking a felucca from Antibes or Nice to Genoa. This, too, had its hazards: the felucca hopped from port to port, risking choppy waters and rocks. Casanova was nearly shipwrecked off Menton, as had been a younger brother of George III, who died in Monaco, it was claimed of sea-sickness.

Perhaps the most salubrious form of travel was that used on the long trek east to the new Russian capital of St Petersburg. Because much Russian trade was with other Baltic and Scandinavian ports, Holland and Britain, the usual approach was by sea, and the city had been designed, primarily, to impress from this perspective. Casanova, however, travelled to Russia from Berlin overland. He left Berlin in the winter of 1765, and returned during the following wet September, in a travelling sleeping carriage, or *schlafwagen*. In Russia these could be hitched on to either a sledge chassis or wheels, but offered travellers a closed, padded, fur-lined double-bed passage. On the way back his travelling companion was a French actress he had met in St Petersburg. She paid her share with her company and – from one reading of a lewd poem he wrote her, with a venereal infection.

As a Venetian sea travel ought to have been Casanova's natural preference; he had grown up with the soft tides of the lagoon lapping the Fondamenta San Samuele; he learned to row before he learned to ride. Yet he suffered severe sea-sickness on the Channel crossings to and from England. He was more used to Venetian punts. The *burchiello* in which he travelled to Padua in 1734 was the preferred style of craft in Venice and the Veneto. In Venice itself, daily transport of goods and people was, of course, by gondola; it has been estimated there may have been as many as twenty thousand in 1750. Although in the paintings of the period these look very much like their modern counterparts, they differed in an important respect: they rose much higher out of the water – original eighteenth- and nineteenth-century gondolas would no longer fit under some of Venice's smaller bridges, and this is only partly explained by rising water levels and the architecture's slow subsidence; the gondolas were then an extra foot proud of the waterline.

Casanova's *History of My Life* is one of the most comprehensive records of what it was to travel in almost every European country in the eighteenth century. It is much wider-ranging than the memoirs of the Grand Tourists, who tended to concern themselves only with France, Italy, parts of Germany and Switzerland. Casanova's tale nevertheless forms a vital counterpoint to their rarified, and Anglocentric perspective. He had hitchhiked, been robbed, journeyed with nobility and courtesans, sailed with slave-galleys to Corfu and Istanbul, and had rowed himself in storms the substantial distances from Murano to Giudecca in Venice. As well as forming a history of travel – the tolls and breakdowns, the twenty-seven different currencies and 471 monetary items he had to negotiate and exchange, the dangers and pleasures of moving around in an age when so few did – his journeys explain much about him. The inveterate traveller, who can find no peace in one place, relationship or career, may seem a modern archetype, but it dates at least to Casanova. He had the same relationship with place as he did with person: an idea of experience or, indeed, conquest that speaks to a restlessness of spirit. But he happened upon an era of relative peace and stability, acceptance of foreigners, notably Venetians, and economic boom in the new cities of the early modern age. He similarly happened upon upon a modern style of fashioning his memoir: as travel-writing. As one contemporary advised, 'Every traveller ought to have two objects in view; the one, to amuse himself, the other, to impart to his friends the information he has gained.'

ACT TWO

ACT II SCENE I

THE ROAD TO ROME AND NAPLES

1743-5

'The man fit to make his fortune in Rome must be a chameleon
. . . He must be insinuating, impenetrable, obliging, often base,
ostensibly sincere, always pretending to know less than he does,
in complete control of his countenance, and cold as ice. If he
loathes the pretence he should leave Rome and seek his fortune
in London.'

Giacomo Casanova

Orsara, on the Croatian coast, was the first stop on one of
the traditional routes south towards Rome, zigzagging
across the Adriatic. It remains a tiny port, 'barely worthy of the
name', but Casanova was befriended there by a red-headed
Franciscan monk who in turn introduced him to a fellow priest
who took him for a meal, and eventually to his presbytery. For
the first time in his memoirs he mentions the power of good local
food to lift his spirits – on this occasion it was fish fried in olive
oil and served with Friulian red wine. He was also taken with the
priest's housekeeper – and embarrassed at being unable to
follow through in what he describes as *her* seduction of *him*
for fear of infecting her. However, his eagerness got the better of

his qualms and, having decided he could take 'certain precautions' to avoid reproaching himself with the 'unforgivable sin' of knowingly passing on an infection, he duly 'gave her the reception she has expected'. A treatise of the period insists that infections could not be passed from man to woman if ejaculation was avoided or took place outside the vagina, which might have been the 'precaution' he intended. By the standards of the period he was well informed – he had arranged before he left Venice for his stash of 'banned books' to be hidden by a friend – but, of course, he was wrong in thinking such a precaution would protect his partner.

Next Casanova sailed to Pula, further down the Croatian coast – the site of awesome classical ruins – in the company of the Franciscan, Brother Steffano, who had promised to show him how to beg his way to Rome in the spirit of St Francis. They sailed on together to Ancona, on the Italian coast, where they knew they would be obliged to stay for some time in quarantine: as there had recently been a plague at Messina, in Sicily, which traded with Venice.

Casanova wrote letters on Steffano's behalf, seeking alms from local churches and others so that they could feed themselves throughout the quarantine period and on the road to Rome. It was the traditional means of underwriting travel for poor clergy, and Franciscans, with their nature-loving ways and vow of poverty, were particularly kindly looked on. Steffano and his companion were soon rewarded with food and 'enough wine to last us all [twenty-eight days of quarantine]'. Things were about to improve further. The next to join them in quarantine was a Turkish merchant, accompanied by a Greek slave girl – slavery was a feature of the Ottoman empire. With little to occupy him, Casanova soon considered himself in love with her. They managed to talk through the 'splintery square five or six inches across' that separated his balcony from her exercise yard and within days had hatched a plot to run away together. They had made strenuous efforts at immediate physical union by tearing away planks from the balcony for her to squeeze through. Casanova clearly convinced her, and maybe himself, that he was in love because she suggested he buy her out of slavery and they run away together with jewels she could steal from her master. But he would have none of it: frustrated by the physical impediments between them, despite her seemingly offering him oral sex whilst he was 'naked as a gladiator,' he balked at the idea of theft and used this to end her dreams of freedom. The impeded lovers were discovered by a guard, and their re-enactment of Pyramus and Thisbe ended comically enough for the young Abate if not for the slave girl. He was released from quarantine, he claimed heartbroken, but set off immediately for Rome by foot.

The road from Ancona was well trodden by rich and poor alike. 'The country is as fine as any in Italy,' wrote one traveller, 'but the road exceeding bad.' Abate Casanova and Brother Steffano planned to go on together, but tensions had arisen between them. They made a comical travelling pair: the lanky, elegant Venetian, with his new pale blue English redingote and summer linen breeches and the red-headed monk, described by Casanova as a loutish and loud-mouthed 'sordid freak,' weighed down by his Franciscan cloak, its huge pockets filled with pilfered sausage, bread and wine. They argued constantly. Steffano's sense of humour amounted to scatalogical and obscene jokes, and he was, Casanova sensed, ill at ease with women. But he had been on the road before, and had much to teach Casanova about the realities of hitchhiking as a cleric. Casanova had figured the 156 miles from Ancona to Rome could be covered in five days by a fit youth, but Steffano declared he would cover the distance over several months, walking at a contemplative pace of three miles a day. Casanova set off alone on the first leg, fifteen miles to Loretto, and covered it in a day.

There, almost immediately, he met with the prodigious good fortune that would be a hallmark of his life – or his memoirs at any rate. The hospitable cloak of the church brought him shelter and succour. He was recognised as a scholar and an abate and welcomed into a comfortable private home. He was bathed, given Chianti and offered a barber – although it is worth noting that despite a sexual confidence and breadth of experience that might be the envy of many young men his age, Casanova, aged eighteen, was still not shaving.

The two young clerics met up again near Macerata, argued and came to blows when Casanova took umbrage at Steffano's renderings of Mass and confession for a local family. They parted company again less than a third of the way to Rome. Subsequently, Casanova was robbed on the road, lost his wallet at an inn table, and suffered the traditional torments of the inexperienced traveller, along with others that were unique to him: after accepting a bed in the home of a provincial watchman, he was joined by his host, naked and drunk, where 'the most honest policeman in the Papal States', Casanova recalled, (not, one assumes, without irony) tried to rape him. Consequently, as the journey progressed, Steffano's pace proved that the tortoise wins over the hare. He kept overtaking the beleaguered Casanova and rescuing him, then pressing on towards Rome at his snail's pace.

Some of the hospitable homes into which Steffano introduced them in the name of St Francis were more welcome than others, and a few proved as lairy for the young men as anything Casanova had experienced. They were set upon by two drunken beggarwomen with whom they were sharing a roadside hovel. Steffano thrashed about with his stick in the dark, injuring a dog and old man. Casanova succumbed reluctantly, he wrote, to an 'ugly woman of thirty or forty' and recalled that at this early stage of his adventuring he had decided that 'without love this great business is a vile thing'. They walked from Foligno to Pisignani to Spoleto; Casanova's record is one of the few testaments to eighteenth-century Italian roads *not* seen from the windows of a Grand Tourist's *vetturino*. Eventually, at Otricoli, Casanova persuaded a passing carriage to take him on to Castelnuovo for four papal *paoli* (Venetian money was not accepted so far south) and proceeded on foot the last miles to Rome. He walked through the night to get there. Possibly he did this out of desperation, or to avoid the heat, but it seems as likely he pressed on by moonlight out of sheer excitement that he would at last realise his dream of Rome . . . and find himself back on the proper road to becoming its bishop.

When he finally arrived at Rome's Minimite Monastery of San Francesco di Paola ai Monti he found that he had missed Bernardis so would have to leave immediately for Naples and the south. It was November 1743. In Naples, too, he was late. Bernardis had travelled on ahead of his new secretary to take up his see in Martorano, two hundred Roman miles further south. He had left a note for Casanova, urging him to follow at his earliest convenience.

Martorano and the new bishop's palace were a sore disappointment to Casanova. The see was bankrupt. The palace was a medieval ruin. There was hardly any furniture. Whatever books there might once have been had been sold or lost, and those ordered for a new library had not yet arrived from Naples. The food was atrocious. There was no one to talk to. Casanova enquired if there was a literary society, or any intellectual life in the town, and the bishop – whom Casanova describes as kindly and warm-hearted – became 'disconcerted' on realising 'what a poor present he had made me'. So shocked was Casanova by the backwardness of Calabria and the prospect of working there that he even suggested to the bishop they run away together to seek their fortune. Bernardis laughed, and released him from his obligations. He gave him letters of introduction to influential churchmen in Naples, his blessing and his regrets – he had seen instantly that Martorano would never be stage enough for an ambitious actor like Casanova – then sent him on his way.

The post for which the bishop had fought so hard in Warsaw turned out to be his undoing. Life was as harsh in Calabria as

Casanova had surmised it would be, and within two years the new bishop was dead.

Casanova set off again for Naples. He was unsure what lay ahead, and wary after his earlier experiences on the road. *En route*, he recalled, he 'always slept with my breeches on . . . a precaution I thought necessary in a country where unnatural desires are common', but as he walked into the Bay of Naples, paved then with Vesuvian lava, he felt himself safely back on the path to Rome and the his manifest destiny in the highest ranks of the Church.

As luck would have it, Bishop de Bernardis had furnished Casanova with an introduction to a man in Naples in want of a poetry tutor for his bookish fourteen-year-old son, a post to which the Abate Casanova was eminently suited. Within days of his arrival, he and his new pupil, Paolo Gennaro Palo, had published some odes, written on the occasion of the entry into a convent of a young débutante. The Abate Casanova's verse, and his name, were spotted by a distant cousin, Don Antonio Casanova, who was a fixture on the Naples social and literary circuit. As a result Casanova was soon taken up by Neapolitan society.

He was, and remained, fascinated by Naples, but on his first proper visit there, he was ill-at-ease in society, insufficiently self-confident to face up to those who suspected he came from nowhere. And when it looked as if he might be presented to Queen Maria Amalia, he decided to move on. He might have fine introductions through the Church, and a friendly, well-placed relative, but his *entrée* to society was through Bernardis and his connection to a far-off working comedy actress, his mother, which the Queen had known as Zanetta had lobbied her mother for Bernardis' appointment. It was a return to reality for Casanova. His mother might have influence but it was bought at the expense of her family's honour. Giacomo decided to press on to Rome, with little idea of what would become of him there but, again, some advantageous letters of introduction.

Casanova's journeys presented him with many actual, and metaphorical, crossroads. Had his road to Rome taken him simply there, to the Eternal City or even to a churchly career, his life would have have been much the poorer, if the purer. And we would doubtless not have a *History of My Life* in anything like its eventual, epoch-defining style. But the history of his life was full of unexpected turns at crossroads, and the frequent accidents of the road that make travelling, again, the compelling metaphor for personal narrative.

As the wheels of the *vetturino* rolled along Naples's Strada di Toledo, the city's main thoroughfare north, Casanova found his knees pressed against those of an attractive young Roman woman returning to her native city with her husband and sister. The name Casanova later gave her was Donna Lucrezia Castelli. Her sister was about to be married in Rome and her husband, an affable middle-aged Neapolitan lawyer, had business there.

Because 'Donna Lucrezia' came to play an important role in Casanova's life, not least as mother to one of his illegitimate children, and because her sexual emancipation, as represented by Casanova, is so striking, she has become the object of particular curiosity for several generations of eighteenth-century scholars. As so often with women with whom he was intimately involved, Casanova went to some lengths to obscure her identity. As he wrote in 1791, 'What afflicts me is the duty I am under to conceal the names as I have no right to publish the affairs of others.' But he changed his mind, as he wrote, as to whose identity he should obscure and how to do so. Often circumstantial or tangential evidence he left in elsewhere in the memoirs leads fairly quickly to a surmise on an identity, which more recently has found the corroboration of unrelated archives. In Donna Lucrezia's case, it has been possible to establish with reasonable certainty that she was one Anna Maria d'Antoni Vallati, and her sister as Lucrezia Monti. Later Casanova records them as daughters of Cecilia Monti, of Rome – whose first name turns out to be correct. The daughter Anna Maria bore Casanova was christened Cecilia Giacoma; and Casanova had more cause than usual to protect her name as 'Leonilda'.

A few patterns emerge in the palimpsest of his use of pseudonyms. Several times he swapped the names of sisters and mothers. Sometimes he used only initials, perhaps not even the correct ones – 'Mme Z. or Mlle X'. Almost invariably, out of gallantry, out of fond memory, or from having been lied to in the first place, he knocks years off the ages of his lovers. Anna Maria, for instance, was in her late twenties, nearly a decade older than Casanova, when she found herself travelling to Rome with the nineteen-year-old abate. She had been married for the best part of a decade, and was childless. All of which puts what happened next into a slightly different context than the one Casanova gave in his memoirs. There is little reason to doubt, however, his assertion that she was one of the great loves, and arguably the first great love, of his life.

The *vetturino* was a standard means of transport for the relatively well-to-do, so 'Donna Lucrezia', or Anna Maria Vallati and her family, are marked out as middle-class Romans. Casanova describes a flirtation between a slightly bored wife and a young cleric flung together for several days in those intimate circumstances. It was not so much that the carriage provided opportunity for dalliance, but that the driver had booked accommodation in advance for the journey, which invariably threw virtual strangers into bed together. At the first inn, at Capua, Abate Casanova bedded down with the lawyer, and the sisters in the other double bed. Later on, at Marino, when a commotion outside the shared room sent the lawyer out to investigate, Casanova tried to hop into the women's truckle bed – perhaps 'by mistake' – only for it to collapse. It was the beginning of an affair that blossomed into a heady entanglement that ended only when Anna Maria became pregnant and returned to Naples with her husband.

As Casanova relates it, however, their liaison flourished from the start under the eye of Anna Maria's easy-going husband, and later that of her mother. 'The road [between] Rome and Naples', another writer pointed out, often provided cover for romantic dalliance as 'a great part of it leads through the pestilential Pomptine marshes' and the windows were 'heavily veiled against the malaria'. Anna Maria responded enthusiastically to a flirtation on the road behind coach curtains and in the bedrooms of roadside inns, and this was an experience Casanova learned from and used later to his advantage as a regular traveller. But, again, he believed himself in love, even if Anna Maria, a full ten years his senior and party to a barren marriage, may have been guided by more complex motives.

It took six days and five overnight stops to get to Rome via Capua, Terracino, Sermonetta and Velletri. At each stop, the horses were of greater concern to the *vetturino* than the accommodation of his passengers, and the inns that catered to them were basic in the extreme. In Italy the scenery, classical ruins and even the food were often admired, by the British especially, but the willingness of even respectable Italians to 'pig down together' in disreputable inns while travelling was considered remarkable – not for the intimacy but for the lack of basic comforts at the inns. If traffic was heavy – as one traveller claimed it was towards the end of the week – the inns might run out of space and house their guests in empty stables.

The road from Naples to Rome, the ancient Via Appia, had not been repaved since Horace had traversed it on his way to Brundisium. It was a rough, slow ride, but the Vallati family's discomfort was eased as would often be the case with Casanova in the future, by the affable charm of their young travelling companion. Though silent for most of the first day, on the second he soon fell into a breezy flirtation with Anna Maria. Her middle-aged husband, flattered, perhaps, by the young man's interest in his wife, encouraged the friendship. The poor food at Garigliano on the second night was compensated for by the 'amusing conversation' between the foursome, and by the third night, in the hilltop village of

Terracino, Casanova was convinced that Anna Maria had more on her mind than chat.

At Sermonetta she took the initiative. On a twilight stroll near the coaching inn, she asked him if she had upset him, and they kissed for the first time. The next day, they 'spoke to each other with our knees more than with our eyes', but when they reached Rome, their flirtation remained unconsummated.

Casanova shared breakfast with the Vallatis in celebration of their arrival in Rome, and vowed to visit them as soon as possible, leaving Anna Maria in no doubt that, cleric though he was, he had every intention of pursuing the affair she seemed to be proffering.

He was dropped off near an inn at the foot of the Spanish Steps, an area that has barely changed since. It afforded then, as now, a perfect ring-side seat to the circus that is Rome – a generation later Keats lodged in the same house, cafés were just beginning to open along the Strada Condotto, now the via Condotti, and the Steps, as intended, drew an international crowd of pilgrims, hawkers and tourists.

The prize letter of introduction in Casanova's bag was to Cardinal Acquaviva 'the one man in Rome who has more power than the Pope', the *de facto* head of the Spanish Church in all its dominions. So Casanova immediately presented himself. Acquaviva found the young Venetian lacking in nothing but languages; his continuing ignorance of French – the language of international diplomacy at the Vatican, and at the best parties in Rome, was a particular stumbling block. Casanova reaffirmed his vow to learn it. He engaged a tutor, who lived nearby at 31 Piazza di Spagna, and attempted to assimilate into Roman life.

Fashion was paramount, he noted. Religion was merely trade, 'like the employees of a tobacco monopoly'. He forsook his cassock and decided to dress in the 'Roman fashion' of his cousin's tailor in Naples. He appeared thus attired in his first audience with the cardinal, who stared at him for a full two minutes, then engaged him on the spot as his secretary with three months' pay in advance. The cardinal had his major-domo show Casanova to apartments on the fourth floor of his residence, the Palazzo di Spagna – then as now sovereign Spanish territory – and Casanova moved his few possessions from the inn at the bottom of the Steps across the Piazza di Spagna to his new home in the lavishly upholstered bosom of the Mother Church. He then went straight to Anna Maria to celebrate.

At first Casanova's main objective was to ingratiate himself with Anna Maria's mother, with whom she was staying. At the widow Cecilia's house, in the Minerva district near the Pantheon, he met Anna Maria's other younger sister, an eleven-year-old, and her fifteen-year-old brother, who was also an abate. 'In Rome,' Casanova wrote, 'everyone either is or wants to be an abate.'

Anna Maria's mother welcomed him into the family, and invited him on weekend excursions outside the city. It was on a trip to Frascati that they finally consummated their affair, in what must be one of the most dramatic and romantic settings imaginable.

The Villa Aldobrandini dominates the hillside town of Frascati, a pleasant few hours' carriage ride from Rome through vineyards along the route of the Maximus aqueduct. A nephew of Pope Clement VIII had built it on the sound principle that there was no point in waiting for heaven when you had the resources to construct a paradise on Earth. The palace gardens, arranged over the whole hillside, were open to well-dressed Romans, and featured walkways, follies, fountains, and grottoes that open out still on to a seraphim's perspective of Rome. Naked gods and monsters grappled with mountain streams and each other, while cascades and even Roman theatrical masks, some large enough to walk inside, were cut into the rockface. The gardens were and are so steep and heavily planted that it was possible to be completely hidden from onlookers while enjoying panoramic views. The gardens remain intensely romantic, exactly as Anna Maria had known they would be.

Standing face to face, intensely serious, looking only into each other's eyes, we unlaced, we unbuttoned, our hearts throbbed, our hands hurried to calm their impatience. Neither of us having been slower than the other, our arms opened to clasp the object of which they were to take possession . . . At the end of two hours, enchanted with each other and looking most lovingly into each other's eyes, we spoke in unison, saying these words, 'Love, I thank thee.'

Once again, Casanova insisted it was true love not just lust: 'Alas for anyone who thinks the pleasure of Venus is worth anything, unless it comes from two hearts which love each other and are in perfect concord.' Again, he pictures himself as no libertine, but a mere facilitator in a woman's seduction of him. He seems surprised to find himself mocked by her: 'Alas for you, I am your first love, you will never get over me!'

Meanwhile Casanova's French progressed fast. He was a gifted linguist, even by the standards of the age when the educated élites of most major cities routinely spoke several modern and one or two ancient languages. He made notes on Acquaviva's correspondence, and could even converse with a Roman socialite, the Marchesa Caterina Gabrielli and compose odes in his newly acquired language. And some time in the winter of 1743/4 – according to Casanova's rendering of dates at this period – he was presented to the pope.

Benedict XIV might have sat easily on St Peter's throne in the modern age: he was affable, good-looking and sociable. Giacomo found that he 'liked a joke', and was voluble, though essentially reactionary. Casanova's lifelong success in inveigling himself into high society and the intellectual and artistic élites of the many cities he lived in was based, doubtless, on his charm but also on an appearance of easy assurance and a quick wit in the presence of the great and the not-so-good. In an age of toadying obsequiousness, his manner must have been refreshing. Benedict claimed he had heard of him, laughed at his stories of the rural backwater of Martorano and its new bishop, and commended Casanova for having landed on his feet in the service of Acquaviva. They met in Monte Cavallo, the primary summer residence of the pope in the eighteenth century, now the seat of Italy's president.

It was the Marchesa Gabrielli who first alerted Casanova to the fact that his affair with the lawyer's wife, Anna Maria, had not gone unnoticed. She even alluded to the gossip that they had been seen in the Frascati gardens and that Anna Maria was pregnant. 'Rome is small,' he was warned by a fellow cleric in the Palazzo di Spagna, 'and the longer you remain in Rome, the smaller you will find it.'

The potential scandal for Cardinal Acquaviva's young secretary was avoided by the settlement of the law case on which Anna Maria's husband had been working and their consequent return to Naples. Anna Maria was carrying Casanova's first child. Her sister Lucrezia was about to marry, and the wedding is one clear marker among the disputed dates in this period of Casanova's life: Lucrezia 'Angelica' d'Antoni was married on 17 January 1745.

The cloud under which Casanova was advised to leave Rome in the winter of 1744–5 he describes as relating to another scandal that only obliquely touched himself, Cardinal Acquaviva and a girl involved with the family of Casanova's French tutor. It seems likely, however, that the Vallati affair showed Acquaviva that his new secretary was unlikely to be a calming presence at the Palazzo di Spagna, and he suggested Casanova take leave of absence from Rome. 'I will supply you with an excuse which will preserve your honour,' he told Casanova. 'I give you permission to tell anyone that you are going away on a piece of business which I have entrusted to you . . . consider which country you wish to go to; I have friends everywhere and I will give you such recommendations as I am certain will procure you employment.'

To Acquaviva's immense surprise, Casanova asked to be sent neither to Venice nor to any of the other great Italian city-states where Acquaviva had contacts. Instead he wished to be entrusted with letters of introduction and despatched to Constantinople.

ACT II SCENE II

LOVE AND TRAVESTY

1745

'Our word *Person* is derived from the Latin for *Mask* or *Vizard*
. . . So that a *Person* is the same that an *Actor* is'

Thomas Hobbes

C asanova was due to sail for Constantinople, via Venice, with letters of introduction for one Count Claude Alexandre Bonneval. First, though, he had to extricate himself from Rome, and Italy. He was waylaid, as ever, by a love affair, one of an unusual hue: he believed himself in love next with a castrated man.

In the memoirs, Casanova details precise financial and diplomatic arrangements made for him to leave Rome in 1745. The pope gave him a token – a rosary of agates worth twelve *zecchini* at most – but the cardinal furnished him with seven hundred *zecchini* worth of Spanish gold, which was international currency, and Casanova himself had saved three hundred *zecchini*. He bought himself a bill of exchange, as was common across currency borders, to be cashed in Ancona and headed north. He had requested to travel via Venice, clearly intending to show his family and friends what fast work he was making up the greasy pole of church politics. He seems also, as the financial details

83

attest, to have kept some sort of diary or record of this period. Although he was talented with numbers, and felt keenly both insult and approbation as they related to payment, the detail is unnecessary and the more interesting for it. It takes up more space than his casual reference to Anna Maria's long desired pregnancy, which he must have guessed at the time was likely to herald the birth of his first child. His record was of turning the world to *his* account, and the tally of gains and losses was a ruthlessly personal audit.

In Ancona he happened upon a family of travelling actors who immediately made him feel at home. They represented all that his immediate family might have been – 'all the verve of the theatre; a pretty playfulness' – if his mother had chosen to take her children on tour. He describes a manageress-mother, two young daughters and two sons, one of whom made a striking impression on him. 'Bellino' was slightly younger than himself, Casanova guessed sixteen, 'ravishingly handsome', and was working as a *castrato* singer on a successful tour.

The Papal States, which included Ancona for much of the eighteenth and early nineteenth centuries, forbade women to take to the stage, just as they were barred from church choirs in Rome. This was one reason why Venetian actresses, like Casanova's mother, forged their careers beyond the Italian peninsula. The papal proscription extended to opera in which soprano and contralto roles could not reasonably be sung by men. In some instances, as in the Shakespearean tradition, boys sang the female roles, but the strength and singular beauty of the unbroken adult male voice had made *castrati* an exotic, highly prized and highly paid novelty on the Italian musical scene.

Castrati – male singers whose testicles had been surgically removed before adolescence – had a long and musically noble heritage in papal and liturgical music. They had sung at Santa Sofia in Byzantium and at the Vatican from at least the sixth century. The supposedly angelic quality of the voice – as high as a choirboy's but with the strength and volume of a grown male's

– had made *castrati* honoured members of the papal court. The development of opera, and of large opera-houses, with an array of mythical 'Metastasian' themes and an immediate issue of voice-projection, favoured the careers of *castrati*. So, too, did an allure that is remarked on even by as stolid a music enthusiast as Charles Burney: 'It was extacy [*sic*]! Rapture! Enchantment!' *Castrati* became superstars. Their voices combined brilliance, limpidity and power with the technique and artistic expressivity of an adult artist – and for that matter a tortured one. These tragedy-tainted divas earned far more than their wholly male counterparts, and composers including Handel, Haydn, Gluck, Lully, Monteverdi and Mozart wrote for the singular three-octave *castrati* range. Their careers often spanned several decades and the entire expanse of Europe.

Casanova's history as a travelling Italian exotic, trailing an aura of sexual mystery and paying court to salon and royal society across the continent, mirrored the career trajectories of contemporary *castrati* – some of whom, like him, were Venetian. It was inevitable that he should come into contact with the ultimate diva/divo Farinelli. It was only surprising that he fell in love with the first 'famous *castrato*' he met.

Bellino was in truth a further rarification of the genre, of a breed that troubled Italian theatre and choirs: a *castrato* in masquerade – that is, a woman disguised as a castrated man for the purposes of her musical career. Indeed, it was so widely rumoured that certain *castrati* were women that many were submitted regularly to the humiliation of showing their mutilated genitalia to satisfy critics, moral pundits or the merely prurient. It was a risky business, to masquerade against the Church and the law in this manner, but *castrati* played a dangerous double-game of sexual titillation anyway. Often, though not always, they took female roles in *opera seria*: goddesses and princesses, suitably attired. Often, though not always, *castrati* developed breasts, displayed to advantage by the theatrical and corsetry architecture of the day. Many plied a separate trade in sating heterosexual and homosexual – or even complicated transgender and transgressive – passions. Several were reputed to perform sexually as men despite the operation, giving them an entirely separate allure to women attracted to extreme sexual adventure or who simply feared pregnancy. And some allowed rumours to circulate that they were women, hermaphrodites or some untouchable third sex, which in a sense they were. In image and in practice, *castrati* were on the shores of sexual and artistic experimentation, desired, despised, pitied and envied; a veritable trinity of godhead, maidenhead and man.

Casanova decided that Bellino was a soprano in disguise. He was right, although at first he was troubled by the apparent likelihood that he was lusting after, and falling in love with, another man. He wrote that he 'made no resistance to the desires which [Bellino] aroused in me', but the piquancy of the 'travesty' was clearly part of the attraction for him, as it had been with the Venetian courtesan Giulietta Preati who had made him try on her dress. Casanova was a born masquerader. He makes some play in the memoirs of rejecting the advances of Bellino's brother, Petronio, a theatrical chancer-cum-rent-boy, who, to complicate things had a career as a '*première actrice*', or female impersonator. Nevertheless, he welcomed the opportunity to travel on with the theatrical family of 'Bellino', promising to escort them to Bellino's engagement in Rimini, via Venice.

There is some evidence that he may have conflated different journeys and experiences from 1744 and 1745 either through misreminiscence or deliberate streamlining of his picaresque narrative. But where he is vague on dates, he is specific on sex: he was increasingly alarmed to find himself besotted with a beautiful 'man'. 'Cecilia' – Bellino's younger sister – was not adequate distraction. Neither was the Greek slave girl whom he met again by coincidence on board a ship at anchor when he arrived in Venice. Casanova and she consummated their lust

fully dressed and in full view of 'Bellino', who was understandably shocked by the Abate Casanova's behaviour.

Bellino's other sister, Marina, also threw herself at Casanova,
as much in the spirit of enterprise as lust: she accepted payment,
which she passed to her mother, who (as was common in the
theatre) elided the maternal role with those of agent and pimp.

In Venice, Casanova threw himself into impressing his new
stage family, showing them around, buying expensive oysters
and arranging a meal of 'white truffles, shellfish, still champagne, Peralta, sherry and Pedro Ximenes', the latter being
fashionable Spanish wines. All of this was to become his pattern
of convivial, conspicuous, homosocial, food-focused seduction
as well as a narrative device that framed sex as just one part of a
sensual travelogue. But quite soon things between him and
Bellino got out of hand. Bellino refused to be examined or
touched by Casanova, explaining reasonably that 'all we *castrati*
have the same deformity' – the breasts that had first caught
Casanova's eye – and raising an eyebrow at his insistence that he
could not believe he was in love with a man. They agreed that
they would never 'consent to [the] infamies' of acting on a
homosexual impulse, but Bellino still refused to 'satisfy [Casa-
nova's] curiosity'. At last, brutally, Casanova used force to
discover what was really between Bellino's legs – and 'it was
at this moment that [he] found that [Bellino] *was* a man'.

Casanova was profoundly shocked and briefly dumbstruck.
In very little time, however, he reasoned that what he had seen in
the breeches of the person he believed to be a woman masquerading as a *castrato* was a 'monstrous clitoris'. Eventually,
however, Bellino became assured of Casanova's love and revealed the truth: that she was what Casanova had only hoped
she might be: a woman masquerading as a *castrato*. The penis
was fake – necessary to avoid detection by the moral arbiters of
the opera and the Church. The penis was revealed to be a
contrivance that 'Bellino', whom Casanova thence reveals as the
singer 'Teresa Lanti' had worn for several years when in danger

of being exposed as a woman. It was 'a sort of long, soft gut, as thick as one's thumb, white and with a very smooth surface . . . attached to the centre of an oval piece of very fine translucent hide . . . five or six inches long and two inches wide . . . fixed with gum tragacanth to the place where sex can be distinguished'. Wearing this, 'Bellino' appeared to have a penis, though no scrotum, in exact parody of a *castrato*.

Once Teresa had come clean with him, he found it amusing to watch her apply her 'apparatus': 'With this extraordinary attachment, she seemed to me even more interesting . . . I told her she had been wise not to let me touch it, for it would have . . . made me become what I am not.' After they had made love for the first time, and he lay watching her sleep; he determined 'to make her the partner of my fate', recognising in her that 'we were very nearly in the same situation'.

Who, then, was the woman masquerading as Bellino? Casanova rarely bothered to give pseudonyms to lovers who had also been actresses: their reputations were already irretrievably lost and their appearance in the pages of a libertine's memoir would not have been seen as authorial indiscretion. The fake *castrato* he names as Teresa Lanti may have been Teresa Landi, born in Bologna in 1731, as Casanova says, whose portrait hangs to this day at La Scala, Milan. Alternatively she may have been Artemesia Lanti, or even Angiola Calori, who later achieved fame and fortune in London in the 1750s and 1760s.

The back story Casanova provides for Teresa is colourful, as would befit a woman forced to dress as a man to play women on stage, but more instructive in his revelation of himself is his desire in the first place for this transgender lover. It is a chapter in his life illustrative more than most of the overlays of theatricality in Casanova's experience of the world. Yet his constant iteration of the theme of rejecting the homosexual potential of a liaison with Bellino, as with her brother, semaphores a contradictory concern that whatever his reasonable curiosity he was attracted as well as, possibly, repulsed by 'her' exaggerated sexual otherness.

What Casanova found so compelling in Teresa seems to have been the element of the actorly to their affair and, in particular, their love-making: he writes, at this stage about the importance to him of *performing* as a lover, 'the pleasure I gave . . . made up four-fifths of mine', but also of the need to *enact* affection for Teresa as 'fresh assurances of . . . our happiness'. They obviously had a good deal in common in terms of background, family, ambition and hazardous prospects. But if Teresa Lanti was indeed 'very nearly the same' as Giacomo Casanova – and she was one of the very few women from whom he accepted, initially, a serious proposal of marriage – then her attraction to him as what would now be termed a transvestite or even transsexual can hardly be ignored.

Their first love-making and her dramatic baring of her soul and fake penis – surely unique in the history of romantic literature – had a strong effect on Casanova. Not only did he contemplate giving up his career in the Church for her, he also made a full confession of his situation, prospects, finances and character. His greatest boast, aged nearly twenty, was only that he was 'my own master, that I am not dependent on anyone, and that I am not afraid of my misfortunes. My nature tends towards extravagance. Such a man am I.' It was not an unreasonable summary, and Teresa was as enamoured of his honesty as she had been of his persistence and passion. In one of his unpublished works found when he died Casanova had written about Teresa and the *castrati* phenomenon: 'Neither women nor men could avoid loving her [Teresa] and nothing was more natural; for amongst women he seemed the handsomest of men and amongst men the loveliest of women whilst dressed as a man.'

They decided to elope to Rimini, outside papal jurisdiction – where Bellino was due to sing but where she might reveal herself to the opera management as a woman. They intended to marry *en route* in Bologna. This impetuous plan fell through at Pesaro, where troops were checking passports. Casanova had lost his. He claims he tried to use the letter he was carrying from

Cardinal Acquaviva as suitable proof of his identity, but was ordered to wait at Pesaro until a new passport could be summoned from the Church authorities.

There are a number of holes in Casanova's story: he is unclear as to why he would diverge from Venice at this stage of his progress to Constantinople, though we might grant him the imperative of love. He is vague about why he and Bellino were travelling cross-country for the sake of a theatrical engagement that fails to fit the known dates of the Rimini opera calendar: the theatre was dark from February 1744 until the autumn of 1745. And the temporary loss of a passport seems an insufficient obstacle to persuade a man like Casanova to forgo an appointment he wanted to keep. Teresa continued on to Rimini, or wherever it was she was due to sing, and thence to Naples. She and Casanova, of course, never married.

'My story,' Casanova here admits, 'is none too plausible,' but aspects of its background politics meet with corroborative evidence. The essential truth, as often with Casanova, was more emotional than geographical. Whichever Italian theatre the unmasked Bellino was next engaged in, and there are several contenders, it is undisputed that Teresa was the first woman Casanova might have settled down with, and the first – he admitted to himself – that he renounced in favour of further adventure and the freedom to travel.

A letter arrived at Pesaro from Teresa: she had found a protector in the fifty-five-year-old Duke of Castropignano. She and Casanova were already moving apart. Perhaps she knew that he would be unwilling to play the role his putative father had with his mother. In a series of letters they agreed to end their liaison, without saying it was over. 'Sharing her lot, whether as husband or lover, I should find myself degraded, humiliated, and forced by my position and profession to grovel. The reflection that in the fairest time of my youth I would have to reject all hope of the high fortune which it seemed to me I had been born for gave the scales such a strong jolt that my reason silenced my heart.' He was nineteen, ambitious and, most importantly, haunted by the image of this parents' marriage – its tawdry glamour and potential for humiliation. His affair with Teresa forced both parties to grow up in different ways. Casanova accepted at last that he could not continue his church career and was not prepared, in his late teens, to marry, while Teresa found herself pregnant. Their son, born later that year in Naples, was christened Cesare Filippo Lanti and was brought up to believe that Teresa Lanti, the opera star, was his sister.

Teresa's example in masquerade inspired Casanova's next mask. In the continuing absence of his lost passport, having absconded from Pesaro to Bologna, he decided upon a different costume for himself. 'Reflecting that there was now little likelihood of my achieving fortune in my ecclesiastical career, I decided to dress as a soldier in a uniform of my own invention.' Life, for Casanova, was truly a succession of roles, Again, the practice of the times puts his impersonation of a professional soldier in its rightful context; armies of the period were dressed in all the colours and materials of the bazaar, and uniform was anything but unifying. The armies in the Italian peninsula were made up of pressed militiamen and paid mercenaries from most of mainland Europe, with the range of national custom in martial attire that that might suggest. Soldiers bought, and often customised, their own uniforms, and a young blade like Casanova, aspiring it would seem to be taken seriously as a mercenary for hire at a decent rate, naturally attempted to look like an officer. Casanova had himself a dandy outfit made of white and blue with gold aiguillettes and silver sword knots, and considered his début as a soldier, in Bologna, quite the entrance he should be making in life. A conversation he records when challenged in his uniform shows him at his imperturbable best: a young man on the make in need only of the right costume to feel confident on the world's stage. The inn he booked into in Bologna required his name:

'Casanova.'

'Your profession?'

'Officer.'

'In what service?'

'None.'

'Your country?'

'Venice.'

'Where have you come from?'

'None of your business.'

Teresa Lanti was already fading in his mind as he made plans for his triumphant return to Venice as an officer *en route* to Constantinople. It was a pattern of acquiesced abandonment that Casanova would repeat. Teresa's affection continued, as did his, but the passion waned, he moved on and, by and large, he was forgiven if not forgotten. Of course Teresa had more reason than most to feel marked by her affair with Casanova. He had led her to unmask herself as a woman – and a triumphant soprano career followed – and he was her first great love. He was also the father of her first child. But, then, when they first met, they were little more than children themselves. When Casanova finally reached Venice with the proper intent of heading to Constantinople, if his chronology is to be believed, it was 2 April 1744: his nineteenth birthday.

TALES FROM THE SERAGLIO, CONSTANTINOPLE

1745

'Never in my life have I been so beside myself or so carried away
. . . It would have been impolite to refuse – I should have shown
myself ungrateful, a thing that is not in my nature.'

Casanova, in an Ottoman harem

The ruse of military attire worked well for young Casanova. His uniform allowed him to dodge Venetian quarantine this time, reimposed since he had passed through with the Lanti family, and he found himself welcomed by the Grimanis, by his 'little wives' Marta and Nanetta, and into a small inn near the Rialto now that he had no real base in Venice. His stay was entirely as any prodigal might want: brief, celebrated and inconsequential.

There was no boat due to sail immediately to Constantinople so he opted to journey via Corfu, for which reason he swapped the cockade in his hat for that of a *bona fide* commission in a Venetian regiment stationed on the island, then a possession of the Doge. The Grimanis arranged introductions for their young ward, now a junior officer, to Venetian noblemen travelling to Corfu on the same ship: Senator Pietro Vendrami, Cavaliere Venier and Antonio Dolfin, newly appointed *bailo* or ambassador to Constantinople.

All three were highly influential men, and Dolfin, besides, was rich. Casanova set sail aboard a twenty-four-gun warship with a 'garrison of two hundred Slavonians' on 4 May 1744, having spent what would be his last night among the tangled limbs of Marta and Nanetta.

The ship put in at Orsara, where Casanova had been before as a poor abate. He imagined he would not be recognised, dressed splendidly as a Venetian officer, but the local barber-surgeon remembered him with unexpected clarity and unusual cause: 'You communicated a certain love token [gonorrhoea] to Don Geralamo's housekeeper,' he recalled, 'who gave it to a friend, who shared it with his wife. She gave it to a libertine who distributed it so effectively that in less than a month I had fifty patients whom I cured for a proper fee . . . Can I hope,' he continued, 'that you will remain here for a few days and give the disease a fresh start?'

Life aboard ship was sociable: Casanova ate well with the large retinue of Antonio Dolfin – but the nobles turned out to be enthusiastic gamblers, which started Casanova on his secondary addictive pursuit, whose consequences could not be cured by barber-surgeons. He gambled away the jewels he had bought or been given by the Grimanis as travel insurance, and much of his money, at faro and basset. 'The only stupid satisfaction I had,' he wrote, 'was hearing myself called a "fine player" by the banker each time I lost a crucial card.'

Some time in mid-May 1745, according to Casanova's chronology, they arrived in Corfu where he boarded the *Europa*, one of Venice's largest warships, and the finest way to sail up the Bosphorus to Constantinople on his first great overseas adventure.

'The view of the city from a league away is astonishing,' he gushed. 'Nowhere in the world is there so beautiful a spectacle.' It was the middle of a sweltering July and Casanova, with the retinue of Bailo Dolfin put up at the Venetian embassy in Pera before decamping to a summer residence nearby at Buyukdere.

Such close detail of diplomatic comings and goings lend both an air of authority while simultaneously casting the cloud of doubt on the precise chronology of Casanova's tale. The retiring and arriving Venetian *bailis* for instance, are miscredited by Casanova, but his local colour is emphatic and his encounter with the Earl Marischal of Scotland, Lord Keith, on his journey to Constantinople dates his story specifically to 1745. He sent his letter of introduction from Cardinal Acquaviva to the former Count Bonneval, now converted to Islam as Ahmed Pasha of Karamania, and was invited into his presence just two days after his arrival.

Constantinople 'is beyond dispute the largest City of Europe', a French diplomat averred in 1718. However, its population was less than that of Paris, and would soon be outstripped by London's, but it sprawled up to thirty-five miles in several directions and consequently was often thought to be the world's most populous metropolis. It overwhelmed visitors when they first arrived, 'its situation [being] the most agreeable and advantageous in the Universe', studded with mosques and minarets but also many gardens along the water's edge that were the backdrop to Casanova's exotic adventures. The triangle of the old city had its apex at the Topkapi Palace, referred to by Europeans with awe and wonder simply as 'the Seraglio', its gilt roof appearing to 'glitter' above the waters 'in a blaze'. To a Venetian like Casanova, however, Constantinople was in some regards familiar: a fading imperial capital built on water, a maritime power, semi-cloistered and segregated but dressed in all the fabrics of the Orient and more vivid yet to a young man on his first great overseas adventure. It was also a city that met travellers' previous expectations based on fiction, and Casanova's telling of his Oriental tales owes much in style to works he later read, to Montesquieu's *Persian Letters*, Diderot's *Bijoux Indiscrets* or, indeed, to the popular translation of *The Thousand and One Nights* then widely available, especially in France, by Galland. But to Constantinople he definitely had gone, if not exactly when he said he did.

At first Constantinople invited Casanova into its exclusively masculine political society. Women, travellers often noted, were rarely seen on the street, and if they were they appeared 'like spectres' in voluminous veils. Casanova's first guide to the city was Count Bonneval. Aged fifty-five and known since 1730 as Ahmed Pasha, his easy-going attitude to religion seems to have been one of Casanova's inspirations in dealing with the challenge to his faith made by the Muslims he met; Bonneval admitted he 'did not know the Koran any better than the Gospels . . . he was a Turk as he had been a Christian' – in other words, he was a secular opportunist. Casanova took note.

Bonneval felt he could be of little practical help to Casanova, but as Acquaviva had introduced him as a student of literature, Bonneval invited him to a sort of literary *soirée* at which only Italian was spoken. Here, Casanova met two Turks who would shape his experience of Constantinople. One was the relatively elderly Yussuf Ali; the other Casanova refers to only as 'Ismail'.

Casanova's new friends at the Venetian embassy and at the summer residence where he stayed that July and August were enormously impressed by the prominent Turks who invited him to their homes, having met him at Bonneval's Italian evening. Bonneval offered Casanova his janissary to help him find his way round the city, and reflected that Casanova was indeed in a fortunate position, 'without either cares or plans or any fixed abode [abandoning] himself to Fortune fearing nothing and expecting nothing'. With older men, he seems to have projected an air of lost or abandoned youth, and the two Turks showered him with avuncular attention.

Yussuf Ali was a philosopher. He was also a very wealthy man. He invited Casanova first to a dinner – Casanova assiduously recorded the honeyed drinks and meat stews of old Istanbul – and thence to a series of theological discussions. It was the sort of sociable discourse Casanova relished. He even confessed that he could be a philanderer and a good Catholic by virtue of frequent confession and absolution: 'I am a complete man and I am a Christian. I love the fair sex and I hope to enjoy many conquests . . . for when we confess our crimes to our priests they are obliged to absolve us.'

Yussuf merely raised an eyebrow. He began to probe Casanova on his interest in Islam, even in conversion, perhaps because the initial introduction had come through the celebrated apostate Count Bonneval, perhaps because his affection for the intellectually omnivorous young man had convinced him of some other sort of find. Yussuf Ali began to sound out Casanova as a prospective son-in-law. Zelmi, his daughter and the apple of his eye, was his only child whose future was insecure – his sons were independently wealthy. She had been brought up as a European intellectual and was deemed by her father to be above the fray of the Constantinople marriage market – which may be why he determined on an arranged marriage between her and the well-connected Venetian who happened to share his interest in philosophising. Casanova, with the promise of riches and a beautiful virginal fifteen-year-old, was sorely tempted, but vacillated over two obstacles that troubled him: that he was not allowed to get to know Zelmi first, and that he would be forced to spend a year converting to Islam. Meanwhile, another side of Ottoman life, much commented upon by travellers in the later eighteenth century, was opened up to him in the person of 'Ismail'.

Ismail had also been at that first Thursday gathering of what might be termed Constantinople's literary society. He was sufficiently connected to the powers in mainland Italy – he had previously been the Sultan's Minister of Foreign Affairs – to have been on the list of Turkish notables Acquaviva had given Casanova and invited the young man to another dinner. All was 'Asiatic luxury', but the conversation was entirely in Turkish, so Ismail invited Casanova to a separate occasion, a breakfast, where they could speak alone, and in Italian. On this occasion, in his garden summerhouse near the Bosphorus, Ismail made a pass at Casanova. The nineteen-year-old, caught off-guard, parried with the clear statement that he 'was not of that persuasion'. However, because he feared he might have offended Ismail by leaving 'rather abruptly', he mentioned the incident to Bonneval, who advised him to feel relaxed about accepting further invitations from the man they both called 'Effendi': Ismail had only acted, he said, in the tradition of a Turkish host and would 'make no such proposal again'.

In narrating his parallel relationships with Yussuf Ali and Ismail, Casanova moves easily between an abstract discussion of chastity with the former and attacks on the same with the latter. They were minor experiences for Casanova in so far as both men were attracted to him intellectually, and in some sense sexually, though with greatly variant intents. His time in Turkey forced him to question his own culture, mores and morality, but the passage is also important for the parallels his story presents to recent research on Ottoman sexual practice, as well as the experiences of other travellers in Constantinople, which tends to support Casanova's rendering of social history.

Ismail's next invitation was to an evening at which Casanova was requested to demonstrate the *furlana*, a racy Venetian carnival dance. Rather like the waltz a generation later, it brought couples into scandalously close contact and involved swinging the woman vigorously round the man. From his harem Ismail provided a dancer, whom Casanova thought Venetian, though dancers for hire in Constantinople were, according to Lady Mary Wortley Montagu, most often gypsies. She was veiled in the Venetian carnival manner and Casanova was pressed to perform. He never found out who his energetic partner was, and left the party out of breath and out of sorts that he was unable to ascertain her identity. Bonneval advised him not to meddle with the harem of an Ottoman grandee. Constantinople, as Lady Mary had noted in 1717, was a 'perpetual masquerade' of sexual scandal, half hidden behind 'muslins' or 'ferigees', now known as burkas, where even women in exclusive harems might have 'entire liberty of following their inclinations without danger of discovery'.

This aspect of Constantinople was familiar to Casanova from Venice, the only difference being that in Ottoman society women were often veiled in bed. 'You may easily imagine the number of faithful wives in a country where they have nothing to fear from their lovers' indiscretion,' wrote Lady Mary, not without jealousy. There is hot dispute over this depiction, in Casanova's writings as well as in hers, of Ottoman sexual licence. It seems most likely that foreigners and well-connected Venetians like Casanova met the element of Ottoman society that was most open to them, while the orthodox morality described by other writers simply existed in parallel. On the Ottoman sexual demimonde, Casanova's has turned out not to be a lone voice.

Next Ismail invited him to a late-night fishing expedition, at full moon, on the Bosphorus. He accepted, but 'His wanting to be alone with me,' Casanova wrote, 'seemed . . . suspect.' Things took an unexpected turn. They put ashore at Ismail's summerhouse and grilled the fish they had caught. Ismail then whispered that certain female members of his household were likely to bathe in the pool and that he and Casanova could watch from an adjoining garden house to which he happened to have the key. Casanova agreed enthusiastically. 'Leading me by the hand he opens the door and we are in darkness. We see the whole length of the pool, lighted by the moon, [and] almost under our eyes we see completely naked girls, now swimming, now coming out of the water to ascend marble steps, where . . . they exhibited themselves in every conceivable posture.' It was a scene from the *Arabian Nights*: three women of the seraglio, naked in the moonlight. Travellers' tales of the period are filled with wonder at the 'ablutions of Mahometans' and in this Casanova appears to conform to literary type. The Ottomans bathed publicly and often. One French writer of the period spent ten pages on these rituals for the delectation of his royal master, including unexpected details considered shocking at Versailles:

both men and women practised complete bodily depilation – men's beards aside.

It is hardly conceivable that Ismail's household's display of a moonlight bathing ritual was unplanned. It is conceivable, as Casanova relates the tale, that Ismail enjoyed watching it especially in the company of another voyeur. Casanova certainly thought the women knew they were observed and that they performed accordingly. Doubtless, too, Ismail had hoped that things would become more intimate between himself and the Venetian. Casanova writes that he 'chose to believe' everything that followed was unplanned on Ismail's part but he was aroused to the point of first following Ismail's lead in pleasuring himself in the darkness, whilst watching the girls, and then he allowed Ismail to touch him. His prose is perhaps deliberately unclear – his emotions and impulses were mixed, as was his regard for his later readers, and their prejudices and expecta- tions of a largely heterosexual libertine. 'Never in my life,' he wrote, 'have I been so beside myself or so carried away,' which he may have considered mitigation for a rare confession of repeated sexual contact with another man, which may or may not have been full penetrative sex.

Like him I found myself reduced to making the best of the object beside me to extinguish the flame kindled by the three sirens . . . and Ismail triumphed when he found that his proximity condemned him to take the place of the distant object to which I could not attain. I also had to submit to his taking turnabout. It would have been impolite to refuse; I should have shown myself ungrateful, a thing that is not in my nature.

The implication in Casanova's description of what went on in Ismail's peep-cabin seems unavoidable. Perhaps he was testing the waters, as it were, with a frank admission of sexual free-ranging. In literary terms, Constantinople was the right place to do this. The 'Sublime Porte' appears frequently in the travel literature of the time as the most likely place in which young men could experience a sexual culture that was entirely foreign to that which prevailed in Europe. Sometimes taken as a deliberate slur on Islam, the testimony of writers from Lady Mary Wortley Montagu and Adolphus Slade to Baron de Tott is consistent in its reiteration of Casanova's experience: Constantinople was as louche as Venice at Carnivale, with the added likelihood of homosexual encounters as a result.

Constantinople was teaching Casanova a great deal about himself. He found that his ambition did not outstrip his attachment to the faith and culture of Europe. He found he could hold his own abroad with admiring older men and philosophers, as he had in Italy. He found the slating of his sexual appetite, at the height of its voraciousness, knew bounds of neither place nor conscience nor, seemingly, orifice or gender. If, as some have suggested, he embroidered the Constantinople episode, it is still revelatory that he should choose to place there the defining of his attitude to the Church, the limit of his avarice – he balked at an arranged marriage – and a first experience, seemingly, of passive and active anal sex, which he glances over in the memoirs with less regard than he gives to Constantinople's filigree jasmine pipes. As for the duplicitous seducer Ismail, Casanova simply concluded, 'We did not know what to say to each other so we simply laughed.' Which sounds authentically Casanova at least.

He left Constantinople richer in life's experience, and in its goods. Although he turned down Yussuf Ali's tempting offer of 'high office in the Ottoman empire' and the hand of his daughter Zelmi, Yussuf said he was as impressed by Casanova's conscience and argument as he would have been happy to have him as a son-in-law, and gave him a small chest of goods to sell in Corfu or Venice. His escapade with Ismail was one of the few adventures in Constantinople he did not relate to Bonneval or Venier back at the Venetian embassy; he lost a letter Ismail gave him for Acquaviva, and sold the cask of hydromel that had been his admirer's parting gift.

Casanova's brief adventures in Corfu on the outward and return journeys to Turkey are now cited as evidence of the essential veracity of his writing on Constantinople. He arrived back in Corfu with a trunkful of goods from Yussuf Ali and Ismail, bought, according to Casanova, at the simple price of their affection for his good company – although a cynical modern eye might trace a pattern of sexually flirtatious chancing. The gifts included wine, tobacco, jasmine pipes and mocha coffee worth hundreds of *zecchini* in Corfu to the naval forces on the island and their sophisticated community of courtesans. In Corfu, also, Casanova had a minor rank, bought in Venice, in the Venetian army. With this, his impressive erudition and an introduction from Dolfin, he was offered a job as adjutant to Giacomo da Riva, governor of the Galleasses, based in Corfu. And in turn this landed him, briefly, in the bed of Signora Foscarini, Riva's mistress.

It was an abortive, frustrating and humiliating affair, an early lesson in the ways of cicisbeism, the Venetian code of gallantry, which could lead to romantic disaster. Such was the experience in any event for Casanova, who, in his frustration with the mistress of his superior officer ended up paying for sex with one of the port's whores, and contracting another bout of gonorrhoea.

It was a chastened man who set sail to return to Venice. His ship dropped anchor near the Arsenale on 14 October and, after undergoing quarantine on board, he set foot in Venice on 25 November. He was broke, thin again, unwell and full of self-doubt. But, in important respects, he had begun to grow up.

PALAZZO BRAGADIN, A YOUNG MAN'S ENTRANCE INTO SOCIETY
1745–8

'I felt ashamed . . . I felt humiliated . . . earning a scudo a day
scraping away at the violin in the orchestra of the Teatro San
Samuele . . . I let my ambition sleep.'

Giacomo Casanova, 1745

As soon as he was allowed ashore, Casanova went to visit
Signora Orio for news of his friends and to visit his 'little
wives'. He had missed much while he had been away. The
widow Orio had remarried, Nanetta had married, becoming a
countess, and her sister, Marta, had by this time entered her
Murano convent. He never saw her again.

Francesco, his brother, now eighteen, was studying the battle
paintings of Simonini out at the Fort Sant'Andrea where Casanova had once been confined. The young men became, for the
first time, almost friendly – once Casanova had taken the
trouble to visit the fort and demand Francesco's return to
Venice.

But Casanova's reappearance in the city was neither happy
nor auspicious. He was acutely aware, at all of twenty, that he
was viewed as a dilettante and a disappointment. His boasted
schemes of a fine career in the Church or the military had

crashed on the rocks of overweening ambition and petty scandal, and former acquaintances around San Samuele openly laughed at him. He took a cheap room with his brother in another lowly theatre district, the Calle del Carbon in San Luca, and found himself thus yards from the centre of Venice, marked at the midpoint of the Campo San Luca, but also penniless. It could be accounted a symptom of a sort of self-abnegating depression, adolescent in its way, or some trait more ingrained in Casanova that he chose to mark the lowest point of his life by making things even worse.

He approached Grimani about returning to the theatre as a lowly fiddler. There was an opening in the orchestra and he had continued to play the violin, intermittently, ever since Dr Gozzi's lessons in Padua. His position in the orchestra pit was a crushing humiliation and a fairly public one, but he chose it and wallowed in his misery. He played in the little orchestra for two musical comedies in repertory, newly identified as *L'Olimpiade* by Fiorelli and *Orazio Curiazio* by Bertoni, in the cramped pit of the San Samuele. But he avoided his former friends. He hid, to the extent he could, avoiding 'fashionable gatherings' and cowled himself psychologically by drinking heavily and hanging with a bad crowd. One of the earliest references to Casanova in the files of the Venetian Inquisition recorded his disgrace: 'After the defrocking of the quondam priest Casanova played the violin in the Grimani theatre San Samuele. This Casanova, according to many people he has encountered during his travels, has no respect for religion.'

There is camaraderie in the professional theatre, and also a complicity and habit of bad behaviour. The orchestra pit of any theatre traditionally spills out straight into the bar, and such was Casanova's experience. The young musicians poured themselves enthusiastically into the all-night *magazzini* near the San Samuele in Campos San Stefano and Sant'Angelo and, emboldened by *malvasie* wine, bonhomie and fecklessness they marauded, drunk, around the Piazza San Marco. They untied gondolas. They woke priests to beg final unction for the healthy, and sent midwives to spinster virgins. They cut bell cords, rang fire alarms and even desecrated the war memorial in the middle of the Campo Sant'Angelo. Casanova recorded all of this without apology or self-defence. He was a lost young man.

However, it was a separate incident with the orchestra, during the carnival of 1746, that put Casanova on an entirely different footing in Venice society and in life. Lucky for him that they were available to play one night on the other side of the Grand Canal, briefly released from their duties at the San Samuele. They made up 'one of several orchestras for the balls . . . given for three days in the Palazzo Soranzo . . . di San Polo' in honour of a patrician wedding. If Casanova had not been there, he would never have met Bragadin.

Senator Matteo Giovanni Bragadin was brother to the *procuratore* of Venice and lived in the sixteenth-century Palazzo Bragadin di Santa Marina near the Rialto. He was at the Palazzo Soranzo that evening in March 1746, with the cream of Venice society, for the wedding celebrations. 'An hour before dawn' the orchestra was paid off and Casanova was about to head home when, in front of him in the queue for gondolas, a red-robed senator dropped a note on the ground. Casanova returned it to the older man, who introduced himself as Senator Bragadin, thanked him and asked if he could give him a lift home.

In the gondola, though, the senator suffered what appeared to be a stroke. First his arm went numb, then his leg, and when Casanova moved a lamp close to him, half of the senator's face had fallen into a rictus of paralysis. He acted quickly. He had the gondoliers stop at the Calle Bernardo, woke a surgeon, who immediately attended the senator in the gondola and bled him as they pressed on towards the Palazzo Bragadin on the far side of the Grand Canal. Casanova loitered, shirtless – he had donated his to stem the bleeding. Servants ran to fetch the senator's two close friends, Marco Dandolo and Marco Barbaro, who arrived within the hour. A doctor was summoned and Casanova was told he could go home. He said he would stay.

The doctor sought to cure what he seems to have misdiagnosed as a heart-attack by applying a mercury poultice to the senator's chest. The senator rapidly deteriorated, and Casanova took one of those leaps in the dark that punctuate his career. He challenged the prescription and removed the poultice. It was breathtakingly audacious in the context of the Venetian class structure and prevailing medical opinion, but the senator recovered, hailed Casanova as a genius and natural healer, and asked him to move into his palazzo.

As Casanova relates it, the key to his appeal to Bragadin, and indeed to Dandolo and Barbaro, was as a healer. They also shared an interest in the esoteric teachings known as the cabbala, not uncommon in Venice at this period and discussed in a later *intermezzo*. Casanova was credited with preternatural powers by Bragadin and when asked where his wisdom and flair for medicine came from he quoted some half-remembered gibberish from Dr Gozzi's collection of illicit books and hoped for the best. His medical genius had amounted to little more than self-confidence and common sense, strong traits in him already, along with an instinctive willingness to risk a throw of the die. If Bragadin had died, he would have been held responsible – but when faced with danger, Casanova tended to play like a *commedia* actor and improvise in the least likely direction. As it turned out, he was *en route* to becoming the man he had dreamed he would be. He moved into the Palazzo Bragadin and the world he had always felt should be his.

There is, however, another possible explanation for Casanova's sudden elevation in society and his fast adoption by a fifty-seven-year-old senator, with confirmed bachelor friends.

Casanova was well aware of the rumour that was soon circulating in Venice:

The close attachment of these three respectable personages to me was cause for raised eyebrows by those who observed it. People gossiped as if it were some strange phenomenon behind which must lurk something sinister . . . wicked tongues invented infamous explanations. This thing, it was said, can't be natural. Slander got mixed in. Surely there was some mystery under the surface which must be exposed?

One Casanova scholar has stated unequivocally that Bragadin deliberately 'picked up' the handsome orchestra boy.

This may seem unlikely: Bragadin's seizure was treated seriously by others, so was clearly not feigned, but perhaps the episode began in different circumstances from those Casanova presents. It is not possible to wander from the Palazzo Soranzo to the canal, the Rio de la Madonetta. The palace has a water gate that opens straight from the *portego*, or water-level hallway, on to the canal. Though gondolas waited in the *piscina* where two canals met, the Rio delle Beccarie and the Madonetta, it takes a deliberate meander through a dark labyrinth of *calles* to walk from the palace to the arcade of the Fondamenta del Banco Salvati where gondoliers loitered. Is this what Senator Bragadin did, glancing furtively over his shoulder down the ravinous Calle Cavalli with Giacomo Casanova following discreetly behind? Was the dropped note the final signal in a flirtation begun earlier rather than an opening gambit? If Casanova was a sexually omnivorous chancer seriously down on his luck in 1746, it makes a degree of sense: 'The association with Bragadin began at least as a simple sale of his [Casanova's] body, the way all his family and everyone else in the theatre, of both sexes, sold theirs.' It certainly helps to explain the tight hold Casanova had on Bragadin from that day forth. Elsewhere Casanova opined that any young man was stupid not to win 'the affection and esteem of men of position . . . by his caresses [and defy] prejudice'. Moreover, he was aware that the Inquisition viewed his instant rapport with Bragadin as suspicious: 'I learned twenty years later that they were having us followed and the best spies of the Tribunal of the State Inquisitors were charged with discovering the hidden explanation of this unlikely and monstrous union.'

The files of the Venetian Inquisition indeed lend credence to Casanova's paranoia about their interest in him and his belief that they had set on him one of their finest spies, and in the theory that Casanova was selling his body as well as his supposed cabbalistic healing powers. The Inquisition files are pregnant with a couched but pointed insistence that at this time Casanova was something between a free-loader, a social climber and a rent-boy:

Those he is acquainted with . . . include Bragadin . . . Barbaro and other noblemen who love him and with some of whom he is intimate . . . It has also been noted that he has numerous foreign acquaintances and a young crowd – men as well as women – with whom he dallies at their homes, and also married women and older men and women whom he also entertains in every sense.

The Inquisition's conclusion was: '[Casanova] is trying to elevate himself in society and make his fortune whilst satisfying his pleasures at the same time.' Last, if Casanova was indeed hoping for a ride home across the Grand Canal that night, why would he have travelled with the senator, whose gondola was heading in the *opposite* direction, north towards the knot of canals around the Calle Bernardo *before* his 'heart-attack'?

Casanova's own account of why he was so rapidly befriended by the troika of patrician bachelors is hardly more creditable to him, depending on your point of view. Bragadin, Dandolo and Barbaro were practising cabbalists, in thrall to the fashionable but illicit divining of fortunes and casting of spells based on ancient Jewish mysticism. Casanova may have known as much about the cabbala at this time as he did about medicine, but he managed to say the right things at the right time, convince the three men of his powers, which, rather than anything vicious,

Casanova claimed had won the 'old men's' hearts (they were middle-aged).

Within weeks, Bragadin had asked Casanova to do more than move in. He asked him become a special private cabbalist healer and occultist to him and his friends, and to become his adopted son.

'I took the most creditable, the noblest and the only natural course', wrote Casanova, not without a hint of irony. 'I decided to put myself in a position where I need no longer go without the necessities of life; and what those necessities were for me no one could judge better than I. That', he claimed, 'is the story of my metamorphosis and of the happy period that raised me at one bound from the base role of a fiddler to that of a nobleman.' He had leaped across the footlights to the centre-stage *jeune premier* role he had coveted. He became, overnight, a young Venetian patrician, with all the privileges of wealth and none of the responsibilities that might have accompanied it had he been an actual, not adopted, son.

But it had not been achieved at the whim of the theatrical gods: Casanova credited his 'invincible self-esteem' that when challenged about his cabbalistic knowledge he had bluffed, then risen to the occasion. He developed genuine affection for the three older men, 'all heaven', as he called them, and if they lavished material kindnesses on him, 'all earth', he returned them in a spirit of protectiveness and boyish affability. He would be the young man they once had been, he said, for their vicarious pleasure. Why not? His explanation of Bragadin's affection, aside from their shared interest in the cabbala, was simple:

The magnanimous Bragadin looked after me . . . he loved my heart and my wit. In his youth he too had been a great libertine, a slave to every passion . . . he thought he saw in me his own image and felt sorry for me. He used to say I was going so fast I would soon burn out but in spite of this expectation he never lost faith in me. He always expected my wildness to wane but did not live to see it so.

Casanova joined that class of Venetian high society that Stendhal would later declare had lived better, more elegantly and more happily than perhaps any other in history. And he had a singular talent for happiness and living the best of times. So begins Casanova's period as a gentleman of leisure in Venice – the image that he has left to the world, but one which he stumbled upon almost by accident, and one which occupied in any event only a few years of his early twenties. It cannot easily be overstated that the accident, whatever it was, outside the Palazzo Soranzo, utterly changed Casanova's life. It elevated him, *deus ex machina*, from the gutter to the starry heights of Venetian society. This Cinderella transformation at once made his life, and risked ruining it. It soon becomes apparent in the files of the Inquisition that it was this class infraction – rather than anything Casanova ever did between bedsheets or with Tarot cards – that alerted the guardians of La Serenissima to the supposed dangerous radicalism of Giacomo Casanova. But that all lay in his future.

For the time being, he set about learning what it was to be rich. Bragadin, Dandolo and Barbaro settled on him a fairly generous allowance of ten *zecchini* a month, which was paid to him for almost the rest of his life. He did a little undemanding legal work for a Leze Manzoni. He had a home again, a new father-figure – or, rather, several. More importantly, in terms of his standing in Venice, he was equipped with his own gondola, a servant and henceforth dressed and acted as if he was the equal of his young noble friends. The Polish Count Zawoiski, the wild young Zorzi Balbi, Angelo Querini, a famed wit, scion of a great Venetian family and a young libertine called Lunardo Venier, whose family *palazzo* stares at San Samuele over the Grand Canal, became his intimates.

A relationship at the Palazzo Bragadin that started out in a theatrical tradition of quasi-prostitution or, as Casanova presented it, the cynical duping of three men obsessed by spiritualism, soon turned into something rather touching. Bragadin and, to a lesser but growing extent, Dandolo and Barbaro clearly cared for the young man. And he, in turn, grew to love and respect them. He turned to them for advice as well as money. As he was aware, Bragadin had lived and loved hard in his youth and knew more about Venetian high society than his young ward from a back alley in San Samuele possibly could. When he found himself implicated in a young noblewoman's flight from a feckless fiancé or when he tried to help a country girl with her dowry, they advised and admonished him. In both instances his gallantry had mixed motivation: the women extended sexual favours in return for his kindness. '[Bragadin] was always giving me excellent guidance', wrote Casanova, 'to which I listened with pleasure and admiration and never ignored. That's all he asked of me. He gave me good advice and money.' Also, as Casanova was well aware, he gave him love.

In and out of the *portego* of the Palazzo Bragadin, under the three stone apostle heads on the *piano nobile* balcony, Casanova soon became a well-known figure around Santa Marina, the little parish dominated by the exquisite palace and, ironically, another theatre: the Teatro Grimani di San Giovanni Grisostomo (now Malibran). As the young dandy stepped in and out of his gondola, he might have thrown a glance back across the canal to the life he had left behind; opposite the *palazzo* water-gate is the theatre stage-door.

With the three older men, he spent the summer of 1746 inland at Padua, though far from his former scholarly world at Dr Gozzi's. Instead, he frittered his time and money at the home of a notorious local courtesan called Ancilla, who ran a gambling den. As a result he came to fight his first duel, with 'a young man as harebrained as myself and with the same tastes;' one Count Medini who was Ancilla's principal lover and also her card-shark. A moonlit sword-fight – Casanova had adopted the noble and military habit of wearing a sword but at no point mentions learning to fence – in which he wounded the count inspired Bragadin to suggest Casanova return forthwith to Venice. He

duly did, and spent the rest of 1746 'at my usual occupations
. . . gambling and pursuing love affairs'.

It is not surprising that the Venetian authorities had become
aware of young Giacomo Casanova. It was – and remains – a
city where it is impossible to achieve any sort of anonymity in
the simple pastimes of the day, and one in which transgression is
immediately the subject of gossip, comment, censure or amusement. Moreover in the eighteenth century, there was an
extensive network of informants in the pay of the Council of
Ten, and, it's sub-committee, the Council of Three, referred to
more often by their feared ecclesiastical title, The Inquisition.
The Venetian Inquisition should not then be confused with the
other inquisitions of religious suppression; the Council of Three
to which most Inquisition material was addressed was an organ
of government censorship.

Giovanni Battista Manuzzi informed mainly on the area
round the Campo San Stefano and Sant'Angelo but also wrote
of affairs as far towards the Rialto as San Luca and even Santa
Marina. He was a drinker, to judge by the wine stains on his
reports, still held in the Frari in Venice, and his deteriorating
handwriting during the writing of his extant reports. He was
also a prude. He took a keen interest in Casanova, who would
inevitably have come to the attention of the Inquisition at some
point, if only for the frolics that went far beyond ebullience into
the realms of danger and bad taste. There would have been
reports on him, as there were on so many of his fellow citizens,
for misdemeanours such as being seen frequently in the company
of those who knew foreigners.

But it was more than that. Because The Venetian Inquisition
was an organ of state more than of religious control, though the
distinction would have been meaningless to an eighteenth-
century Venetian, it was primarily interested in Casanova for
his sudden elevation to the ranks of quasi-nobility.

One of the main functions of the Inquisition, and arguably of
the Venetian governance, was to preserve Venice's oligarchy –

the tight circle of patrician families entered in the doge's Golden Book and entitled to government and Church positions, to sinecures and commercial monopolies – untouched by the rest of Venetian or international society. One of the earliest of Manuzzi's reports on Casanova illustrates how ill-advisedly he played into the Inquisition's hands by behaving conspicuously badly in the company of the well-connected:

Under an obligation to the Venetian [Inquisition] to address the issue of Giacomo Casanova, son of a comedian and comedienne [Casanova's] character can be described thus: cunning; one who takes advantage of other people's generosity, such as Sig Bragadin who has helped him financially due to the fact that Casanova is unemployed. Most of his travels have circled around people with similar leanings to his own, but from all walks of life; from nobles to petty gamblers. Don Pio Batta Zini of the church of San Samuele, a friend of Casanova, told me in private and confidentially however that one should not underestimate Casanova's intelligence; he is a capable gambler who is able, in town, to con the nobility of money through his numerous acquaintances [among them].

Possibly aware that he was being closely monitored, Casanova left Venice in January 1748 and travelled across northern Italy to Milan, whose principal attraction was that 'No one paid any attention to me.' It would not be so for long. He had borrowed four hundred *zecchini*, most likely from Bragadin, was 'well supplied with jewels [i.e. credit], in excellent health and at the happy age of twenty-three.' He dressed himself well, and he went to the theatre.

The performance, an opera, was unremarkable but for the appearance to 'general applause' of Teresa Lanti's younger sister Marina, now 'grown-up, filled out, and in short all that a pretty seventeen-year-old should be.' She was all that a pretty sister of the Lanti family should be indeed, in that she was under the 'protection' of a self-styled Roman count, Celi, who made her sleep with men he intended to dupe at cards. When Casanova introduced himself as a relative of Marina, Celi said, 'She is a whore,' to which Marina rejoined that it was very true 'and you can believe him for he is my pimp'. Mixed impulses of gallantry and opportunism led Casanova to 'rescue' her from him and offer to travel with her to Mantua, where she had a further engagement as a prima ballerina. In extricating her, he again found himself asked to fight a duel. The man who stood as his second was to become a lifelong friend, the French actor-singer-dancer Antonio Stefano Balletti, a year older than Casanova, who was engaged to dance opposite Marina in Mantua.

At this stage of his life Casanova was repeatedly drawn back into the circle of the professional theatre – he was even travelling under his mother's maiden name, Farussi – and evidently he found the company of musicians and performers suited his amused take on the world and his rootlessness. Marina, however, set her eyes on Antonio as the three travelled together to Mantua, via Cremona. Casanova's habit of seeking out a theatre crowd may also have been a simple preference for the city at night, and soon enough, with Marina and Antonio busy at rehearsals and all three in separate lodgings, this again got him into trouble.

Mantua was under partial curfew. The city was patrolled by militia of the Austrian army, but the officer who questioned Casanova for being out late was of Irish descent in the Imperial Infantry, one Franz O'Neilan. Casanova and O'Neilan instantly recognised each other as kindred spirits and were drinking together within hours of Casanova's 'arrest'. O'Neilan, however, was a dissolute of a darker hue. He boasted that he had given up trying to cure himself of gonorrhoea, picked fights and quarrels, thought nothing of knocking down old ladies while galloping through the city and had a particularly unattractive interest in sexual sadism that led him to wear a ring with a spike to inflict greatest pain at the moment of greatest pleasure. This turned out to be too much information for Casanova who, however catholic his tastes, was never intrigued or aroused sexually by violence.

They eventually fell out over their different philosophies of womanising. Casanova offered the syllogism that love without love was worthless, and O'Neilan teased him for having caught the clap, yet again, from fifteen minutes with a whore he had not even found attractive.

Casanova's understanding of his own sexuality was evolving: he acknowledges at this point in his memoirs that his compulsion for sexual adventure was not entirely or even mainly physical, but for the joy in giving joy, in performing and in a pathological desire to please sexually and otherwise – then move on. The idea of chasing sex to inflict less than pleasure, or indeed pain in the case of O'Neilan, 'well set up for love . . . tall and handsome' as he might be, was anathema to Casanova.

He spent two months in Mantua, curing himself of gonorrhoea with his usual doses of *eau de nitre* and a Spartan diet, while attending the theatre frequently to watch his friends Balletti and Marina dance out their passion on stage.

On what was to be his last night, he again attended the theatre where he saw Signor Manzoni, in whose law firm he worked if somewhat inattentively, in Venice. Manzoni was with Giulietta, the famous courtesan whom Casanova had met years earlier at the Palazzo Malipiero. Through them he was introduced to the local Austrian military grandee, General Spada. It might have been an unremarkable meeting of acquaintances old and new, and achieved nothing more than a footnote in the memoirs, had it not been that later that night Casanova met the woman with the clearest claim to have been the love of his life.

YOU WILL ALSO FORGET HENRIETTE

1749

'They who believe that a woman is incapable of making a man equally happy all the twenty-four hours of the day have never known an Henriette . . . It is impossible to conceive the extent of my happiness.'

Giacomo Casanova

There was a commotion in the corridor of the Cesena boarding-house where Casanova was staying such as might have formed the opening scene of a play of the period, be it farce, romance or drama. Indeed, the brouhaha heralded all three. A Hungarian officer, as Casanova deduced from the articles of uniform strewn about, was arguing with the Italian landlord; the officer was attempting to communicate in Latin. Another man was in bed in his room, but the landlord was threatening the Hungarian with the Inquisition – known to be particularly severe in Cesena – because he suspected the interloper to be a woman. He had already called the *sbirri*, the Inquisition constables who reported to the local bishop.

Casanova, attracted by prurience, gallantry or his instinctive interest in a drama and in supporting an underdog, chose to side with the foreigner against the locals and act as translator. 'The ardour with which I embraced the affair,' he claimed '[sprang] from my innate sense of decency, which could not bear to see a foreigner treated in such a fashion.' He was also, of course, intrigued by the person in the Hungarian's bed. He went to ask General Spada, his acquaintance from the theatre, for help with the *sbirri*, whom he believed, rightly, were being used by the landlord as a means to extort money from the Hungarian. It worked in the old Venetian way: a little charm, a few contacts, some wry eyebrow-raising at the errant ways of men and at the commonality of fleecing tourists . . . and all was resolved.

Back at the inn, the Hungarian disclosed his bedmate: a tousled, crop-haired Frenchwoman, dressed as a soldier, who called herself Henriette. She spoke neither Italian nor Latin; the Hungarian spoke no French. Nevertheless, they were travelling companions and bedfellows in an arrangement that was as unconventional as it was dangerous. To pass oneself off as a soldier was not unheard of; Casanova had done the same. To sleep with a woman who dressed as a man was to invite more than curiosity from the Inquisition for, unlike Bellino, Henriette made no real attempt to hide her femininity; her transvesticism was a signifier of sexual and social emancipation; she expected to be treated like a man and was travelling semi-openly as the mistress of an older foreigner with whom she could not converse. They were heading for Parma, and Casanova immediately reconsidered his travel plan.

If any memory of the transvestite Bellino was triggered by the vision that emerged from beneath the Hungarian's sheets, Casanova does not refer to it. But in *The History of My Life* he is soon calling the sparky, wilful Henriette the 'masquerader'. And it was her stage-honed wit that first alerted him to her class background, education, and singular attractiveness. The next day, Henriette parried a series of enquiries from Giulietta, who assumed she was a courtesan on the run or, as Casanova termed her, an 'adventuress'.

' "It is strange," ' said Giulietta to the 'masquerader', ' "that you [and the Hungarian] can live together and never speak to each other."

' "Why strange, Signora? We understand each other none the worse for speech is not necessary in the business we do together." '

At this the whole company fell about laughing.

' "I do not know of any business in which speech, or at least writing, is not necessary."

' "I beg pardon, Signora. There are businesses; gaming for instance?"

' "Then you do nothing but play cards?"

' "Nothing else. We play faro. I am the banker."

This time, Casanova wrote,

'The laughter lasted until everyone was out of breath; and Signora Querini [La Giulietta] could not help laughing too.

' "But does the bank have large takings?"

' "Not at all. In fact what the bank receives is so small it is barely worth accounting." '

This final put-down, Casanova remarks, was left untranslated by the company to spare the Hungarian's pride.

Casanova had been intrigued by the drama of the hidden bed-fellow and attracted when he found she was a pretty, tomboy-ish woman, and was now smitten by 'a kind of wit I greatly admired' – a mixture, as he described it, of licence and love of language. She had already revealed herself to be an adventuress; he decided to win her from the Hungarian, having correctly surmised that the affair was some flag-of-convenience in her travels. For him, the key elements of a romantic adventure were present in Henriette: an air of mystery, an element of transgression, not to say transvesticism, a name that turned out to be false and some extra need for independence, born of previous misadventure. There was also physical beauty, an apparently liberated attitude to sex, and the promise of a passion both immediate and evanescent.

Henriette confessed to Casanova that she had made 'three follies' in her life, for which she was paying. One was her marriage – she described her husband and father-in-law as monsters. She was *en route* to Parma having picked up the Hungarian as a sort of escort near Rome. Casanova made his first move: he asked the Hungarian if he might engage Henriette as his mistress. The Hungarian agreed. Casanova suggested to Henriette that she carry on to Parma with him as her replacement protector: 'Not only do I feel friendship for you,' he argued, '[unlike the Hungarian] I love you in such a way that it is absolutely necessary either that complete possession of your person should make me happy or that I should remain here, letting you go to Parma with the officer . . . Know Madame that a Frenchman may be able to forget [you, as you suggest], but that an Italian, to judge by myself, has no such power.' The force of his passion, which had won him Teresa/Bellino at a pivotal moment in her life, at first made Henriette laugh. (From the start she treated him as if he were an infatuated boy – she may have been his elder by almost a decade.) This maddened him and he demanded, petulantly, that she decide immediately who should escort her to Parma. She continued to tease him: 'Let me laugh I beg you, for I have never in my life conceived of a declaration of love being made in anger. Do you understand what it is to say to a woman in a declaration of love, which should be all tenderness, "Madame, one or the other, choose this instant"?'

Love is often to be found between laughter and loneliness and Henriette was one of the few women Casanova allowed to laugh *at* him, to know his essential neediness, and to enter into a liaison with him as an equal. When forced to declare his need of her, 'Be sure that I love you. So choose. Decide', he handed her the power in their relationship, to begin it and therefore to end it, which was part of course of what made him angry, as well as aroused:

'Still the same tone!' She laughed at him again. 'Do you know that you appear to be in a rage?'

Her eventual answer was clear, if equivocal: 'Yes,' she said. 'Come to Parma.'

He could join her if he wanted to. Or not. She would go anyway; the Hungarian would take his own path. The next day, in an inn at

Reggio, between Bologna and Piacenza, Casanova and Henriette became lovers. The apparent comfort with which men of the period might exchange or negotiate the favours of women once their respectability was lost is shocking to modern sensibilities. In dealing with a Greek slave, Russian serf or apparent courtesan, Casanova exhibits the objectification of women as befitted his epoch, culture and sex. However, after he had won Henriette physically from the Hungarian, he 'swore that he would never even ask to kiss her hands till I had won her heart.' He was a libertine on the cusp of being a romantic, and Henriette's allure and status were undiminished for him by her predicament or that she was with another man. The women Casanova found most attractive were strong and unorthodox, though often displaying a vulnerability that brought out either the pleaser and protector in him or the exploiter. Seemingly, with Henriette, as with Teresa, he felt twinned by a woman whose predicament matched his own, and his affair with Henriette, marking the end in a sense of the first act of his life, began out of a shared sense that their lives might go in any direction, perhaps even onwards together.

The Parma Casanova and Henriette entered in 1749 was also at a pivotal point in its history. The previous year, by the treaty of Aix-la-Chapelle, the town had been ceded to Don Philippe, Infante of Spain. However, at the same time he had made a most propitious match with the daughter of the French king, Louis XV, Princess Louise Elizabeth. When Casanova and Henriette arrived, the previously Italian city was becoming increasingly French. The shopkeepers were pleased to serve an Italian in Italian (rather sweetly he bought clothes for Henriette, who was still attired as a soldier, as well as 'gloves, fan, earrings . . . all of which pleased her') and engaged a tutor to teach her Italian. The opera, which they attended frequently under the assumed names of Signor Farussi and Madame Anne d'Arci, was full of French and Spanish, asserting their new social dominance to the dismay of some locals. 'The new Duke of Parma,' wrote one British diplomat 'has disgusted all his new subjects; he [behaves] so horribly French that they cannot please him.' Which makes nonsense of Henriette's insistence that she had to avoid Frenchmen: when Casanova met her, she had been heading for the most French city in Italy. However, she refused to rouge her cheeks when they went to the opera, as any Frenchwoman would have done in public at this period; she asked to sit at the back of an ill-lit box, and to follow the score but without the aid of a tallow wick. She sent out mixed signals. In one episode, she offered, shyly at first, to play the viol de gamba at a recital and sight-read an entire concerto, then quipped afterwards that the mother superior of the convent where she had been educated had worried about her learning an instrument that required so unladylike a posture. Overcome by a mixture of relief, pride, adoration and amazement that he should be on the arm of such a prodigy, Casanova recalled that he had gone outside alone after the concert and burst into tears.

Little by little she let slip details of her past, and during three months of what Casanova later described as the happiest time of his life, he was able to piece together some of her background – and likely future. Henriette had run away from an abusive husband, and, seemingly, father-in-law. She did not admit to it, but she had perhaps left small children in France – two of the three women who might have been 'Henriette' were mothers. She was waiting for some sort of rapprochement with her in-laws or her husband, perhaps the granting of an official separation or the right to see her children without bringing further scandal on the family. Now she had happened upon a wild young adventurer who shared her outlook on life and love, but could not, realistically, share her future. Perhaps that, too, had attracted Casanova: Henriette had no intention of living with him in the long term.

With her, he dropped his guard: he admitted his precarious finances and future without bombast, 'for Henriette', he allowed, was not playing a part – she *was* the character she represented, which demanded the same of him; something he rarely offered in life or love. Even their lovemaking, for him usually the supremely enjoyed performance, 'seemed always as if it were for the first time'.

Of course, it is difficult to surmise what Henriette made of him, except that he seemed for several months to succeed in ensuring that his lover was happy. Henriette blossomed in the gaze of an attentive and assiduous lover. He was attentive to her needs, exercising some of his own taste in what she should wear, but basking in the reflected glory of her success as a wit, beauty, musician and, in a city in thrall to all that was French, as an educated Provençal aristocrat. She worried about what he spent on her, and dropped hints to a man she may have felt was less versed in love and in the world than herself that the flower of their happiness came seeded with the likelihood of its ending. 'Those who say that one can be happy all one's life talk to no purpose,' she told him. 'Pleasure, to be such, has to end.'

It was a Monsieur Antoine-Blacas of Provence, who may indeed have been related to Henriette and was in the suite of the new Duke of Parma, who recognised her. It was at an evening garden party at Colorno, the ducal summer residence outside Parma. A tortuous interview followed, then an agonising wait for Henriette and Casanova after she and Blacas despatched a letter to France, presumably to her family. Three weeks passed before their reply arrived. They must have acquiesced to her terms because Henriette told Casanova that they must part:

It is I, my only love, [she wrote], who must forsake you. Do not add to your grief by thinking of mine . . . let us boast of having succeeded in being happy for three months on end; there are few mortals who can say as much. So let us never forget each other, and let us often recall our love . . . and if chance brings you to know who I am, be as if you did not know it . . . I do not know who you are; but I know that no one in the world knows you better than I do . . . I wish you to love again and even to find another Henriette. Adieu.

Casanova was distraught. He locked himself in his room and wallowed in misery. Henriette's family had allowed her to draw a substantial sum from a Swiss bank – a thousand French *louis* from Tronchin's in Geneva – so Casanova agreed to accompany her over the Alps to Switzerland. From there he would return to Italy, she to her life in the South of France. It was a bleak journey.

At the Hôtel de Balances in Geneva they parted. 'During the last twenty-four hours the only eloquence we could muster was . . . tears . . . Henriette held out no illusory hopes . . . she asked me not to inquire about her and to pretend that I did not know her if I should ever meet her [again].' She sent him a letter from the first staging-post at Châtillon, simply 'Adieu', and scratched a message in the glass of the bedroom window with the diamond ring he had bought her in Parma. As late as 1828 the inscription was pointed out to Lord Malmesbury: '*Tu oublieras aussi Henriette*' (You will also forget Henriette).

She had read Casanova well, it might seem, but on that last point she was wrong. He never forgot her. Years later he committed their affair to paper as one of the most memorable of his life, and one of the more arrestingly modern romances in literature. He also recalled his promise not to reveal her identity or their shared past should they ever meet again, when chance brought him many years later to the door of her Provençal home. 'When I consider what makes me happy in my old age it is the presence of my memory and I conclude that my life must have been more happy than unhappy . . . and I congratulate myself . . . No, I have not forgotten her and it is balm to my soul every time I remember.'

END OF ACT II

CASANOVA AND SEX IN THE EIGHTEENTH CENTURY

'Madame, I am a libertine by profession.'

Giacomo Casanova

'When it comes to vice, acting must be as old as mankind.'

Giacomo Casanova

First, the bedpost notches: let's get them out of the way. In his *History of My Life*. Casanova records sexual experiences with well over a hundred women – 122 to 136, depending on how one computes certain group and semi-consummated experiences – and with a handful, as it were, of men. The history of his sex-life runs from the loss of his virginity, at seventeen, through the following thirty-five years covered in his memoirs; an average of, say, four partners a year. Although he lived twenty-four years beyond that, not without romantic adventures, it is reasonable to suggest that the history is a near-complete overview of his sexual prime, during which, by his estimation, he had 'turned the heads' of several hundred women across Europe. Some, therefore, never made it into the *History of My Life*, any more than those he slept with after the 'end' of the *History*, or the Venetian common-law wife with whom he settled down in his fifties. But while it would be fair to say that this incomplete tally was probably outside the norm then, as it might be now, a series of factors puts the number of sexual encounters in the *History* in a specific new context. Nor, in any case, is it the *amount* of sex that justifies Casanova's place in a history of it, but rather the manner in which he writes of it.

For what it is worth, some of Casanova's contemporary memoirists and diarists, from James Boswell to William Hickey and John Wilkes appear to record or refer to more sexual encounters than the man whose name is practically synonymous with serial womanising, and Lord Byron alludes to more conquests in a couple of years in the Palazzo Mocenigo in Venice than Casanova did in an entire lifetime. Casanova was certainly very sexually active in his twenties and early thirties but, for an almost constantly travelling bachelor of his era and background, his sex life begins to appear more modest. In the classic eighteenth-century sense, Casanova is a poor example of a libertine in that he had so little interest in conquest or coercion. He was no Valmont or de Sade. He is outclassed ten to one by his fictional *alter ego* Don Giovanni with his catalogue of 1800 conquests. Casanova's is not a compulsion or sex addiction. Indeed, he might not register at all as having a 'Casanova' complex in the sense in which the term is used today. Rather, he enjoyed the game of love and seduction, a sport or art of unsurpassed fashionability in the generation that preceded the French Revolution. He narrates affairs, rather than one-night stands. Romantically, he was indefatigable.

He paid for sex from time to time throughout his life but did so considerably less than seems to have been the norm at this period for many urban men. Nor did he put himself in the first rank of sexual athletes, some of whom he encountered and witnessed, any more than he accounted himself handsome, well endowed or of abnormal libido. He was aware that his singular interest in humankind, and womankind in particular, was considered unusual and attractive, and until his late thirties he proceeded in life and love in the unquestioning faith that for him, anything and anyone was possible; a credo that transubstantiates its own reality. That he was an attractive man has the witness of figures from the Prussian king Frederick the Great to Madame de Pompadour, connoisseurs of masculine beauty both. Yet he did not conform to ideals of sexual allure of that or any age. He had a large, beaked nose and bulbous, heavily lidded eyes, thick dark eyebrows and a swarthy complexion, minuses all in the lexicon of eighteenth-century ideals of beauty. He looked almost a caricature of an Italian, was uncommonly tall and unusually muscular for a man who never laboured at anything; there are also references to the thickness of his neck and the prominence of his Adam's apple, which suggest a solid man; a manly man for all he swathed himself in lace. Despite his bulk he moved, it was said, like a dancer, unsurprising, when his family were all in the theatre. At his prime, his only boast was that he was convinced he – or any man – could conquer any woman, if she was the sole object of his undivided attention. He focused completely on those he was with, a sort of charm in itself, and perhaps an unusual experience for women in the eighteenth century.

That said, he was aware – when he was writing towards the end of his life – that his sentimental, romantic and sexual journeys had been at least as adventurous as his travels, and he turned his pen often to matters of the heart and loins. Of all the sensory aspects of his writing it was romance that had amused, confused and enervated him most. His memoirs come alive when he is on his favourite subject – sex. For sheer numbers, pornography or extremes of taste, one must look elsewhere, to de Sade, or to the indefatigable Lords Lincoln or Byron. It is Casanova's unjudgemental overview of his life and times, including sex, that makes him worthy of study in terms of the history of sexuality. Without apology or blush he ranked his sexual and romantic adventures on a par with the rest of his intellectual, professional and geographic odyssey, the first great writer of the modern period to do so.

He spent most of his life as an exotic stranger in foreign cities. He rarely lived anywhere for more than two years, and spent only six to nine months in his more famous destinations – St Petersburg, Rome, London. The context in which his promiscuity must be seen, therefore, is that of the travelling salesman in a differing landscape of travel. Much new work has emerged on this aspect of the eighteenth century in the collation of diverse short memoirs compiled by other travellers of the age – mainly single young men on routes familiar to Casanova. The age of the Grand Tour saw not only the invention of tourism but also of a sort of sex tourism. It has taken some decades for the work on eighteenth-century sexual attitudes, the adventures of the Grand Tourists, or the other frank memoirs of the times, to influence Casanova studies. Set beside Boswell, Hickey, the Earl of Lincoln and his Grand Sex Tour, not to mention the men he knew, such as Andrea Memmo or the Prince de Ligne, Casanova's sex life can now be revealed as far from monumental. It is perhaps instead typical of a certain type of eighteenth-century urban man, especially the rootless travellers who peopled Europe's capitals at a time when anonymity and self-invention was possible, even normal. Casanova knew that de Ligne and Memmo would find what he wrote believable because, in spirit and most likely in detail, it was. What shocked, amused, inspired and aroused them was the unique manner in which he suggested that an understanding of his sexual journey was vital to understanding him. Few writers had ever been so candid.

How typical was Casanova of his era? The question hinges between the man and his times. While putting Casanova's sex life in context and making a case for its singular importance because of his writings about it, it would be disingenuous to avoid his framing of his life in love affairs, his overarching narrative of romance and his fascination with sex. That he relates his fears and failures is less well known. He expressed extreme concern about disappointing a lover or losing an erection. He suffered premature ejaculation. He noted a decline in his interest in sex from his late thirties and enumerated a series of encounters when he turned down the offer of a bedmate. He suffered at least six gonorrhoea infections or outbreaks, possibly eleven, which led to long periods of abstinence. His *History* also suggests that by the end of his life he was suffering from syphilis. His long prescription from the German venereologist Dr Peiper on his return from Russia appears to address the uncomfortable undertow to the travelling libertine's tale – haemorrhoids, anal and possibly genital chancres, and warts.

The risks he and his contemporaries took may shock today but speak equally of a compulsion, linked to his womanising, his gambling and his travelling; a desire Casanova had to take risks, and to feel himself punished. His self-administering periods of enforced solitude and 'clean-living' – with which he treated his gonorrhoeal urethritis – coincided with his first periods of writing and self-reflection. Later still his syphilitic depression also informed the pattern of his literary endeavours. His sexual memoir, like his sex life, was shaped by a more vivid and dangerous world than ours where a libertine's overstated sexual machismo risked radical punishment: disease, genital mutilation, impotence, death. His writing sought meaning, a story of a life framed in sensuality, but there was also a rake's progress in contemplation of risk.

In further regards the sexual landscape in which Casanova moved was different from our own, perhaps never more so than in attitudes to children's sexuality, and to sex between adult men and young girls. Privacy as it related to human functions was impossible in eighteenth-century cities. Children were exposed daily to the sight of adult flirtation and even sexual activity, certainly in Venice, and Casanova found little difference in this between the back-streets of London's Soho and the court at Versailles. He and his contemporaries were also bombarded with images of sexualised children – the 'nice big omelette of infants' in the paintings of Fragonard and his ilk, as lampooned by Diderot. There was more naked child flesh in the paintings, frescos, sculpture and decorative arts of the period than any other representation of human corporeality. This reflected an attitude wildly different from our own. Neo-classicism, in its rococo form, harked back to an aspect of ancient civilisation obsessed with Eros, and images of putti, amorini, cupids: the anarchic spirit of sex represented in naughty children. Casanova expressed in his memoirs both the wrongness of what would today be termed paedophilia, but also an erotic vista he shared with his contemporaries, which included young girls. It is difficult to assess the ages of some of the girls and women with whom Casanova had sex. There is no doubt, however, that he regarded those in their early teens as fair game and, more, a connoisseur's prize. This was in keeping with contemporary attitudes: Casanova notes that Lady Harrington's daughters were considered suitable for the London marriage market in 1763, including her thirteen-year-old.

This was all the more the case in the demi-monde and sex-trade, where such huge prices were put upon actual and near-virginity that madams in London and Paris were known to have numerous tricks available to fake intact hymens. On the one hand, some of these country girls in city *bagnios* must have been victims of the grossest form of human trafficking. On the other, in terms Casanova might have understood, an *'education d'amour'* – the first sexual experiences of a young woman – might just empower them in a harsh era of the sexual economy. From Casanova's point of view, the only redemptive feature of what he confessed to Feldkirchner was a 'compulsion' to seduce virgins – in a letter that has only recently come to light – was that he may have believed he could save them from the worst of what might befall them, by treating them more kindly than most, as sexual equals who could thence use their power over men for as long as it lasted. In modern times, Casanova would, of course, be considered a criminal.

Perhaps his acts of incest should be seen in a similar context. The Church did not bother to countenance incest as a major sin in an era when there was so much early sexual experimentation within the family environment, and the marriage of cousins, nieces and uncles was commonplace at all levels of society.

Venice, in particular, was lax on the issue of consanguinity: the caste system dictated a relatively narrow gene pool for the great patrician families. That Casanova had sexual relations with at least one and perhaps two young women whom he represented as his likely daughters ranks among the more controversial areas of the memoirs. The contexts, in these cases, are specific to Casanova, though some of the background is not. He allowed for himself and his readers the possibility that the whole story was not quite true; another shifting perspective of Venetian mirrors, but hinted more shockingly at a complicit enjoyment in the act. But this, too, is not so surprising in that the young women who turned out to be possible daughters had grown up not knowing him, or he them. This is now understood as the classic situation for acts of willing incest: when, for instance, brothers and sisters have been brought up separately or with no knowledge of each other and a reunion kindles some shared flame of personality and familiarity, a dangerous frisson un-dampened by the realities of real family life.

Casanova was, first and foremost, a Venetian, and this is never more so than in his attitude to sex. There was a different concept of personal space in Venice. It was then probably the most densely populated city in the world. At its historic core it remains, architecturally and geographically, a city that demands a com-plete realignment of modern ideas of privacy and interpersonal relations. Lovemaking, snoring, arguing and laughing are clearly audible across small canals and smaller *calles*, even with the additions of glass and air-conditioning. Then only the masks, and covered gondolas 'like floating double beds' created small oases of privacy. This, with the related fact that Casanova's earliest sexual experience was with two sisters, helps to explain a recurrent motif of sexual encounters that might seem, to modern eyes, somewhat public. From Nanetta and Marta, to the Greek girl with whom he coupled in full view of Bellino, to his long-standing ménage with Caterina Capretti, M.M. and de Bernis, then his voyeuristic enjoyment of, and later participation with, his Roman landlady's daughter and her well-endowed tailor, all feature as signals in his sexual odyssey. Casanova was instinctively serially monogamous but was repeatedly allured by or inveigled into experiences that tended towards a more communal enjoyment of sex. Sexual intrigue was heightened through the voyeuristic gaze, an endlessly iterated theme in the art as well as the pornography and erotic literature of the period. Because the game was half clandestine, half witnessed, in a semi-staged tradition, Casanova behaved within the confines of much of the erotic literature of his day – part of what made his writing suspect to some.

The voyeuristic aspect to Casanova's sex life and his recording of it may be seen in this Venetian light, but also reflects erotic literary concerns of the period. Libertine novels that preceded Casanova's sentimental memoir inform our understanding of this aspect of his sex life also. Fictional pornography, such as *La Putain Errante*, *L'Academie des Dames* and *Venus dans le Cloitre*, foreshadowed some of his erotic experience with nuns and school-girls – a prefiguring that is one function of erotica in the first place. If any theme typifies the libertine writings of the period, though, it is voyeurism, and Casanova was, so far as it is possible to tell, reflecting in his practice what was written and thought of as the language of desire. Everywhere in libertine tales, characters observe each other from behind muslin and masks, through keyholes or spyholes, in gardens or via mirrors. All styles are to be found in Casanova's sexual narrative. And it is the style of eighteenth-century Venice – half hidden, furtive, a world of mirrors, grilles and semi-obscured identity. It gave, as one cultural historian has written, 'an air of theatricality to the whole business [of sex]. Sex, in the *livres philosophiques* was rococo.'

Venice also informed Casanova's attitude to women and theirs to him. In eighteenth-century Venice the fashion or cult of cicisbeism or the *cavaliere servente* had been at its height. Visitors to the city made much of it but Casanova barely mentions it, except in Corfu with the Venetian military. The *cicisbeo*, or *cavaliere servente*, in the tradition of medieval knights, paid court to an older woman, usually of higher social station. Some regarded this as safeguarding her honour, and it was said the women treated the men as they would their hairdressers: they were allowed privileged access to the boudoir and gossip but little more. Others were accepted by husbands and by Venetian Society as the sexual and romantic partners of the women involved, a situation of sophistication such as to impress Lady Mary Wortley Montagu when she visited Venice in 1716 and again in the 1740s. Casanova grew up in a city where many women thus enjoyed a degree of sexual freedom that was ahead of its time. It was another reason why Venetian style was so admired in an age that, broadly speaking, gave greater emphasis to the idea of female sexuality than the age that followed. And women across Europe would have been instantly alive to the sexual danger, knowingness and likely wide sexual experience of a travelling Venetian like Casanova: he would have been thought more courtly, more gallant and more sexually adept than his fellow men.

The danger as stated of the furrow of life ploughed so assiduously by a traveller like Casanova was venereal disease. Casanova, for this reason, provides unexpected detail on condom manufacture and etiquette in the period, again very much in parallel with his fellow-travellers, the Grand Tourists.

They all seem to have admired English-made condoms. Though they were well known on the Continent, their importation into Italy at this period seems to have followed in the wake of the British interest in combining art history with sex. Venereal disease was a scourge of travellers in Casanova's Europe, and condoms the only resort for the promiscuous. As Casanova well knew, they had been an insult to any but the most 'weathered votaries of Venus', but were nevertheless becoming, it seems, an object of connoisseurship. It is possible, indeed, that his memoirs address a fundamental shift in attitudes to them: Casanova saw condoms as more than prophylactics.

The Murano nun, M.M., kept her own supply from which

Giacomo Casanova, aged twenty-five. Casanova claimed he was never
handsome, though others – from Madame de Pompadour to
Frederick the Great of Prussia – disagreed. The portrait is by
Casanova's artist brother, Francesco.

Venice in the eighteenth century had a reputation as Europe's most hedonistic city. The parish of San Samuele where Casanova grew up is ringed by the bottom curve of the Grand Canal. The *ridotto*, or state gaming house, was to the left of the

iazza San Marco and the prison to which Casanova was taken is visible to the
de of the Doge's palace on the far right. He escaped from under the lead roof
f the palace itself.

Venice's San Samuele theatre where Casanova's mother worked as an actress. Giacomo later played violin in the orchestra.

Venice was a theatre capital in Casanova's lifetime, boasting numerous comedy and opera houses since demolished or converted. He grew up surrounded by *commedia* actors.

Visiting time at a Venetian convent. There were seventy-nine convents and monasteries in Venice, some more open than others. Casanova had affairs with at least two nuns.

Casanova's mother and grandmother foresaw for him a career in the church. As an 'abate' in minor holy orders, Casanova had privileged access to the young women of Venice.

Casanova became a dedicated food writer. Coffee and drinking-chocolate, both of which he counted as aphrodisiacs, were crazes in Casanova's Venice. He drank his coffee black, often in the Piazza San Marco's newly opened Florian's and Quadri's cafés.

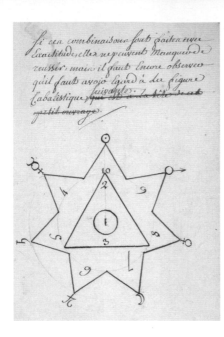

Casanova was a devotee of the cabbala and left voluminous notes and diagrams explaining the divinations he based on cabbalistic prophesy. It was this interest, along with his flouting of Venice's strict caste rules that put him in the sights of the Venetian Inquisition and landed him, ultimately, in prison.

In November 1756 Casanova escaped from the Venetian Inquisition's prison, The Leads. The story of his break-out became his most polished anecdote and later the only literary success he enjoyed in his own lifetime.

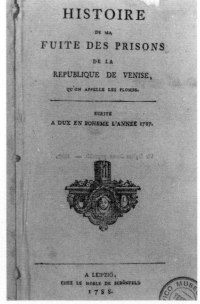

HISTOIRE
DE MA
FUITE DES PRISONS
DE LA
REPUBLIQUE DE VENISE,
QU'ON APPELLE LES PLOMBS.

ÉCRITE
A DUX EN BOHEME L'ANNÉE 1787.

A LEIPZIG,
CHEZ LE NOBLE DE SCHÖNFELD
1788.

Sentenza esequita il giorno 28. Marzo del corente Anno 1757. nella Piaza di Greve in Parigi per mano di 13. carnefici contro la persona di Roberto francesco d' Amiens.

Fù tenagliato il petto, le braccie e coscie. 4

In ciascuna ferita li fù gettato piombo ligefatto.

I quarti e il busto furono gettate nel fuoco

ROBERTO FRANCESCO D' AMIENS

fù Strascinato per la Piazza e poi Squartato da 4. cavalli la piu atroce pena, che durò 14 minuti.

Viene esaminato per piu ore. Fig. 1

Fù condotto aualla la Chiesa a dimader perdone

Fù condotto alla Piazza di Greve. 3.

Casanova arrived in Paris on the day Robert François Damiens attempted to assassinate Louis XV. Casanova's record of Damien's brutal execution is one of many examples of his memoirs' foreshadowing the age of Revolution.

Madame de Pompadour spotted Casanova from her theatre box at Fontainebleau. The king's mistress controlled the faction of Versailles politics and finance into which Casanova was drawn.

The singer Teresa Lanti or Landi: dubbed 'Bellino' by Casanova, was working as a fake *castrato* and dressed as a man when he fell in love with her. She went on to a successful career as a conventional soprano and bore Casanova his first son. This portrait now hangs in La Scala, Milan.

Casanova appears to have attempted to steal. Made from rendered sheep gut and tied on with a small ribbon, usually pink, they were designed for repeated use; some only became malleable when moistened with water. However, it seems Casanova's were so finely wrought that they did not require lubrication. If Casanova suggests a certain reticence about trying to 'render happiness . . . enveloped in a dead skin', he recognised their usefulness in avoiding pregnancy as well as disease. He writes about condoms as the most important tool in allowing his *partners* to relax, 'preservatives that the English have invented to put the fairer sex in the shade of fearlessness', and 'so precious to a nun who wants to sacrifice herself to love', vital in avoiding 'fatal plumpness'. He made his lovers laugh with his euphemisms: 'English riding-coats', 'a prophylactic against anxiety', 'the coat that gives peace to one's heart'. For M.M., he wrote verses in their honour. With his second M.M., the pregnant nun from Chambéry, he had a detailed conversation about condoms that shows he viewed them as they are today, not the exclusive property of demi-mondaines and sex-workers but part of his repertoire of attentions meant to please women: 'I took from my wallet a little vestment made of very fine skin and transparent and about eight inches [*huit pouces*] long, open at just one end like a purse, tied at the open end with a pink ribbon. I showed it to her, she contemplated it, and she laughed, and said to me . . . she was curious.' It is worth noting that Casanova's use of the old or new measure – *pouces* meaning thumbs or inches – is unclear, as also is the snugness of intended fit; surviving examples tend to be capacious, but then that may be why they survived – his lover later put another condom on him, unfurled and inelastic. There followed a conversation of striking modernity about the pros and cons of the condom: Casanova stated that 'the little fellow pleases me less well in costume', before they settled on one of 'better fit' and set to with abandon. Louis XV of France was also of the opinion that the best condoms were English and had his specially imported.

For many, though, the condom remained, as Casanova's

second M.M. suggested, shocking and demeaning – to both lovers. But Casanova was on the cusp of a change. The condom had been derided earlier in the century as 'the only preservative our libertines have . . . and yet by reason of its blunting the sensation [men] acknowledge that they often chose to risk the clap rather than engage *cum hastis sic clypeatis* [with sword thus shielded]'. By mid-century it was deemed, 'though commodious, and peculiarly adapted to the country of Merryland [the vagina]', and a source of some wonder due to its 'extraordinary fine thin substance, and contrived so as to be all of one piece, and *without* a seam', still not something to show a lady. The Grand Tourists brought higher-quality condoms with them, exactly as Casanova described: 'of different sizes from six to seven or eight inches in height . . . and from four to six in circumference' but those such as Casanova appeared to prefer, 'of much larger dimensions, [are] very rarely to be met with'.

What the Grand Tourist brought south largely as a prophylactic against foreign diseases became, in the hands of Casanova and his lovers, a key to sexual liberation as vital in its time, according to the *History of My Life*, as the contraceptive pill in the 1960s:

> Unknown big belly, and squawling brat
> Happy the man who in his pocket keeps
> Whether with green or scarlet Ribband bound
> A well made Cundum.

It was a sea-change.

Casanova's is also a unique record of the eighteenth century's attitudes to fertility – mostly to the business of avoiding unwanted pregnancy although he is also informative about conception on the rare occasions when he and his partner were trying for a baby. He was involved in one unsuccessful abortion, attended at least two births and fathered eight children he knew of while thanking his *redingotes d'Angleterre* that he did not see his own 'visage more often across Europe'. It was singularly cavalier, but again is mirrored by the Grand Tourists, among others, who considered the accident of conception an inconvenience unlikely to rebound on them if they kept travelling. Women were more circumspect, informed and practical about the risks. There is one death, and one near-death in labour in the *History*, and in both instances Casanova showed extreme concern: as a gallant and as an aspiring medic. He was touched, intrigued and shocked by the plight of women. He took care of one labour single-handed in Paris, though the woman's pregnancy was not by him, and exposed himself to great personal danger in trying to procure a termination for another.

The risks for women, however, as with his own hazarding of venereal disease, speak of a different age of personal safety, comfort and control: pregnancy was part of the game. On one occasion, Casanova was persuaded to try a luxury contraceptive preferred by some women, a 'small golden ball . . . about 18 millimetres in diameter', which fitted like a contraceptive cap. He liked the idea, though not the expense or practice, writing that the device precluded several sexual positions – for the *three* cousins involved in his ambitious sex-education experiment as well as for him – because the ball fell out of position.

It is an item of record, from *The History of My Life* and Casanova's notes, that he had sexual relations with men. This is not part of his 'legend' and certainly makes up only a small part of his sexual experience. It is telling of the man, but his handling of the material, his literary relationship with what would now be termed his bisexuality, is telling too. He was open, frank and exhaustive in his detailing of heterosexual experiences, but covert, circumspect and oblique when it came to sex with men. The notes found after his death included intended passages on affairs with a man called 'Camille', the Duc d'Elboeuf, a known homosexual, and the famous mention of 'Pédérastie avec X. à Dunquerque'; here, historians have noted Casanova's need to disguise the name of someone important when he was working clandestinely for the French government. Meanwhile, as the memoirs show, he had sex frequently in the company of other men, but also more direct, intimate and exclusive homosexual contact in Turkey, Russia and elsewhere. It was not an area, however, that he was comfortable with as a writer, and it seems not to have attracted him especially.

There is a school of thought that Casanova's womanising might indicate a counter-phobia, a misogyny or even latent homosexuality, as may be the case with some serial womanisers. In conforming, to some extent, to the genre of libertine memoir and expectation of him as an 'adventurer', Casanova was at liberty to detail the dehumanising trade in sex and favours that was a clear part of the theatre economy and eighteenth-century cityscape. But he was not at ease with expressing the totality of his experience. 'Why did you refuse Ismail [in Turkey],' repined de Ligne, over his friend's apparent lack of candour, 'neglect Petronius and rejoice that Bellino was a girl?' De Ligne wanted all the details. Casanova was unusually guarded. Little else in his notes has been left out of the finished memoir. Casanova, who censored so little and told so much drew a curtain over an area of sexuality that was being colonised by politics, prurience and censure.

In every other regard his *History* furnishes one of the most fulsome, unabashed and unapologetic accounts of a sex life, from his own or any other period. Perhaps he felt the need to touch so many as a way to feel more alive: the memoirs often seem written in a yearning key but, then, they were written by an old and lonely man. Whatever inspired him to dedicate quite such energy to the pursuit of a very eighteenth-century style of loving is not necessarily as interesting as his testimony to the centrality of sex and sensuality in one construction of self, one appreciation of living.

ACT THREE

ACT III SCENE I

THE ROAD TO FRANCE

1750

'Every young man who travels, who wishes to know society, who does not wish to be inferior [or] excluded . . . should be initiated into . . . Freemasonry.'

Giacomo Casanova

I n the wake of his break-up with Henriette, Casanova fell into what he had begun to establish as his regular style at the end of a love affair. His depression and self-loathing led him into an ill-considered rebound encounter that seemed almost designed to convince him he was unworthy of love in the first place. It was a pattern he would repeat again and again. On this occasion he accepted the proposition of an actress in Parma at the theatre where he had spent so many romantic nights with Henriette. 'I considered myself justly punished,' he admitted, when he realised she had infected him with a venereal disease.

This time the cure was more than his usual diet of abstinence and water, with which he had successfully treated gonorrhoea. The Duke of Parma's doctor and dentist, Frémont, diagnosed the pox (syphilis) and prescribed six weeks of mercury che-motherapy. The harsh, ineffectual and unnecessary treatment left Casanova temporarily weakened in mind, spirit and libido, sufficient, he wrote, to convince him for a while that he would lead thereafter a celibate and religious life. It was not to be.

Letters arrived at his lodgings from Bragadin, containing good news: Casanova's name had been dropped from the lists of those displeasing the Serene Prince, in the state of Venice, and he could return. This time, he would not stay long in the bosom of his adoptive patrician family, or, indeed, in that of the Church.

Even in midwinter Venice was its alluring self. There was the familiar round of theatre and coffee-houses – Casanova was keen to reacquaint himself with the glories of the Piazza San Marco cafés. But there was also gambling. It was a feature of the restrictive nature of Venetian society that a patrician household such as Senator Bragadin's at Santa Marina could not be entered by a foreign diplomat. Moreover, as the bankers at the *ridotto*, or state-sanctioned gaming salon were drawn by law only from the ranks of patrician families, it followed that foreigners with any status in the city were obliged to avoid it and to play in small private apartments, known as 'casinos'. There was an added furtiveness to these venues, evidenced in the single surviving example, the Venier, with hidden doorways, escape routes, spyholes and screens behind which the orchestra sat so that its members could not see the gambling – or anything else that took place.

Casanova invested a small win from a *terno*, or Venetian lottery, to set up as banker at a tiny private casino. He was soon able to bank a thousand *zecchini* with Bragadin, and buy a quarter-share in a patrician's faro bank – a noble's private table for playing 'faro' or 'pharoah,' the eighteenth century's rui-nously addictive card game – at the official *ridotto* near San Marco. These monies represented the foundation of his first, minor, fortune, and funded his visit later that year, in some style, to Paris.

That February of 1750 his friend Antonio Balletti came to Venice to dance and help manage the season at the Teatro San Moisè, one of the most fashionable Venetian theatres in the carnival season. Teresa Lanti's sister Marina was with him, but she and Antonio were no longer lovers. Antonio was making plans for after the carnival, and inveigled Casanova into joining him. Even as the scion of a patrician like Bragadin, and with money in his pocket from gambling, Casanova was nevertheless sufficiently drawn to the theatre to accept an invitation to travel abroad with actors. Antonio's mother, the Parisian actress Sylvia Balletti, had sent word that the Comédie Italienne would be central to the intended celebrations for the birth of an heir to the French throne. (The Dauphine was pregnant with the expected grandchild of Louis XV.)

Thus Casanova, aged twenty-five, left Venice again, with little purpose in mind but to swim in the wake of the famous, and with little to trouble him financially or emotionally. He had no ties. He noted that his brothers, Francesco and Giovanni, were setting themselves up in trades as artists, but did not pause to reflect his talents had as yet no clear direction. It was 1 June 1750. His travelling companions were ideal: a theatre troupe, and a friend of almost exactly his age with whom he clearly had a stronger affinity than he shared with his brothers: 'I could not choose company more agreeable and more apt to procure me countless advantages in Paris and a quantity of brilliant acquaintances,' he wrote. And somewhere around the company of Antonio Balletti and his dancers, Casanova threw off the cloud that had hung over him since Henriette's departure, and began again to play the role of the young adventurer and Venetian masquerader that the world was beginning to expect.

His theatre background was soon of use to him. At Ferrara's Albergo San Marco, Casanova immediately assumed a new role very much in the *commedia del'arte* improv' style. A dancer, Cattinella, who knew Casanova glancingly and whom he knew by repute, introduced him to everyone as her cousin. He was no such thing. 'I see that she is making me play a role,' he wrote, 'for the sake of a play of her own dénouement,' and chose to play along. It is a signal encounter in his memoir; it shows his ease with improvisation, even before he is aware of any profit for himself. He found himself unwittingly her accomplice in fleecing the innkeeper, who had been extending her credit and awaiting the arrival of a 'mother', who was meant to be Casanova's 'aunt'. Gallantly, Casanova even tried to pay her bill once she had fled, but he gained for his troubles – and impressive performance – little more than a fumble in her bedroom. It seemed not to concern him: he had enjoyed the make-believe.

Next, in Turin, he narrates an characteristically earthy encounter with the daughter of the washerwoman at his lodgings. He remembered her for piety and a coyness unexpected in a profession whose representatives were regarded as fair game in inns. Perhaps her coyness could be explained, he reasoned, by a singular characteristic she displayed when she had succumbed quickly to his advances: in the absence of underwear and any better offers, she proceeded to fart in time to his every thrust. She continued to do so 'like the bass of an orchestra marking time in a piece of music', thereby reducing him to helpless and impotent laughter. 'I remained there sitting on the stairs for more than quarter of an hour before I could shake off the comedy . . . which makes me laugh even now every time I think of it.'

His comic-theatrical rendering of his travels continued in his description next of Lyon. Here he met Ancilla, the Venetian courtesan and dancer, just back from London and a successful run at the King's Theatre, Haymarket. His well-connected theatrical companions almost certainly gave him entrée to the salon of the elderly lieutenant-general of the city, François de la Rochefoucauld, Marquis de Rochebaron.

Rochebaron was seventy-three in 1750, but immediately struck by the twenty-five-year-old Italian, his fine manners, amusing companions and easy spending, and sponsored Casanova in his initiation into the Freemasons. It is likely that Casanova's travelling companions rendered him acceptable to Rochebaron and the Lyonnais Freemasons but also his knowledge of the cabbala, a frequent topic of conversation among Venetian actors in a way it was not in wider society. The Lyonnais Lodge of Freemasons into which Casanova was inducted by Rochebaron was a so-called Scottish-rite lodge, credited as such supposedly for its connection to a tutor of the exiled Jacobite court, Chevalier Andrew Ramsay, and known as the Grande Loge Écossaise, its motto *Amitié, Amis Choisis* (friendship and chosen friends). It had clear links with medieval Rosicrucianism, which, in turn, acknowledged the power and meaning of the cabbala.

Casanova writes little about this, but the importance of joining another semi-closed but international fraternity, rather better connected than that of actors, cannot be overestimated. At the time, though, he was pressing on to Paris, and more immediate quests than that of divine enlightenment.

Casanova and Balletti reached Paris in the high summer of 1750. Antonio's mother, the star of the Comédie Italienne, near the Palais Royal, rode out with Antonio's little sister Manon to Fontainebleau to meet them and, rather high-handedly, swept up her son to return to Paris, leaving Casanova to continue alone in the low-slung *diligence*. His consolation was to be invited to dinner that evening, and by the time he reached Paris Antonio had sufficiently sung his praises for the Ballettis to send a hackney coach to collect him from his lodgings on the rue Mauconseil.

MADAME DE POMPADOUR'S PARIS

1750

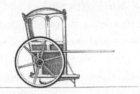

'At the beginning of my stay in Paris, it seemed to me that I had
become the guiltiest of men, for I did nothing but beg pardon
. . . *Non* is not a [Parisian] word . . . give it up or be prepared to
draw your sword in Paris at every moment. Say "*pardon*".'

Giacomo Casanova

The rococo age of libertinism had its centre in Paris, and
Casanova found himself well placed to enjoy and profit by
the new Parisian attitude to life. 'Paris,' he noted, 'despite all the
wit of the French, is and will always be a city in which impostors
will succeed . . . a characteristic which . . . comes from the
supreme influence of fashion.' The fashion of the times tended
towards sexual freedom and metropolitan cynicism, and a
delight in a monarch, court and royal mistress that encouraged
both. Crébillon the younger recalls in *Les Égarements du coeur
et de l'esprit* (1738) that 'You told a woman three times she was
beautiful, no more was needed; upon the first she quite believed
you, upon the second she thanked you, and upon the third she
rewarded you.' The hero of this work, which Casanova read, is a
seventeen-year-old introduced to the ways of the world by an
older woman, the Marquise de Lursay, over several hundred

diverting pages of engaging moral turpitude, described at the time as 'providing an education *d'amour*'.

Within days of arriving in Paris, Casanova was exposed to several of the key figures and sites in playground Paris. Prosper Crébillon – the playwright father of the more famous novelist – became his French tutor after they had met at the Balletti house. The Palais Royal gardens, with their cafés, tarts and gossip, became his outdoor salon, and he soon found his own Marquise de Lursay in his friend's glamorous mother, the actress Sylvia Balletti.

A twenty-one-year-old French lawyer he met at one of the fashionable cafés adjoining the Palais Royal gardens, Claude Pierre Patu, was one of the first to point out to Casanova that, having been embraced by the Ballettis, he had landed squarely on his feet in Paris. They were well known in Bohemian Paris, shouted to in the street by the names of famous *commedia* characters they played. Their dinner table, at which Casanova ate nightly for the first few months of his stay in Paris, consisted of Antonio, his parents, Sylvia and Mario, an elderly aunt, Flaminia, who was as garrulous as she was opinionated, and Antonio's little sister Manon. There was also an ever-changing crowd of Paris's literati – Marivaux, another playwright, whose comedies, Casanova loyally opined, 'but for Sylvia would never have come down to posterity', and the older Crébillon, Prosper Jolyot, who was sufficiently impressed with Antonio's new friend to offer to improve his written and spoken French. Casanova attended thrice-weekly lessons in the rue des Douze Portes in the Marais with Crébillon, who was then an eccentric seventy-six-year-old – yet another example of Casanova's easy relationship with all generations and classes but his surprising attraction to the elderly. The lessons took place amid twenty ill-trained cats, who belonged to the playwright: two enormously tall men – Crébillon was three inches taller than Casanova's six foot two – huddled over French verses. Casanova credited Crébillon with some of the best advice he received as a writer:

'tell amusing stories without laughing, be witty, respect the rules of grammar', and that the *je ne sais quoi* of great writing was what separated a lover from a *castrato*: balls.

Casanova's descriptions of Paris in the middle of the eighteenth century, during the glamorous reign of Louis XV, with Madame de Pompadour at her peak, remain some of the finest examples of his travel-writing. He was fortunate to be there at that time, with the company he had chosen, but even so his outlook on life and manners is as refreshing as it was ingenuous. Not for the last time, he presents himself as the foreign maladroit finding his way in the big city; and for a man who had chosen to write in French and pursue much of his later career in France or with French-speaking élites, the experience of being schooled in French ways was the genesis of another Casanova. He was a son of Venice, but he aspired to be courtly in the French manner. He lost the last vestige of his moral innocence with the actresses and courtesans who laughed openly at churchly ideas of rectitude. Where Venetians might be all masquerade and unsaid knowingness, Parisians blatantly followed their own moral codes. One actress, Marie Le Fel, gaily explained her children's different features by telling Casanova that they had been fathered by three separate lovers. Casanova remembered blushing. Such things were widely known in Venice but not talked of. 'You are in France, Monsieur,' a retired actress explained, 'where people know what life is and try to make the most of it.' It was the philosophy Casanova was adopting in affairs of the heart but also of the world. Paris in 1750 was the perfect backdrop for the next scene in Casanova's *commedia*.

The Ballettis and Crébillon took him to the theatre; he saw celebrated productions of Molière's *Le Misanthrope* and *L'Avare*. He attended *Le Joueur* and *Le Glorieux* by Regnard and Destouches respectively, starring great names of the Parisian stage now long forgotten but fresh in his memory when he wrote of the pleasures of their performances, and their backstage companionship. The Italian community in Paris also began to open to him again, partly because he was Zanetta Casanova's son. His lodgings in the rue Mauconseil were at the centre of the increasingly Italian neighbourhood of Paris, its focal points the Hôtel de Bourgogne and the Théâtre Italien. Carlino Bertinazzi, who had worked with Casanova's mother in St Petersburg in 1736, was in Paris and welcomed Casanova, whom he had not seen since he was a schoolboy in Padua, to his table. Carlo Veronese, who had played Pantalone opposite Casanova's mother, also invited him to dinner and introduced his actress daughters, Anna Maria and Giacoma Antonia. Seemingly, it was through Anna Maria, known as Coralina in Paris after the character she played in the *commedia del'arte*, that Casanova met her lover, Charles Grimaldi, Prince de Monaco. Giacoma was the mistress of the Count de Melfort, a great favourite with the Bourbon princess, the Duchesse de Chartres. Casanova's circle extended rapidly. As well as their theatrical connections, some to Casanova's mother, all of these nobles were Free-masons and the duchesse was head of France's female masons. How or if Casanova communicated to her his status as a Freemason is as unclear as masons have always intended, but she seems to have been made aware of it and of his interest in the cabbala.

In one of Casanova's few indiscreet meanders, he tells of the Prince de Monaco pimping for the Duchesse de Ruffec. This 'elderly' lady – she was forty-three in 1750 – was introduced to Casanova by his new friend Grimaldi. As soon as they were left alone the duchesse asked him to sit beside her and tried to unbutton his breeches. Horrified by her advances, and possibly Grimaldi's imputation that Casanova was so easily available, he blurted out that he had the clap and was thrown out. It was the first of several stories that, he said, began to make the rounds of Paris, none of which reflected him in a particularly good light but they made for amusing anecdotes, then as now. Mainly, his French let him down, though in a way that suited the lewd, frivolous times. In attempting to ask a friend how she had spent the night, he inadvertently enquired what she had 'discharged' in the night, and in explaining the proper placing of the Italian '*vi*' preposition to a young lady, he said that the '*vi*' must go '*derrière*'. '*Vi*' 'or '*vis*' was slang for penis. He was said to be fun company, this try-hard, slightly gauche charmingly faux-naïve new Venetian in town. Word spread. More invitations followed.

On 7 October 1750, a few months after Casanova's arrival, the Ballettis were due to decamp with the other court players to Fontainebleau for the hunting season. The court was based primarily at Versailles, but Louis XV's other great passion, after women, was *la chasse*. Each day's hunting was followed by musical or theatrical entertainment. The Ballettis invited Casanova to stay with them in the house they were renting near the palace, which afforded him his closest view yet of the royal centre of French life, and of Louis XV's mistress, Jeanne Antoinette Poisson, then a marquise and soon to become a duchess but known universally as Madame de Pompadour.

Within days of his arrival, Casanova had acquired tickets for a performance of a Lully opera but, by either design or accident, found himself seated in the *parquet*, the stalls, directly under but in view of La Pompadour's box. She asked who he was, perhaps because she had noticed his height and bearing, or his inappropriate laughter at some of the recitative of Lemaure, a famous French opera singer of the period not noted for her acting. She was told that the young man was Venetian, leaned over her box and asked him if it was true that he was from 'down there'.

'From where?'

'From Venice,' she reiterated

'Venice, Madame, is not *down*,' replied Casanova, bravely and curtly. 'It is *up*.'

Such arrogance and self-assurance in the presence of the *de facto* Queen of France might have made Casanova's name but was closely followed by a much more amusing exchange that became, Casanova wrote, 'celebrated'. It was another of his ill-tutored double-entendres; the Duc de Richelieu, La Pompadour's companion in her box, asked which of two actresses he preferred. Casanova indicated his choice. 'She has ugly legs,' opined Richelieu. 'One does not see them,' replied the cocky young Venetian, 'and in any case, in assessing a woman's beauty the first thing I always put aside are her legs.' Later he claimed his use of the French '*écarter*', to put aside or, alternatively, spread apart, was inadvertent, but in the competitively witty bear-pit of court theatres it was the sort of thing to get a young man noticed. And it did. Francesco Morosoni, the Venetian ambassador, asked to meet the daring Italian everyone was talking about. So, too, did the Jacobite Lord Keith, who had not seen him since 1745 but recalled him warmly and instantly from then.

Again, Casanova's testimony is rich in detail and first-hand impression; an innocent abroad in the far from innocent world of the French court. He sketches the court ladies, whom etiquette forced to wear heels 'half a foot high' while in attendance on the Queen, and even run, in hooped skirts and doll-like makeup, when palace protocol demanded their presence.

At this time the Venetian courtesan Giulietta Preati, Signora Querini, made an unexpected appearance at Fontainebleau, attempting to attract the attention of Louis XV, who was famed for his wandering eye. Though Madame de Pompadour was indubitably *maîtresse en titre*, her longevity in the King's affections, if not in his bedroom, was predicated on her willingness to support his wider harem of court ladies, and turn a blind eye to his '*parc des cerfs*' to which extremely young girls were recruited for his pleasure. The King rejected Giulietta's subtle advances: 'we have prettier women here', Casanova records him saying cruelly to Richelieu, but Casanova at this stage may well have made a mental note that it was not the practised charms of a professional courtesan like Giulietta Preati that impressed the King, but something altogether more akin to his own taste for very young women.

Casanova soon returned to Paris, and his lad-about-town existence, supported still by Bragadin's allowance, his winnings from cards and the generosity of friends. He could justify this only to the extent he was learning French and gaining a reputation at court but neither, of course, brought him money or definite prospects. Here, unexpectedly, his story crossed with both court sexual intrigue and art history via the unexpected person of Claude Patu, his libertine friend. Patu introduced him to the pleasures of Parisian brothels and, for the first time, Casanova's love life – or, more accurately, sex life – was dominated by visits to one: the Hôtel de Roule at the Porte Chaillot. Given that there was a dress code and expectation of gentlemanly behaviour – clients were expected to be entertaining company through dinner with the girls of their choice – it might have been an expensive habit, but, unblushingly, Casanova proves otherwise. Decades later he recalled the prices: six francs for breakfast and sex, twelve for dinner and sex, a *louis* to eat and spend the night. Sex without food was anathema.

The girls were dressed identically in white muslin shifts, like Grecian votaries, and sat sewing demurely while the men chose their dinner and bed companions. On their first evening, Patu and Casanova bought the company and services of three different prostitutes during a long, debauched and well-fed evening. Thereafter, Casanova was tellingly 'loyal' to one prostitute, Gabrielle Siberre, known as La Saint-Hilaire. During a trip to the Saint-Laurent fair, Patu took a fancy to a Flemish actress of Irish descent, one Victoire Morphy or Murphy, known as La Morphy. She accepted two *louis* from Patu for sex in her house nearby at the rue des Deux-Portes Saint-Saveur, and Casanova was obliged to tag along. It was late, and he asked for a bed to sleep in, either for the night or for as long as his friend was attending to his business. He was offered the mattress of La Morphy's filthy teenage sister for half an *écu*. The bed was not to Casanova's liking but something about the girl intrigued him, not least her willingness to be seen naked, to be touched and even washed. She would not however submit to anything more intimate for less than twenty-five *louis*: she was a virgin, and her sister had told her that the going rate in Paris for such was far more than that sum. In the end, through Casanova, she scored Louis XV himself. Having washed her, Casanova considered her 'a perfect beauty [with] a countenance which instilled the most delicious peace into the soul which beheld her'. The truth of this is verifiable because of what happened next. He paid the Swedish artist Gustaf Lundberg, of the School of Boucher, to paint her naked with her bottom raised towards the viewer.

A copy was made for Patu, which found its way to Versailles and Monsieur de Saint-Quentin, procurer to the King. The King asked to meet 'O-Morphi' – the name Casanova had given her, a play on the Greek for 'beautiful' or 'feminine' – whereupon she was asked to join the *parc des cerfs* and sacrifice her virginity to her country for somewhat more than the going rate in Paris. Word spread that she had particularly pleased the King while she sat on his lap, 'after his royal hand had assured him that she was a virgin', by noting that he bore an unusual likeness to the head on the six-franc piece. Louison O'Murphy or Morphy was then thirteen. She bore the King one child, a boy, titled le Conte d'Ayat, before an indiscretion about the Queen put her out of royal favour.

The story has elements of verifiable reality – the connection between Patu and the Morphy sisters, and the painting, which exists in various forms, of the child-like siren whose appeal was not restricted to Louis XV and Casanova. Nevertheless, Casanova exaggerated his own pre-eminence in the rise of the newest addition to Louis's harem. Though he may have washed her in the house she shared with her sister – it was an act of reverence, connoisseurship or personal invasion he favoured all his life – she found her way by other means to Boucher's studio whence it would have been an easy leap over the walls of the *parcs des cerf* with or without the help and testimony of Giacomo Casanova.

Patu, nevertheless, was impressed – not least with his friend's self control and forward thinking in not bargaining for Louison Morphy's virginity himself.

Casanova's first Parisian sojourn reveals an increasingly worldly and cynical young man, ingratiating himself into a venal, sophisticated society, and adopting, for a while, the mercenary libertinism inspired by the court of Louis XV and La Pompadour. He not only launched, in part, the career of Louison Morphy but tried to do the same for a beautiful Italian who moved into lodgings near his on the rue Mauconseil. In later life, some part of him repined that he could encounter youth, beauty, need and promise in a young woman and, at twenty-five, seek not to take her for himself but, rather, support her in floating her assets on the amorous stock-market of Paris. 'If you have virtue,' he remembered telling the Italian beauty, 'and are resolved to keep it, prepare to suffer poverty.' He advised her to present her inaccessibility conspicuously to raise her price, then play a waiting game with the rakes of the Palais Royal. It was cynical but not without kind intent – and he was wretched when the beautiful Italian gave herself to someone he felt beneath her, or beneath his part in her creation. The idea of love as a game, and a mercenary one at that, is very much in the spirit of the age, and in the Paris of the 1750s Casanova, chronicler of the eighteenth century, became well schooled in the most cynical aspects of libertinism. However, the machinations of the Parisian love-market, which had put La Pompadour into the Trianon and Mademoiselle Siberre from the Hôtel de Roule brothel into Casanova's arms for a *louis* a night, were not of instinct or inclination truly Casanova's. He wore his Parisian fashions well, but uncomfortably. Years later his regret at attempting to sell his Italian compatriot, Antoinette Vesian, into a near-mismatch with the Conte de Narbonne continued to trouble him – less for the sake of traditional morality as for his part in what might have been her downfall. Narbonne, it turned out, had no money. Casanova and Vesian sat sadly on her bed as she contemplating selling herself. In a long, half-remembered conversation, Casanova reveals himself to be more of a romantic than his times, reputation, or the necessity of helping a courtesan to pimp herself should have allowed: 'Pleasure is immediate sensual enjoyment; it is a complete satisfaction which we grant to our senses in all that they desire . . . the philosopher is he who refuses no pleasure which does not produce greater pains and who knows how to create pleasures.' He went on to say that one should avoid any duty 'for which we find no reason in nature' a romantic argument in the style of Rousseau. The employment of philosophy, Casanova continued, 'should be the study of nature'. They are the axioms of revolutionary times – the age of Voltaire and the destruction of old venal ways – but hardly the counsel an aspiring courtesan might expect from a qualified libertine. Though her tale ended well enough – a match with the Marquis d'Etrehan and a box at the theatre where he might exhibit his conquest on a better stage than the stage itself – there is an elegiac note in Casanova's telling of it that makes apparent his heart was more in the romantic spirit of his advice to Antoinette Vesian than in the mercenary realities of a rococo love affair.

Casanova gradually became aware that he had failed again, in Paris, to capitalise on a brilliant opening scene or two, some excellent lines and, of course, a supporting cast well placed to push him centre stage. His French improved. But his small income failed to meet his outgoings – which included regular whoring with Patu, a working lawyer – and through 1751 he looked with increasing desperation for something to justify his Parisian existence.

The Duchesse de Chartres, a cousin of Louis XV and a noted society figure, was on the fringe of Casanova's theatrical and masonry circle: her favourite, the Conte de Melfort, had a lover who was daughter to Carlo Veronese, the Italian *commedia* star 'Pantalone'. The duchesse was almost exactly the same age as Casanova, and, unusually perhaps, she had had far more lovers than he had, but suffered, some said as a result, from an ailment of the complexion that might simply have been acne. Whatever its cause, it gave her even more grief than the regular, for her presence was required at court and in society, and on the occasions when her complexion suddenly cleared, she was accounted a wide-eyed beauty of the aesthetic favoured by the period and its painters. Doubtless through Veronese and Melfort, who were Freemasons, she discovered that Casanova was rumoured to know some secrets of cabbalistic healing. She asked for an interview with him in apartments she kept in the Palais Royal. Casanova was smitten: 'She was adorable, extremely animated, without prejudices, gay, witty in conversation', qualities, indeed, that appealed to him. In a veiled comment, he may also have alluded to her suspected position as Paris's leading libertine, 'loving pleasure', as she did, 'and preferring it to a long life – short and sweet was an expression which was forever on her lips'.

She wanted to ask him various questions, written, as would always be the case when consulting the cabbalistic oracle, to which Casanova would respond in writing. At least one of her questions related to her complexion. Casanova took pity on her – or saw an opportunity for advancement: he prescribed a strict diet, daily washing in fresh water, and the avoidance of *pomades*, or cosmetics. He also made it clear the cure would not be instant. It worked. Her confidence in him grew, and his in her. They continued to meet in the apartments at the Palais Royal. She asked him more questions and devoted more and more time to him and his prophesies. He began increasingly to believe in the system of cabbalistic prophesy. It hit upon truths 'which I did not know I knew' and she promised him 'a post which would give me an income of twenty-five thousand livres'. Here it becomes apparent that he knew he was largely a fraud. He suspected there were some truths to be deduced from the cabbala but he also knew he was faking the difference between surmise and certainty. He could not tell her how it worked because he did not know **and because**, he claimed, 'I was madly in love with her [yet] **thought** such a conquest beyond me.'

Casanova's love life in libertine Paris during the early 1750s was relatively uneventful. He had rejected the advances of the 'ancient' forty-three-year-old Duchesse de Ruffec, decided that the Duchesse de Chartres was beyond him, and had left O-Morphi and Antoinette Vesian to sell their honour elsewhere. Of course, he had been paying for sex with Mademoiselle Siberre, 'La Saint-Hilaire', in the company of Patu – but he had also, on occasion, been sharing his bed with his landlady's teenage daughter. She came to him, he recalled, (and later swore as testimony), 'whenever she felt the need', and 'such as I am,' he reasoned, 'I shall never have the ill-grace to refuse my caresses to a girl who . . . comes to my room to submit to them – especially when she has come with her mother's consent.' Mimi, 'an ambrosial fifteen or sixteen', became pregnant, however, and Madame Quinson brought a suit against her tenant to marry her daughter or pay damages. Casanova pointed out that Mimi had been far from a novice, that he might not be the child's father, and that the mother's consent had been evident from the start, which could only count against the suit. He felt, perhaps rightly, that he was being entrapped. At the initial arraignment in front of the district commissary the case went against him, but when the case was presented to the lieutenant general of police, Casanova was cleared of any wrong-doing, with the costs awarded against Madame Quinson. A man of his times, inclinations and perplexing complexity, he generously paid the court fees for both sides, while never acknowledging that the child, a boy, was his. Yet he must have known or suspected, and certainly Mimi persisted in her claim that he was the father, for it was Casanova who 'allowed' the baby boy, probably his third child, to be presented to the military founding hospital opposite the Hôtel Dieu 'for the benefit of the nation'. They never met again.

In the summer of 1752, Francesco Casanova, then twenty-four, arrived in Paris. He had been advised by his brother that his skills as a battle painter might be marketable in Paris, where few artists were dedicating themselves to the genre, despite the regime's rumbling bellicosity. It may well have been that Casanova paid for Francesco's journey in the hope of acting as his agent, but if so, both brothers were to be disappointed: at a *salon* at the Louvre, a painting by Francesco was heavily criticised. He fled almost in tears, had the painting collected by a servant and 'slashed it twenty times with his sword'.

It was Francesco who suggested that he and his brother travel together to visit their mother in Dresden. Casanova had not seen her since 1737, when he was a skinny twelve-year-old emerging as a precocious social talent. Zanetta was well established at the court of the Elector of Saxony – a celebrated actress but also well respected in Dresden society and at court. Perhaps the brothers thought they might benefit from her contacts. Perhaps they wanted to distance themselves from recent social and artistic embarrassments in Paris. Perhaps, in the continuing absence of any true love or vocation, Casanova felt the need to address her neglect of them in his early childhood. Most likely they merely wanted money.

A police report of the period notes that Casanova had been living off the Balletti family – possibly even been kept, in all senses, by Antoine's mother, Sylvia. Casanova rigorously denied this, but he had found a new family of a sort, a mirror of his own, and a mother-figure who had set him on a successful social career in Paris. He had also noted Antoine's younger sister, whose effusive letters to him still bulk out the Prague Archive. But in 1752 Manon Balletti was only twelve and waved him and his brother off from the rue Mauconseil with the rest of their Italian friends.

The Casanovas set out together in the autumn, travelling through Champagne, Metz and Frankfurt, arriving in Dresden in October. Their mother greeted her eldest sons warmly, and they were able to reacquaint themselves with their sister Maria Maddalena Antonia, then twenty-one and recently married to the court harpsichordist, Peter August.

Francesco devoted himself to serious study of art, and soon moved on to Rome to study further under the celebrated Raphael Mengs. His elder brother meanwhile, wrote a play. Admittedly it was based firmly on Racine's *La Thébaïde*, and may therefore have originated in work Casanova had done with Crébillon in his Paris translation lessons. In fact, it was the second play to be performed in Dresden with Casanova's name attached to it. The first had been a straight translation into Italian of Cahusac's *Zoroastre*, commissioned by the Saxon ambassador while Casanova was in Paris and therefore at the instigation of his mother. Zanetta and Maria both appeared in it, almost certainly in February 1752, and its success may have been partly responsible for Casanova's arrival in Saxony. He retitled his new Racine translation *La Moluccheide* and overstepped the bounds of translation by reimagining it as a dizzy Italian comedy with two harlequins and 'filled . . . with comic incongruities'. It was presented under his name, not Racine's – Casanova's first public work – and was greeted warmly by the theatre-loving court, in particular King Augustus III, who rewarded him in cash for his endeavours.

His first true literary success attracts scant record in the memoirs. Comedy, at which Casanova excelled in conversation, was not where he set his ambitions as a writer – it was too much the family trade, as was music, which likewise, he later told Catherine the Great, was of no interest to him. Perhaps this explains why another modest triumph was accorded only a passing reference in the memoirs: before he left Paris Casanova had suggested to the Abbé de Voisenon, a colleague of Crébillon, that he might try his hand at oratorios in verse in the Venetian style for a concert at the Tuileries. They were the first oratorios performed in France and therefore his name is attached to an important footnote in the history of French music. Casanova, however, decided his fate lay neither at the Saxon court nor in its cultured music and theatre scenes. He decided to return to Venice.

ACT III SCENCE III

LUST IN CLOISTERS

1753–5

'I returned to Venice in the year 1753 well informed, full of myself, giddy, loving pleasure; happy, hardy, vigorous and mocking . . . I partied night and day, gambled for high stakes . . . owed no one. I didn't disturb the peace. I steered clear of politics and the personal quarrels of others, and that's every virtue I possessed . . . my libertine ways could at worst make me guilty to myself, and not a single regret clouded my conscience . . . I was entirely happy.'

Giacomo Casanova

'The day fades, night envelops me . . . great Gods, how I long for you to come again . . . push, enter me. . . . I am dying of love.'

Venus dans le Cloître, Anon.

Ascension Day, when Casanova arrived home in 1753, was the greatest day in the Venetian calendar. The launching of the Buccintoro, the gargantuan state gondola, for the ceremonial marriage of Venice with the sea saw the doge with the entire senate, the ambassadors to Venice and the papal nuncio rowed out in the perilously top-heavy gilded showboat to the edge of the Lido so that the Doge could throw a golden ring into the waves. Flotillas of gondolas accompanied it from the Piazzetta San Marco for a view of the ceremony.

Casanova threw himself straight back into Venetian life, and into the next great affair of his life. After two years of playing a Parisian libertine, he found himself, perhaps ironically, falling in love with an innocent Venetian virgin, declining her brother's attempts to act as her pimp, and even going so far as to propose marriage.

He found his books and papers as he had left them in his room in the Palazzo Bragadin in the summer of 1750. The senator was out of town to avoid the mayhem of Ascension Day and Casanova therefore returned briefly inland to visit him. He was on his way back to Venice, late on the Saturday before the delayed Buccintoro ceremony – the weather had been too poor on Ascension Day itself – when his life took another unexpected turn. As he pointed out, if he had left Bragadin's seconds sooner or later, things would have been very different. On the road by the Brenta canal a cabriolet overturned immediately in front of Casanova's carriage. He helped the shaken occupants back to their feet, no harm done, beyond the lady having had her skirts upturned in the face of Casanova – a sight he recalled happily decades later – and they went on their way. The next day he went to drink coffee under the Procuratie on the Piazza San Marco – in the café now known by the name of its then owner, Signor Florian. Casanova was masked, as was the lady who passed him and tapped on his shoulder. Later, when he arrived on the Riva Sepolero bridge, where Bragadin's gondolier was waiting for him, the lady reappeared and chided him for not having recognised her from the day before. He was being offered, of course, a rather different view of her.

He suspected some sort of adventure was afoot, but could not place the lady's relationship with her companion, a Venetian in a German uniform, who accepted the invitation to join Casanova in his impressive senatorial gondola for a trip to the Lido. The man turned out to be the son of a well-to-do family down on his luck with heavy debts. His identity, 'P.C.' in the memoirs, has been deduced as Pietro Antonio Capretta, the thirty-two-year-old son of Christoforo Capretta, a Venetian merchant. In fact Casanova had had financial dealings with him as early as 1748, but in 1753 he was drawn into an affair with Capretta's younger sister, Caterina, 'a prodigy' of 'unspoiled nature brimming over with candour and ingenuousness'. He was instantly attracted to her and even allowed Pietro to dupe him into making substantial loans he could ill afford in the hope of spending more time with her.

Through the carnival season of 1753, Casanova, a *soigné* twenty-eight-year-old, took Caterina on her first tour of Venice and its attractions; through her eyes he saw it all afresh. He bought a box at the San Samuele theatre, where he had once played in the orchestra, took her to the gardens of Giudecca, watched with her the monstrous illuminations in the *teatro del mundo* light-boxes. Unexpectedly, but deliciously, the worldly Parisian libertine found himself in love. He tried to protect Caterina from her brother's designs on her innocence: Pietro was so keen to solicit Casanova's approval that he even booked a casino for Caterina, Casanova, himself and his mistress, and had sex in front of his distressed sister and Casanova, presumably in the hope of selling Casanova the girl's virginity. Casanova believed at first, as with Vesian in Paris, that he could proceed with Caterina 'neither as an honest man nor as a libertine', because he knew himself to be 'incurably' in love with her, felt he could not afford marriage with her and was unwilling to take advantage of her. It was an unforeseen quandary. Caterina forced the issue, mentioning marriage, on any terms, early in their relationship and admitting freely that she was in love with him.

Casanova, the rake, is reinvented in his telling of their affair as a young man in love; running races with her in the Giudecca gardens, buying her gloves, stockings and garter buckles on the Rialto, eating ices on the Fondamenta San Marco, 'sick with love and in a state of excitement [I felt] could not continue'.

To be in love always troubled him. He was fatally drawn to innocence and youth, and was utterly aware of the irony of his seemingly inevitable role in the destruction of what he adored. 'The more innocent I found her to be,' he wrote of Caterina, 'the less I could make up my mind to possess her.' He knew what he was and what he needed; he also knew what was right. His 'soul', he wrote, 'was struggling between crime and virtue, to defend her from myself.' Caterina ended the struggle. In the Giudecca gardens, where private rooms and hideaways could be booked, she told him she was willing to be his wife 'before God, in His presence; we cannot have a truer or more worthy witness than our Creator'. Casanova could no longer resist 'the compelling force of nature' and made love to her in Giudecca's gardens calling her his 'wife'. He knew what he was doing and was almost immediately regretful. They made love through the night, and eventually he rowed her back over the Giudecca canal with 'dark circles under her eyes as if she had been beaten up . . . having sustained a combat that has changed her into [a woman]'.

Naturally enough, her debauched brother guessed what had happened, then tried and failed to blackmail Casanova into lending him money. Perhaps, at this stage, Casanova again seriously contemplated marriage to Caterina and he plotted to get her pregnant, and thus force her parents' hand towards a generous dowry. They aimed assiduously and often, he writes, at what was believed to assure conception: mutual orgasm.

By the time Christoforo Capretta returned to Venice, some time in the early summer of 1753, Pietro was in prison for debt, and Caterina was indeed pregnant. Casanova persuaded Bragadin to plead his case to Capretta, which would have been suitably impressive to a mere merchant, wealthy though he was. However, even the blandishments of a grandee could not alter the fact that Casanova was a nobody with few prospects and a dubious background in the professional theatre. Capretta not only refused but, not knowing of the pregnancy, he had his sister remove Caterina to the convent of Santa Maria degli Angeli on Murano where, by mid-June, she had been enrolled as an *educanda*.

Murano served as a repository for unwanted orphans and wayward girls, like Caterina. It was the site of several convents, and Santa Maria degli Angeli was one of the oldest and largest, on the leeward tip of Murano's main canal. Little remains but the church and some garden walls, and several small doors that lead down to the quayside that retain a certain air of furtive escape. The entry portico is arched over with a relief sculpture of the Virgin Mary flirting with the Angel Gabriel from behind a book. The door to the side was a rendezvous point for Casanova in his later illicit adventures with Caterina, or 'C.C.', as he dubbed her in the memoirs; with Laura, a lay-sister helped him make contact with her, and an older nun, whose identity remains uncertain; he called her 'M.M.'.

In the eighteenth century, the *traghetto*, or ferry, that went back and forth to Murano from the main islands of Venice, as well as gondolas for hire, waited by the Calle de la Malvasia – the irons that tied up the larger vessels remain on the bridge. It was a part of Venice that Casanova would come to know all too well in his pursuit of Caterina and the intrigues into which it led him. Nearby is the tiny church of San Canzian where travellers could wait and, indeed, pray for safe passage. Here, Casanova met the lay-sister, Laura, who acted as courier for the worldly, well-connected Venetian nuns at Santa Maria. She agreed to smuggle Casanova's letters to Caterina with her regular cargo of shopping, and hers to him. In time she would do more. There are six pillars around San Canzian, a traditionally formed Venetian church, and confessionals on the right as you go in. In these confessionals Casanova could exchange notes and even food and clothing as Caterina's pregnancy became the main concern of the young couple, and to the nuns who made it their business to connive in its secrecy.

All this might present Casanova in a very different light: a young man, a father-to-be, in love, alone in the Palazzo Bragadin, suicidal, he claimed, and denied marriage by the older generation and the traditional stage device of nunnery walls. Things were neither so simple nor so pure.

Back in San Samuele, Casanova called on his mother's former lover Giuseppi Imer, the theatre impresario, and there he met his childhood friend, Teresa Imer. She had long since left Venice and the small business of displaying herself from the house on the Calle della Duca Sforza. She was married to a choreographer, Angelo Pompeati, and working as an opera singer in Bayreuth. She had continued her Venetian-style career as singer and courtesan, and was kept by both the Marquis de Montpernis, who ran Bayreuth's opera house, and the ruling margrave Frederick von Hohenzollern, brother in law of Frederick the Great; meanwhile, she had two children with Pompeati.

Her love life should have been complicated enough, but on her trip back to Venice in 1753 she slept with Casanova – they had not seen each other since their adolescent fumblings in the Palazzo Malipiero in 1740 – and their night together resulted in her conceiving a child. This was in the middle of Casanova's torrid affair with Caterina, such that two young women, unknown to each other, were pregnant by him at the end of the spring of 1753. Caterina's father was right that he was not marriage material, but it took Casanova a long time to realise it himself, and make the truth clear to Caterina.

Caterina's pregnancy did not go well and at the end of July 1753 she miscarried. By this time Casanova had briefly moved in with Laura, to be nearer to Caterina, and with her help smuggled in large amounts of absorbent linen, bought in the Jewish quarter. He was aghast at the miscarriage, which led to haemorrhaging and Laura bringing blood-soaked linen out of the convent to her house. Caterina recovered, aided by the older nun who, if her letters to Casanova were to be believed, was probably bisexual and a little in love with Caterina herself.

Casanova returned to Venice but on major feast days and some Sundays he would have himself rowed out in the Bragadin gondola to Murano for mass at the convent church. Here, he could be seen by Caterina, whom he also called his 'little wife', and the nuns from behind their grille, though he could not talk to her. There was a visiting room, but Caterina was denied its use. He sent her a miniature of himself, hidden behind one of St Catherine mounted on a ring.

In November 1753, things at the convent took an unexpected turn. On All Saints Day, Casanova was visiting and was passed a note as he left to return to Venice. 'The letter was white and sealed with wax the colour of aventurine [the tawny glass made on Murano].' It read:

A nun who has seen you in her church every feast day for the past two and half months wishes you to make her acquaintance . . . she does not wish to obligate you to speak to her before seeing her so she will give you the name of a lady you may accompany to the visiting room [to be introduced]. Then, if [you wish], this same nun will give you the address of a casino here in Murano where you will find her alone at the first hour of the night on the day you indicate to her; you can stay and sup with her, or leave a quarter of an hour later if you have business.

It was a direct invitation to an intrigue.

Because of what followed – a full-blown affair with the nun, who turned out to be Caterina's older friend 'M.M.' – this passage of the memoirs has been cited as possible fantasy, but the balance of evidence is weighted in Casanova's favour. Although M.M., unlike 'C.C.', has not been conclusively identified, the affair, more or less as Casanova chronicles it, fits now into the confirmed broader picture of sexual practice in Venice at the time.

Casanova's portrait of M.M., a woman to whom he was powerfully attracted and who ended the likelihood of his marriage with Caterina, was of a sexually confident and politically empowered woman, far from our image of those cloistered in convents. The later involvement of a French diplomat in the affair, one Cardinal de Bernis, whom Casanova had met briefly in Paris a few years before, lends extra credence to his rendering of the story. François Joachim de Pierre de Bernis was a renowned voluptuary, much favoured by the Venetian government: his sexual peccadillos put him in their debt to a degree only surpassed by the equally libidinous British ambassador, John Murray. Both men were known to have conducted affairs, at one time or another, with women who had notionally taken the veil and were attached to religious orders. It is not quite as shocking or irreligious as it might at first appear. The convents of Venice – which included schools, musical academies and lying-in hospitals, as well as confined contemplative orders – were quite different from the modern concept of a convent. Although Signor Capretta could reasonably expect his daughter Caterina to be kept safely at Santa Maria in expectation of delivering her virginity intact to the merchant for whom he intended her, the surety on this was financial, not religious. He paid to have her kept away from Casanova and other men. Many nuns had different arrangements and lifestyles, in particular those nuns from patrician families who had brought with them substantial dowries: they were owed a two-fold debt – from the house that had profited by their wealth, and from the families who had denied them the right to marry in order to protect lines of inheritance and oligarchical marriage deals. Some such nuns, those Casanova met gambling in the *ridotto*, or masked at *carnivale*, were sometimes engaged in affairs conducted with extreme discretion for the purposes of the religious houses and families involved, and viewed sympathetically by all but the most orthodox. The women were, as the saying went, Venetians first and Christians second.

Casanova was always aroused, intellectually as well as sexually, by a proposition from a woman. He reasoned that an affair with a libertine nun would be 'an infidelity of a kind' to Caterina, but one that 'even if she were to discover it, could not offend her because it would only be meant to keep me alive and so to preserve me for her'.

He agreed to meet M.M. at the convent, with an elderly aristocratic lady, the Contessa Segura, in the visiting room. On that first meeting, in November 1753, they did not speak. M.M. chatted with the contessa as Casanova watched. 'She was a perfect beauty, tall, so white of complexion as to verge on pallor, with an air of nobility.'

An assignation was arranged at a private casino in Murano. Casanova realised immediately that he was dealing with a nun either of independent means or kept by a wealthy man. M.M. served him a meal, with pink *oeil de perdrix* champagne, on plates kept hot over steaming water – the culinary details were important, perhaps, as M.M.'s casino turned out to be owned and staffed by a Frenchman. Through the accidental knowledge that the perfume she wore was only available from, in effect, the French embassy, Casanova deduced that her protector was none other than the French ambassador himself: de Bernis. That first night, M.M. arranged a sofa and pillows at an angle that struck Casanova as odd, and let him unlace the 'six wide ribbons' of her corset – but, despite his attempts to manoeuvre her hand 'to the place where she could have convinced herself that I deserved her mercy', they did not make love.

The next day this puzzling encounter was made more so by a note from Caterina that Casanova collected from Laura on the way back to Venice. She had seen Casanova talking to M.M. and wished him to know that M.M. had been her special guardian in the convent, party to her miscarriage and its cover-up. Although this knowledge made Casanova 'uneasy', he was by no means put off his stride in chasing an affair entirely predicated on sex, although he was in theory engaged to Caterina. Intoxicated by M.M.'s social class and her patron, the French ambassador, almost as much as by the prospect of a clandestine affair with a courtesan nun, he set about play-acting the patrician.

He rented an expensive casino in which to entertain M.M. It had been owned by Lord Holderness, the British ambassador until 1746, and was decorated with erotic Oriental tiles, mirrors and a 'revolving blind waiter . . . such that masters and servants could not see each other'. It was yards from the now long-vanished San Moisè theatre, near the Piazza San Marco.

He arranged to meet M.M. by the famous equestrian statue of Bartolomeo Colleoni in the Piazza dei Santi Giovanni e Paolo. She kept him waiting 'in delicious anticipation', smiling under the three-pear shield of the medieval Venetian hero, less famed for his military exploits than for his singular anatomy: he had three testicles. She arrived dressed as a man, which thrilled Casanova yet more. They walked in arm in arm across the Piazza San Marco towards San Moisè and the rented casino where they 'unmasked'. She was impressed – mainly by the multiplicity of mirrors that reflected the expectant lovers from every angle in the flickering light of candles, by a bathtub and 'English water-closet', the boudoirs and annexes that opened off the central mirrored octagon. After the carefully prepared supper – ices, oysters, punches and Burgundy wine – they undressed and made love through the night. Though M.M. 'taught me nothing new so far as the physical side of the performance was concerned . . . I showed her . . . what she did not think she was entitled to ask me to do to her; I taught her that the slightest constraint spoils the greatest of pleasures'.

After their first night together, Casanova dedicated himself to stage-managing his first purely sexual hedonistic affair. M.M. was a patrician's daughter, rich in her own right, and kept in some style by de Bernis when she was able to slip away from Santa Maria degli Angeli. Casanova felt he had found a better audience for his sophisticated *mise-en-scène* than the shopgirls who were impressed with ribbons. He bought clothes and jewels for M.M. – on the Bragadin allowance and his occasional win at cards – and kept the casino at San Moisè well stocked with food bought from Lord Holderness's chef. In his narrative of the affair Casanova adds details of the tides of a Venetian winter, the unmasking and masking before and after Christmas, the closure of the theatres for the novena, or nine days of prayers for the grace of Our Lady of the Sea, M.M.'s hanging of blue ribbons by the quayside of the Murano casino to announce to Casanova her presence, the series of occasions through Advent when he could legitimately attend mass at Santa Maria in full view of both his lovers . . .

At Christmas, M.M. presented him with a new twist in their lubricious affair. She had confessed to her protector, de Bernis, that she and Casanova were lovers – there seems little doubt that he had asked her to take a lover in the first place – and told Casanova that de Bernis was happy for the affair to continue if he could watch their lovemaking through a peep-hole in the Murano casino. Another image of Casanova is brought into sharp focus: Casanova the happy performer and compliant participant in voyeuristic orgies. It was organised with consummate worldliness. The casino was stocked with a small library, mainly though not entirely erotica; M.M. left Casanova waiting there for several hours until she arrived on the designated day, New Year's Eve. She appeared in her habit, but soon changed into a muslin shift embroidered with gold. She had, Casanova noted, a supply of condoms at the casino – de Bernis expected her to avoid pregnancy, so she and Casanova had been practising, seemingly, *coitus interruptus*. She pointed out the peepholes in the plasterwork flowers of one wall, and they made love, Casanova having costumed himself in an Oriental turban and nothing else, with 'a pillow under her buttocks and one of her knees bent away [which] must have afforded a most voluptuous vision for our hidden friend'. They continued on the Persian carpet, standing in front of the mirror: 'I lifted her up to devour her chamber of love' . . . and so on through several hours, narrated over numerous paragraphs. The next day Casanova went to commission another portrait of himself to be hidden behind a religious image: in the Annunciation, the image outside the convent as it happens. The painter represented him as Gabriel and the Virgin as a swooning blonde.

These passages in the memoirs, which bear close resemblance to the pornography of the period in their details of nuns and voyeurism, have been questioned. There is, of course, little corroborative evidence on the precise nature of Casanova's affair with C.C., who certainly existed, and M.M., who has not been conclusively identified.

De Bernis, of course, is an easily identifiable figure, later a grandee of the Church, some of whose apologists have tried to pour scorn on Casanova's character sketch of him. In 1753 he was in his late thirties, a Jesuit by training, with a reputation as a worldly and witty churchman. He found favour politically at the French court through Madame de Pompadour. He knew her first when she was plain Madame d'Étoiles, and it seems to have been through her – it is possible they were lovers – that he was given apartments in the Louvre and in 1751 appointed French ambassador to Venice. It was here, in 1755, that he took the full priestly vows that put him *en route* to a career in the Church's hierarchy, but when Casanova knew him he was merely an *abbé*.

Though de Bernis saw a good deal of Casanova, largely unclothed, throughout January 1754, it was not until 8 February that M.M. allowed them to meet. Casanova recognised him from Paris – they had met in the company of Earl Marischal Keith four days before de Bernis left Paris for Venice.

It was entirely likely that the Venetian authorities would look kindly on an ambassadorial affair with a Santa Maria nun – the diplomatic community, of course, was forbidden contact with the patrician class (their own class) – but M.M. had as much at stake as de Bernis in keeping it discreet; the affair put him, to some large degree, in debt to the Venetian authorities. And de

Bernis was clearly involved with a woman in a religious order: he states as much in a letter of 1754, in which he refers to his 'nun who evaded the walls of her convent . . . I have been to see and she will come to dine at my house,' while Casanova's later friend the Prince de Ligne, who knew de Bernis well, recorded 'an adventure that he had with a nun in Venice'. Yet more corroboration is given by the separate philanderings of another member of the diplomatic community, the British ambassador, John Murray, described in 1757 by Lady Mary Wortley Montagu as 'a scandalous fellow in every sense . . . always surrounded by pimps'. He arrived in Venice later in 1754, and was convinced by the end of that year that any nun in Venice could be had for 'a hundred sequins' – though no records directly support this.

Through the carnival of 1754, until May, when de Bernis was recalled to France, M.M. enjoyed her two lovers. To begin with the men went out of their way not to meet, although they were aware of each other's existence, and in some sense enamoured of the triangular relationship. After the New Year's Eve assignation de Bernis sent Casanova a gold snuff box – it was decorated with two portraits of M.M., one in a habit, the other naked beside a smirking cupid with a quiver at his feet.

It was perhaps inevitable that Caterina would be dragged in. M.M., a dedicated adventuress, seems to have taken Caterina as her lover within the walls of Santa Maria. There is only Casanova's word for this, and he could hardly have been witness to what happened between them, but when Caterina recognised in M.M.'s Annunciation the work of the artist who had created her secret image of Casanova, she guessed at Casanova's infidelity and was drawn into the circle. M.M. effected this. With relatively easy access to gondolas and exeats as a patrician, and by virtue of the influence of de Bernis, M.M. smuggled her out of Santa Maria and took her to the Murano casino. Here, Caterina waited, puzzled, watched over by de Bernis and M.M. from behind the plasterwork roses. When Casanova arrived, expecting to find

M.M. – he was dressed as a pierrot for carnival – he was shocked and none too pleased to find Caterina. Immediately he knew he was the object of some plot, but felt 'played with, tricked, trapped, scorned' by both women: he had been exposed as a cheat. If M.M. and de Bernis had expected another sex-show they were disappointed. Caterina's cool acceptance that she had been superseded in Casanova's affections by her own lover – she seems to have suggested they deserved each other – was followed by night of tears, remonstration, pleading and regret. Casanova gave her his key to the Murano casino and told her to pass it to M.M., assuming he would never see either woman again.

Outside a terrible storm had whipped up the lagoon and many of the carnival revellers who had been partying on Murano faced a hazardous journey back to Venice. Casanova nearly drowned, and took to his bed in the Palazzo Bragadin with a fever that lasted several days.

On 8 February, recovered, Casanova entertained M.M. and de Bernis to dinner at his San Moisè casino. De Bernis protested not to recall the young Italian from Paris, but declared that 'from this moment we can never forget each other. The mysteries which unite us are of a nature to make us intimate friends.' In accord with this pact, he and M.M. decided to try to reunite the younger lovers. Or so they claimed. From the start they may have entertained far less altruistic and romantic ideas, for a *ménage à quatre* developed. Casanova was powerless to keep his 'little wife' away from the debauched and sexually omnivorous coterie he lived among. He vacillated only briefly – in his memory of events – before he agreed to introduce Caterina to de Bernis and thereby set in train a series of increasingly outrageous orgies for the delectation of the voyeuristic ambassador.

It is the stuff of pornography to this day but that, of course, hardly proves its lack of basis in fact. Casanova, to his credit, does flesh out, as it were, the characters and their motivations in involving themselves in other than dual sexual relationships: the waned love, the sexual hedonist, the possibly bisexual, the voyeur, and, at the centre of it all, the bemused but celebratory priapic performer himself.

On their first night together, Casanova, M.M. and Caterina – de Bernis was not there – began with the usual lavish meal, the perusal of classical pornographic literature. (Meursius' amorous encounters between women) and ended in a threesome that 'played havoc with everything visible and palpable which Nature had bestowed on us, freely devouring whatever we saw and finding that we had all become of the same sex in all the trios which we performed'.

The next day Casanova admitted, as he often did, to 'a certain remorse', though whether this was for the further debauching of the recently virginal Caterina, the fact that they had eschewed birth control when they had particular reason to fear pregnancy or, indeed, as he wrote, that 'I have never been able to decide whether I was truly ashamed or merely embarrassed' he leaves unstated.

It was an intrigue he was not as well equipped to deal with as he had thought. His resources, financial and emotional, were not as robust as those of de Bernis or M.M. He had been drawn happily into a world of hedonistic excess, with the ever indulgent Bragadin picking up some of the expense of the Holderness casino, but had not intended Caterina to become involved. However, once de Bernis had colluded in arranging for M.M., Caterina and Casanova to enjoy a threesome, Casanova knew he was beholden to the other man, and the price would be Caterina's coupling with de Bernis. This he had little desire to witness or participate in. He did nothing, however, to prevent it. At the last minute he bowed out, pleading a sudden engagement at the Palazzo Bragadin. M.M. wrote suavely to him later that he had 'made a splendid present' to their friend de Bernis, and that Caterina's mind was now 'as unprejudiced as ours . . . I have completed her education for you'.

The extent to which the episode, through the winter and carnival of 1753–4, was engineered and sponsored by de Bernis is revealed by the problems M.M., Casanova and Caterina experienced once de Bernis had left Venice, temporarily, in Lent 1754. They had to bribe the gardeners at Santa Maria to help with the women's comings and goings. Caterina was moved to another part of the convent, when they all feared they might have to cover up another pregnancy (it was a false alarm) and Casanova even dressed as a gondolier himself to row M.M. around the lee side of Murano. As the love affair with Caterina waned, Casanova's relationship with M.M. intensified – at least sexually. The attractions of a patrician hedonist like M.M. trumped the potential of future happiness with Caterina. Though, in fairness, it would seem Caterina let Casanova go with an equanimity beyond her years or position. She seems to have married a Venetian lawyer and merchant a little while after this, exactly as her father might have wanted, and was still in correspondence with Casanova years later, like so many of his past loves. The Prague Archive contains two notes, found in his study when he died, which purport to be from her.

Through the rest of 1754 the affair with M.M. continued. Casanova gambled, often with her money. Once de Bernis realised he would be away from Venice for much longer than he had originally intended – he was heavily involved in the negotiations between France and Austria that ended in the Seven Years' War (1756–63), he closed up the Murano casino and dismissed the servants. Casanova had been forced to let go the Holderness casino, and must have confessed to M.M. the shaky state of his own finances: she gave him her diamonds with which to gamble. Sometimes he won, sometimes not. De Bernis had been right in his concerns about Casanova's affair with M.M. and its potential for scandal – not for its flouting of Church rules but those of class. M.M., almost certainly a member of the prestigious Morosini family, and certainly a high-born patrician heiress, was frequently in Casanova's company at the *ridotto* and around Venice. She was masked, necessarily, but by virtue of her manner and bearing was likely to have been acknowledged as a member of the Venetian establishment. It was late in this year, 1754, that the name 'Casanova' begins to feature frequently in the Inquisition files at the Frari. Though M.M. or, indeed, any impropriety with women in religious orders was never mentioned in accusations against Casanova, de Bernis was right to distance himself, at this time, from him and M.M.

Since his return to Venice in 1753 Casanova's circle had included Andrea Memmo, the well-regarded son of one of Venice's oldest families, a young man of easy charm, impeccable pedigree and of whom great things were expected. The Memmos had been among the founding fathers of Venice; there had been a Memmo doge as early as 979, and although the family fortune was much diminished, Andrea and his brothers, Bernardo and Lorenzo, were princes in their way. They were Venetian blades exactly as Casanova had dreamt of becoming, and took up the actor's son as a drinking companion around the Campo San Stefano coffee houses and *malvasie* – the wine shops that sold the fashionable sweet malmsey. They attended the *ridotto*, perhaps in the company of Casanova's enigmatic masked companion, M.M., played cards and were enthusiastic theatre critics, arguing over the new comedic styles about which Casanova, the comedienne's son, had reason to be opinionated, and the works of Abbé Pietro Chiari, the playwright.

All this might seem innocent enough, in the spirit of the roustabout carnival city, but Casanova's socially aspiring choice of drinking companions, rather than his unorthodox sex life, put him directly in the sights of the doge's spies.

It turned out that the Inquisitori di Stato – the triumvirate of patricians who oversaw internal security in Venice, kept a close eye on those associating with young members of the Venetian establishment – the Memmos, in particular – and viewed Casanova, who had already caught their eye with his theatrically seditious pranks, as a dangerous young radical. The hefty dossier they compiled on him remains in Venice's Archivio di Stato. Giovanni Battista Manuzzi wrote a series of reports on what Casanova and the Memmo brothers were doing and saying. It was not good. Manuzzi summed up the *arriviste* Casanova as 'a man with a tendency to hyperbole who manages to live at the expense of this or that person on the strength of his lies or his ability to cheat'. This was not far from the truth, of course – or one way of looking at it. Another spy noted that Casanova's relationship with Bernardo Memmo was particularly voluble, and that he 'alternately loves [Casanova] and thrashes him'.

The records form part of three separate pieces of the Casanova jigsaw. They corroborate repeatedly what Casanova wrote about this period. They point out the dark undertow of Venetian society: the city of pleasure was also a police state, and though libertinism was far from unusual, Casanova's lack of respect for class rules of Venetian society put him out of favour with the formidable system of state informers. The Inquisitori files also make up the dossier of 'crimes' which would eventually lead to Casanova's complete downfall.

A number of factors conspired to put Casanova on the wrong side of the law – or, more exactly, on the wrong side of the establishment. Through 1754 and early 1755 he used his cabbalistic influence with Bragadin to dissuade the old senator from a marriage that was being pressed upon him. Another member of the family let it be known that Casanova was responsible for ruining the match, which might well have been the case, and for introducing Bragadin to the cabbala, which most certainly was untrue. Lucia Memmo, the Memmo brothers' mother, also formed the opinion that the low-born Casanova, who spent so much time in her *palazzo* and at the *ridotto*, was corrupting her sons and bringing them into gambling losses as well as disrepute. It seems to have been she who added to these slurs that Casanova was a Freemason and an atheist, one of which was certainly true, and only a crime of class, and the other was also possible: he had been heard composing lewd anti-clerical and anti-religious verses as part of his *commedia* routine in late night *malvasie*.

At the same time, Casanova had become embroiled in a literary dispute. He had sided loudly, and often in public debates at the Campiello San Zulian café, with the playwright Zorzi and mercilessly mocked those who found poetry in the work of Abbé Chiari. Unfortunately, one such was Antonio Condulmer, the 'Red' Inquisitor – appointed by the doge himself.

It was a mere sideshow that in the spring of 1755, when Casanova was up to his ears in debt, he borrowed some money from the neurotic Contessa Lorenza Maddalena Bonafede, who subsequently went mad and ran naked through the Campo San Pietro shouting his name. In Venice that name was beginning to mean 'trouble', which the Inquisition found dangerously close to the oligarchy. Chiari has left us with an image of Casanova at this time, in his fictional portrayal of a young man who was conspicuous, ridiculous in his way, enough of an egotist to put many noses out of joint:

He is a dandy, full of himself, blown up with vanity like a balloon and fussing about like a watermill. He has to be working his way in everywhere, paying court to all the women, grabbing every chance to get his hands on some money or use his conquests as a ladder to social success. He plays the alchemist with misers, the poet with pretty women, and the politician with important people – all things to all men, though to anyone with a grain of sense he only makes himself ridiculous.

At this time Casanova had a small suite of rooms just behind the fleshy carytids of Santa Maria dei Derelitti, on what is now the Calle Luigi Torelli, though he often stayed at the Palazzo

Bragadin. He may have wanted his privacy – he was twenty-eight, after all – or more space for his books, of which he was an avid collector. Or he may have wanted more freedom to associate with foreigners by putting himself outside the household of a patrician. It is as likely that he preferred to be near the Piazza San Giovanni e San Paolo for its easy access to Murano and the Colleoni rendezvous point he favoured with M.M. In any event, it was this address to which the Messer Grande, the chief of police, Matteo Varutti, was despatched to investigate a claim that Casanova was in possession of contraband salt.

Casanova had been wandering the *erbaria*, the early-morning herb-market, as Venetians with hangovers do to this day, disconsolate at another night's losses on the tables with M.M.'s money, when he heard of this. He went to Bragadin to complain, and flew into a fit of self-righteousness, only for the older man to point out that this was a clear warning. The police chief would not have been sent on such an errand in the normal course of events: spies could easily have informed him that Casanova was elsewhere. The message was clear. The Council of Three, on which Bragadin had once served, could mean only one thing: *leave Venice*.

Casanova, obdurate and proud, refused to take Bragadin's advice. He returned to San Giovanni e Paolo. The old senator and his young ward never saw each other again.

On 26 July 1755, the day after Casanova's last interview with Bragadin, nearly forty men arrived at his rooms. They arrested Casanova. The interest of the Inquisition was clear: his shelves were searched and dozens of his books confiscated, two key works on the cabbala – the *Key of Solomon* and the *Book of Zohar* – and others on astrology, along with his translations of Ariosto and Petrarch, and the little book of Aretino's erotic postures – famous *inter alia* for being small enough to hold in one hand. They ordered him to dress, which Casanova did with slow and studied care. He put on his best ruffled shirt, a fine floss-silk summer cloak and a dandy hat, trimmed with Spanish lace and a large feather. With exaggerated *sangfroid*, or over-arching stupidity, he decided to play his scene with the Inquisition as neither threatening nor tragic, but merely ridiculous. It was a fateful error of judgement.

PRISON AND ESCAPE

1755

'A man shut up by himself where it is impossible for him to do anything, alone in near darkness where he does not and cannot see anything . . . or . . . stand upright . . . longs for Hell if he believes in it, just to have some company . . . [it is] solitude that drives men to despair.'

Casanova, 1755

That day, 26 July 1755, which had begun so dramatically for Casanova, went from bad to worse. He was taken into the Prigioni Nuove, the new prison on the far side of the Bridge of Sighs. It was designed to intimidate with its impenetrable architecture and mysterious reputation. He passed across the blinding white courtyard, overlooked by nearly a hundred barred windows, into the cool, damp Istrian-limestone corridors. 'We then climbed a number of steps, which lead to a closed bridge [the Bridge of Sighs] that links the prison with the Doge's Palace on the other side of the canal.'

As a suspect of the Inquisition, he was heading to a part of the palace much more feared than the Prigioni Nuove or Il Pozzi, the Wells: the inquisitorial offices high in the ducal palace, and their special prison 'Il Piombi', the Leads, so named because they were directly under the palace's lead roof. Freezing in winter, the cells were ovens in summer. 'Once over the Bridge we came to a flight of stairs to a corridor that leads into one room and then another [the Deputato alla Segreta and the office of the Notaio Ducale].'

Casanova was yards from the epicentre of the secretive Venetian government. On the one side, at this level, there were the paintings, gilding and frescos that served as backdrop to the official business of senators, Tribunal and secretaries. Behind the façade was, and is, a warren of cramped dark offices and secret passages in which the Inquisition carried out its sinister work.

In the office of the Notaio Ducale, Casanova was formally identified by the Secretary to the Inquisition Domenico Maria Cavalli as the man that Manuzzi had been following. Then he was handed over to the gaoler at the Piombi. Next he was taken to the Sale dei Tre Capi, the room where the delegated inquisitors of the Council of Ten – the Council of Three – met, only at night, under ceilings rendered by Veronese. It has barely changed in the intervening centuries except that in 1755 the walls were lined with Cardinal Domenico Grimani's gift of Hieronymus Bosch's triptychal visions of hell. These would be Casanova's last view of 'freedom' for many months.

He was escorted up ever narrower staircases and along smaller corridors to the cavernous space above the Sala del Maggior Consiglio, the Great Council Room. Here, under twenty-metre larch beams, which supported both the roof and Tintoretto's half-acre ceiling below, the gaoler, Lorenzo Basadonna, scrambled for a key. He took Casanova the few yards back into the loft space to a larchwood-lined cell, one of only half a dozen, about eight feet by ten but only five feet high, entered by a door that, at three feet tall, was only half the height of the new prisoner. During all of this Casanova, as was the custom with Inquisition suspects, was told neither the charges against him, nor the sentence that the Council of Three had passed: five years' imprisonment. His crime was recorded as 'a question of religion'. He had no trial.

'Bewildered and in a state of shock', he heard the door slam behind him. He was beyond the help of his family, his young noble friends and, even Bragadin, whose generosity towards Casanova, according to the Inquisition files, was one of the reasons he had been under suspicion in the first place. His first cell was above the Sala degli Inquisitori, with a view of sorts, through a six-bar iron cross-hatch and a corridor, to the top of the palace courtyard. He gave way to despair, then anger:

I realised I had ended up in a place where the false seemed true and reality seemed some sort of bad dream; where the mind seems to lose its abilities and a deformed imagination can make one the victim of either chimaerical hope or terrible desperation. I made a decision to keep all my wits about me, drawing upon all the philosophy I had in my soul but which I had never had occasion to use.

There was a 'private' gaoler, who ferried messages, sometimes food and even books from the outside world. The first thing Lorenzo had asked him was what he wanted to eat. There was light and air, for all it was bitterly cold in winter and almost unimaginably hot in summer. But food was delivered regularly, some basic furniture provided, books – Casanova was given Maria of Agreda's improving *Mystical City of God*, which he claimed was the one thing more depressing than his surroundings – while prisoners had the bizarre status of living in the same palace as a potentate, and within feet of the judges who had condemned them.

Little by little, Casanova came to realise that his incarceration was not going to be of the short-sharp-shock variety he had experienced at the Fort Sant'Andrea. Little by little, his febrile mind turned to thoughts of escape. It had never been done. But, then again, he was not behind the metre-thick stone walls of II Pozzi: he was inside the palace, the throbbing heart of Venetian corruption and political cupidity. Surely, he reasoned, if he could get beyond the cell floors or ceiling – mere wood and terrazzo, or on to the lead roof, he might find a way out through the bustling palace.

Days turned into weeks turned into months, and summer

moved towards winter. After a full nine months' imprisonment, a pallid and back-sore Casanova was finally allowed out of his cramped cell for regular exercise. He took this not in the open air of the Pozzi courtyard but in the half-dark of the brick-floored undercroft beneath the medieval corner of the palace, above the senators' loggia. The roof here is supported by a small forest of Byzantine brick pillars, and behind one, with trunks full of medieval trial records, Casanova found an iron spike. It was of the sort from which hangs the heavy Tintoretto ceiling under the loft space to the side – there were hundreds of them – and this he secreted back to his cell.

It shows a new side to Casanova's character, and also to his writing, that these months of imprisonment only rarely dented his positivity or the later jauntiness of his style of recording it. He was convinced he would escape. The instinctive imaginative leap to success, which had helped him already to sexual and professional conquests now pulled him forward to improbable freedom. With the patience and perseverance borne also of long solitary confinement, he worked away at the floorboards of his cell with the spike. Under them, he found the usual Venetian layer of terrazzo and mortar. Over several weeks, he worked through this, with the spike and some vinegar (terrazzo is an organic resin corroded by even weak acids) brought to him by the compliant Lorenzo with his food. If he had known he was above the Sala degli Inquisitori, it did not put him off his plan to escape one night, bribe, swindle, charm or simply walk out of the palace.

By the end of August 1756 he had made a hole almost big enough to break through; it was hidden from below by the ornate ceiling and Tintoretto's paintings. Each day he hid the night's progress, the growing hole, the detritus of larch splinters and ground-up terrazzo, under his bed. Then, on 25 August 1756, without warning, Lorenzo informed him that he would be transferred to another cell. Ironically, Bragadin's intercession had won Casanova this small favour, but at the worst possible moment. He had time only to hide the iron spike in the chair, which he guessed would be transferred with him to his new cell. Of course, the hole was soon discovered.

When asked where he had procured tools to dig his escape, Casanova replied coolly, 'You provided them.' It was a stroke of genius. Lorenzo, fearful for his job in the prevailing atmosphere of suspicion and easy denunciation, decided it was safer to cover the hole at his own expense, but keep a closer eye on Casanova; the cell he was moved to was next to the guards' room.

This new, larger cell was above the Sala dei Censori on the far east of the palace, overlooking, when he strained to see it, the Rio del Palazzo, the Pozzi prison and what is now the Hotel Danieli. He was allocated a cellmate, a bona-fide spy called Soradaci, with whom he did not get on. He also began a book-exchange friendship with a prisoner now housed quite near him. On the other side of the corridor, which slopes off into the palace labyrinth from the guards' room, there was a renegade priest, Marino Balbi. Balbi's cell was over the Sala della Bussola. Casanova and he managed to communicate by scribbling notes in the books they exchanged, and each soon confessed his interest in escape. After his previous attempt at digging his way out, Casanova's cell walls and floor were checked regularly, but not the ceiling. He had noted that Balbi was allowed a large collection of religious canvases and drawings with which he papered his cell and its ceiling, and reasoned that Balbi might hack through his ceiling into the shared void space above, concealing his progress with a picture – it was indeed a bizarre prison. He smuggled the iron spike to Balbi, hidden in a Bible under a plate of butter-soaked gnocchi – Casanova was never one to forgo a culinary detail – and, over the next few weeks, Balbi got through his ceiling.

From here, with little difficulty, he squeezed himself into the tight space between the larchwood cell ceilings and the lead roof of the palace. On the night of 31 October 1756 he broke through into Casanova's cell and together they scrambled through the roof void, testing to find a weaker spot in the leading above. Neither Soradaci nor Balbi's cellmate could raise the alarm: at night, Piombi prisoners were left to sweat, scream or die unattended. So, Casanova reasoned, they had a full night to work through their escape plan, and 1 November, All Saints' Day, took the Inquisitors and nearly all of the Chancellory and Inquisition staff away from the palace. Venetian government ran to churchly calendars.

Casanova broke out of the roof, peeling back the lead. That night the moon was full, and he feared that if he pulled himself through the hole he would send long shadows down from the roof. The pair bided their time. Eventually, either cloud or the moon's movement gave them reason to believe they would not be seen. Casanova and Balbi struggled out on to the roof. Eventually they found a skylight that let them back into the palace, exactly as Casanova had intended. *Histoire de ma fuite* – (*History of My Escape*), published in 1787 – and *The History of My Life*, which also dealt with it, relate an action-hero's vertiginous adventure, which involved bedsheet ropes, a well-placed ladder and Casanova hanging on to the roof above the Rio di Palazzo ninety feet below. Artistic licence, partial memories from a terrifying night, and embellishment may have been burnished into true recall by a practised anecdotalist – even his enemies admitted his telling of this tale was superb. But his contemporaries believed every word. Even the Venetians. The damage he and Balbi occasioned to the palace was repaired, the costs noted in the accounts, stored in the Venetian archives.

By whatever route, they found themselves inside the palace on the night of 31 October/1 November, then discovered a narrow stone staircase and went down another flight of stairs that ended at a glass door. 'I opened it and found myself in a chamber that I recognised [from the arrest]'. He was in the Inquisition offices. From there corridors connect to the Atrio Quadrato, or Square Atrium, at the top of the Golden Staircase in the Doge's Palace. Dignitaries would usually turn right into the state apartments and council chambers, rather than left into the offices of the Inquisition but it was here, as dawn was breaking on 1 November 1756 that Casanova and Balbi found themselves – locked in. They were stuck there, contemplating their prospects, which must have seemed bleak indeed, with little to look at but Tintoretto's rendering of Doge Geralamo Priuli footling with the Sword of Justice. They still had the clothes they had been arrested in to change back into, and they had cut each other's hair and beard as best they could before they left Casanova's cell (Soradaci had been a barber), which was why, when a night watchman spotted them at the window of the Square Atrium, high above the Giants' Staircase of the Doge's Palace, he assumed they were courtiers who had been locked in overnight – perhaps it happened now and then in a building that was Byzantine in every sense.

He let them out, and Casanova, with Father Balbi, walked calmly between the giant marble buttocks of Neptune and Mars, through which doges passed after their coronation, and down the Giant's Staircase to the Piazza San Marco.

There, Casanova hailed, loudly so that passers-by might hear, a gondola to take them to Fusina. Once they had rounded the Customs House by the Salute – the view of Venice known to the world from the works of Canaletto – he changed his instruction: they were to head for Mestre because once the escape was discovered, they would be looked for at Fusina and the Brenta Canal. As the oars turned in their *forcolas* down the Giudecca canal by Zattere, Casanova was suddenly overwhelmed with relief and racked with sobs as the gondola pushed onwards towards the mainland.

Next they headed straight for Treviso. They had a little money, some begged from other prisoners, and Casanova gave all of it to Balbi when he decided they would best evade capture if they travelled on separately. To complete the devil-may-care brilliance of his story, Casanova decided to seek shelter for the night nearby, and when the woman who answered his knock told him it was the home of the local police chief who was out hunting for one Casanova and an escaped monk, he knew he had found the perfect place to hide. He slept for twelve hours.

Dressing quickly the next morning, he went on his way,

walking for up to nine hours a day, heading north towards Brenta and the borders of the Venetian territories. Using skills that the Franciscan Brother Steffano had taught him, he lived off the land and the kindness of peasants who took him for the poor cleric he had once been.

Within a week, on a donkey he had borrowed from a stable in which he had slept, he was crossing the border at La Scala near Brenta. He would not see his homeland again for nearly eighteen years.

ACT III SCENE V

COMÉDIE FRANÇAISE, PARIS

1756–7

'I am going to respond directly to your last letter: you start as the harbinger of your great love, and I believe you sincere; I am flattered . . . but I want it to last, to last until I can see you revolt against the worldly life you lead . . . but I know my fears also distress you.'

Manon Balletti to Casanova, Paris, 1757

Casanova's escape was soon the talk of Venice and beyond, recorded by contemporaries as 'prodigious'. He was quite open about it in Paris; it fast became a polished anecdote and key to his new persona as a dangerous man of action, and wronged scion of the Serene Republic. He stopped at Bolzano just long enough to collect some money sent from Bragadin – who had recently begged for Casanova to be pardoned, only to have him turn outlaw – and went on over the Alps to Munich, Augsburg and Strasbourg, then Paris. He arrived on 5 January 1757 – impressive winter progress by the standards of the period – on the very day, as it happened, that there had been an audacious assassination attempt on Louis XV, by a man called Damiens.

188

The aspiring regicide's execution, which Casanova witnessed with thousands of Parisians, was a spectacle of epoch-defining barbarity – though recalled by Casanova, typically, for its unexpected effect upon the women he was with. But that was months away. On arriving in Paris, a criminal also, unshaven, unwashed, all but penniless but unusually well connected, Casanova went first to the rue du Petit Lion by the Comédie Italienne. Here he sought out the Balletti family, and later his companion in *amour*, de Bernis.

Prison changed Casanova irrevocably. He was entering his thirties and had left not just his youth behind but, more vitally, his home: he was an exile from Venice for as long as it pleased the Inquisition to name him such, and it was reasonable now to assume that he would be an exile for some years to come, no matter how much he trumpeted his innocence. In 1757 in Paris, he made no attempts, as he would in the future, to ingratiate himself with Venetian diplomats. 'I saw that to accomplish anything I must bring all my physical and moral faculties into play, exercise strict self-control and play the chameleon.' He was ever more determined to make money, fitter, stronger, steelier and more focused than before. He cut a swathe through mid-century Parisian society: its politics, finances, theatres and boudoirs. These years in Paris laid the foundations for his posthumous fame.

He had not written ahead, but news of his escape had reached his friend Antonio Balletti, who consequently claimed he had been expecting him. They arranged rooms for Casanova in a house near theirs, belonging to the wigmaker at the Comédie Italienne. Casanova was immediately struck by two key changes in the Balletti household: Sylvia the matriarch's worsening health, and the beauty in maturity of Manon, Antonio's younger sister. For the present, though, he had more pressing concerns: he had to present himself as soon as possible to de Bernis to ask for help, patronage and work. De Bernis was obliged to Casanova with multiple ties of complicity, as fellow Freemason, bedfellow, lover of M.M. and Caterina, and as the man who had inadvertently put Casanova in the sightlines of the Venetian Inquisition.

Casanova took the hackney coach – so uncomfortable it was known as the 'chamber pot' – from the Pont Royal to Versailles in search of him, but did not find him as the court had been thrown into confusion by the assassination attempt on the King. He caught up with his old friend at the Palais Bourbon where de Bernis was conducting his new business as France's foreign minister. They met in private, and de Bernis greeted him warmly, pressing a hundred *louis* into his palm and promising to be of every assistance.

Casanova was conspicuously and immediately elevated in French society by the workings of somebody very well placed to do so and it seems now that that person was de Bernis, who had already heard of Casanova's escape from M.M. and said he had been expecting him: the story was the talk of Paris. Casanova claimed he was frequently stopped and quizzed about it, occasionally obliged to spend two hours detailing the tale; some, including Madame de Pompadour, were already encouraging him to write about it.

De Bernis sent him to meet Jean de Boulogne, the King's comptroller-general in charge of the treasury, who subsequently suggested Casanova meet Joseph de Paris-Duverney, a noted financier. It is a feature of eighteenth-century government finances that much central fiscal business was farmed out to the private sector, especially in France, where even the right to tax could be bought by 'tax farmers'. It is a feature, likewise, of Casanova's career that his fast thinking when an opportunity arose was based on research and some innate ability. When Giovanni Calzabigi suggested a lottery to de Boulogne in Casanova's presence, Casanova pounced on the idea, added some mathematical calculations of his own, and found himself hired as director of a French national lottery. Calzabigi was its administrator, and some of the start-up costs were offset by de

Paris-Duverney and though Casanova made the first of his real fortunes out of the scheme, the French government felt safe too. Had it failed, it would have been passed off as the work of foreigners.

De Boulogne and de Paris-Duverney had to raise money to finance Madame de Pompadour's scheme for a French military cadet school. Although Casanova's involvement in the first full-blown lottery in France was partly serendipitous, partly a result of his ease with numbers, it came about also because he had introduced Calzabigi and his brother Ranieri to de Paris-Duverney. International speculators and artists – Ranieri wrote the libretti for Gluck's *Orfeo ed Euridice* and *Alceste* – they had much in common with their fellow itinerant Italian, Casanova, but they were ill-at-ease socially: Ranieri suffered appalling eczema, and their French was not good. Years in the company of French actresses and high-born sybarites like de Bernis, as well as his lessons with Crébillon had paid off: Casanova could dazzle Parisians in their own tongue and fashion.

Casanova set about explaining to those who would buy tickets – *many* tickets in an age of gambling addiction – the terms of his 'Genoese' lottery. With the Calzabigis, he fixed the 'house' always to gain slightly over the winners, with a fixed set of ninety numbers and the ability to buy up to five. One correct number in a set returned the stake, three correct numbers or a '*terne*' returned the stake eight-thousand-fold, four correct numbers, or a '*quaderne*', brought a sixty-thousand-fold return, and a '*quine*', or full house, created France's first instant millionaires. It was a runaway success.

Casanova effected one of history's more remarkable come-backs. Within a few months he had reinvented himself as a fixture on the Parisian social scene, *en route* to creating one of the fastest fortunes in mid-eighteenth-century France. A Venetian who knew him described him in a letter from Paris:

[Casanova] has a carriage and lackeys, and is attired resplendently. He has two beautiful diamond rings, two tasteful pocket watches, snuff-boxes set in gold, and always plenty of lace. He has gained admittance, I don't know how, to the best Parisian society. He . . . has a stake in a lottery in Paris and brags that this gives him a large income . . . He is quite full of himself and stupidly pompous. In a word, he is unbearable. Except when he speaks of his escape, which he recounts admirably.

Casanova's years in Paris were to be among the most glamorous, certainly the most prosperous, of his life. He was coining more than 120,000 francs annually from the lottery – his immediate haul on the first draw was four thousand – and as one of the co-founders he had negotiated the right to open six lottery offices himself, all in Paris, though the lottery eventually sold in several major cities. He ran the most exclusive himself, in sumptuous rented apartments in rue Saint-Denis. This became the headquarters of his business and his life, a privileged salon where he sold dreams of fortune, dabbled in cabbalistic forecasting, and seduced Parisian society with his affable charm and tales of adventure. 'Paris was and remains,' he wrote, 'a city where people judge everything by appearances. There is no other [place] in the world where it easier to impress people.'

Casanova's memories of Paris, with de Pompadour at the height of her influence, the rococo salons of the mysterious Comte de Saint-Germain, the theatres and races, sex-games and gambling of an idle aristocracy, may read like a well-costumed dance of death. One episode in particular stands out, unusually prescient of the horrors that would come to Paris and typically Casanovan in its pitch-perfect re-creation of humanity *in extremis*. The would-be regicide and former soldier Robert François Damiens was due to be executed on 1 March 1757 at the place de Grève. There are several descriptions, and engravings of the event. Damiens took four hours to die. His skin was ripped off with heated pincers, molten lead was poured over him, he was castrated, and the end to his sufferings came only when he was tied to four stallions, which were sent in different directions, tearing him asunder.

Casanova, never a fan of violence, took an interest instead in the reaction of the crowd and, in particular, the aged libertine Angelica Lambertini. As she watched she allowed her skirts to be lifted from behind by Conte Eduardo Tiretta of Treviso – an acquaintance of Casanova from Venice, known around Paris as 'Count Six Times', '*le compte six fois*' a title Lambertini had recently insisted he live up to with Casanova as witness when he happened to visit them for breakfast. Tiretta had made love to her 'merely' five times through the previous night – a limit, it might be noted, deemed absolute and medically inviolable at the time.

But Casanova was more impressed with Tiretta's other attribute as Paris's favourite-titled gigolo: his endowment. At Damiens' execution Casanova records he first pleasured and finally entered Lambertini as the torture continued. It is a moment of sadistic prose in terms of its free mingling of horror and the darkest elements of human sexuality – but also a moment of *Grand Guignol* prescience in its way.

Then something happened to Casanova that was as unexpected as it was unfashionable. He and Manon Balletti fell in love. And, unusually in Casanova's story, *her* feelings about their affair are preserved because he kept more than forty of her love letters till he died. Manon was his near neighbour for the first months he was in Paris, and he ate most days with her family. She captivated him from the first meal, and the surviving Nattier portrait of her at this age, seventeen, hints at one reason why. She was the very model of beauty expected of the age; pink-lipped, poised, as delicate as the bloom placed at her bodice, with a clear, kind, direct gaze. She admitted quite fast to being in love with Casanova, in letters preserved in the Prague Archive. She wrote usually late at night, signing off with kisses as if they were already lovers, and was open, passionate, adoring – 'Oh how I wish this absence [of yours] would end . . . I believe I love you.' But he held back, wisely, promising marriage one day, knowing that the nearest thing he had to a family would never forgive him if she became just another of his conquests. Her letters throw new light on Casanova in love: her girlish hand narrates a drama from her first infatuation through increasing infuriation to resigned despair.

Manon, like Henriette, was a gifted musician and Casanova was captivated by the highly educated but playfully theatrical young woman; she put on plays of her own devising, with props and costumes from the family store on the fourth floor of the rue Petit Lion house, with Casanova, among others, as audience. Her imagination alive with romantic adventures for the stage, she could hardly fail to be impressed by the dashing stranger, beloved of her brother and mother, whose reappearance in her life could not have been better stage-managed – in a midwinter storm after a prison escape, trailing sexual and romantic danger.

But she was engaged to someone else. Her family had accepted a marriage proposal on her behalf from the musician Clément: it was a good, safe match, and well meant, but Manon fell headlong in love with Casanova. 'If only you knew how hard I fought to vanquish the tenderness I felt towards you', she wrote, '[but] I did not succeed.' Knowing from her brother, or sensing simply that the age and experience gap between them was too great, she had the intelligence to recognise that what she felt was a sort of hero-worship, but also that she was experiencing something altogether more intoxicating. 'I enjoy myself with you more than anyone else . . . but I tell myself he's merry, he's clever, this isn't surprising, but in the end I become uneasy if a day passes and I do not see you . . . I become sad, dreamy, and I find that when I dream it is only and always of you.' Her pain echoes down the centuries, as does her exquisite pose between infatuation, propriety and pride. She was desperate from the start to know Casanova loved her too. 'What will become of me? How stupid am I to love someone who is indifferent to me . . . but then sometimes I thought that perhaps you might love me but that you dared not show any signs of your love because of circumstances [her betrothal and family]?'

Manon has sometimes been written of as one of Casanova's more pitiable 'victims' but her letters, even from early in the affair, display a cool sense of self-worth and a serene unwillingness to risk much in love. Every time she states her infatuation with Casanova, who was thirty-one to her seventeen, with a world of experience and learning behind him, she asserts her equality. And in one respect at least she was right: for Manon, like Casanova, being in love was at least partly a performance in which she expected to be centre stage and adored. It set their romance on an uncomfortable footing, not just because she held out for a proposal of marriage – which she received.

In her self-penned dramas, she had always been rescued and placed on a pedestal; her own adoration of Casanova shocked her as much as it troubled him. 'The friendship and esteem which I felt for her family kept me from harbouring any idea of seducing her,' he wrote. 'I could not conceive what the outcome would be as every day I fell more and more in love with her.'

It became, at first, that most eighteenth-century of intrigues: an epistolary romance. Madame Obert, the Ballettis' maid, ferried letters back and forth between Casanova and Manon through the early spring of 1757. In this, he was all stage-rhetoric, which Manon recognised, adored and teased him for: 'You begin by exaggerating your love greatly to me . . . but [I choose] to believe it is sincere, as it flatters me and I desire nothing else than to see it last for ever.' In her way she was careful and calculating: she was determined not to be just another of Casanova's passing infatuations. 'Always love me . . . never neglect to take care of my heart', she wrote to him, perhaps unwisely, and 'Burn all our letters'. On neither point did he oblige.

Although Manon may have reminded Casanova of Caterina, whom he had so nearly married, and the many young women to whom he was attracted, in the end the more lasting ties on his heart and mind tended to be to older, more worldly, sexually confident and experienced women, like M.M. or Henriette. He knew and enjoyed the aspect of hero-worship that was a necessary part of his initial attraction to Manon – he was, after all, enjoying his first period of real fame and, linked to it, some true prosperity. It was not a likely time for him to fall in love or settle down, but he played with the idea that Manon might be a perfect partner. She had an extra attraction for him, in marital terms, rather as Bellino had; an extended family into which Casanova could happily fit, who loved him already.

The letters, and brief moments of privacy – some kisses but little more – continued through the spring and into the summer of 1757. Manon broke off her engagement to Clément, without telling her mother why. She and Casanova argued. Her insecurities began to surface. She doubted Casanova loved her, and blamed herself in letters to him, as if to solicit his encouragement: 'Your love has lessened but I don't think this is a crime of yours, no, I have a thousand faults, I know, and the more one knows me the more one discovers them.' It seemed so, for Casanova: 'Falling in love with Manon every day but never intending to ask for her hand in marriage, I had no clear idea at what I was aiming.'

The rows intensified. She was jealous of Casanova's time away from her – often on lottery business – and by June she wrote that she was 'desolate'. She suggested they draw up a list of issues that annoyed the other party, like a married couple, and Casanova laughed in her face. By July, he was feeling pestered, often sullen in her presence, and was apparently critical in his letters to her – only her replies survive: 'Your letter which I am reading again makes me see all my faults and eclipses those that I imagine you have yourself,' she wrote. Manon and Casanova felt the world thought them well suited, but could not, in private, get on.

Why did Casanova string her along for so long? First, Sylvia was dying: Casanova hadn't the heart to break hers with a wedding, of which she would not approve – the Paris police were of the opinion that Sylvia and Casanova were or had been lovers – and had no interest in rocking the Ballettis' domestic boat. Perhaps, also he hoped that things would become easier with Manon in time and they would marry – she certainly was expecting such an outcome through that difficult summer.

In the meantime, he was a man of strong sexual appetite and limited interest in fidelity. He was at the height of his fame and wealth – and Manon was determined to remain a virgin. She was right that he was away a lot for reasons other than business: he was conducting a series of affairs with the sort of women, *au fond*, he preferred: those who had no interest in him as a husband. 'You go and enjoy yourself elsewhere,' she wrote, '[just] do not keep my heart in perpetual chains.' At other times she would try to rouse his jealousy, swearing devotion, 'Despite all the bad talk, rumours and calumnies, nothing can take my heart away from you,' and reminding him that she had been invited by a Monsieur St-Jean to a dinner *à deux*. Casanova refused to be drawn, and it is for this that he deserves criticism: his cowardly or self-interested disinclination to tell her sooner that it was not going to work left her confused and desperate for the best part of a year.

Things dragged on while Casanova had affairs of greater or lesser duration with the actress Giacoma Antonia Veronese, who worked with the Ballettis at the Comédie Italienne, with a Dutch heiress, when he was in Holland on business, with a shopkeeper's wife called Madame Baret, not to mention in Dunkirk some affair noted for a chapter in the memoirs that was never written. Nor did his 'engagement' to Manon restrict him, he wrote, in his interest in the 'mercenary beauties' of Paris. He was a busy boy.

On 16 September 1757, Sylvia Balletti died, with Casanova and Manon at her side; she unexpectedly commended the latter to his perpetual care. As Sylvia drew her last breaths, he told her he would marry her daughter. Manon, then, continued to believe there would be a union one day and continued to write to him as her 'cher mari'. The Balletti family thought she should go the convent while her mother's estate was wound up, or eventually go on the stage – the more classical Comédie Française – or make one of several advantageous matches put forward by the Marquise de Monconseil, a family friend. Manon began to see the volatile Casanova again as a potential saviour: 'Always remember that you have a very loving little wife who expects the greatest fidelity from her husband,' she reminded him as he was en route to Dunkirk.

What he was doing there remains a mystery; he may have been on his first foray into espionage – he presented it as such in *The History of My Life*. Notionally he had been sent by de Bernis to report on the French fleet there, because it was thought that the King, who controlled the navy, was being less than frank with the Foreign Ministry and the Treasury over his ships' state of readiness for war. There may have been more to it than that. At some time around this period, Casanova flirted with the idea of becoming a French subject – indeed, he may have taken what would now be called dual nationality – to further himself within the establishment and as a small player in French diplomacy, espionage and international finance. For the time being the semi-autonomous, stateless Casanova was useful to de Bernis for missions in Dunkirk and later in Holland from which the French government could distance itself if necessary.

Whatever he was up to, he came back to Paris substantially richer, with a twelve-thousand-franc 'honorarium' from the government. Soon after this, he had a fortuitous, not to say comic encounter *en route* back to Paris that indirectly further improved his fortune. It was October 1757, Casanova was returning to the city from an evening near the Barrière Blanche.

He was paying court to La Veronese, the actress courtesan known as 'Camilla'. She had several lovers 'surrendering now to love, now to money, and sometimes to both at once', as Casanova elegantly defined the theatre courtesans of Paris, 'free women in almost every respect.' He was sharing a small coach with the young Conte de la Tour d'Auvergne, a 'dancer' named Babet sitting on their laps in the jostling dark. Casanova reached for her hand, kissed it, and pressed it into his crotch. The hand obliged, but 'just at the moment of crisis' de la Tour broke the silence: 'I am obliged to you, my dear friend, for this courteous and unexpected Italian handshake; a greeting I was neither expecting nor deserving of,' and laughed himself hoarse. It took Casanova some time to see the joke, which de la Tour spread around town, but the men became close friends. In the winter of 1757–8, de la Tour fell ill with sciatica. Casanova offered to cure it with the Talisman of Solomon – the star of David; he drew it in his memoirs and noted that he had no faith in it. Whatever Casanova's investment of faith at the time his 'cure' worked on de la Tour, who made a rapid recovery and told his friends of the unexpected cabbalistic powers of the wealthy young man known mainly for his wild past and high living.

One person who made particular note was de la Tour's aunt, the old Marquise d'Urfé, an ardent devotee of the cabbala and one of the richest women in France. The day after Casanova had effected de la Tour's cure, she invited him to her townhouse on the Quai des Théatins and received him there 'with all the grace of the old court in the days of the Regency'.

ACT III SCENE VI

'THE MASK OF A MAN OF NO CONSEQUENCE': THE MARQUISE D'URFÉ AND EXPERIMENTS IN NECROMANCY

1757–60

'The Marquise d'Urfé, still seeking the powder that will trans-form lead into gold, lives only to discover the elixir of life, barely leaves her laboratory . . . but has fallen into the hands of the Italian called Casanova who has convinced her she will fall pregnant, aged sixty-three, by the actions of the stars, himself and his cabbalistic numbers and give birth *to herself* as nothing less than an immortal being.'

Souvenirs de la Marquise Créquy

The Seven Years' War was bankrupting France. The financial crisis formed the undertow of Casanova's adventures there in the middle of the century, as the government, in particular the faction headed by Madame de Pompadour and those in her patronage, like de Bernis, sought ever more resourceful ways to generate revenue. The lottery, of which Casanova was director and salon-keeper, had been devised to help support de Pompadour's military academy. His trip to Dunkirk, in late 1757, had been at least in part to evaluate the worth of the French fleet, not just in military terms but in case assets had to be sold. Now Casanova was to be despatched on an even more daring, and clandestine, international errand for the French government. It was important, again, that it was undertaken by a 'foreigner', but one loyal to de Bernis and La Pompadour. Casanova would go to Amsterdam to negotiate how much cash and gold could be raised against French government-issued bonds up to a face value of twenty million francs. Those who doubt the more exuberant financial claims of Casanova's *History* need look to this, just one of many passages, where the faith of contemporary businessmen is matched by the dull record of finance to reiterate Casanova's varied talents and fiscal reliability. He was in Amsterdam, as he says. He sold private shares to the value of seventy-two thousand francs on 5 December 1758. He agreed sales of French bonds at only eight per cent discount and made a further private deal, possibly based on cabbalistic prediction, that a ship thought lost would return, which netted him many thousands of francs in profit. He returned to Paris not only with the prospect of official approval and further commissions but with an enhanced personal fortune based on percentages of all his deals.

After his return from Holland, Casanova felt on sufficiently secure ground financially to rent two new properties: one in the rue Comtesse d'Artois near the rue Montorgueil, the other in the up-and-coming neighbourhood of new townhouses known as Petite Pologne north-west of Paris, beyond the city walls. There, he took a large pleasure-palace, called Cracovie en Bel Air. The house, near where the current Gare Saint-Lazare now stands, had two gardens, stables, a good cellar and an excellent cook, Madame de Saint-Jean, known as 'La Perle'; it also boasted several baths – a sign of the changing fashion in personal hygiene and plumbing. Casanova kept two carriages and five fast stallions known as *enragés*, thoroughbreds from the King's own stud reknowned for their speed and whipcord musculature. Casanova's greatest pleasure in Paris, beyond women, food and theatre, became 'driving fast' down the capital's well-made streets. His household was soon infamous in Paris society for its gambling, loose living and late nights, but also for its *macaroni al sughillo* and *pilau ris in cagnon*: exotic tastes of Venetian carnival.

Casanova's sojourn in Amsterdam brought him more than just financial success. There, he found his old friend Teresa Imer. She was working as a singer, with her two children in tow: a truculent twelve-year-old boy, and five-year-old Sophie, Casanova's daughter from their 1753 fling in Venice. Casanova claimed Teresa was turning them into little monsters by training them to cry and overact. The boy in particular seemed to displease him, but little Sophie was the image of her father. He offered Teresa a thousand-ducat investment in her new venture in London – a club in Soho – if Sophie could come with him to Paris. She thought about it for a minute, said no, but offered him the boy instead. Giuseppi Pompeati was in need of a father figure – and Giacomo Casanova, for reasons that became clear all too soon, was in want of a son.

In 1734, at the age of twenty-eight, Jeanne de Lascaris d'Urfé de La Rouchefoucauld had inherited the entire d'Urfé estate, one of the oldest and richest in France. She had lived her life, unusually for the era, as an independently wealthy woman, free-thinking, free-spirited, without the chains of responsibility or domesticity. She had an income of eighty thousand *livres* a year, much of which she spent on books – the d'Urfé collection formed one of the cornerstones of the later Bibliothèque Nationale – owned numerous properties in and around Paris and a portfolio of châteaux. Politics bored her: by virtue of her incomparable wealth and learning, she preferred to absorb herself in philosophy, alchemy, theosophy and magic. The Marquise d'Urfé had moved beyond the constraints of her sex and society into an alternative universe of occultism, high art, high finance, high fashion and high maintenance. She was widowed young, disinherited her only surviving daughter, and committed her to an asylum. As Casanova became intensely aware, she was not only in search of the Philosopher's Stone, an elixir for eternal youth or a means to regenerate herself, she was also, as a fall-back, in search of an heir.

When Casanova was first invited to her home, he found there a laboratory in which she was conducting alchemical experiments and attempting to create a quintessence – a powder of projection or catalyst – that would speed the supposed 'natural' evolution of substance. This *opus alchemicum* or 'great work' was one of the primary goals of alchemy, the area in which chemistry overlapped with the search for the Philosopher's Stone. It took resources, determination and patience, all of which the marquise had in abundance.

She was not a hermit: she held a salon most evenings for twelve dinner guests to discuss the paranormal as well as what today would be considered 'science' in an age when there was no clear distinction between the two. According to the Marquise Créquy her evenings were 'choked with quacks and people stampeding after the occult sciences'. Others were more generous. The Abbé de Bernis was a regular, so too Madame Bontemps, the reader of cards to Madame de Pompadour. The Conte di Cagliostro, a chemist and hypnotist was a *protégé*, also Mesmer who linked – wrongly – electricity to trance but nevertheless was a skilled hypnotist, and the bizarre Conte de Saint-Germain, of indeterminate age, state and origins who claimed to be several hundred years old and have the ear of the King.

Into this privileged but unhinged world stepped Giacomo Casanova, known already among Parisian dabblers in the occult for his successful treatment of the Duchesse de Chartres' acne in 1750. He was now an altogether more intriguing figure: he had escaped from an impregnable prison; he had created a fortune from lottery numbers; numerous society women were said to be in his thrall, such as Madame du Blot, Madame de Boufflers, ladies-in-waiting with much time and some money on their hands. The marquise decided quickly that they had all under-estimated the wealthy Italian: she believed he had powers that only she might unlock. Together, they began one of the more bizarre attachments of his bizarre career – an apparent mutual dependency of faith in the occult sciences, to which Casanova later said he paid mere lip-service but may at the time have believed. Her family claimed he did this for one reason only: he cost her 'millions'.

The marquise and her coterie, Casanova wrote,

had chimerical plans and by making them hope for their success I hoped at the same time to cure them of their folly by disillusioning them. I deceived them to make them wise; and I did not believe myself to be guilty, for what prompted me was not avarice. I was merely paying for my pleasures with money which was destined to acquire possessions that nature makes it impossible to obtain . . . It was money destined to be spent on follies; I merely diverted its use by making it pay for mine.

It was one of his most sophisticated self-justifications for fleecing an ageing, vulnerable and stupendously wealthy wo-man. The deception, if such it was, went on for years. He asked for jewels to use in his own 'experiments' and as crystals to guide astral powers, with the help of the cabbala. He translated Latin texts for her, and spent so many hours locked with her in her laboratory that rumours circulated they were lovers, which may have been so. She showered him with gifts and compliments, specifically that he was 'a genuine adept under the mask of a man of no consequence', a line that stuck in his memory though not perhaps in the sense she meant. Perhaps the key to Casa-nova's relationship with the marquise, as with the occult, was the attraction the arcane and esoteric had to a man who needed to feel elevated beyond the ranks and rules of society. The marquise chose to believe that Casanova had generated a fortune on the lottery to disguise his real identity as a messiah of the occult. He, at least briefly, must have hoped it was true. He decoded some texts of Paracelsus for her, the sort of cabbalistic cryptograms he had dealt with at the Palazzo Bragadin and with the Duchesse de Chartres. He told d'Urfé that he had a guardian angel and oracle called 'Paralis' – the name he had used before – who guided him; it was this 'secret', shared between them, 'that made [me] the arbiter of her soul . . . her heart and mind and all that remained of her common sense'. He became consultant on every aspect of existence to the richest woman in France.

The secret the marquise divulged to Casanova in return was that she was seeking reincarnation, a central tenet of the Rosicrucian order of which she was a member but heretical in a Catholic country. She believed her soul could be rehoused in the body of a young boy. Rattling back from Holland to Paris after his reunion with Teresa, it was clear to Casanova, if not the twelve-year-old boy seated opposite him, that great plans might be laid if the marquise could remain convinced of his powers and insights.

Quite how he thought he could pull it off is unclear. However, Giuseppi Pompeati was redubbed the Comte d'Aranda and moved into the palace on the Quai des Théatins as the marquise's latest experiment. He was bought a pony and taught to ride, given clothes and jewels, and enrolled in Paris's premier academy for boys, Viard's. Casanova invited the marquise and his ward to his new house in the Petite Pologne, and acted as 'godfather' to the boy.

Giuseppi was only one of several projects that occupied the marquise in her scattergun approach to eternal life. She took to wearing a giant magnet round her neck, for instance, on the advice of the Comte de Saint-Germain, whose unscrupulous prophesying makes Casanova look like an amateur – in the hope that it would attract a lightning bolt to her and elevate her to the sun. Gradually, Casanova's plans for her eclipsed all others.

Through 1758 and 1759 the lottery was failing to meet the ever-growing expenses of Casanova's extravagant lifestyle, and he turned increasingly to the marquise for financial support. What may have begun as a mutual interest in cabbala and necromancy turned into a long-term, incremental leaching of her resources. The detail of the confidence tricks and experiments Casanova performed over several years occupies many chapters of the memoirs; in retrospect, he enjoyed the ridiculousness, the ingenuity, the fecundity of his own imagination and stagecraft. Though it is one of the more fabulous tales in the *History of My Life*, the essential truth of what went on between the marquise and Casanova has rarely been questioned as it provides insight into the credulousness of the era. It also helps to explain Casanova's ability to travel and intrigue with no visible means of support. Casanova returned repeatedly to the Quai des Théatins between 1758 and the early 1760s, each time with a plan more extreme, and more expensive, for the marquise's investment.

Casanova's Great Work with her became an attempt to transmute her soul into a boy-child born of a union between himself and a virgin, conceived and born in her presence. The brothers of the Rosy Cross were said to believe in such miracles; so, too, did the marquise. For this Casanova needed an accomplice, someone willing to play the role for nine months or more of surrogate mother to the marquise's *golem* or soul-carrier. Where to turn for such a 'virgin'? Naturally the theatre.

It was in Bologna, and through his old flame Bellino, now a successful soprano, that he met a dancer called La Corticelli. She and her mother, Laura Gigli, were recruited to be part of the ever more elaborate preparations for a regeneration of the marquise. In Prague, she had a message from Casanova, asking her to join him in Metz, whence they would proceed to Pontcarré, near Paris, where she would be introduced to the marquise as the Contesse Lascaris – a family name with ancient ties to the d'Urfés. In the Gothic setting of the old château of Pontcarré, the 'virgin comtesse' would conceive a child, whereupon the marquise would 'make a will in due form leaving everything she had to the child, whose guardian I [Casanova] was to be until his thirteenth birthday'.

This first part of the elaborate deception of the marquise proceeded according to plan. Casanova 'deflowered' the virgin comtesse in the presence of d'Urfé at a mid-month point after the April moon – his cabbalistic texts had a fair amount to say about fertility and lunar cycles. She did not conceive. Casanova excused this by claiming his mysterious oracle, Paralis, which spoke to him in the form of algebraic codes, was communicating to him the fact that conception would be impossible with the continuing presence of the Comte d'Aranda, Teresa Imer's teenage son, in the château. It was all nonsense: Casanova wanted him to be sent away, and he duly was. Then La Corticelli began to lose faith in the plot and nearly ran off with the sixty thousand francs' worth of jewellery the marquise had lavished on her.

Casanova decided the party of 'spiritualists' should journey south at the marquise's expense, avoiding Paris and her understandably alarmed extended family. *En route* to Aix, Casanova arranged for a spirit he called 'Selenis', who lived on the moon, to write to the marquise in the form of a floating letter, which appeared while they were in a moonlit bath together. It informed her that the regeneration would have to wait another season, and would take place in Marseille. This required a call on her purse to the tune of a further fifty thousand francs in travel expenses, and rumours spread, understandably enough, that something truly bizarre was going on in the marquise's household at the instigation of the charismatic Venetian.

Next La Corticelli spilled her story to a friend of the marquise, the Comtesse de Saint-Giles, a well-known Paris socialite. Casanova was obliged to acquire a supporting cast of two bogus clerics; one was his younger brother Gaetano, a failed priest, and the other a spurious cleric of Casanova's imagination, whom he titled 'Querilinte of the Rosicrucian Order'. In truth, the role was played by the low-born Giacomo Passano. They all put up at Marseille in the most expensive hostelry, the Auberge des XIII Cantons, along with Gaetano Casanova's mistress, another dancer called Marcolina, who was soon also Giacomo Casanova's lover. Here they awaited the stars' alignment in favour of another attempt at regeneration.

D'Urfé's continuing faith in Casanova and in reincarnation is baffling. Meanwhile the entourage grew restive, and the potential profits were being diluted. Casanova sold jewels he had been given by d'Urfe – caskets of crystals dedicated to particular planets with healing powers. Passano threatened to expose him, as La Corticelli had before, this time writing the marquise an eight-page letter that must at least have planted suspicions in her mind. Casanova decided to bring her more fully into complicity in the regeneration ritual. He dropped the plan of rebirthing the marquise's soul within the bodies of either Giuseppi Imer or a child born of the 'virgin' comtesse. Instead, Casanova informed the marquise that Paralis had told him he himself should impregnate her with a child who would carry her soul. It may have been a desperate and even murderous plot; in this version of reincarnation, the old woman would have to die in childbirth for her soul to migrate into that of the immortal being in her womb, conceived by the 'adept' Casanova, who would then be guardian of the child – and its fortune. For one last time, d'Urfé agreed to Casanova's stratagem.

Marcolina was to officiate as a 'spirit' in the conception ceremony in which Casanova would have sex with the marquise. The dancer was to perform as a naked and gyrating altar-server thus helping to maintain Casanova's ardour as he played sacerdotal stud. It makes for hilarious, irreligious and troubling reading. For reasons best known to himself, Casanova claimed 'Paralis' had insisted that the conception would require three orgasms, a task he felt less able to achieve 'at the age of thirty-eight [when] I was beginning to see I was often subject to the fatal misfortune [of losing an erection]'. He came once, but towards the end of an hour of attempting a second orgasm with the marquise he 'finally determined to finish, having counterfeited the signs which appear at that sweet moment', which he followed shortly with another faked orgasm, 'accompanied by an agony and convulsions which ended in motionlessness, the necessary outcome of [such] an agitation'. The marquise, unaware she was partnered in literature's first known faked male orgasm, immediately believed herself pregnant, and even subsequently convinced her doctor it was the case.

But the whole bizarre spiritualist episode was also reaching its disappointing climax. The sixty-three-year-old marquise was not pregnant. Paralis had failed her. She was inundated with letters of complaint against Casanova from Passano, who even took the trouble to write to Teresa Imer in London asking her to help blacken Casanova's name. After years of to-ing and fro-ing on the business of Paralis and the regeneration, common sense and the failure of black magic put an end to the Marguise d'Urfé's regeneration ambitions and also her relationship with her 'adept'. Giacomo Casanova did not have the quasi-divine powers she thought she had sensed in him. He was not a healer, an adept at alchemy or in possession of the recipe for the Philosopher's Stone. Just what he was she never resolved, partly because she felt both affection and admiration for him, partly because their worlds grew apart. Rather than finding a magical eternal life, she placed her faith in the future in a grandchild, a boy named Achille, born in the traditional manner to her estranged daughter, whom she eventually took into one of her Parisian homes and brought up to inherit her vast fortune. Though he eventually sided with Thomas Paine as an anti-monarchist, he was guillotined. It was the French Revolution, rather than Casanova's ridiculous, disingenuous and fraudulent regeneration plans, that ended the d'Urfés.

CASANOVA AND THE CABBALA

'Those who possess this treasure, who call themselves adepts, have many other small privileges by knowing the Cabbala. The cabbala they say signifies that by knowing the secret of the word God cabbalists are rendered masters of all the elemental spirits, their knowledge to be used for guiding everything they desire from the cabinets of state down.'

Giacomo Casanova

'The doctrines of mathematicks have such an affinity with Magick that they who do possess one without the other . . . labour in vain.'
Second Book of Occult Philosophy,
Henry Cornelius Agrippa, 1651

That Casanova was a believer, in the broadest sense, in the cabbala is no secret or revelation. He was open, if not clear, about his fascination with this ancient core of revelations long before he committed his dealings with and some thoughts on it to paper in the *History of My Life*. Lorenzo da Ponte was fully aware of Casanova's deep involvement with Freemasonry, Rosicrucianism and the cabbala when he wrote of them and used their discussions as part of the material behind his satirical take on them in *The Magic Flute*; the Venetian Inquisition was sufficiently alarmed at Casanova's interest in the more esoteric shores of Judaeo-Christian mysticism in Venice in the 1750s to put one of its top spies on his tail and confiscate his books.

Previous biographies of Casanova have tended to gloss over his interest in the cabbala for the good reason that it is particularly difficult to disentangle belief from confidence trick, as it may have been for the man himself, and to care about the

workings of the eighteenth-century mathematico-magical algebra that made such an unlikely fellow-traveller with Enlightenment rationalism in the Age of Reason but was eventually, of
course, outflanked by it. Odd to relate then that two hundred
years later there is renewed interest in this fusion of Gnosticism,
Egyptian mathematics, neo-Platonism, Judaic mysticism and
personal revelation. Perhaps the cabbala can teach us more
about the happiness with which Casanova lived his life than
has previously been assumed as much as it can explain the
workings of his elaborate tricks, prophesies, diagnoses and
attempts at reincarnation. It can certainly illuminate the singularly foreign landscape that the past sometimes reveals, while
bringing an unexpectedly spiritual dimension to this most fleshly
of men and of times.

The word cabbala comes from the Hebrew for 'reception' or
'received doctrines' or simply 'tradition'. It refers to an oral
tradition of mysticism related to Judaism, and possibly dating to
Abraham. One of the frustrations from the historian's point of
view is that cabbala cannot easily be discussed in language. Its
essentials are abstract, expressed in parables and images, in
poetry, signs and numbers. Its teachings or, rather, revelations
may date to as late as the twelfth century AD – at least, that was
when the first written record appeared. It is widely assumed to
date, in the historical sense, from much earlier in the related
history of Judaism and the Christian gospels. To believers
cabbala's 'origins' are celestial and therefore beyond a mere
historian's timeline.

At its simplest the key cabbalistic revelation is that the
Creator is not separate from the world we live in or from
ourselves but manifest in creation and in humanity. God is
everywhere. The means by which He may express himself, or
might be addressed, can be approached, among other paths,
through the perfection of numbers, and through letters and
equations based on them – codes created for the elect. In terms of
personal revelation – the God within us and the importance of

assigning meaning to individual self-realisation – this chimed with many Enlightenment concerns. More specifically, this cabbalistic 'algebra' – the codes that uncovered further meanings in texts – had great impact in the mathematically and scientifically credulous eighteenth century. Until a hypothesis is tested it is just that, and the cabbala was put to use by many, including Casanova, and found to be helpful in matters beyond the obviously spiritual.

The differences between the name of something and the thing itself became defining issues in cabbala long before Nietzsche chose to regard them as linguistic fictions. And from this emanated Casanova's singular fascination with the cabbalistic tradition in deciphering the workings of God in language and in mathematics, and of interpolating spiritual significance into the posited relationship between the two. More modern debates about the relationship between thought and language have absolute analogue in this conceptual concern in the cabbala: if God is manifest in his name, and a word can be both vessel and essence of the divine, then believers must turn to imagery in addressing God. The cabbalistic tree – a map of divine and human powers often personified over a prone body – and the use of imagery relating to building (masonry) and geometric mathematics take the place of words in the cabbala. It is no surprise to find the visual and literary works of Casanova's close contemporary William Blake littered with ideas and images from the cabbala, in which the intercessionary place of prayer is replaced with the transcendental value of idea-in-image.

Casanova's first and main attraction as a young man to cabbala was as a tool of prophecy, divining and prescribing as a code to success and happiness in pretty materialistic terms. It came to mean more. He had a particular fascination with cabbalistic formulae that connected the letters of the Hebrew alphabet and their supposed numerical equivalents. Cabbalists would take a phrase or a word from Torah, then deal with it letter by letter, count the numerical value of the letters – each letter equals a number, a system known by the Greeks as *gematria* as it related to their alphabet – receive the total that would be reduced to a singular number, then find the letter or word that had this number as its numerical equivalent. Thereby a new and hidden meaning within the phrase would be revealed. This, reductively, was the cabbala code, and as potent to Casanova and his contemporaries as it had been to the Gnostics, the sect suppressed by the early Christian Church for its apparent heresies and competition with the teachings of Christ. It was the *gematria*, alchemical and code-breaking character-istics of cabbala that attracted Casanova and his contempor-aries, only some of whom, Casanova perhaps among them, came to explore further what cabbala offered in terms of personal enlightenment. To the more spiritually minded admirers of the cabbala today it would be anathema to conflate this cabbala as used and misused by Casanova and his contemporaries with the wider spiritual concerns of cabbala, but it was nevertheless the first step towards cabbalistic enlightenment for Casanova.

The twenty-two letters of the Greek or Hebrew alphabet and the twenty-one in French, were also assigned planets and signs of the Zodiac: D, or Daleth, became assigned to Scorpio and numbered 4, while A, or Ayin, was assigned to Mars and numbered 16, and so on. To many this overlay of zodiacal mysticism is a distraction from the central concerns of the ancient cabbala, but this was both the strength and the danger of an oral tradition: it was open to adulteration, misapplication and misunderstanding. Cabbala has meant, and continues to mean, many things. However, in Casanova's mind and practice, as in many of his contemporaries', there was no shibboleth to divide the differing realms and intentions of mystic knowledge. Or, at least, it would be fair to assume that Casanova, perhaps like many others, filled that hiatus between hope and effect with, on some days, pragmatism and, on others, maybe faith. For him, after all, the cabbala often 'worked'.

Casanova was familiar with the cabbalistic pyramid of letters and numbers before he met Bragadin so it was clearly openly recognised in Venice. Since the twenty-two letters of the Hebrew alphabet express both letters and figures it was possible to arrange two different *arcana* (from the Latin *arcanum* or secret) in the form of triangles, the so-called 'great *arcanum*' with the twenty-two letters and 'lesser *arcanum*' of the figures 1 to 9. From the Orient, and indeed via Constantinople and Venice, the *arcana* passed into European medieval alchemy – a vital concern to many eighteenth-century 'scientists' – to the occult and thence to the writings of the Rosicrucians. Agrippa von Nettesheim (1486–1535) treated the subject of numbers, pyramids and their mystical power at length in his *De occulta philosophia* (1510) and there is no doubt that Casanova had read this, whether from the collection of Dr Gozzi, Father Tosello, Senator Malipiero, or a copy bought illicitly from a book store around the Piazza San Marco. He seems also to have read the 1700 *De la Cabella intellective, art majeur*, which explains how to construct a magic pyramid such as the one he mentioned to Bragadin, then abstract an answer to any question. It worked with the alphabets of modern romance languages too. It took a while, of course, which was why Casanova replied in verse – an impressive skill in itself to modern minds but expected of a polished eighteenth-century gentleman. It served, however, to obfuscate the calculations involved and, like modern astrology, could go a long way to seeming pertinent by clever suggestion and by attention to the needs of the listener. It was central to cabbala that God could be present within letters or numbers, and the first cipher system used to relate one to the other was a simple parallel of equivalents, which worked for the French as for the Hebrew and Greek alphabets, thus:

a	b	c	d	e	f	g	h	ij	k	l	m	n	o	p	q	r	s	t	uv	x
1	2	3	4	5	6	7	8	9	10	11	12	13	14	15	16	17	18	19	20	21

or more often, and as Casanova drew out, the vowels went first in numerical order, followed by the letters used by more modern languages

a	e	i	o	u	y	h	b	c	d	f	g	j	k	l	m	n	p	q	r	s	t	v	w	x	z
1	2	3	4	5	6	7	8	9	10	11	12	13	14	15	16	17	18	19	20	21	22	23	24	25

There were a number ways to manipulate this supposed relationship, and the divine revelation it might contain. The letters themselves might have value; so, too, would the number of letters in a word, then retranslated into a letter. The geometry of the cabballistic oracle depended largely on the arrangement of the numbers deduced from letters into a pyramid.
Thus:

Ou est ma nouvelle clef dorée?

is rendered first as:

2   3   2   8   4   5

and then as:

$$2$$
$$3 \quad 2$$
$$8 \quad 4 \quad 5$$

The pyramid had thence to be extrapolated to six rows, at the discretion of the reader of the oracle – the numbers might be additions, subtractions or digital sums of the first rows, into, say,

$$2$$
$$3 \quad 3$$
$$8 \quad 4 \quad 5$$
$$13 \quad 9 \quad 10 \quad 8$$

This 'system' of numbers could either be used to divine some message or, more likely – to a fast thinker like Casanova – to create a message in the same way as a ouija board may be manipulated by achieving desired numbers using the variable patterns his pyramid allowed. An answer,

'Dans votre tabatière'

could be construed out of

36   75   78

or

4   20   19

combinations simply wrought by any clever nine-year-old or, indeed, a grown man with a facility for mental arithmetic, words and wiles. Women were rarely taught mathematics, and upper-class women were even less likely to have picked up a facility with numbers, such as any tradeswoman would have needed. Casanova kept all his life a *'trésor cabbalistique'*, mainly to divine auspicious numbers and dates for lotteries, but drawn out with exactitude and faith in the fluidity of meaning between letters, numbers, time and place. He also drew out, in old age, systems of cabbalistic *gematria*, which lends further credence to the idea that on some level he had faith in the cabbala despite exposing his cabbalistic work in his *History* as the cynical imprimatur of the grifter upon fools. He renders his consultations with his oracle for the benefit of the Duchesse de Chartres or the Marquise d'Urfé as a flummery of words and numbers. The much more intriguing question is how much he actually believed.

The cabbala is first introduced in the *History* with relation to the three patricians Bragadin, Dandolo and Barbaro who later adopted Casanova as their house guest and *protégé*. The relationship became complex, but one early point of commonality was their shared interest in the cabbala, and the belief of these educated, worldly men that Casanova had real powers and insights. Casanova himself refuses to associate the intricate *gematria* of the cabbala with his previous experiences of folk medicine and the occult, but they are different colourings of the same motif in his narrative: he understood people, he may have had the indefinable gift of healing – or, to be more cynical, he preyed on the intellectual and emotional insecurities of men as willingly as the romantic yearnings of some women. Which, from the anticlerical perspective of the times, is exactly the God-shaped hole filled by religion in the first place. His writings and his unpublished notes give little clue as to his true philosophical investment in cabbala beyond the clear indication that he had a ready facility with numbers, language and people just as he did with alchemy/chemistry, which he also used as a duping tool.

At the same time, the origins of his interest and possible belief in cabbala may have been deep-rooted and familial as faith so often is. The cruciform imagery of the famous cabbala Kircher Tree (1652), the so-called Tree of the Hermetic Cabbala is used to this day in the stagecraft of *commedia* actors, each stock character of the harlequin troop given their own place – both metaphorical and actual on stage – as laid out within the power structure of this tree-shaped image of classical cabbala. Brought up by a folk-healer, Marcia Farussi, within an extended family of *commedia* actors in eighteenth-century Venice, Casanova would almost certainly have ingested cabbalistic mantras and subsumed caballistic imagery with his mother's milk. Later he chose to present himself as a worldly cynic, who still placed ultimate belief in the catechism of the Roman Catholic Church and who struck a dandy-pose of ironic detachment from the belief system that had inspired so many of his adventures and so many of his contemporaries.

But the truth may address an essential issue about the boy within the man.

Nor would it have passed unnoticed by Casanova that for the cabbalist 'the ultimate sacrament is the sexual act'. Some of the key texts in cabbalistic literature on the mysteries of love emanate in modern translations from Venice in the sixteenth and seventeenth centuries; the city was easily persuaded that there was a spirituality of sorts in the unfettered expression of love in all its forms. The cabbalistic view of love, which includes sexual love, (eros, beyond the usual Christian definitions of charity) is of a vivifying spirit that speaks of God's transcendence throughout the world but, of course, it is a love that needs to be made manifest. In cabbala, to make love achieves its full linguistic, spiritual and physical potential. Love, the lover and the beloved are all one in love-making and in God, according to at least one text probably known by Casanova which speaks of 'a copulative felicity with God which may only not be continuous . . . for the matter of the fragile body'.

As well as presenting Casanova with an alternative cosmology that celebrated both his libertinism and his intellectual élitism, the cabbala presented something altogether more potent. It attached to his long-standing interest in alchemy, chemistry and medicine and, by extension, to the creation or re-creation of life. The hidden name of God was taken to give its speaker the power that this name contains. The Marquise d'Urfé, like many others, was trying to evoke spirits and rule them as well as assuming that there was a conflation between religious secrets and codes and others that would now be addressed 'scientifically'. One of the consequences of this was the emergence in Casanova's time of the legend of Golem, a homunculus created by a cabbalist; usually, it is said, by Rabbi Loew of Prague. 'The creation of the Golem was, as it were, a particularly sublime experience felt by the mystic who became absorbed in the mysteries of the alphabetic combinations described in the Book of Genesis.' In other words, the secrets addressed gematrically might even lead to the creation of new life, with all its attendant horrors and glory. Mary Shelley's *Frankenstein* was understood by some at the time as a comment on the cabbalistic Golem. For Casanova reincarnation, or the creation of new life, found expression in the parallel phantasmagoria of rebirthing an old crone into a young boy through a dark ritual of sex, bathing, moonlight and lightning.

His Freemasonry and the Marquise d'Urfé's Rosicrucianism tied Casanova more securely into an international élite of fellow-travellers than even his later assumed title of 'Chevalier de Seingalt' might. For him, they were part of the same need for a lead role in society that he, as the bastard son of a Venetian comedienne could hardly aspire to without such props. The title itself, 'Seingalt' or 'de Seingalt' has been addressed as a Casanovan joke based on the cabbalistic love of anagrams – it may be an anagram of '*genitale*.' The man who wrote that 'Paradise *means* etymologically an idea of a place of voluptuousness, the term being Persian', who made dream-notes featuring cavorting sex organs, and whose current fame rests on something similar, may have invented a title out of an anagram of his 'cabbalistic' Rosicrucian title of '*Paralisée Galtinarde*' but also forming intertextual jokes on '*genitales*' or '*des parties genitales*'. These can variously form '*Paralis de Seingalt*' or '*Paradis genitales*', '*des parties genitales*', and Paralis itself, his title as a diviner, further plays on *paracelsus*, the system of symbolic representation in cabbala, and indeed on *paradis*, a concept common to cabbala as to Judaism, Islam and Christianity. The *gematria* fit even when the anagrammatic connection fails. More specifically, the cabbala's connection to alchemy and the discovery of the Philosopher's Stone, which promised so much more than merely turning base metal into gold, was accepted by all those who chose to study this now largely ridiculed branch of chemistry.

Alone in his rooms in old age, Casanova returned to many of his lost pleasures, those he could no longer afford or enjoy but could re-create in his memory, and in his memoirs he turned again to the joys of pure mathematics, to cabbala and to lottery numbers. He wasted many hours and countless sheaves of paper on cubic geometry and *gematria*. He laughed in his writings at his attempts to discover the Philosopher's Stone, but also credited his faith in a cabbalistic fatality with weighting the die at every gambled moment in his life. Cabbala, its associated disciplines as well as its attachment to atavistic faith and personal self-fulfilment suffused Casanova's pleasure-principle in living, delineating a path from cradle-side folk medicine to Enlightenment metaphysics. 'I am infinitely happy,' he wrote, 'when in a dark room I see the light coming through a window which opens on a vast horizon.' It is the view from the library at Dux castle and the words are from the *History of My Life* that he wrote there, but they are also from the cabbala's *Book of Zohar*.

ACT FOUR

CONVERSATIONS WITH VOLTAIRE

1760–61

'On Thursday 7 September a parcel was sent by market canal boat from the Hague to Amsterdam, where it was not delivered. It contains a LOTTERY TICKET numbered 14934 on which a prize of 20,000 gilders has fallen . . . two obligations of the account of the East India Company one worth 6000 gilders, and 45000 worth of French Billets d'Annuities . . . a reward of 100 silvers ducats is offered, no questions asked.'

Casanova's Lost and Found notice,
Amsterdamse Courant

C asanova's early thirties, spent mainly in Paris and Amsterdam, were typical of his itinerant middle years. His unconsummated affair with Manon Balletti dragged on until the winter of 1759–60. She lived briefly under his roof in Petite Pologne, helping to nurse her brother Antonio, who had suffered a bullet wound in a stage-stunt mishap. She and Casanova wrote constantly to each other in French, but she addressed him as her 'Giacometto' and her 'little husband' until she acquired an actual husband in the summer of 1760: the royal architect, François Blondel. Casanova was distraught when he received the news, he claimed, in Amsterdam at Christmas 1759 – but in truth he must have heard later. Sylvia was dead, Mario Balletti in debt and Antonio still ill – and Manon made the best of her precarious situation by deciding that Casanova was never going to marry her. His final break with Manon unguyed him yet further from the ties of family life and seems to have been the catalyst in a sort of mid-life crisis; it generated a wanderlust that did not let up for more than a decade.

As Manon moved into Blondel's much-admired house on the rue de la Harpe, Casanova left Amsterdam for Cologne, then went on to Stuttgart, Zürich, Baden, Lucerne, Fribourg, Berne and Geneva. He made a great deal of money, quite how, as ever, he fails to make clear. In a summary of his life written in 1797, Casanova estimated that in the late 1750s he had been a millionaire. While travelling in Holland he seems to have been impressed with the prospect of profiting from some sort of industrial monopoly: his letters to the Venetian authorities of this period – he was beginning to court them in the hope of a pardon – express his willingness to share with the factories of Murano industrial secrets he had acquired in northern Europe: 'My research, my travels, my studies have allowed me to be a master of the secret [silk dyeing] which I am offering to my country. I can offer the dye for real cotton more beautiful than that of the Orient and which I can sell at 50% reduction.'

But Holland was not impressed. The French ambassador wrote to the Duc de Choiseul, who had succeeded de Bernis as foreign minister, that his *protégé* from Paris, Casanova, had not entirely won over the Dutch: 'He appeared most indiscreet in his purposes . . . he went to Amsterdam after [The Hague] and lost heavily at play.' Even so Casanova considered settling in Amsterdam as a better headquarters for his financial dealing, and he had entered into a relationship with a young Dutch woman, whom he calls 'Esther' who seems to have been a relative of the wealthy Jewish Symons family or the merchant Thomas Hope. But Paris kept calling him back, even as his lottery fortune dwindled. One reason for this appears to be the arrival in the French capital of a young woman from Venice, whose dramatic re-entry into Casanova's life is documented not just by Casanova but in a series of letters which have more recently come to light.

Giustiniana Wynne was a beautiful half-English, half-Venetian adventuress with a slightly dubious past whom Casanova had met in Venice, briefly, through his friend Andrea Memmo. After Casanova's arrest and imprisonment, she and Memmo had become lovers, their torrid, secretive affair documented in fraught, explicit letters – some of which Memmo daubed dramatically with his own blood and semen – that survive to this day. Their love remained clandestine because Memmo was a young patrician, and Giustiniana was the legitimised daughter of a foreigner, an English baronet, and a Venetian courtesan. Because Lucia Memmo was instrumental in preventing their marriage, as she had been in paving Casanova's route to The Leads, when Giustiniana arrived in Paris Casanova was understandably welcoming and sympathetic to her. But he was dragged almost immediately into the heart of a complex scandal: Giustiniana was pregnant with Memmo's child, but her scheming mother had arranged a dazzling match for her beautiful daughter to an elderly but wealthy tax farmer, Alexandre La Pouplinière. Giustiniana knew that the marriage must take place quickly if the child was to be passed off as his heir. Otherwise a more drastic solution would have to be found.

Casanova refers to this story, of a woman he called 'Mlle XCV', as one of the central dramas of his Paris years. It was long assumed that he had heavily embroidered it, but recently it has been corroborated, not only in the letters that descended through the Memmo family, but in a letter that was sold on the open market in 1999: in it Giustiniana gives a rare female perspective on the price of sexual emancipation, and on Casanova. Because it details, not from Casanova's perspective, but from that of a desperate young woman some of the reasons women turned to him in adversity and in faith of his good nature and worldliness, it is worth quoting at length. It was written from Giustiniana from the Hôtel de Hollande, and sent to her lover's former friend, Casanova. They had remet the week before:

You wish me to speak, to tell you the reason for my sadness. Well then I am ready to do so. I am putting my life, my reputation, my whole being in your hands . . . I beg you to assist an unhappy soul who will have no other resource but to seek her own death if she cannot remedy her situation. Here it is, dear Casanova; I am pregnant . . . You think like a philosopher, you are an honest man . . . save me if it is still possible and if you know how. My whole being and everything I possess will be yours if you help me . . . If I go back to my original state my fortune is assured . . . provided I free myself of the burden that dishonours me. Casanova dearest, please do your best to find a surgeon, a doctor . . . who will lift me out of my misery by delivering me with whatever remedy and if necessary by force . . . I trust you. I have only you in the world . . . I have never had anyone to confide in and you are now my guardian angel. Go see some of the theatre girls, ask them if they've ever found themselves in the need to deliver themselves the way I wish to do . . . Save me. I trust you.

It was as astonishing then as it is heart-grabbing now. She was soliciting Casanova in an enterprise that was both mortally dangerous for herself and of course highly illegal: the procuring of an abortion. Though Giustiniana later promised her diamonds to the surgeon, and her person to Casanova, it was an appeal to his gallantry. He had noted her arrival in Paris when Giustiniana and he had re-met at the opera after his return, newly enriched, from Holland. He was now touched, and spurred into action, by her helpless faith in him. She had been right in her instincts: not only was he inspired to help, he knew just who to ask.

A plan was enacted, both theatrical and dangerous. They met at at a ball, wearing prearranged disguises (Casanova had on a

Venetian mask with a single rose painted under the left eye), dashed over the Seine to a *vendeuse* of oral abortives, and were back, on the dance floor before, they thought, anyone might spot their absence. They were mistaken on two counts. First the pharmacist, a Madame Reine Demay, knew the precariousness of her trade, and the potential to blackmail rich clients, and did not remain discreet. Second, their absence was noted for the wrong reasons: it was assumed they had absconded as lovers. And they had taken too long: Giustiniana was shaking with cold, hunger or the effects of the abortifacient, and asked Casanova to stop at Petite Pologne, where, sweetly, he made her an omelette, and opened champagne and less sweetly, where he made a pass at her.

Back at the ball, she danced till dawn in the hope of losing the baby, but the plans failed, and Madame Demay called on Giustiniana's fiancé to spill the beans in the hope of being paid for her indiscretion.

Fortunately for Casanova and Giustiniana, the tax farmer had reason not to believe those who claimed his fiancée was pregnant and trying to abort a child: he knew his family was desperate to blacken her name and keep his fortune intact, but he had fallen in love with her. But he was suspicious and the pressure increased, as Giustiniana's pregnancy began to show, for her to rid herself of the child of the man she loved. Meanwhile a memorandum on 'the whole Wynne affair' was being prepared for the Duc de Choiseul, the minister of foreign affairs – the Wynnes were resident aliens – which, of course, would blacken Casanova's name also.

Giustiniana asked him if he knew of any more potent remedy – she seems to have been hinting at an invasive termination, which was yet more hazardous. Casanova turned to the Marquise d'Urfé for advice. She knew exactly what to do: consult the works of Paracelsus, who, incredibly, lists an abortifacient in a work on esoteric mysticism.

The *Aroma philosophorum*, better known as an '*aroph*' is mentioned in several forms in alchemical and cabbalistic writings, including the *Elementa Chemiae* of Herman Boerhaave then also widely available in Holland where Casanova had been working; the key ingredient was saffron, believed to bring on menstruation and/or weaken the lining of the womb, and the cervix. It was usually mixed with myrrh and honey. 'The woman who hoped to empty her womb,' Casanova read, 'was to put a dose of this opiate in such a way as to stimulate' its opening. It was to be applied – and, to his credit, he laughed when he read this – at the tip of a suitably sized cylinder inserted 'into the vagina in such a way as to [reach] the round piece of flesh at the top of her such-and-such'. This application was to be repeated three or four times a day for a week.

On the one hand his dealings with Giustiniana show him at his most manipulative, taking advantage of her gullibility and desperation. On the other, though, the *aroph* was widely credited as working, and saffron and myrrh were traditional abortifacients, even taken in a less direct fashion. But when he presented the results of his researches at the Marquise's library to Giustiniana at the Hôtel de Hollande, he added his own ingredient to make sure she understood what 'cylinder' he had in mind: the *aroph* only worked when applied with freshly ejaculated semen, he informed her, so, as their mutual friend Andrea Memmo was in Venice, he himself would supply the equipment and all ingredients for the course of treatment. Giustiniana looked him up and down, smiled a wry smile and then laughed, too. But she did not challenge his prescription. Although it has been suggested that this was a cruel or, at least, opportunistic coercion into sex, the prescription of *arophs* and other unguents with invasive techniques, including penetrative sex, were established methods of procuring an abortion. Giustiniana agreed to meet him in the garret at the hotel when the household was asleep; when Casanova discovered the garret was being used by two servants for an illicit affair, he blackmailed then into silence and found an adjacent attic. Here, he and Giustiniana set to 'like a surgeon getting ready to perform an operation and the patient who submits to it'. It was hardly the stuff of romance:

Both of us concentrate on our roles and we play them to perfection . . . By the light of the candle which I am holding in my left hand she puts a little crown of *aroph* on the head of the being who is to convey it to the orifice where the amalgamation is to be accomplished . . . after the insertion was completed, [she] blew out the candle.

They made love a second time, which Casanova recalled as a 'remedy of quarter of an hour' and soon after again.

As with the previous 'remedies', the alchemical application also failed to procure an abortion, and Giustiniana realised she would soon need to hide the birth from her fiancé and from society, not just her pregnancy. Casanova, in self-justification – it is never clear if he felt there was any legitimacy in the claims of the *aroph* – wrote that he won from Giustiniana on their several nights of determined sex a 'promise to think no more of suicide' and to entrust herself to his aid. It is clear from her letters and actions as well as his memoirs that this is what happened. Casanova helped her run away, to the alarm of her family, fiancé, her lover in Venice and Parisian society – 'I cannot remember,' wrote one socialite to Andrea Memmo, 'anyone being talked about so much.'

Casanova went to the Comtesse du Rumain, fellow cabbalist and friend of the Marquise d'Urfé: he had reason to believe she would know of some discreet convent where gentlewomen might disappear for the purpose of giving birth, and he was right. She suggested the one at Conflans and, as a middle-woman and travelling chaperone, a Madame de Mérinville, who seems to have been related to the convent's Mother Superior and may have made a career of such assignations. On 4 April 1759, Giustiniana disappeared.

Her family immediately suspected Casanova, and within days her mother and the Venetian ambassador, Erizzo, issued a writ against him for conspiring to kidnap. Mother Eustacia, of the Conflans convent, smuggled out letters from Giustiniana assuring her family of her safety, and her need to hide for fear of her life and the enemies she had made as intended bride of the tax farmer, La Pouplinière. Letters to Casanova assured him of her thanks and comfort, but asked for books. Her reading requirements were low on Casanova's list of priorities, though, as the authorities, diplomatic and civil, were closing in on him. He had been seen to leave the masked ball with her, and there was the question of his contact with Madame Demay, a known abortionist. In the short term he was rescued by his well-placed friends: the Comtesse du Rumain visited Antoine de Sartine, soon to be chief of police, and explained, quite simply, that Miss Wynne was in hiding to have an illegitimate child, which, she pointed out, proved no abortion had been carried out. Madame Demay, meanwhile, asked Casanova for a hundred *louis* to retract her evidence against him and say she had simply misremembered.

At the end of May, Mother Eustacia sent word to Casanova and to the Comtesse du Rumain that Giustiniana had been delivered of a boy, then wrote to Giustiniana's mother:

May 27 1759

MLLE JUSTINIANA [sic] Wynne finally opened up to me yesterday evening. She told me, Madame, that you are presently at the Hôtel de Hollande . . . had I known this before I could have spared you so many worries. She has been with us since coming here on 4 April. I was certain that someone would soon claim her but nobody came to ask for her . . . she has received no letters.

Sister de Mérinville, abbess of Conflans

The abbess had indeed been a 'princess' of discretion, as Casanova described her. But things were no longer on a comfortable footing in Paris. He also lost, at exactly this time, his powerful ally and patron, de Bernis, who was appointed a cardinal by the new Venetian pope, Clement XIII, and effectively exiled by the French King to Rome, as he had fallen out of favour with Madame de Pompadour.

Perhaps as a result, Casanova threw himself more assiduously into the role of *cavaliere servente* to the Marquise d'Urfé, who took a fancy to extending her cabbalistic interests into something more modern and enlightened, and suggested she and Casanova go out to Montmorency to meet Jean Jacques Rousseau, the *philosophe* and writer, then aged forty-seven. He was beset by debt and had been forced to accept the hospitality of the Maréchal de Luxembourg in his château there. Casanova's account is of a writer in financial decline, forced to copy music brought to him by Parisian ladies, like the Marquise, for whom he was an exotic of the avant-garde: 'People paid him twice as much as they might have paid another copyist, but he guaranteed there would be no errors and in this way he made his living.' Casanova was struck by the contrast between international renown and the humiliation of Rousseau's living conditions. Not for Casanova the stony path to literary acclaim.

It was in a similar manner, a year later, when Casanova had an extended encounter with Voltaire, then in his mid-sixties and enjoying Olympian fame and semi-retirement in Switzerland. 'He was,' as Casanova noted elsewhere, 'not a man at that time one might ignore.' Notorious not just as the philosophico-political interlocutor with Russian tsarinas and French radicals, he had repolished his notoriety only the year before with the publication of a *faux*-anonymous satire on Church, state, philosophy and picaresque travels: *Candide*. The meeting, outside Geneva, made a deep impression on Casanova; he records a sally of Voltairean wit that one would wish to believe, but may bear more relation to Casanova's polished anecdote on his meeting than reality – Voltaire barely bothered to mention that he was visited by the voluble Italian at all. 'This is,' said Casanova, 'the happiest day of my life; it is twenty years, Monsieur, since I became your pupil.' He was thirty-five and had certainly *not* been reading Voltaire as a fifteen-year-old in Padua.

'Honour me with another twenty,' replied Voltaire, 'and then pay my wages.'

It was important to Casanova to present himself in his memoirs as equal to Voltaire at least as far as salon wit was concerned, but even so, as with the pen-sketch of Rousseau, he provides a breezy, Everyman perspective on the man who embodied the philosophical spirit of the age, noting Voltaire's love of gardening and the English.

He had a small theatre nearby, in Lausanne, and was an enthusiastic supporter of Italian *opera buffa*. He was keen to talk to Casanova about Italian theatre and Venice, assuming that the former jail-bird would support his view that Venice was exactly the sort of infamous oligarchy that should be crushed. He found instead that Casanova thought Venetians among the freest men in the world – he may have meant sexually as much as politically. By this stage Casanova had doubtless read *Candide*, which was published across Europe in 1759. Its breezy, scandalous mélange of sexual knowingness, philosophical and political satire and preposterous adventure cannot have failed to appeal to Casanova, who must also have been struck by the strong parallels between his own life and that of the young bastard *Candide*, set adrift on the world with little but his wits to rely on in a dazzling sea-tossed adventure.

The best satires, of course, have reality at their core, and the later criticism of Casanova's writings as being too closely modelled on the picaresque adventures of *Candide* – through the hazards of harems, royal courts, prisons and venereal disease – is clearly unfair: evidently it was possible to live such a life. Casanova proved so.

The two men spoke for a long time on Italian literature, ancient and modern, and Voltaire took Casanova outside to admire the view of Mont Blanc. Tiny details verify Casanova's memory of events: he recalled the vast pile of letters and Voltaire's boast that he was keeping up with thousands of correspondents – today there are more than twenty thousand extant Voltaire letters – that his 'niece', his mistress Madame Denis, was the most assiduous host, that conversations and arguments ranged over all subjects, in several languages during many visits. Voltaire's Château at Ferney in Switzerland provided him with a mini-court, an intellectual Versailles, and where Casanova found himself immediately at home as salon jester, polymath and flirt. Voltaire was beginning a new theatrical work, *Tancrede*, which would première on 3 September 1760 in Paris. It resembled his earlier work *Zaïre*, and it seems likely that he and Casanova, an expert on stage comedy, discussed it; a few years later, Casanova named his Russian maid Zaïre in memory of his time with Voltaire.

The meeting of these two great figures of the eighteenth century is detailed not just in the Casanova's posthumously published memoirs, but in other of his works *Confutazione*, *Scrutinio* and *À Leonard Snetlage*, all of which contain elements of a lost work on Voltaire. Casanova was an admirer, but not a humble one. He took Voltaire to task for his disinterest in Mantuan poetry, Merlina Coccai's in particular, and they disputed on monarchy, the occult and the need in men for faith. Much later he attacked Voltaire for his radical politics, but when they met it was his anti-clericism that alarmed Casanova, who felt faith to be an instinctive part of living: 'You should love humanity' he told Voltaire, 'as it is.'

His encounter with Voltaire forms more than just another celebrity anecdote, though it is perhaps his most famous. It reaffirmed, in Casanova's mind, his own unfulfilled ambition and potential. Voltaire was working on the second volume of his *History of Russia under Peter the Great*, as well as the play and responding to the criticism of *Candide*, and may have helped seed the idea in Casanova's mind that he could profitably travel to St Petersburg.

But something more had troubled and inspired Casanova. He was staying in Geneva at Les Balances, the inn on what is now the rue du Rhône where he and Henriette had parted thirteen years before. It was not such a coincidence: it was the main and best inn for visiting Francophones. He saw the etching in the window-pane of the room where they had last made love. '*Tu oublièras aussi Henriette*.' It made his hair stand on end, he wrote, not just for the memory of lost love or even the cold realisation that she had been right: when he compared himself to the man he had been, he found his thirty-five-year-old self wanting. It was the beginning of the breakdown that would grip him later in London, stemming partly from the realisation that his sexual and physical powers were waning – 'what horrified me was that I knew I did not have the same vigour' – but also that he lacked now 'the delicacy which was then mine and exalted feelings which justify the errors of the senses, considerateness. A certain probity.' The dreamily ambitious young man, had become calloused by life, love, opportunism and wasted opportunity.

What Casanova was doing in Geneva in 1760 is less easily answered than what he was thinking or feeling. From mid-1759 into the early 1760s he was increasingly away from Paris. To begin with, there was government and financial work in Amsterdam, as well as a burgeoning affair with 'Esther', which carried on, intermittently, for several years. His financial deal-ings have been called into question in this period, in an attempt to prove that he was living off the Marquise d'Urfé but this turns out not to have been the case. Within the last few years, more evidence has come to light in Holland to support Casanova's previously suspect detail of his time there: for example he was telling the precise truth when he wrote that he had helped to discover a lost wallet by cabbalistic means: an advertisement has been recently unearthed in the *Amsterdamse Courant*, placed by one Emanuel Symons, for a lost wallet containing money. Casanova was closely linked with the Symons family, likely to have been Esther's, (as further evidenced by two notarial acts also extant in Amsterdam).

But all was not well on Casanova's occasional business trips to Holland. For one thing the French ambassador, Conte d'Affray, discovered that Casanova, despite appearances, was the son of a Venetian comedy actress. He took a dim view of dealing socially or financially across class barriers and though it was hardly a secret among the cognoscenti that Casanova's background was suspect, his long-burnished polish as a darling of Parisian salon society had allowed the French establishment to forget that he was a low-born Italian. D'Affray was affronted at having to work with him. At the same time Casanova unwittingly accepted a false bill of exchange from a gambling creditor, and had to flee Amsterdam's courts.

Casanova was soon consoling himself in the arms of the wife of the mayor of Cologne, Mimi van Groote, on the first leg of what turned into a long trip through central Europe. The principalities of Germany in particular welcomed the cultured, well-dressed and entertaining Venetian. At Bonn, indeed, the Elector so adored all things Venetian that he employed gondoliers and Italian pages and spoke Venetian-dialect Italian; Casanova was the ideal *schloss*-guest.

The 'Chevalier de Seingalt', as Casanova now introduced himself, became well known in the tiny courts of middle-Europe; perhaps simply as a social fixture, perhaps involved in covert espionage for the French, reporting on the shifting allegiances of the minor players in the ongoing Seven Years' War (1756–63). The title was part of the game. He bestowed it upon himself, perhaps in recognition of his close ties to the French throne, perhaps as his own joke. It gave him the aura of a cosmopolitan aristocrat. If it reads today more like imposture, to a Venetian the title 'chevalier' was nothing more than a recognition of his *de facto* status. As one visitor to Italy remarked, 'the majority [of Venetians] give themselves the style of *cavaliere*, which does not actually denote knighthood [but rather] as the denomination *Squire* now is in England'.

At Soleure in 1760 he cautioned a friend not to 'read or so much as touch any of my papers as I am the depository of secrets of which I am not free to dispose', and in Bonn in the same year an Austrian military attaché described him as 'a most dangerous spy, capable of the greatest crimes . . . linked to a spy ring and to badly disposed Dutch officers'.

Unfortunately none of this amounts to much more than circumstantial likelihood that Casanova was working, part-time, as an informant for the French, or that he had secured some promises of money, a retainer of sorts, against future usefulness. This appears to have been the career of his contemporary, the Conte de Saint-Germain, and the web Casanova spun round himself, as self-created aristocrat, stateless Franco-Venetian and occult diviner, allowed him to support a wayward, directionless existence. For some, it amounts to proof that Casanova was primarily supported by the Freemasons as a roving recruiter and spy, but their resources were not as great as Madame de Pompadour's, nor their need for a 'special envoy' as great. The court of Versailles was quite sufficiently secretive to need a diplomat of Casanova's unique skills.

From Bonn, Cologne and the court of the Elector, Casanova proceeded in the spring of 1760 to Württemberg and the court of its duke, Charles Eugene, at Stuttgart. He went on to Zürich, via the Benedictine abbey of Einsedeln, where he considered joining the order of contemplative monks, and returning to his academic and literary studies rather than his gadabout life. Instead, he ran into Baroness de Roll, who later made an impression on James Boswell, and decided he would rather follow her to Soleure than his faint calling to the monastic life.

In the spring of 1760 Casanova was at a low ebb. That April, in Zürich, he was obliged to pawn some of his possessions and pledge effects against a loan of a mere eighty gold *louis*, at a time when his net worth in Paris was estimated at silver equivalent to more than a hundred thousand *écus*, six-hundred thousand *livres tournois* or many thousands of *louis*. He travelled on to Berne, then back and forth between there, Lausanne and Soleure, Switzerland having no capital to its cantons and society therefore being spread between its rival centres. A letter survives in Berne Library that sheds a sidelight on Casanova at this staging-post of his journey. His memoirs are full of amorous skirmishes, mainly in the chase of the Baroness de Roll, and on details of the naked baths at Berne. Meanwhile the locals had recognised a one-off in Casanova, someone both fascinating but elusive. The letter is from the Berne magistrate to an academic in Roche, Albert Haller, to whom Casanova wished to be introduced:

'We have here [in Berne] a foreigner named the Chevalier de Seingalt . . . who was strongly recommended [to us] at the instance of a prominent lady in Paris. He left here the day before yesterday for Lausanne, and from where he proposes to visit you. This foreigner is worthy of being received by you and is certainly a curiosity, for he is an enigma we have been unable to resolve here, nor discover who he is. He does not know as much as you, but he knows much. He speaks of everything with much fire, appearing to have seen and read prodigiously. It is said that he knows all . . . languages . . . He receives each day an abundant number of letters by post, writes every morning . . . He speaks French in the Italian manner having been reared in Italy. He tells me he is a free man, a citizen of the world . . . His dominant taste is natural history and chemistry; my cousin Louis de Muralt, who is strongly attached to him . . . imagines he is the Comte de Saint-Germain. He had given me proofs of his knowledge of the cabbala which are astonishing if true and make him something of a sorcerer . . . in sum he is a very singular personage. He could not be better dressed or equipped.

Such was the impression made by the thirty-five-year-old Chevalier de Seingalt – without mention, it should be noted, of his previous fame as an escapee or subsequent notoriety as a supposed libertine.

CHEVALIER DE SEINGALT

1761–3

'"I think nothing of those who attach importance to titles,"
said Emperor Joseph II one day to Casanova [the "Chevalier de
Seingalt"] and he, Casanova, whose every word was a thought
and every thought a book, replied: "So what are we to think of
those who sell them?"

Prince Charles de Ligne

Casanova travelled almost constantly through the early
1760s. As Europe concluded the Seven Years' War – which
one might have thought would prevent easy travel – the Chevalier de Seingalt lived briefly and variously in Aix-les-Bains,
Grenoble, Avignon, Marseille, Menton, Monaco, Nice, Genoa,
Florence, Rome and Naples. Then, working his way north
again, he stayed in Rome, Florence, Bologna, Modena, Parma
and Turin, where he picked up work with the Portuguese
government that took him to the intended peace congress at
Augsburg in 1763. He went there via Chambéry, Lyon, Paris,
Chalons, Strasbourg, Munich and Paris again, whence he proceeded to Aix-la-Chapelle. Thence he moved on to Besançon and
Geneva, to Lyon, Turin, Milan, Genoa, Antibes, Avignon, Lyon
and Paris, before finally deciding in 1763 to base himself in
London.

The house in Paris was packed up, and his life became increasingly that of a stateless wanderer. He became a gentleman of the road in a style that perhaps only the pre-revolutionary eighteenth-century might support.

After his extended visit to Voltaire, Casanova crossed the Alps to head towards Rome and Naples. The latter was the real draw: a city that had always been kind to him in the past and, indeed, where he had reason to believe he had at least two children – his daughter by Anna Maria Monti-Vallati and his son by 'Bellino', Teresa Lanti. He stopped at Aix-les-Bains, then Aix-en-Savoie, in July 1760 where, taking the waters, he met an aristocratic nun he at first mistook for M.M. She was not, but in the memoirs he gave her the same pseudonym. She resembled his former lover in looks and habit, but also because she, too, was a libertine of sorts and was 'taking the waters' in the sense often implied in the eighteenth century: she was in Aix for a clandestine pregnancy. Casanova aided her in this, assisting in finding opium with which to drug her chaperone – a plan that backfired when they overdosed her and she died. Two fugitives, they were briefly lovers, Casanova, as so often, mixing altruism and opportunism to construct an affair from near disaster: 'In the light of my character it was impossible that I abandon her, but I had no merit in so doing; I had become amorous of this new M.M. with black eyes and was determined to do all for her, and certainly not to allow her to return to the convent in the state in which she was.' Yet return she did and Casanova travelled on to Grenoble.

Here, he had a letter of introduction from the Marquise d'Urfé, with whom he was still on good terms, to a Mademoiselle Roman-Coupier. The story might seem a meander in the memoirs, but is entirely in accordance with the facts of a drama soon played out in Paris. Casanova drew Mademoiselle Roman-Coupier's horoscope and cabbala numbers – decoding her name, birthdate and so on – and predicted she would become mistress to Louis XV. He presents the story as an attempted seduction but, based on the faith he had instilled in her – though he never achieved his objective of sleeping with her himself – she proceeded to Paris and by May 1761 was indeed one of Louis XV's many mistresses. She bore him a daughter in January 1762. It was the second time Casanova had contributed to the royal *parcs des cerfs*. All this might look like *post-hoc* fantasy, but for the fact that Casanova details Mademoiselle Roman-Coupier's unhappiness after her elevation from provincial Grenoble to the Versailles boudoir in the same terms that came to light much later in her own memoirs.

From Grenoble Casanova travelled to Avignon to see the sites associated with Petrarch at Vaucluse, and to tarry on the route south for the purposes only of entertaining himself cheaply. The provincial theatre allowed him easy access to the Avignon demimonde, such as it was, and he met there the actresses Marguerite and Rosalie Astrodi, one of whom he had already slept with in Paris, the other of whom he engaged in Avignon in a three-way sex session featuring, exotically, her hunchbacked dresser. In Avignon also he introduced himself to a couple passing themselves of as 'the Stuards', who were staying in the same inn. At the same time that Casanova was emptying his purse in the pursuit of theatrical debauches, he opened it also to the impecunious Stuards on whom he took pity for less carnal motives. They were an eloping couple, possibly both married to others, and their story makes a counterpoint to Casanova's apparent insouciance and amorality. Within months of assisting in a hidden labour, the disposal of a child to a foundling hospital, the accidental manslaughter of a nun and the soliciting of two actress-prostitutes, not to mention a disabled dresser, Casanova was moved to tears by the plight of a woman on the run, and gave her most of his ever-depleting funds.

He travelled on to Marseille, then Antibes, where he left the carriage he had recently bought – he would reclaim it three years later – to travel by *felucca* down the Italian coast. He took with him a maid he had met in Marseille, one Rosalie, whom he dressed and passed off as his lady-companion. They put in at Nice, due to bad weather, but arrived at Genoa in high summer, disembarking to be met by a Venetian *commedia* star, who immediately recognised Casanova

arriving from Antibes in a splendid equipage and in the company of another traveller [Rosalie]. Gritti [the famous Pantalon] saw him and ran towards him with open arms. The adventurer assumed a grave air, and darting a stern eye at him said, 'You are mistaken, I am the Chevalier de Saint-Galle.' [Gritti] was astonished but before he could recover from his surprise the pseudo-knight gave him a wink as much as to say, 'Listen, look, and keep quiet.'

Such was the style in which Casanova travelled. The Venetian Luigi Gritti soon made Casanova's proper acquaintance, once he had realised the importance of playing along with Casanova's improvised title. Casanova offered him his own Italian translation of Voltaire's *Écossaise*, which Pietro Rossi, Gritti's manager, offered to produce. Some time late that summer, Casanova himself trod the boards in a reading of his work, playing Murray, the lead.

From Genoa he set out for Florence, Rome and Naples, passing through Livorno, and Pisa that winter. He intended to end up in Florence for Christmas. There 'Bellino', on stage as Teresa Lanti, presented him with his son, Cesare Filippo, now sixteen. The unconventional family was entertained by the British consul, Horace Mann, resident in Florence since 1737 and a later fan of Casanova's literary works. In the long tradition of English Italophiles, he collected antiquities and studied Italian – he subscribed to Casanova's translation of *The Iliad* – and Casanova left a deft description of his gardens, paintings and genteel lifestyle.

The sense of drift in Casanova's life was almost subverted at this moment by another chance encounter, this time with a political cleric he had known in his youth at the Vatican: the Portuguese Abbé Gama, who suggested he worked for Portuguese interests at the upcoming Augsburg Congress, due to realign Europe in the event of the Seven Years' War concluding. In the meantime, Casanova was again running short of money. He was forced to leave Florence after a financial scandal in which he was implicated – police records survive to this effect, though Casanova may have been innocent – and he arrived in Rome for Christmas.

It was fifteen years since he had left, but he went again to the Piazza di Spagna and found it little altered. He lodged at the Villa de Londres at the bottom of the Spanish Steps, on the recommendation of his brother, Giovanni, also an artist, like Francesco, and then studying in Rome under Raphael Mengs. It was through Giovanni that Casanova encountered a slightly different Rome on this trip. He spent time with Mengs, head of Rome's Academy of Painting, and also with Johann Winckelmann, credited with having immense impact on the creation of the style now known as Neo-classicism. Winckelmann was keeper of the vast collection of antiquities in the care of Cardinal Alexander Albani, at Villa Albani. Casanova had a personal tour of the collection and saw the work in progress on a ceiling, painted by Mengs, as well as his brother's work for Winckelmann's *Monumenti inediti*.

Casanova, the increasingly dedicated bibliophile, also went out of his way to revisit the Vatican Library, and there presented the curator, Cardinal Passionei, with a valuable book, *Pandectorum liber unicus*, still in the Vatican collection. This won him an audience with the new pope, Clement XIII, in whom he raised laughter, as he had in his predecessor, with tales of lesser clerics. The pope and Casanova had known each other slightly in Padua, and his family *palazzo* in Venice, Ca'Rezzonico, was and is directly opposite the Malipiero and the Campo San Samuele where Casanova had played as a child. It was as a result of Casanova's gift to the library, rather than his amusing company one would assume, that the pope conferred on him the Papal Order of the Golden Spur. It was not the highest of honours, but it was quite something for an actress's son and, moreover, it gave Casanova the right to use the title 'Chevalier' under which he had been travelling for several years.

While in Rome, he made enquiries in the Minerva parish for the Monti family, Cecilia and her daughters, in particular Anna Maria Vallati. The mother was dead, and the family dispersed, but Anna Maria, now a widow, was said to be near Naples, which was one of Casanova's reasons for travelling on south.

In Naples, as ever, Casanova attended the theatre. His account is historically precise and verifiable: it was a tenth-birthday gala for the boy-king, Ferdinand IV of Naples and I of the newly unified Kingdom of the Two Sicilies. It was 12 January 1761, and the performance was Metastasio's *Atillio Regolo*. The Duke de Matalone introduced him to his mistress, whom Casanova names Leonilda, a titular mistress only, as the Duke was widely known to be impotent. His first encounter with Leonilda was a *coup de foudre* for Casanova, or so he presents it in his memoirs. Perhaps something about her uniquely frustrating, artificial situation attracted him, but he decided fairly quickly he was in love with her and asked the duke to release her. This is a clue that he was not negotiating, as he later wrote, for Leonilda's hand in marriage, but to replace the duke as her lover. He was told he would have to ask Leonilda's mother, who lived near Naples.

When they met, everything changed. Leonilda's mother was Anna Maria Monti-Vallati and the girl was Casanova's own seventeen-year-old daughter. Casanova put aside any idea of negotiating for Leonilda's favours, but the incestuous undercurrents of the situation did not abate. Anna Maria took her former lover, now a man of thirty-six, to her bed but she did so in the presence of their daughter – according to Casanova. What seems certain is that they talked about re-establishing their affair, and even marrying. Anna Maria continued to write to him for the rest of their lives – and offered him solace and retirement in years to come – but in 1761 she offered marriage only if Casanova consented to settle in Naples.

Settling was never part of Casanova's plan. He left the bemused Leonilda – reunited with her father but in the most unsettling circumstances – five thousand ducats towards a possible dowry. She was still a virgin, despite her position, and he wanted to see her married, or least better placed than as mistress to an impotent man. Then he boarded the Rome *vetturino* at the Strada di Toledo, as he had eighteen years earlier, with the six-day journey to Rome ahead of him.

This time he stayed only long enough to arrange letters of introduction and commendation from friends new and old. His brother Giovanni gave him a cameo to present to Dr Maty of the British Museum in London; it may have been the onyx forgery of an ancient Sostratus still in the collection. He was clearly intending to try his luck further north.

From Florence he travelled to Bologna, thence Modena, Parma and Turin, where he stayed until May 1761. Here he corresponded again with Abbé de Gama about the position with the Portuguese delegation at Augsburg. It was the beginning of Casanova's complex relationship with the politics of Portugal, Spain, the Holy See and the Jesuits – who would soon be banned from Europe, except in 'enlightened' Russia, and even South America. De Gama was working with the Portuguese Marquis de Pombal – with whom Casanova would collide later in his travels – and needed men like Casanova – multilingual, schooled in Church and secular politics, mercenary – among the delegation to argue Portuguese interests.

Casanova wound his way towards the peace congress, via Chambéry – where once again he met M.M., the nun from Aix-les-Bains, and threw a lavish dinner party for her in her convent – with a table set half in the sequestered nunnery, and half-out – and on to Lyon, Paris and Munich. In Turin, while awaiting instruction from de Gama, he fell in with the local libertine and Freemason crowd including one Count Gian Giacomo Marcello Gamba della Perosa (de la Perouse in the memoirs), who wrote to Casanova for the rest of his life.

In Paris, *en route* to Augsburg, Casanova convinced the Marquise d'Urfé to forward to him a letter of credit for fifty thousand francs. He also arranged the commission of jewelled snuff-boxes and watches as presents for delegates at the congress. He told her that it would give him the opportunity to arrange with Lord Stormont the release from the Lisbon Inquisition of the fictional Rosicrucian 'Querilinth', who could officiate with him at her regeneration. She acquiesced, but Casanova received only the cash. The jewels were stolen by a secretary he had engaged.

He went on to Augsburg, only for the proposed congress to be abandoned. Negotiations between Frederick the Great and Britain had broken down and the war dragged on for another three years. It was a low point for Casanova too. He could be of no immediate use to de Gama or the Portuguese government, and he was again unwell, having caught another venereal infection in Munich on the way to the congress from a dancer named Renaud. It can have been little consolation that his infection, like his politicking, was nothing if not well connected: Renaud was married to the jeweller Boehmer, who was ruined by the diamond-necklace affair in Paris that so damaged the reputation of the French queen Marie Antoinette.

From Paris back to Metz to collect La Corticelli, and to Pontcarré, the d'Urfé château, and thence Aix-la-Chapelle in the extended business of the d'Urfé 'regeneration'. It was at this stage, 1762, a profitable business. He was in Aix-la-Chapelle in early May 1762, with its easy crowd of *curistes*, one of whom, seemingly a Mademoiselle Lambert, Casanova seduced while waiting for the arrival of the Marquise. They travelled together to Besançon before separating temporarily while Casanova went to Geneva to gamble her money, and continue an affair begun earlier with 'Hedwig', niece of a Protestant pastor, and her cousin Helen. His three-way affair with both women – probably an Anne Marie Maya then aged thirty-one and her unidentified cousin – is among the more erotic passages of the memoirs, and the more often disputed as a result. Unfortunately the early and unsympathetic editor Laforge lost the original copy, so we have only his rendering of events.

Casanova returned to Turin in September 1762, via Lyon and Chambéry, and made it his home through the winter of 1762–3, spending the marquise's money and that which he could garner from the city's gaming tables. He became friendly with Lord Hugh Percy, Baron Warkworth, son of the Earl and Countess, later Duke and Duchess of Northumberland, who was on the Grand Tour but tarried longer than the art treasures of Turin might justify to share the favours of a dancer called Agathe with the Chevalier de Seingalt. Eventually the two men in effect swapped mistresses: Percy tempted Agathe away from Casanova: he promised her two thousand guineas at the end of their liaison. He also gave Casanova a diamond-framed miniature of his own likeness, a love-token usually, but it was destined for Percy's mother as a 'letter of introduction' for Casanova in London. Only an Englishman, Casanova noted approvingly, would essay such a grandiloquent gesture with its recognisable theatrical flourish and gentlemanly disdain for money.

Early 1763 found Casanova in Milan, which was meant to put on a finer carnival than Turin. Here he entertained again in lavish style, buying dresses for masqueraders and throwing expensive dinners. He spent some time outside the city, at the castle of the Attendoli-Bolognini family near the village of San Angelo. When the sister of the châtelaine, Angela Gardini, whom Casanova called variously Clementine and Hebe turned out, like Hedwig in Geneva, to share his love of literature and theology, he bought her half a library of books with his gambling profits. When he escorted both sisters to the Milan carnival, he bought costumes for everyone, then had them ripped to pieces and sewn back together with more expensive interlinings to dazzle the locals with his wealth. His reward, of course, was that Angela readily went to bed with him, as her sister slept – or pretended to sleep – beside them.

He went to Marseille at the behest of the Marquise d'Urfé and the call of necromancy, which in turn took him to Genoa, by boat, and back again to Antibes with his growing team of fellow conspirators: his brother Gaetano, their shared mistress Marcolina, and Passano, the secretary, who would soon turn against him. On the way back to France the sea passage became so difficult that the *felucca* put in at Menton, then part of the principality of Monaco. It was a not uncommon refuge and, subsequently, Casanova travelled on towards Paris via Aix-en-Provence.

His carriage, however, broke down just beyond the Croix d'Or staging-post near Aix, which nearly landed him back in the 'Henriette's' arms. Hospitality was offered to strangers off the high road in a local château – the Château of the Albertas or Gueydan Margalet families. 'Henriette' had returned there to her difficult marriage and her children after her affair with Casanova in 1749. This time they did not meet: she heard his name announced and, desperate to avoid scandal, sent a note, though Marcolina, addressed to 'The most honest man of my acquaintance', implying her continued need for his discretion. She had nothing to be concerned about: his regard for her was such that he had burned her letters exactly as she had asked. The carriage repaired, he travelled on to Lyon and Paris

When Casanova finally returned to his lodgings on Paris's rue du Bac in May 1763 after a sixteen-month absence a great number of letters awaited him, none very welcome. As he sat, in his travelling clothes, opening and reading them, two caught his eye. Both were from Teresa Imer, in London, now signing herself 'Mrs Cornelys'. In the first she politely requested the return to London of Giuseppi, her son. In the second, written when there had been no reply to the first, she insisted that Casanova send him to her immediately.

Casanova had long contemplated a trip to Europe's fastest-growing city, but Teresa's letters forged his determination to make a new fortune in London. Not that this intention prevented him drawing on substantial sums in bankers' drafts, yet again from the Marquise d'Urfé, as well as packing jewels and clothes she had lavished on him, which would allow him to present himself in London as an aristocrat.

Giuseppi, the 'Comte d'Aranda', was persuaded or, rather, hoodwinked to come too.

LONDON
1763

'A Single . . . Lady may be immediately accommodated with a genteel and elegant furnished first Floor . . . to which belong some peculiar Advantages; it is agreeably situated in Pall Mall . . . it may be entered on immediately, and will be let on very reasonable Terms . . . more for the Sake of Company than Profit. Please to enquire exactly opposite Mr Deard's Toy Shop in Pall Mall'

Casanova's advert for a mistress, 5 July 1763

Casanova's advertisement for a lodger, ideally a single woman who could read between the lines, appeared on the second page of the *London Gazetteer and Daily Advertiser* of 5 July 1763, along with others aimed at a worldly readership, between a notice for 'Flat Razor Straps "be sure to ask for Cudworth's Strap",' and one for the new Dog-&-Duck-Pleasure-Baths and their 'Grand Antivenereal Tincture'. The *Gazetteer*, clearly, was not read by parsons' daughters in the provinces. Why would a notable, wealthy and well-connected Italian, renting an expensive house on Pall Mall, advertise for a lodger?

Casanova was nothing if not catholic in his approach to love, life and adventure. His nine-month sojourn in Europe's largest and richest city saw him conduct affairs with his Portuguese lodger, a family of aristocrats and a Soho-based prostitute who broke his heart. By the time he left he was thousands of pounds poorer, had been arraigned in front of Bow Street magistrates for affray and had contemplated suicide from the parapet of the new Westminster Bridge. It was a dramatic visit.

Casanova had arrived in England by private-hire packet from Calais on 11 June 1763, with the Duke of Bedford, the returning ambassador from Versailles, travelling as his guest. He was immediately taken with England, its roads, its carriages, its people, for all 'they think they are superior to everyone else'. London was clean, orderly and, despite everything he had heard, open to foreigners and those who sought lodgings. He found a large townhouse with a housekeeper on Pall Mall within just two hours of arriving in London, though in fairness this was as a result of clear directions from the Italian author Vincenzo Martinelli, whom he met on his first day in the Prince of Orange coffee-house on the Haymarket, a club for the West End's large Italian community. The house was 'perfect' in every way, with much admired water closets in every bedroom. It was not, however, where Casanova had intended to stay. He had assumed, in reuniting the young Comte d'Aranda with his mother, Teresa, now living as Mrs Cornelys on Soho Square, that he would be welcomed as a favoured house guest. After all, Teresa and he had a ten-year-old daughter, Sophia, and Casanova had arguably acquitted himself well enough in providing for eighteen-year-old Giuseppi a highly polished Parisian education, a fictitious but widely accepted title, and, for some years, the doting interest of one of the richest women in Europe. However, although he made straight for the house on the east side of Soho Square – it stood opposite the then Venetian embassy – he was not welcomed with open arms. Indeed, Teresa kept him waiting so long that he eventually wandered off into Soho.

What was Casanova doing in London – or what was he planning? One clue lies in the manuscript version of the *History of My Life*, which has relatively few crossings-out for such a long document; those that are visible are especially beguiling. When Casanova narrates the story of his presentation at court to King George III and Queen Charlotte, which took place at St James's Palace later that summer, he explains that he was announced by the French ambassador 'because of my naturalisation'. This he has subsequently crossed out. Not only was he using a French-style title, 'Chevalier de Seingalt', he had actually acquired, by 1763, a French 'passport'. In the memoirs he has deleted this. He denied his French naturalisation in later life, which may have been due to his disgust with all things French after the excesses of the Revolution, or to protect details of his past that he still had reason to deny: that he had been a spy in the pay of the French. There is more specific detail in the files of the Inquisition in Venice, to whom Casanova began to write more pressingly at this period in the hope of a pardon based on his usefulness abroad. In one letter from London dated 1763, he offers industrial secrets – silk dyeing again – that he believes could be of use in Venice. However, it is reasonable to suppose that he was offering the same know-how, based on new Spitalfields technology, to the French as well, in whose pay he may have continued to be.

He went back to Soho Square later that evening – it was Monday, 13 June – to the house where he had left Giuseppi sleeping and waiting for his mother. There, eventually, Teresa Cornelys, née Imer, London's premier club hostess, finally made her appearance.

The years had not been kind to her physically: she was now forty and getting stout, but London had seen her make, and risk, several fortunes in the new business of running what amounted to a private club in her lavish house on Soho Square. There was a positive craze in London for Venetian-style masquerades and *ridotti*. In the 1750s they had been mounted at Ranelagh

Rotunda or Vauxhall Gardens, but both venues proved too open of access for London high society. It was Teresa's stroke of genius on arriving in London a few years earlier to found the Carlisle House Masquerades, which were apparently 'private' parties thrown at the house she rented for the purpose on Soho Square; access was expensive and strictly guarded by society ladies. The possibility that one might be denied entry proved, as always, the greatest attraction, along with a price that allowed lavish hospitality inside. 'I give twelve suppers and twelve balls to the nobility every year,' Teresa enumerated to Casanova that first evening, and his recall is confirmed in the *London Public Advertiser*. 'The expense,' she went on, 'is enormous.' Casanova estimated she was bringing in more than twenty thousand pounds a year.

The scene at Carlisle House on Soho Square should not be thought of as louche, although everyone was masked in the style of Venetian carnival. Teresa Cornelys might have lived and loved all over Europe and have had children by more than one father, but to the world she presented a solidly respectable demeanour. Eventually her subscription concerts, mixing high-society exclusivity and her own wide-ranging musical connections, had a profound impact on the history of music in London. She had an encyclopedic knowledge of Italian and German music and introduced London to the works of Johann Christian Bach. She even tried to arrange a Carlisle House concert for the 'infant phenomena' children of Leopold Mozart, little Maria-Anna and Wolfgang. She was a promoter and producer, in modern parlance, a club impresario, and with that came profit and risk. Once the girl-next-door in San Samuele, when Casanova turned up on her Soho doorstep, Teresa Cornelys had become a woman of style, fashion and substance.

She invited him to the last ball of the season – in truth, the season was over, much of the aristocracy had left town for their country seats, but she needed to eke out as much profit as she might before the quiet summer months, and told Casanova he could come as her son's tutor and her friend, even though he was not an aristocrat. It was the last straw in a series of minor insults that, Casanova claimed, he only bore in the hope of being allowed to spend time with his daughter Sophie, 'a prodigy' of ten. He and Teresa were understandably cautious of one another. Where he had hoped she would help him with his *entrée* into London society, he found instead that she was in a precarious financial and legal position, and fighting an expensive law case against 'Lord Fermor' to whom she owed money for the costly furnishings of her 'club', Carlisle House. There is some doubt over Casanova's rendering of events, in that although Teresa Cornelys eventually fell foul of angry creditors, she was relatively successful in 1763, and seems to have had other reasons for giving him scant welcome. She did not approve of Giuseppi's Parisian ways – she seems to have been a remarkably strict mother – and forbade Casanova a reunion with Sophie for a week. She suspected, rightly, that he wanted access to her friends in fashionable West End society and in the City, for the purposes of setting up another lottery, but was disinclined to help.

Casanova returned to Carlisle House the following weekend, invited for a dinner that was to include his daughter. He took a sedan chair from his house on Pall Mall – in the company of a footman called Jarbe he had hired that week because he was fashionably black and also trilingual – and wore his most expensively foppish Parisian lace. The company was duly impressed. Teresa, however, had instructed her daughter to greet the Chevalier de Seingalt with cold formality, and Casanova spent a tortuous evening trying to persuade the embarrassed ten-year-old to talk to him. To some extent Sophie warmed, but only after a series of criticisms from both parents. It is an example, however, of Casanova's avuncular but erratic regard for his off-spring, and his willingness both to lavish affection upon Sophie and use her as a pawn in an unseemly spat with an ex-lover, her mother. He kept all his life a note from her, written in French on paper she had lined for the purpose; it expresses formal thanks for a present, and also bemusement at an allegory she had not understood. Sophie was somewhat careful and prim all her life.

Casanova's London narrative flows with the easy confidence of one who remembered key details and knew he had made a strong impression on a famous city, as it had on him. He saw Garrick at Drury Lane, he met and spoke to Queen Charlotte, whose French was good, though almost certainly not on the date he mentions. Through his friends Dr Maty of the British Museum and Vincenzo Martinelli, he met Dr Johnson. The two men discussed etymology, possibly in St Paul's Cathedral, according to one source, and the origin of the word 'committee'; it was the sort of question on the mind of the great dictionary compiler, if not often on Casanova's. He went back and forth to the City to try to sell his plans for a lottery, and leaves us in the memoirs a unique testament to all London had to offer a fashionable foreigner in the 1760s, its food, furnishings, high and low culture. Until his money ran out.

The house he set up was among the most lavish of his establishments outside Paris. As well as the housekeeper, who came with the property, and the 'blackamoor', Jarbe, there was Clairmont, a *valet de chambre*, brought from Paris, a house-maid, Fanny, and later a French cook. It all cost him more than twenty pounds. He went out to Ranelagh Rotunda, in Chelsea, where society and the demi-monde met for concerts, dances and flirtations – 'the enchanted palace of a genius'. It was an unremarkable evening, except for an incident on the way home, comic for its reflection on Casanova, the times, and the English. He was offered a ride by a lady who said she would deliver him to Whitehall. It was dark. He kissed her hands in gratitude. She laughed, so he kissed her face, then her bosom, while she, as he recalled, giggled. He then gave her 'the greatest proof that I find her perfectly to my taste', and she told him they would meet again. When they did, at Lady Elizabeth Germain's home, 16 St

James's Square, Casanova was shocked to find the same hand he had pressed to his 'greatest proof' unwilling to shake his. The lady, 'of the highest nobility and reputation', retorted that though she remembered him perfectly 'such escapades are hardly grounds for claiming acquaintance'. English snobbery was an unexpected stumbling block to Casanova's social and sexual progress.

Taking the advice of another Martinelli contact, Henry Herbert, Earl of Pembroke, Casanova initially turned to the professional services of various ladies of Covent Garden and St James's. Pembroke recommended a series of courtesans, and even suggested to Casanova he let some of the small upper rooms in his house to a live-in mistress, explaining that this was quite acceptable for London bachelors. He pressed Casanova to visit the infamous Shakespeare's Head in Covent Garden, a pub and *bagnio*: French was spoken, girls and private rooms could be ordered with beer. Casanova found the ale and the girls bitter. Eventually, also through Pembroke, he found a courtesan called Miss Kennedy, recorded in Harris's List of Covent Garden Ladies, the guide to West End whores, at rather less than Pembroke's recommended six guineas. According to the memoirs, Casanova had not had sex in several weeks and set about doing so in the style of the city as he found it. Though he famously described the sex trade in London as the most sophisticated in Europe and a bargain deal – 'bed, bath and bedmate; a magnificent debauch!' – it paled for him after a while, and he sought more fulfilling affairs. Not before, however, he had sampled the *bagnios* with Pembroke, the available charms of the infamous Garrick sisters, Mrs Welch's brothel in Cleveland Road, and even been offered a quickie with Kitty Fisher, London's most renowned courtesan, 'covered with diamonds to the value of 500,000 francs', and awaiting a royal duke. Casanova declined, not because of the price – he was told he could have sex with her, assuming the duke did not turn up, for ten guineas – but because they had no language in common: 'love without language is an ugly business.' Perhaps he was meant to feel flattered by the proffered bargain: he was given to understand that Kitty had that morning 'swallowed a banknote of a thousand guineas . . . or,' as he sagely put it, 'so she *claimed*'.

It is testament to Casanova's apparent wealth and standing at this period that his London acquaintances were not just from his usual round of demi-mondaines, opera stars, cabbalists and Freemasons, but rather from those ranks of the aristocracy with whom he felt at ease: fast-living noblemen and -women, like Pembroke, Bedford and, later, various members of the Hervey and Fitzroy-Stanhope families, the earls of Bristol and Harrington respectively. Lady Harrington, née Fitzroy, was the recipient of a letter of introduction Casanova had with him from the Venetian Francesco Morosoni. She introduced Casanova to the Countess of Northumberland, for whom he had the miniature of her son, Hugh Percy, Lord Warkworth, whom he had met in Turin earlier that year. This landed Casanova in the middle of the wild set. Lady Hervey, the long-secret wife of the earl to whom Casanova became most firmly attached, had been the notorious Miss Chudleigh, once maid-of-honour to the Princess of Wales, ruined, supposedly, by her early marriage to Hervey, but mistress, by 1763, to the Duke of Kingston and a favourite of the King. Lady Hervey and Teresa Cornelys were longstanding friends. Lady Harrington had been widely famed in her youth for 'her gallantries' as, according to Casanova, she had been so promiscuous and democratic in her favours she was known in London as 'Messalina of the Stable Yard'. Her daughters followed her example – several slept with Casanova – and at Northumberland House on the Strand he almost immediately fell into the agreeable company of Lady Rochford, 'whose numerous [affairs],' he recalled, 'afforded a fresh topic of conversation every day'. Casanova became intimate with almost every member of what became later the 'most notorious [British] matrimonial scandal' of the eighteenth century when Elizabeth Chudleigh was accused of bigamy with the Duke of Kingston for having been legally married to Augustus Hervey, later Earl of Bristol, who in turn shared a mistress, Kitty Hunter, with Casanova's friend Henry, Earl of Pembroke. He had found his milieu: the sexually dissolute, leisured and cultured London upper classes of the mid-eighteenth century – or so it might have seemed.

It was not as Teresa's son's tutor that he came to the ball at Carlisle House, but as Lady Harrington's elegant new escort. Teresa played society hostess, as was her role, but introduced Casanova as the man who had looked after her son in Paris. Lady Harrington immediately recognised the frisson between the famous Mrs Cornelys and Casanova, and teased him when Sophie, who bore a marked resemblance to her father, was brought down to say good night to the guests. She and Casanova danced a minuet in the ballroom – an odd sight surely, the tall dark man and the shy ten-year-old girl. Giuseppi, now known as Joseph Cornelys, cut an even odder figure: he was unable to speak much English and was homesick for Paris and the *hôtel particulière* of the Marquise d'Urfé and spent the evening in a corner of the room.

Casanova took more of Pembroke's advice and advertised for a 'lodger' for the upper rooms in his house – he remembered them as on the third floor, but in fact it was the first. It would have been apparent to anyone reading the notice that there might be another situation vacant in the household in question. The woman who answered his advertisement was beyond immediate hope of respectability, labouring under the twin disadvantages in London of being an abandoned fiancée and a Catholic Portuguese. Nevertheless, she arrived in a sedan chair, spoke several languages, including Italian, and settled quickly into the small rooms in the Pall Mall house, requesting that anyone asking for her be turned away. An affair began that ran in the style familiar from the *History of My Life*, an affair of convenience, in which one party, Casanova, willed himself into believing briefly that he was in love. He play-acted with Pauline, as he referred to her, the *pater familias* of Pall Mall, with little Sophie as reluctant daughter; once she was sent to beg money from Casanova for her indebted mother, Teresa. Sophie spent nights in the house with Pauline and her father, all three playing the roles assigned to them by the locals of mother, father and daughter.

Pauline was noble, educated, beautiful, but also vulnerable: like Henriette, she had run away from a sort of domestic imprisonment. It seems unlikely that she was in love with her landlord. Neither did she yield quickly in the game they played of domestic flirtation, until a well-timed riding accident near Green Park put him to bed for some days, with Pauline as his nursemaid and little reading material but his collection of 'philosophical', or erotic, literature.

Doubt lingers over Casanova's description of the dark-haired woman who lived with him on Pall Mall, for although he claimed that her story would be familiar to anyone who knew Lisbon society, her identity has eluded researchers. Though elements of her background were almost certainly her or Casanova's fiction – her connection with the Marquis de Pombal and a Brazilian princess – in unexpected ways Casanova grounds his story in verifiable truths. The chapel where she and the Portuguese community attended mass by Golden Square exists to this day, and on the night he says he saw her naked for the first time through muslin bed-curtains in Pall Mall – 24 July 1763 – the moon was indeed full.

The affair continued until early August when she returned to Portugal via France. In the memoirs the story is intermingled in the London narrative with Casanova's continuing interest in acting the role of father to his Sophie. It was an unhappy episode in the bizarre trajectory of Sophie's life – she was used as a pawn in her mother's various stratagems and ended up a royal almoner in Cheltenham. In 1763 she suffered an illness or depression that involved serious weight loss – it has been suggested she was anorexic. Casanova stepped in to try to help, spoke sternly to

Teresa, who agreed with him that they would send 'their child' to a Hammersmith boarding school for young ladies.

Casanova and Teresa never saw each other again after 1763 though he met her son, Giuseppi, in Italy six years later. Her life was a pleasure garden in the eighteenth-century sense, full of gaiety and spectacle, debts and deviance. She was briefly one of London's richest commoners, but ended her days selling asses' milk in Knightsbridge before a short stint in Fleet prison and a pauper's grave. Sophie's continuing story was related to Casanova years later by a schoolfriend, but they, too, never met again.

Italian opera, Jewish painters, multilingual African servants, Venetian club-promoting: Casanova sketches a diverse, cosmopolitan London, so it is not surprising he came upon other Continental economic migrants he had met before. One such, Marie Anne Geneviève Augspurgher Boulainvilliers Charpillon, a French-Swiss courtesan, very nearly ended his life and certainly changed it for ever. If London was the site of Casanova's mid-life crisis, Marie Anne Charpillon was its catalyst.

Casanova had known her and her family in Paris, where they had been called Boulainvilliers. Marie Anne was of such arresting beauty, even in her early teens, that a rake like Casanova was certain to have noticed her – as, indeed, was her intention. She, her mother, aunts and grandmother were all professional beauties. Decades before the grandmother and her daughters had been expelled from Berne, in Switzerland, for immoral behaviour, and by 1763 the rent-books of Holborn prove they were established as working girls on Denmark Street in the parish of St Giles – Soho, in effect. It was here that Casanova reacquainted himself with the family. Marie Anne was only eighteen, but had already been kept by the Venetian ambassador Morosini, who had given Casanova a letter for her when they had met in Lyon. It was a recommendation of sorts, in the courtly and epistolary style of the eighteenth-century sex trade.

Anne Marie Charpillon played the game of love and lust with a professional and cynical eye. Pembroke warned Casanova against her: he had paid her to walk with him in one of Vauxhall Gardens' dark alleys, landscaped for such assignations, but Anne Marie escaped with the money and laughed at him. It showed her willingness to play tough and dirty in the family business. She knew her worth. She was young, doe-eyed, with abundant chestnut hair, and those admired attributes of the age, exquisite hands and feet. If her breasts were small, noted the expert Casanova, they were perfectly formed, and she had grace and courtliness, supposedly inherited from the Marquis de Saint-Soire, her natural father. She was set on a career as London's premier *grande horizontale*, a fantasy Frenchwoman, and had little time for Casanova.

She told Casanova she intended to torment him, win his love and abuse him. Was it a love game – a dominatrix mask she felt she should don for such a player as Casanova? More likely perhaps she sensed what he had only begun to guess, that beneath his dazzlingly confident carapace something more vulnerable was emerging: a man who recognised the ridiculousness of his position, his self-aggrandised fantasy, the preposterousness of male vanity and the evanescence of lust. And she sensed her power to mock his sexual prowess at the moment when it was turning from its full tide. 'I knew,' he declared melodramatically, 'that aged thirty-eight, I had begun to die.'

The drama unfolded in the scripted manner. He invited her to his house. He began to hint at terms. As it happened, because they were all European travellers, some members of her extended family owed Casanova money. Things progressed quite quickly. La Charpillon made it clear that she expected to be set up as his mistress in a fine establishment in Chelsea, such as she had enjoyed when Morosoni had been her protector. There must be a stipend and servants. To all this Casanova agreed. A contract was produced by La Charpillon's mother, her madam, who received a hundred guineas from Casanova as down-payment. If this looks coldly financial, it is no more than a clear recollection of exactly the manner in which demi-monde contracts were sorted out in

Manon Balletti, musician and daughter of Sylvia Balletti, France's most celebrated actress. This portrait by Jean-Marc Nattier was painted during Manon's engagement to Casanova in 1757.

Louison O'Murphy or the 'O'Morphi' became Louis XV's mistress having been talent-spotted by Casanova. He suggested that this pose for her portrait would catch the King's eye.

The eighteenth century cult of love, personified by *putti*, cherubs and cupids, or representations of the god Eros, known in French simply as Amour, adorned every fashionable interior in Casanova's lifetime. They were emblematic of the light-hearted attitude to love and sexuality expressed also in his life and writings.

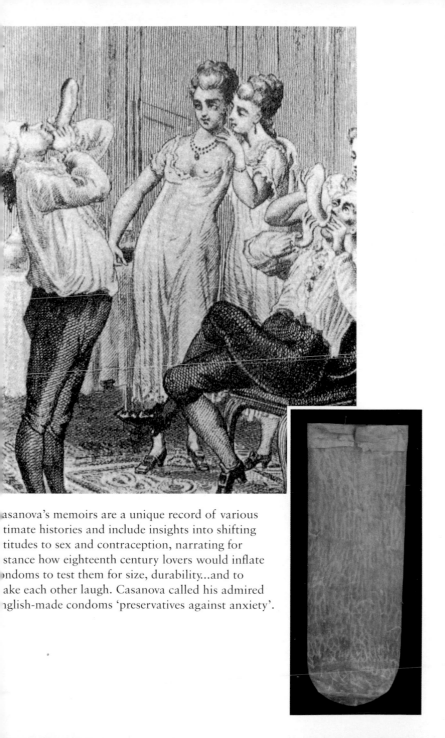

asanova's memoirs are a unique record of various
timate histories and include insights into shifting
titudes to sex and contraception, narrating for
stance how eighteenth century lovers would inflate
ndoms to test them for size, durability...and to
ake each other laugh. Casanova called his admired
nglish-made condoms 'preservatives against anxiety'.

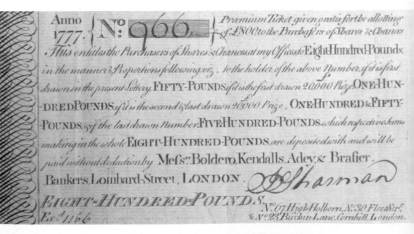

Casanova was a leading player in setting up a French lottery and he made a fortune as its director, but his success was not replicated in London or the many other capitals where he attempted to set up lotteries. His surviving papers include thousands of calculations on lottery and gematria: the cabbalistic association of numbers and letters.

Casanova became a Mason in France in 1750. At the time, the concerns and imagery of Freemasonry were seen to overlap with the cabbala. In London, Russia, France and elsewhere Casanova was introduced into society by local fellow Masons.

Westminster Bridge, London. Casanova intended to commit suicide from the parapet after a disastrous love affair with a Soho courtesan.

Part of the original Summer Gardens, St Petersburg, on the banks of the Neva where in 1765 Casanova met Catherine the Great several times.

The Tsarina Catherine II (the Great) 1729–1796, usurped the Russian throne only three years before Casanova came to St Petersburg to seek preferment at her court. He tried to convince her that he could help with calculations for a new Russian calendar.

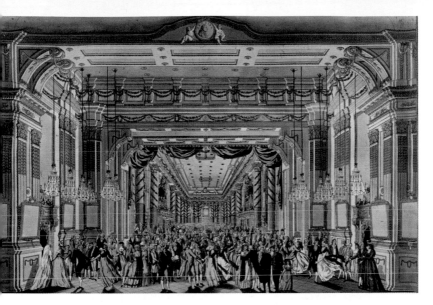

Prague, 1791. The Estates Theatre Ball, in honour of the coronation of Emperor Leopold II. Casanova was in the throng at the theatre, where *Don Giovanni* had recently premièred.

he castle at Dux – north-east of Prague – where Casanova worked as a librarian from 1785 to his death in 1798. The room where Casanova wrote his memoirs, and later died, is the first window from the right behind the castle railings.

Don Giovanni; Casanova's notes for Lorenzo da Ponte's libretto to Mozart's opera were found in Dux castle after his death. Prague musicians had always claimed Casanova had collaborated on the libretto in the final days before the première in 1787, thus linking the man and his myth.

London between well-to-do gentlemen and professional courtesans well into the nineteenth century. Casanova kept Marie
Anne's letters and they survive in the Prague Archive: an unexpectedly petulant and immature tone obtains to many – she
objected often to his mood and ill-attendance even after she had
accepted money from him for the support of 'her mother, grandmother, aunts and a man she gives out is her father'.

However, she decided to ignore key aspects of the contract.
She did not want to have sex with Casanova. Indeed, she fought
him off when he discovered she had lied about a menstrual
period. It became ugly: she hit him, screamed abuse; he gave her
a bloody nose; she and her mother threatened court action and
hinted that they would accuse him of sodomy – a far more
serious crime than battery and not, seemingly, among Casanova's catholic catalogue of sexual predilections.

After a few days it made some sense. The Augsburgher-
Charpillon family wanted Casanova to return the bills of
exchange in which they were implicated – the proof that they
owed him more than four thousand *livres*.

Marie Anne and Casanova wrote flowery apologies to each
other, things seemed patched up. She said he could sleep with her
if he gave up the bills of exchange. He did so. She wept with
gratitude, they retired to bed, but she denied him, again, her
person. For Casanova, it was an unfamiliar experience. It was
also a breach of contract, but Casanova knew he was obliged to
play-act the persuasive groom rather than the righteous custo-
mer. He sent more presents. She wrote pretty thank-you notes in
misspelled French.

Eventually Casanova felt it had gone beyond a joke, but while
claiming, to Pembroke and Chevalier Ange Goudar among
others, that he was smitten, it seems more likely that his pride
and masculine vanity were hurt, along with his purse. He
wanted Charpillon for more now than the usual reasons.

At a *fête champêtre* based partly in Richmond, at the Star and
Garter gardens with their famous view of the Thames, and later,

it would seem, at Hampton Court Palace, in the Tudor maze, La Charpillon continued her perplexing war of attrition on Casanova's pride. She first launched a 'full scale amorous attack' on him, rolling with him on the grass and allowing him full view of her person, so that 'everything made [him] sure that she was to be' his. Again, she pulled away at the last minute. In a moment of madness he instantly regretted, Casanova threatened her with his penknife, then got up, retrieved his 'hat and walking stick' and they proceeded back into more open public spaces, assuming the air of lost tourists.

They returned to London. Casanova demanded the return of his bills of exchange. The family refused, and said they would consider returning them through Marie Anne once Casanova had learned to 'respect' her. He went to Denmark Street in a fury, burst in, and found Marie Anne naked with her hairdresser, making together – he noted, in a Shakespearean phrase he had recently picked up – 'the beast with two backs'.

What happened next landed Casanova in Bow Street magistrates court. Mainly he smashed furniture and decorative porcelain. Again, he repented and even offered to pay for the damage. In a telling letter in the Prague Archive he pleaded innocence while musing on his own behaviour, as well as Marie Anne's: 'I have too much respect for good manners as well as morals and I had mistaken too abjectly these women [the Charpillon family] to find myself blackening my own name with such a frightful crime.'

Then Marie Anne, diagnosed with what was considered a life-threatening stress-induced 'interrupted period', took to her bed, demanded ten pounds from Casanova for doctor's fees, and put out to Soho that she would soon die as a result of his violence. Her health deteriorated rapidly and, within a few days, Casanova heard that Marie Anne was not expected to live. This news set off a sudden, catastrophic and self-abnegating period of depression. Almost immediately, Casanova recalled, he contemplated killing himself. 'At that moment,' he later wrote, 'I felt, as it were, an icy hand clutching my heart.' He returned to Pall Mall, convinced that he was responsible for the early death of a woman he – in a strange sense – loved and set about about putting his affairs in order. He wrote a letter to the Venetian resident in London to pass on to Bragadin with his personal effects. These – his diamonds, snuff-boxes, purses, money and 'portfolios' – he put into a strongbox to be discovered after his death.

Then he went out in his sturdiest overcoat – it was November – bought lead shot with which to load its large pockets, and walked to the Thames. He planned, as the London saying goes, to make a hole in it. 'I walked slowly,' Casanova remembered, 'because of the immense weight I was carrying in my pockets.' He went to Westminster Bridge, the new Thames crossing built, as it happened, out of exactly the sort of lottery speculation he had been hoping to profit from in London, and there he contemplated the grey waters.

He was on the brink of killing himself through a depression born of sexual rejection and guilt that his frustrated rage had, apparently, led to the death of a young woman for whom he had a strong feeling – or even loved. Of course, there was more to it than that. Marie Anne was not the first woman to reject Casanova. She was not even the first professional courtesan to do so: it was part of the helter-skelter cotillion of love and lust that both parties might move away unexpectedly at the very last moment. It was part of the thrill, mirroring a 'real' seduction, one unsullied by commercial exchange but, like a true romance, the outcome could never be assumed.

Casanova was more vulnerable in London than he chose to admit. His money was running out – and the business with the Charpillons had not been inexpensive. He had neither the power nor the influence to resolve the matter to his satisfaction, as clearly Morosini had before him. The price of Marie Anne's favours was the ability to support her entire family. Where often before he had overcome all obstacles by force of positive energy, charm and determination, Marie Anne Charpillon presented an implacable resolve against him. He felt old and ill-judged. The terror that, he admitted, gripped him when someone simply looked him up and down, or when he feared his 'steed' might not rise to his 'reputation', the terror of being rejected by a woman whose favour he sought – the atavistic terror of the boy abandoned by his mother – for some reason overwhelmed him in this foreign city where he could not speak the language. He may also have been suffering an early bout of his later recurrent depression – symptomatic, if so, that he may have contracted, in the *bagnios* of Covent Garden, the dreaded pox, or syphilis, and its companion psychosis 'blue devils'. He alludes to the 'great treatment' or mercury cure he underwent at this time, perhaps thinking he had primary-stage syphilis.

As the lead weighed in his pockets, on the bridge where Boswell would later copulate with whores, he was interrupted by a friend. It was the extravagantly christened Sir Wellbore Ellis Agar, twenty-eight-year-old playboy son of a minor MP, and friend of Pembroke. In the familiar tones of affable British boors, he noted that Casanova looked glum, and said he'd take him for a drink. Though Casanova claims he intended for several days to try again to kill himself, Sir Wellbore's singular prescription for lightening a heavy heart put him back on the track of writing his memoirs, and for that we should thank him – as did the melancholy Chevalier de Seingalt – eventually.

Sir Wellbore thought he knew exactly what Giacomo Casanova needed: a drink, a woman, beef and Yorkshire pudding. It is typical of Casanova's style that the precise detail of the provision of all four in 1763 – at the Cannon on Cockspur Street, near the site of the later Trafalgar Square – should be stirred into the narrative of a mind and man in turmoil. Sir Wellbore could not tempt Casanova with the meal, but only because there was no soup to start, and Casanova was already in thrall to the French orthodoxy that meals were unhealthy without it. He ate some oysters instead. Neither could Sir

Wellbore inveigle Casanova out of his depression with two French dancers, who performed for Casanova naked in an attempt to raise his spirits. Sir Wellbore paid up and had sex with both of them – in the presence of a hastily contracted band of blind musicians, such discreet orchestras apparently being *de rigueur* at London orgies. Casanova was too depressed to become aroused, became more so by disappointing the girls and his own reputation, but the drink helped to some extent, and the oysters, and he agreed to go with Sir Wellbore to Ranelagh Rotunda. He left his pistols and his lead weights at the Cannon and headed for Chelsea, saying he would pick them up the next morning and kill himself. He never did. At the Rotunda, dancing among a crowd of admirers and wearing a dress he had given her, he saw Marie Anne. She bolted.

Though Casanova took a few days to recover his *amour propre*, things moved swiftly, with the help and interference of Sir Wellbore. Casanova issued a warrant against the Charpillon family for the return of bills of exchange that were rightfully his. A deal was done where by they paid him two hundred and fifty guineas, with Sir Wellbore acting as go-between. He ended up as Marie Anne's protector on the principle that he was willing to pay Casanova his money *and* look after the entire family for the pleasure of Marie Anne's attentions. All would have been at an end, were it not for the family's anger with Casanova for shaming them publicly with Marie Anne's tricks. It was this that led to his arrest, after their sworn testimony to his violent behaviour at Denmark Street. The blind judge Sir John Fielding, brother of the famous Henry, first found *against* Casanova and sentenced him to indefinite imprisonment on the principle that Mademoiselle Charpillon had feared for her life. However, once Casanova was allowed to speak – in Italian, which Fielding had learned in childhood – he was freed on condition that two London householders stood surety that he would never again assault Marie Anne. The court records are clear for 27 November 1763: John Pagus, tailor, and Lewis Chateauneu were willing to stand surety for Casanova and, after two hours in Newgate, he was free.

He took the only revenge left to him. He bought a parrot, which he left at the City's Royal Exchange once he had taught it to say, 'Mademoiselle Charpillon is more of a whore than even her mother.'

Marie Anne Charpillon went on, after Wellbore, to become the mistress of one of England's premier rakes, the fascinating and complex John Wilkes. Her epitaph is perhaps best written by him, as it was he who succeeded where Casanova was all but destroyed: 'Having proposed to write pieces on such as, to use my Lord Rochester's expression, come home to men's business and breeches . . . we ought first to know that the Science of Woman is of all Sciences forever the least understood.'

Casanova was only partially aware that he was on the brink of a collapse. He had been contemplating a trip to Portugal, partly in pursuit of Pauline, or across the Atlantic even, but the pox got in his way. Oddly he eschewed a trip to America for exactly this reason: the disease was widely and correctly assumed to have originated there, and it was thought it attacked the body more efficiently west of the Azores.

It was not only disease and depression that put an end to Casanova's London visit. The mercury cure was expensive, but the Charpillon affair had been much more so. With his lavish lifestyle and the many gifts he had bought for his short-lived seraglio on Pall Mall, he was running out of money. The lottery schemes had failed – or, at least, there was no place for Casanova to profit with efficiently run lotteries already established. He may have contributed to the 1763 lottery as one of its guarantors but he was never again in the position, as he had been in France, to work at the highest levels of lottery speculation. He wrote to Bragadin for help but catastrophically, at the same time, was either duped or complicit in a forged bill-of-exchange scandal that nearly sent him to the gallows.

He left London owing perhaps £520 in worthless bills-of-exchange, that he may or may not have realised were forged. If he had been intending to stay he must have been innocent as it would have ruined all prospects for him in the lottery business in the City if he had been suspected of being an accomplice. If, conversely, he was already set on flight, it is, of course, possible that he was willing to leave a trail of chaos behind him.

Jarbe packed for him, and said he would join him at the Channel with his precious cargo of linen, which was in Islington being washed. The shirts, the lace and Jarbe never re-appeared. Casanova crossed the Channel in a mercury-and-syphilis delirium and, after several days of being bled in every sense in Calais, he limped on, ill, bankrupt and at a loss what to do next, to await money from Bragadin in Brussels.

ACT IV SCENE IV

FREDERICK THE GREAT

1764

'Diminishing their ages is a sort of duty for those in the theatre; because they know that, despite all their talent, the public turns against them when it becomes known that they are old.'

Casanova, 1764

From Brussels, recovering both his health and a bill of exchange from Bragadin, Casanova travelled on to Brunswick to see its prince. Here, he rallied and made plans for the future; hoping to find favour or employment as a fellow Freemason: he and the Prince of Brunswick had met in Soho Square, possibly through Teresa Cornelys, who had thrown a picnic party to mark the prince's arrival in London the year before. His plans came to nothing. Freemasonry was a useful *entrée*, but no more.

In Paris, his friend Balletti explained Casanova's financial straits to the cabbalist Comtesse du Rumain who sent money to Brunswick with which Casanova travelled on alone to Berlin. First, though, at Wolfenbüttel, Casanova spent some days in its famous library studying the texts on *The Iliad*.

He pressed on to Berlin, and the prospect of an interview with Frederick the Great of Prussia.

The Seven Years' War, concluded in 1763, had cost Prussia dearly and Casanova was among many who thought they might profit from its rebuilding.

At Berlin he knew he would see the Scottish Lord Keith, by then in the service of the Prussian crown. Frederick recruited his army and administration staff without regard to nationality and on an unorthodox range of criteria. He believed himself a great judge of character, and a meritocrat. He had founded a regiment of immensely tall guardsmen, and was in the process of establishing a cadet school to be staffed by Europe's finest tutors. Casanova was set on convincing him of the merits of one of his lottery schemes. However, Lord Keith persuaded him to seek a royal audience and simply impress by his person, in the way Frederick admired.

It was not as difficult as one might imagine to gain an audience of the great victor of the Seven Years' War. After 1763 Frederick was famous, one of the monarchs who would glory in the term 'enlightened despot'; he was in correspondence with Voltaire while reforming a state and army that became standard-bearers of martial efficiency. He was also widely assumed to be homosexual. Casanova, an enthusiastic supporter of Frederick's politics and military prowess, wrote a scurrilous poem in his honour, eulogising the King's sequestration of Silesia by personifying the country as a woman desperate to be taken by her rampant monarch. When Casanova read it to a cardinal who knew the King better he laughed for ten minutes at the idea.

Keith, Earl Marischal of Scotland but exiled for his Jacobite sympathies, was well versed in handling Frederick and coached Casanova in how to approach him. Casanova dressed in black and attended the King in the gardens of Sanssouci, his pleasure palace outside Potsdam. The King appeared unattended, and asked Casanova bluntly what he wanted. Frederick had received his letter requesting an audience, and seemed short of time.

Of Casanova's sketches of contemporary 'celebrities', the one of Frederick is especially compelling. It was embellished later with the minute detail that contemporary writers tended to leave out but Casanova's magpie memory retained: that Frederick, for instance, slept at night still wearing his parade helmet 'which must have been awkward'.

Frederick, who was fifty-two, 'had astonished Europe by his warlike ideas . . . with an air of confidence that could not be opposed' was in the middle of a series of family reunions and court ceremonies relating to the proposed nuptials of a Brunswick Princess, and his own son. Casanova was a witness to one of Frederick's rare appearances in court when he was *not* in military attire, at the opera with his sister 'wearing a coat of lustrine with gold braid [when] only the very old could remember seeing him appear in public except in uniform and boots'.

His military style was emulated by all the royal houses of Europe, and he was in army uniform when Casanova met him at Sanssouci. Initially the conversation was stilted. When Casanova admired the gardens, Frederick retorted that they were not a patch on Versailles, with which Casanova was obliged to concur. When the King mistook him for a 'hydraulician' he thought he might have to parry his small knowledge of fountains into a pitch for work. Frederick thought a lottery was a tax on stupidity: 'I consider it a swindle, and I should not want it even if I had material proofs that I should never lose by it . . . the ignorant people could not risk their money in it unless they were carried away by a fallacious confidence.' Enlightened, Frederick the Great certainly was.

Casanova did not give up hope and Frederick's concerns turned out to be posture. A lottery was set up – not by Casanova but by his rival from the Paris lottery, Giovanni Calzabigi. He made a profit in the first year of three hundred thousand crowns and ran it for three years; Casanova noted bitterly and regretfully that Calzabigi still died bankrupt and never thanked him for his part in helping to convince Frederick of the scheme. Lord

Keith informed him that he had made good impression upon the King, and should await some form of preferment. This did not entirely surprise Casanova, but neither did it please him, because of what had been said in the gardens.

As he had been leaving Sanssouci Frederick had turned to him, looked him up and down and then, 'after thinking for a moment', said, 'You are a very fine figure of a man.' Casanova affected to be a little shocked. He had thought he was being taken rather more seriously. His later rendering of Frederick the Great as 'a catamite . . . who made no secret of it' perhaps showed pique that the King should make such a comment when Casanova was hoping for a job. Frederick the Great may or may not have been a practising homosexual; Voltaire made jibes at his expense, and the British ambassador had noted his 'unnatural tastes', but Casanova was probably wrong to feel insulted. The King had stated merely what was true: that Casanova was physically imposing, even when he was down on his luck and thin from recent illness.

Five or six weeks later, the King offered Casanova a job. The lottery had gone to Calzabigi, but Frederick had been informed, correctly, that Casanova was as well read as he was well travelled. He offered him a post as tutor to the new academy of officer cadets. Casanova seems to have taken offence at this too: in his memoirs he describes the barracks as spartan, the wages insulting, and the post minor. But this was far from the truth: the cadet school was to be an exclusive and royally favoured institution; it would take fifteen of the brightest and best young men each year, with five tutors in various arts and languages, including the polymath Chevalier de Seingalt, to polish their manners and instruct them in international relations. Casanova, still smarting from losing the lottery commission to Calzabigi and wary of official posts that might involve too much hard work, turned it down. There is a point in self-made or self-fantasised career when it is harder, perhaps, to face cold financial and professional realities than to struggle on in the dream that some huge win will redeem all past losses and failures. Casanova, gambler, spendthrift, internationalist and dilettante was faced with such a moment, and chose to press on.

At the same period in his life, we are presented with a quite unexpected light on Casanova from none other than James Boswell, travelling through Germany and himself the recipient of Frederick's hospitality. He met Casanova in an inn, and Casanova's intellectual chippiness, at this time in his life more than most, is immediately recognisable '[we] dined at Rufin's' writes Boswell, 'where Neuhaus [the German rendering of Casanova] an Italian wanted to shine as a great philosopher and accordingly doubted of his existence and of everything else'.

While Casanova awaited Frederick's favour in Berlin, the usual cavalcade of internationalists seem to have passed through the city. A dancer, named La Denis but known to Casanova as Giovanna Corrini, immediately caught his eye: they had been acquainted as children in Venice. She was now knocking ten years off her age, and desperate to solicit Casanova's complicity in her lie (she was only three years younger than him, but claiming to be in her twenties). She was Zanetta's goddaughter, and had last seen Casanova when he was a lanky abate and she a child dancer. Again he became part of the louche theatre scene, mingling with the itinerant Italians at the Charlottenburg Orangery theatre where the entire assembly knew his mother and extended family.

Pierre Aubry was a French dancer Casanova had known in Paris through the Ballettis. He had meanwhile been in Venice and attained some fame both on stage and off, where he had become lover simultaneously to the wife and husband of a patrician family and been exiled by the Inquisition. He had gone to St Petersburg and married there. Also in St Petersburg he had met Guiseppi dall'Oglio, a famous violoncellist, another Venetian, who had found favour with the Tsarinas Anna Ivanova and Elizabeth. It was this man who had immediate effect on Casanova's travels and career. Dall'Oglio, too, had found a wife in St Petersburg, success, acclaim and a small fortune at the imperial court. 'It was dall'Oglio and his wife who made me think of going to Russia', wrote Casanova, 'if the King of Prussia did not give me such employment as I wanted. They assured me that I should make my fortune there, and they gave me excellent letters.'

He waited several weeks to make a move. He and La Denis resumed a theatrical flirtation, begun decades earlier backstage at the San Samuele theatre where Casanova had paid to watch her undress. He saw much more of her in Berlin.

Baron Treyden, another companion in Berlin, offered to write to his sister, the Duchess of Kurland so that Casanova might be received in Riga on the way east, and Casanova wrote to the ever-munificent Bragadin to request that funds be sent for him to set up home in St Petersburg. Imagining that there would be riches in the new city, with a new lottery, perhaps, he left Berlin towards the end of 1764, with a new French-speaking valet he had contracted for the purpose to impress in Russia, Franz Xaver Lambert, an aspiring geometrist with 'a score of books on mathematics'.

ST PETERSBURG
1765

'Of course one thing you *do* have is better than two things you *might*.'

Catherine the Great

'In Russia only men who are expressly sent for are regarded. Those who go there by their own choice are not esteemed. Perhaps this is right.'

Giacomo Casanova

C asanova left Riga for St Petersburg on 15 December 1764. It was a bold time of year to be travelling as the weather was 'atrocious' and he could not even leave the confines of his *Schlafwagen* – a sort of giant bed on wheels – for the sixty hours it took to get to the new Russian capital. Nor did his travelling companion, the young valet-mathematician Lambert, please him: he prattled endlessly about geometry, convincing Casanova that he would have to get rid of him as soon as he could in the socially competitive scene he was rightly anticipating in imperial St Petersburg. At this point in the memoirs Casanova lies about one key date, in that he claims to have been in Riga when the Tsarina Catherine II (the Great) visited, a story that would have been much in circulation when he was there. His assessment of her character, style and intellect on the four occasions when they did meet, later in 1765 in St Petersburg, were described by the Prince de Ligne, who knew Catherine intimately, as among the finest sketches in the memoirs, and among the truest and clearest renderings of the famous monarch then on paper. So it is odd that Casanova should introduce her, and by extension his relationship with her, in Riga, which she visited not when he was there but several months before. It was bold piece of journalism but disingenuous; everything he states is verifiable, but not to when he might have witnessed it as such.

To his putative European readership, however, Catherine II, glorying in title of 'Empress and Autocratrix of all the Russias &cetera' *was* Russia in 1765, and it makes narrative and stylistic sense to position her first on the fringes of her empire, when her image and impact were just beginning to be felt by the travelling Italian and his companion.

Casanova arrived in St Petersburg on 21 December 1764, the winter solstice, when the sun rose above the Neva for only five and a quarter hours. Everything about Russia was and remained disconcerting to him. He engaged a French-speaking Cossack valet and took lodgings at 28 Millionnaya, between what would become the Hermitage and the Summer Gardens of Peter the Great. It was the fashionable place for foreigners to stay: central, but not ostentatious as it was a mews at the back of buildings that faced the Neva to the north and Nevsky Prospekt to the south. In his rooms he was bemused to find Russian stoves that seemed inadequate to heat them. He had to buy furniture as he was provided with nothing to write on. And having thought he would be at ease with his fine command of French, and in an area where many Italians, French and British had lodgings he found that German was the language 'known to everyone in Petersburg . . . which I understood with difficulty'.

St Petersburg, the capital of a country of twenty-eight million, was not yet a generation old and housed most of the estimated half-million Russian aristocrats. Its 'infancy', as Casanova described it, gave it the appearance of 'ruins built on purpose'. As a Venetian, he was qualified to comment on the haste with which buildings were being inadequately underpinned on marsh in 'a city which a man in a hurry must have had built in haste'. Axonometric maps of the period show a capital of hastily laid out streets, wooden façades and rickety bridges amid the palaces, churches, formal and market gardens. It was a bustling port, as well as Europe's newest capital, exporting the raw materials of the empire – iron, skins, hemp and sailcloth. According to one ambassador, it smelt of fish factories and rhubarb. Nevertheless, he soon settled in, seeking out theatre contacts, Freemasons and inveigling himself into society by the many letters of introduction he had solicited since leaving London. A chain of epistolary delegation took him from Colonel Pyotr Ivanovich Melissino, a Greek in the Russian army and former lover of Signora dall'Oglio, to a twenty-six-year-old guards officer, Stepan Zinoviov, whom he met at Melissino's. Zinoviov was a cousin of the powerful Orlov brothers, all implicated in the coup that had brought Catherine to the throne in 1762, and one of whom, Grigori, was Catherine's reigning lover.

Zinoviov was also a friend of the British envoy, Sir George Macartney, 'a handsome young man of great intelligence' – he was twenty-eight – who had had 'the English impertinence' to get one of the Tsarina's ladies-in-waiting pregnant. For this misdemeanour he was eventually recalled to London, his lover banished to a convent. She had danced impressively at a court ball along with one Mademoiselle Sievers, who behaved with more circumspection and married a prince much younger than herself, Nikolai Putyatkin. She was friendly with the *castrato* Putini, who brought to St Petersburg the Buranello chapelmaster Galuppi, who had known Casanova's mother. So, Casanova's circle in St Petersburg began to form in familiar fashion; army officers, expatriates from Italy and Greece and, of course, the local theatrical crowd, made up in large part by French and

Italians. He renewed a Prague contact in Giovanni Locatelli, a Milanese theatrical impresario, who had turned in St Petersburg to managing a restaurant for the well-to-do, Locatelli's, in the former imperial residence of Ekaterinhof. Here, 'for a rouble a head, without wine', he served 'excellent meals'. Casanova was also introduced around town by his Greek banker Demetrio Papanelopulo, who hosted him to dinner every day, apparently for the pleasure of his company and that of his alluring coterie of newly met St Petersburg Bohemians.

Casanova soon found that the Italian dancers he came to know had influential friends. Giovanna Mecour, née Campi, from Ferrara, was dancing and whoring in the city and introduced Casanova to Catherine's secretary of state. Ivan Perfilievich Yelagin, whose island home now bears his name, was also St Petersburg's leading Freemason, with a grotto for secret cabbalistic ceremonies hidden under the waterside pavilion of his palatial *dacha*. Doubtless Casanova knew it well, as he became a close associate of Yelagin and, through him, of Count Panin, who had the dubious distinction of being implicated in the murders of both Peter III and Paul II, Catherine's witless husband and son respectively. It was probably also through Yelagin that Casanova came to be aware that Princess Dachova – Catherine's right-hand woman during the coup and Russia's most eminent academician – was not Panin's lover, as was often stated, but his daughter. Dachova and Casanova were introduced quite soon after his arrival and it was through her father/lover, Count Panin, that he was introduced, eventually, to the Tsarina.

Casanova's first actual view of Catherine the Great was at a masked ball held at the Winter Palace within hours of his arrival in St Petersburg. His landlord on Millionnaya had informed him that a ball for five thousand was to be held that evening. It is mentioned by the British envoy Macartney, among others. They did not speak – indeed she was not presenting herself as a monarch but as a lowly masquerader in a cheap outfit – she once courted a lady-in-waiting while dressed as a man. Only two years into her reign when Casanova arrived in St Petersburg, Catherine was assiduously playing for public and aristocratic approval, and kept the latter happy, as well as the better-dressed population of the new capital, by throwing lavish parties to all who might come appropriately attired – she had recently spent more than fifteen thousand roubles on a masquerade in St Petersburg's Baum Park when her yearly income before she had become tsarina had amounted to thirty thousand. Nobles and visitors were all well versed in how to behave '*à la* Venetian'; codes dictated how they should equip and costume themselves, and tables were laid 'upon which there were plentiful numbers of pyramids with sweets and candies, as well as cold and hot meats'. The masquerade mentioned by Casanova, on 21 December 1764 was to be in the Venetian style, one reason, perhaps, why he decided to go. He suggested that his dullard companion should stay put. Casanova was travelling with a traditional Venetian 'dominoe' cape, but had to send for a mask. He then made his way the few hundred yards along Millionnaya to the Winter Palace.

'I walk through the rooms . . . I see a great number of people dancing in several rooms where there are orchestras . . . I see buffets at which all those who are hungry or thirsty are eating and drinking . . . a great profusion of candles . . . and as I should expect I find it all magnificent.' It was a glittering court, even when in masquerade, described by many at the time as outshining, quite literally, all the other royal courts of Europe with which Casanova was familiar. The men wore French suits, and the ladies had adopted the Versailles styles of high hairdos and heavy makeup, but nothing was so striking as the profusion of precious stones adorning the courtiers' dress. Of course this was a feature of court fashions in Europe at that time, but in Russia, where gems were mined as well as sold on the open market, men would outdo women. Russians at Winter Palace masquerades were described as 'bestrewn with diamonds gleam-

ing everywhere: on buttons, buckles, epaulettes and even hats
. . . adorned with diamonds studded in several rows.'

A profusion of food and drink was available – guests were
'treated to various vodkas and the best vinaceous wines, as well as
to coffee, chocolate, tea, orgeat, lemonade and other beverages' –
and there was dancing from eight p.m. until seven a.m.

A few hours after his arrival at the ball, Casanova became
aware of a whisper that the Tsarina was in the room, masked
and costumed, with her lover Orlov. 'I [am] convinced of it',
wrote Casanova, 'for I hear more than a hundred maskers say
the same thing as she passes, all of them pretending not to
recognise her.' The Empress had deliberately worn a simple
costume that was noted by onlookers as 'not worth ten kopecks'
and was eavesdropping on what she chose to believe was
uncensored comment on politics and her governance. Of course,
it was a charade: if anyone failed to recognise her, Grigori
Orlov's height and bulk gave him away, and courtiers did well to
hide any criticism they might have of him or her.

The German-born princess who had married into the
Romanov dynasty, then usurped its throne, was described
by Casanova at this time as 'not beautiful [but] whoever
examined her had reason to be pleased, finding her tall, well
built, gentle [and] easy of access'. It was a feature of which
Casanova intended to take full advantage. Catherine was at
the head of one of the most autocratic and repressive states in
Europe yet was determined to be seen as enlightened, modernising and open in government, at least to the extent that it
flattered her image abroad. The St Petersburg project, begun
by her father-in-law, Peter the Great, continued apace to
create an imperial capital in the style of the European baroque
and neo-classical. Meanwhile, Catherine chose to inveigle
foreigners in her affairs and that of her city in order to
promulgate abroad an idea of an enlightened new Russia.
Casanova was right in thinking St Petersburg might be an
advantageous place to be.

He had arrived in Russia, moreover, in the immediate wake of one of the most successful reinventions of the Venetian masquerade on the international stage. Catherine had commissioned the Volkov brothers, Feodor and Gregori, the founding fathers of Russian classical theatre, to ignore the Russian styles for which they had recently been ennobled and create instead a court extravaganza in honour of her new reign and in the Venetian masquerade style. It was titled *In Celebration of Minerva* but was so excessive that Feodor literally worked himself to death on it. The vogue, however, continued, which explains the ease with which Casanova obtained a mask at short notice, and St Petersburg society's familiarity with the different forms of masquerade costume.

Casanova immediately recognised the other true Venetian in the crowd from his authentic beaked-mask costume. He turned out to be from Treviso. He also bumped into a Parisian woman whom he had last encountered between the sheets in the late 1750s; she was plying a parallel trade in Russia as an 'actress' under the name La Langlade. They renewed their affair half-heartedly: they were both aware that Casanova 'no longer had money', and La Langlade was a professional mistress, but it was through her that Casanova became embroiled in the French demi-monde of St Petersburg.

The Winter Palace ball was the perfect introduction to the city of Petersburg in that it promised all the intrigue and adventure Casanova might seek, with the added frisson of a new and volatile regime in which reputations and careers were being forged, especially among the foreign community, and where Casanova had an instant network of talented and well-placed friends, as well as some disreputable ones who would soon lead him into the sort of trouble he enjoyed.

To begin with in Russia Casanova had no lover. Soon after his arrival, however, he met two women who would dominate, in their different ways, his experience of sex there. One, Mademoiselle La Rivière, turned up on his doorstep with her lover, a Frenchman called Crèvecoeur. The other, a Russian peasant, revealed herself to have the figure of 'the Psyche which I had seen at the Villa Borghese [in Rome]' when she took Casanova to the Russian *bagnio* she attended each Saturday where 'both men and women [were] all stark naked'. He decided to cast her with him in his own version of the classical myth of Pygmalion, teach her Italian and pass her off as a member of his own family, at which he succeeded. When he left, she became lover to Catherine's architect in chief, Antonio Rinaldi, who was working on landmarks that dominate St Petersburg to this day: St Isaac's Cathedral, the Marble, Gatchina and Orienbaum palaces.

Casanova met the Russian girl in the park around the royal palace of Ekaterinof. He was there with a small coterie of his new friends whom he had generously invited to dinner at Locatelli's; Zinoviov was the only Russian, the rest a mix of Italian singers, musicians and a French courtesan, La Protée, whom Casanova was pursuing. Zinoviov, perhaps feeling himself the outsider, went out into the park, one of several used by the imperial hunt and well stocked with game. Casanova decided to accompany him. It was Zinoviov who explained to Casanova that the peasant girl they met in the woods was a serf so could be 'bought' as his servant if he negotiated with her father. Because she was still a virgin, her father, who lived nearby, held out for a hundred roubles. Casanova was disturbed by this: he claimed he would never sleep with the girl unless she was willing, but was sufficiently intrigued to enter into a deal. He and Zinoviov returned the next day, and Casanova availed himself of the possibility to hire a housekeeper-bedmate for the price of a periwig. He named the girl Zaïre, after the eponymous heroine of the play he had discussed with Voltaire and she became his *protégé*, someone to dress, to advise on the ways of society, and to teach the Italian language and French manners. She also became his mistress, once he had assured himself of her virginity in the presence of both her parents.

Zaïre moved into the rooms on Millionnaya, and Lambert the mathematician left. Gradually, Casanova taught her Italian, basic table manners, and dressed her in French fashions. In return she taught him a little Russian. She also took him to the new steam baths, opened in 1763, at Malaya Morskaya Street for 'sweating and treating fluxes', which had so shocked and impressed him with its easy commingling of the sexes. A rapport grew between them, which seems credible, for all its one-sided narration. She was violently temperamental, and on several occasions threw heavy objects at Casanova. She could also be petulant and jealous – but strength of character was only ever attractive to Casanova and the unlikely pair became a familiar sight along Millionnaya: the tall urbane Italian and his Russian doll.

The equilibrium of the household was jolted by the next actors to join the Casanova coterie in St Petersburg: two French chancers out to make their fortune in St Petersburg. Their real names have never been established, but Casanova remembered them as Monsieur Crèvecoeur and Mademoiselle La Riviere.

They had letters of introduction from Prince Charles Ernst in Riga, which impressed Casanova, but had arrived in the Russian capital with nothing more to recommend them; no money, no job offers and no plans but to avail themselves of all free entertainments, and to 'offer [their] charms for sale'. Casanova assured them he could not introduce them on such terms, but saw La Rivière turn her first trick in his lodgings with a bisexual German acquaintance of his called Baumbach, who happened to call. Zaïre was less impressed with 'French manners', but said if they were due to make up a party to go to the beer-gardens at Krasni-Kabak, she wanted to go too. Casanova agreed. He did so, he wrote, because he 'feared the consequences' of Zaïre's 'ill temper, tears and fits' if she was not allowed to come, so he, the two French adventurers, the Russian peasant and the German made up the party. The evening was gay, lively and drunken. Zaïre was treated as an equal, which pleased her and Casanova.

There was friendly gambling. Crèvecoeur allowed Baumbach to flirt openly with La Rivière, the woman who travelled as his mistress, but seems to have been anyone else's for the price of one of Krasni-Kabak's famous waffles and Zaïre witnessed the unexpectedly loose morals of the travelling French, whose manners she had been taught to respect.

The next night Casanova chose to leave Zaïre at home; he claims he did so because he knew Baumbach had organised a party involving several Russian officers, and wanted to avoid having Zaïre in the company of fellow Russians, speaking her language beyond his comprehension. In the light of what happened later, however, he may have been aware that Baumbach's invitation implied a further understanding of the traditions of Russian machismo and culture, for the evening seems to have been designed to devolve into an orgy. The Lunin brothers, officers in the prestigious Preobrazhensky regiment, were at the party first; they went on to great fame in the Russian army, but when Casanova met them the elder, Aleksandr, was twenty, and Pyotr Mikhailovich only seventeen. In 1765 Pyotr was 'blond and pretty as a girl'. Casanova writes that he had 'been loved by the Secretary of State Teplov and 'like an intelligent youth he not only defied prejudice he deliberately set about winning the affection and esteem of all men of position'. According to Casanova, Pyotr had already worked out that Baumbach was bisexual, and assumed that Casanova was too. He decided the well-connected Italian was worthy of his sexual-social climbing, and insisted on sitting next to him. In an episode reminiscent of his early attraction to Bellino/Teresa, Casanova began to believe – or wanted to – that Pyotr Lunin was in fact a girl masquerading as a soldier. He found himself attracted to him and declared his suspicion to the boy that he was a girl. Pyotr Lunin unbuttoned his breeches to prove the point, and put 'himself in a position to make himself and me happy'. La Rivière declared them 'buggers'; they responded that she was a 'whore'. When the elder Lunin and Baumbach came back from a walk, they had recruited two more officers – or met up with others from the regiment in some pre-planned arrangement; all four men had sex with La Rivière through the course of one long vodka-fuelled debauch. Casanova, meanwhile, and Pyotr watched 'like two virtuous older men who look on with tolerance at the extravagances of unbridled youth'. Crèvecoeur, meantime, had made himself scarce. It was an arrestingly unCasanova evening – not just for its anonymously orgiastic excess (two of the Russian officers are not even named) but for Casanova's passive voyeurism and implied preference, that night, for homosexual 'sins against nature'; his own, that is, or God's.

On his return Zaïre was wild with jealous rage. She claimed she had divined his infidelity in astrological cards, but she might as easily have heard gossip from fellow Russians of what was likely to have taken place between a gang of drunk men, a *bagnio* and La Rivière. Casanova dodged what was thrown at him, went to bed, and in the morning decided to assuage her anger, or his guilt, by taking her to Moscow. 'Those who have not seen Moscow', Casanova believed, 'cannot say that they have seen Russia.' It was an expensive trip for a man living off a diminishing store of Venetian and French credit: eighty roubles for the six-day, seven-night *Schlafwagen* trip with Zaïre. There were seventy-two stages, or changes of horses, making up, Casanova calculated, some five hundred Italian miles.

They set off in early summer – dated by Casanova's reference to the beginnings of White Nights in St Petersburg, when the end of each day was signalled by cannon fired from the Peter and Paul fortress because the sun never set. They reached Novgorod in forty-eight hours and Moscow by the end of the week.

There, Casanova found lodgings and a hire-valet, who spoke French, and went about delivering the half-dozen letters of introduction that were meant to open the doors of Moscow to him. As ever, they did. He was there as a tourist: Moscow was no longer the capital, but a mysterious throw-back to old Muscovy, heavy with bell-tolling and incense, superstitious and backward. So Casanova noted the food (plentiful but bland) the women (prettier than in St Petersburg and flirtatious) and the 'manufactories, old monuments, natural history collections, libraries . . . and the famous [Kremlin] bell'. He took Zaïre everywhere with him, happy to pass her off as his daughter, but within a week he had decided to return to St Petersburg and concentrate on an audience with the Empress and the prospect of profiting by her.

He had imagined that being a well-connected and self-educated Italian polymath would be enough to lord it over the Russians in their Franco-Italian themed capital. But he was wrong: 'In Russia, only men who are expressly sent for are regarded. Those who go there by their own choice are not esteemed. Perhaps this is right.' Meanwhile, he made sure he took in the sites of the great new building projects around St Petersburg, the imperial palaces at Tsarskoe-Selo, Peterhof, Oranienbaum, the imposing naval base of Kronstadt, and waited for the summons to the Winter Palace, which never came.

Eventually it was Count Panin, Princess Dachova's mysterious friend, who effected an introduction by the simple expedient of having Casanova loiter in the Summer Gardens, where the Empress walked on clement mornings. The gardens, on the bank of the Neva, had been designed by Peter the Great to give access to the monarch in a suitable setting and encourage metropolitan discourse in the European style, an outdoor salon where princes, nobles and the well-to-do might mingle easily 'particularly in the evening, after meals, even until midnight'. In 1765 Count Panin told Casanova that his best chance of gaining an introduction to the Tsarina would be to skulk among the Italian statues and grotto. He seems to have had plenty of time to do this, sufficient to allow him to note that many of the marbles, about half of which remain, were ludicrously mislabelled, either out of ignorance or as a Russian joke against classical pretentiousness: the sign 'Sappho' was attached to a particularly gnarled old man.

Eventually Casanova saw the royal entourage approaching –

probably on the central gravel promenade of the gardens, a long tree-lined vista. Gregori Orlov was in front and two ladies behind, one possibly Princess Dachova. Count Panin was on the Empress's right, so he doubtless pointed out the tall Italian among the curtsying crowd, and Catherine engaged him in small-talk about Russia. She was, Casanova noted, not exactly beautiful, but handsome, relatively small and stout but of direct gaze and imperial bearing, altogether the impressive autocrat of whom Voltaire had spoken to him. They conversed in French. Hers was excellent, possibly better than his, though she had her letters corrected before they were sent, especially to Voltaire. Casanova claims they spoke for an hour. This is unlikely, given Catherine's responsibilities and energy. When she mentioned that she had not seen him at her regular musical *soirées*, or *courtags*, Casanova remembered that she was well known to be bored by music: having once heard a Haydn quartet Catherine had beckoned a courtier and said, 'When somebody plays solo, I know when one ought to applaud, but I feel quite lost with the quartet . . . Please, look at me when the play of the musicians or the work of the composer needs appreciation.' The Empress would often say that music produced in her the same impression as street noise. Explaining his absence from her musical evenings, he shared with the Empress his regret that he found little pleasure in concerts. She smiled.

Thereafter, Casanova went every morning to the gardens in the hope of seeing her again. It was the fast route to preferment in imperial St Petersburg, though he was unsure what function might suit him, and became less and less keen to remain in Russia as weeks dragged into months. On the second occasion he saw her, however, Catherine signalled to one of her soldiers to bring him over. They talked about Venice, which Catherine had never visited but which she wished to include in the tour her son would undertake, semi-incognito, as 'Count of the North'. This led to a conversation about the differences between the Russian and Venetian calendars.

Casanova pounced: he had a great deal of background in

astrology and date-work from his years in Paris divining
fortuitous times and places for the superstitious Versailles
aristocrats who trusted his cabbala so he was better able than
most to discourse on the new Gregorian calendar; it reset the
dates of most of western Europe in the early eighteenth
century in accordance with new knowledge of the true length
of a year: a little more than 365 days. This was done by
knocking eleven days off the calendar, and instituting the
system of leap years. It caused riots, however, among the
superstitious, observers of saints days, and anyone who
thought their demise, and its date, pre-ordained, and felt
short-changed of eleven days of life. (One of the manuscripts
Casanova left at his death with his memoirs was a 'Rêveries
sur la mesure moyenne de notre [temps] selon la réformation
grégorienne', written nearly thirty years after his conversation
with Catherine; he was still doodling with calendar arithmetic
and making his own calculations on bisextiles and leap years
just a few years before he died.) He reminded Catherine that
Peter the Great, her father-in-law, had intended adopting the
Gregorian rather than the Julian calendar when the Russians
had abandoned the eastern Orthodox calendar, and had only
been dissuaded from doing so as it had caused riot even in
Protestant England. When Catherine rejoined that Tsar Peter
had not been wise on all subjects, he again recognised a
moment to flatter royalty and opined that he had been a
genius among men. Tellingly, it was Catherine who ended the
conversation, with the intention of continuing it when she had
had an opportunity to brief herself on the detail. She was
clearly contemplating taking Casanova's advice as another
way to stamp her mark on her country. For Catherine,
though, the balance between modernising western ideas
and the intransigence of the powerful Russian Orthodox
Church was delicate, and only skilfully manipulated. In the
end, she let go this one item of modernity for fear of a
religious backlash, not least as the Russian calendar was

barely a generation old. Casanova's dream of finding himself pensioned off as calendar-maker to the Russian court was not to be.

It was ten days later, again in the Summer Gardens, that he met the Empress again. In the interim she had been impressively briefed on the implications for the change of Easter, of the equinox, and the 'embolism of the Jews which is said to be perfect'. Easter, as in the West, was eventually to be set by the phases of the moon, and the dates changed in accordance with the movement of the earth, but none of this would sway the Russian peasants or the oligarchy from their love of the old ways in Catherine's lifetime. 'She had the pleasure of seeing me surprised and of leaving me in surprise', wrote Casanova, who 'felt sure that she had studied the subject in order to dazzle me'.

It was typical of Catherine. For her, an itinerant Italian like Casanova, whom she knew to have recently met both Frederick the Great and Voltaire, was less useful in St Petersburg than out of it. She hoped, and she was right in this, that he would talk and write of their encounter, and further burnish her image as an enlightened and educated monarch – but also one who thoroughly understood Russia. His memoirs record more than ten pages of conversation, mainly around the study of calendars, but ranging over Venice's time-keeping, and their thoughts on death. Could he have remembered such detail thirty years later? Perhaps. It seems, as with his close and verifiable detail on weather and travel costs, for instance, that he was taking notes on what might one day make a personal memoir, and he knew Catherine would be a star cameo – 'this great lady who was able to reign for thirty-five years without ever making a crucial mistake and without ever parting from moderation'.

Late in the summer of 1765 Casanova was planning his departure from St Petersburg. There was clearly to be no court appointment, and he may have been anxious not to suffer another Russian winter. He met a French actress, La Valville, who had played in J.F. Regnard's 1704 comedy *Les Folies amoureuses* for the Empress, but had not been well received. She solicited Casanova's help in securing her leave of absence from the court – a necessary request for a royally indentured actress – and suggested they travel west together. Casanova recognised a kindred spirit and wrote to her accordingly: 'I wish, Madame, to enter into a liaison with you . . . having to leave for Warsaw next month, I offer you a place in my sleeping carriage, which will cost you only the inconvenience of letting me lie beside you. I know how to obtain a passport for you.' La Valville immediately accepted.

It was necessary for foreigners such as the Chevalier de Seingalt and the actress La Valville to advertise in the *St Petersburg Gazette* their intention to leave town. This was what allowed foreigners easy credit in the city as it was impossible to evade debts and make the sea-crossing via Kronstadt or the land journey via the city's gates without official sanction. Even so, it has been impossible to identify La Valville with complete certainty, a reflection of the relatively large number of foreigners coming and going in the pursuit of their various trades.

Their arrangements complete, the police and passport checks in place – Count Alexander Galitzin delivered to Casanova a passport bearing the name of 'Graf Jacob Casanov de Farussi' and dated 1 September 1765 – Casanova engaged an Armenian travelling cook, bought a *Schlafwagen* and furnished it with mattresses and furs. La Valville laughed when she saw it 'for we were actually in a bed'. He left Zaïre in the care of the architect Reynaldi. He had decided to try his luck in Poland, and arranged for Bragadin's money to be forwarded by Papanelopulo and for various St Petersburgers to write him glowing letters to introduction to the grandees of Warsaw. He arrived there on 10 October 1765.

ACT IV SCENE VI

POLISH DUELS
1765–6

5 March 1776 5 a.m.
'My Lord, yesterday evening at the theatre you gravely insulted me, having neither the right nor justification to behave so. That being so I can and will satisfy you.'

Casanova challenges Count Branicki to a duel

'It is pleasant for a Venetian to see Casanova transformed into a hero; like a a worm who had suddenly changed into a butterfly.'

Melchiore Cesarotti

Casanova was well received in Poland: his letters of introduction to Prince Adam Czartoryski and the Anglican minister in Warsaw ensured that. Again, he sought and gained audience of the reigning monarch, King Stanislas Poniatowski, former lover of Catherine the Great. In 1765 Poland was all but a vassal state of Russia, dependent for the security of its borders and its crown on one or other of its neighbours, and in constant danger through the late eighteenth century of the partition and destruction that would later be its fate. Politics fascinated Casanova to the extent that he wished to understand the shifting power structure of Europe in the hope of turning his knowledge to account. He went on a sort of fact-finding tour of Poland, staying at the homes of the many nobles to whom in St Petersburg and Dresden he had been given letters of introduction. Countess Catherine Kossakowska at Leopold (Lemberg) gave him hospitality, as did Count Wenceslas Rzewuski and Count Franciszewski Potocki in Christianpol – forgotten names, except that they are mentioned or thanked in Casanova's *Istoria delle turbolenze della Polonia – History of the Polish Troubles* – published in 1774.

Casanova made fast progress into the Polish court and theatre. He had dreams, as before, of lottery riches, but seems to have first made money at the card tables. The King, who wanted news of the court of St Petersburg from one who had just been there, gave him his time but no work. Casanova spent his mornings at study in the library of a Monseigneur Zaluski and ate at the home of the Russian Prince Palatine, thus, he reasoned, economising and learning much. It was another sign that, as his energies and wealth subsided, he would turn more and more to his bibliophile and literary interests, partly in the hopes of literary fame but also out of unalloyed pleasure in academe. 'I read' he wrote, 'authentic documents concerning all the intrigues and secret plots whose purpose was to overthrow the entire system of Poland.'

Five months after he had arrived in Warsaw, an event took place, however, that all but ruined his fortunes in Poland, though, ironically, it assured him lasting literary fame. On 4 March he was dining at court, with the King among others, and was invited to attend the theatre to witness the two great divas of the Warsaw ballet who were due to dance in the same production. They were both, of course, known to Casanova as they were Italian, and one, Anna Binetti, may have shared his bed in London. Now she had a Polish lover, one Count Xavier Branicki, her protector. Casanova knew the courtly rules of such situations, and after the performance he went to pay his respects to both dancers, only to find Binetti fuming that she had not been visited first. She set Branicki to pick a quarrel with her old Venetian friend. He accused Casanova of being a 'coward', which only provoked Casanova to retort that the term was 'rather strong'. When he turned away,

Branicki called him, publicly, a 'Venetian poltroon'. This was too much for Casanova: he told the aristocrat that a Venetian poltroon was quite capable of killing a Pole – thus, in effect, challenging Branicki to a duel.

It was an unexpected turn of events. Although Casanova had fought duels before, they had not been a frequent occurrence in a life littered with danger. He had some skill as a swordsman, but was one to nurse deep resentments rather than resolve them with violence. Not since Count Celi in 1749 had he been called to arms. And the world had moved on since then: Branicki wanted to fight with pistols. Again, though Casanova fails to record where and when he learned to shoot, he mentions carrying pistols regularly in London and handling them in Paris during the 1750s. But he must have known he was risking life and reputation, and flouting the law by fighting with the Polish nobleman – something so shocking in class terms as to render the item newsworthy as far away as London.

The two men met at the appointed hour, and were both wounded – Branicki with shrapnel in his stomach from which, surprisingly, he recovered, and Casanova in the skin of the left arm. It could, of course, have been much worse. Casanova fled to seek refuge in a monastery outside Warsaw, and the story went almost straight to the King. Count August Moszynski, the foreign minister, was charged with investigating the alien 'aristocrat' who had broken Warsaw's strict anti-duelling laws, and his report survives to this day. First among the Chevalier de Seingalt's crimes was, of course, that he was not a knight but the son of an actress. This did great damage to him when it became public knowledge, not so much for his standing in society, where he moved with a theatre crowd anyway, but in his hope of being treated seriously by the government. He is described in the report as an intriguer and gambler.

He was falling further and further into debt. He awaited funds from Venice, some of which were travelling via St Petersburg. He saved where he could, but still kept, he notes, two servants and had to dress well to attend court. It became clear, however, fairly quickly, and especially after the duel, that he would not be able to persuade King Stanislas to support a lottery any more than he had Frederick the Great or Catherine. In the end, though, the fellow Mason charged with investigating him, Moszynski, had only sympathy for a man who had acted honourably by the codes of the day in being forced to duel, and who was living otherwise on his wits. Moszynski even loaned him a thousand ducats, which he never saw again: 'For M. Casanova. You are a man of your word. I have found you as such. May a better fate await you in the countries to which you are going, and remember that you have in me a friend. A Moszynski'. This note was found after Casanova died, along with another, attached to it: 'Having received a thousand ducats from the King of Poland when he ordered me to leave Warsaw [because of the duel] I sent his minister the bills of my creditors. He wrote me this letter and I left the same day. 8 June [actually July] 1766'.

The duel in Poland was a watershed for Casanova. It brought him both applause and notoriety and a new, not altogether welcome, fame as a dangerous and volatile presence in any city. In years to come he and Branicki became great friends and Casanova dedicated to him his 1782 work *Ne amori ne donne* (*Neither for Love nor Women*). In turning the tale of the duel, of which he was ultimately rather proud, into one of his prize anecdotes Casanova became convinced that one day he should publish.

He was briefly lionised. As a literary figure who had also acted out some of the quixotic ideals of the age, he turned heads, and this was not just the case in Poland. He was described at this time as 'a man known in the world of letters, a man of profound knowledge'. Which was precisely how he had always wanted to be regarded – outside the bedroom that is. Unfortunately, of course, he still had no real source of income, and less of an idea of where he was heading in life. But that he had taken on an old-world aristocrat in a game he was not meant to play, and stood his ground, impressed many as the tale spread through the salons of Europe where he was known. He had been cruelly exposed in so doing as the mere son of an actress, but had achieved a sort of self-generated nobility that was itself in the spirit of the age. The undercurrents of resentment that would sweep away the old order – from which Casanova, it should be said, still strove to profit – were stirring. Abbé Tartuffi, an Italian cleric in Warsaw at the same time, saw Casanova briefly as a sort of hero, but not for long. As he wrote to the Paduan poet Melchiore Cesarotti:

It is a pity that the illustrious Casanova, formerly a hero and fictitious nobleman and, above all, a so-called wit, had not had the ability to sustain his great role . . . shortly after his brilliant feat, some unfortunate anecdotes from his past, well authenticated, faded his laurels; wonder was replaced by contempt, . . . There, in consequence, is our glorious butterfly, transformed suddenly into the state of a worm.'

END OF ACT IV

CASANOVA – FOOD-WRITER

'He carries three small pieces of paper with him [at all times] that allow him to write comfortably whenever he desires.'

The Venetian Inquisition remarks on Casanova, writer

'I am insatiable . . . always questioning, curious, demanding, intolerable.'

Casanova, to Crébillon

C asanova was a highly original writer, in both the historical and literary sense. There is nothing else quite like the *History of My Life* from his period, and in some respects it is a one-off: a work of resounding singularity by virtue of the unique experiences, and unselfconscious frankness of its author. One aspect that is particularly refreshing is Casanova's writing about food: an example of his inclusive approach to social history as well as, of course, a simple statement of personal interest. He loved to eat. Later in his life friends noted with concern his gargantuan appetite on the increasingly rare occasions when good food was available. It was one of the last sensual pleasures left to him as his health declined.

But his interest in food has given Casanova a place in the history of gastronomy. He is an invaluable source on what was eaten across Europe at a time when few were bothering to record such. If his gourmet's guide was almost always interrupted by his romantic intrigues, food was nonetheless a vivid colour in his memory. There is a sad and heartfelt note that somehow survived in Dux castle from late in Casanova's life with a recipe, in effect, for Venetian, perhaps Buranese, biscuits. He claimed they were good for his digestion. In truth it was soul-food for an old man: '. . . these are the biscuits that I long to eat,' he wrote, 'soaked in wine, to fortify the stomach . . . composed of a little flour, an egg yolk and a lot of sugar . . .'

Like Don Giovanni in da Ponte's libretto, Casanova barely distinguished between the love of food and of women. He used the language of love and sex to describe food and vice versa. 'For men,' he wrote, 'sex is like eating and eating is like sex: it is nourishment . . . and just as there is always a different pleasure in trying different sauces [*ragoûts*] so it is in the game of love/orgasm [*la jouissance amoureuse*]. Though the effect might seem the same at first, one learns that every woman is a unique experience.' 'The sense of smell,' Casanova was likewise fond of saying, 'plays no small part in the pleasures of Venus.' Perhaps it was this eagerness to taste all life's pleasures, and Casanova's uninhibited confidence in recalling them in prose, that has made him such a first-rate food writer. At every inn, capital city, ballroom or *ridotto*, he recalls in his memoirs what he put into his mouth, from the omelette he was greeted with when he first saw Rome, Parisian ices, London's beer, oysters in Naples, imported from the Venetian Arsenale, to Corfu comfits. He never set out on the road without thinking of his stomach and even suggested packing a roast hare as companion-able finger food.

This may bear witness to careful note-taking in the first place: a diary of consumption and appetite that pre-dates the *History* and has been lost. But it may instead evidence a singularly sensory and sensual memory, and the parsimony of flavours on offer to him in old age. Casanova was reliving the tastes and smells of his past. The *History of My Life*, as a result, records more than two hundred meals, at least twenty different wines from all over Europe, many dozens of foodstuffs and otherwise lost gastronomic arcania, such as the availability of macaroni in

Louis XV's Paris, polenta in Bohemia, gnocchi in Venetian prisons, the cost of a hundred oysters in Rome and the vodka and orgeat at Catherine the Great's Winter Palace.

In his youth, Casanova lived through the last great age of Venetian cooking, the last florescence of a unique melting-pot of cultural influences: the fulcrum of the original spice routes. Casanova sprinkled his pasta – probably rather like spaghetti, though he also ate macaroni – with cinnamon and sugar, as would have been the case in the late middle ages, a style that is long forgotten even in the more remote and unspoilt islands of the lagoon and was seen nowhere else in Europe.

On his first visit to France, aged twenty-five, he was struck with the semi-public royal residence the Palais Royal not yet the site of restaurants as it would become later in the century, but by its cornucopia of choice for the discerning drinker: ratafia, a fruit liqueur, orgeat, the barley and almond cordial, popular in Georgian London also, and bavaroise, sweet stewed tea thickened with egg yolk, milk and kirsch. All were offered to him, as well as coffee, '*au lait*', though it was served in the morning only, *never* after meals. His Parisian friend Patu took him to the Civette tobacco shop, opposite what became the Café de la Regence. Here his memoir becomes almost a modern guide to the delights of Parisian café society – he even notes the cane chairs – with the additional information that his French friend knew by name not just the cafés and their signature dishes but the 'light' ladies of the Palais Royal, who plied their trade in rooms above.

In London, Casanova was at once wildly impressed by British produce, and somewhat less so by the ability of chefs to deal with it. He reasoned that the British cooked meat simply because they had such an abundance of it, but London innkeepers concentrated on the meat of the matter at the expense of other courses – English meals were like eternity, he complained: they had no 'beginning or end'. His French-educated palate missed soup, which London taverns in the 1760s considered an effete Parisian extravagance.

Casanova employed a French chef in Pall Mall and ate at home a good deal. Nevertheless, he praised the simple bread and butter, tea and lemonade at Ranelagh Rotunda. He noted that the *bagnios* of London – the brothels of St James's that pre-figured the gentlemen's clubs later in the century – served excellent food, as part of the all-in sex deal. Inevitably, perhaps, he admired Italian food more than any other, especially Nea-politan cuisine. 'Everything [there] is delicious; greenstuff, all the products of the dairy, red meat, veal, even the flour, from Sorrento, which gives all the pastries their specific flavour . . . ices flavoured with lemon, and chocolate, and with coffee and pot cheeses more delicious than can be imagined.'

Casanova linked sex, food and smell constantly in his writing: 'I have always found the one I was in love with smelled good . . . and the more copious her sweat, the sweeter I found it,' he observed, and went on in the same sentence to his opinion that cheeses only reach perfection 'when the little creatures which inhabit them become visible'. It was a different olfactory age – richly, or revoltingly, more vivid than our own. The most erotic passages of the *History* are larded with descriptions of food. Casanova's seduction of the nun M.M., or hers of him, is punctuated with more detail on what they eat than of their sexual acts:

I commented to her on all the food but I found everything excellent; game, sturgeon, truffles, oysters, and perfect wines. I only reproached [the cook] with having forgotten to set out hard-boiled eggs, anchovies and prepared vinegars on a dish, to make a salad . . . I also said I wanted to have bitter oranges to give flavour to the punch and that I wanted rum not arrack.

This on a night when he knew he would be making love to a highly experienced voluptuary. On another occasion he put hair from a lover's locket into sweets they could eat in their love-making, finding a Jewish confectioner who would make comfits of 'sugar combined with essences of ambergris, angelica, vanilla, alkermes and styrax' and ground hair. Few lovers can have gone to quite such lengths to make a recipe of romance. Later he poured the lot into his mouth, in his lover's presence, yet somehow managed to enunciate that he would die if she did not kiss him. Food was part of the *mise-en-scène* of any seduction, and his memory of it.

On aphrodisiacs, he is surprisingly unspecific. He had the usual confidence of the age in chocolate – one of his favourite drinks – coffee and champagne. He may be the originator of the reputation of oysters as an aphrodisiac. He gives one clear recipe, as it were, for long lovemaking, warning one mistress that he was in danger of exploding with desire because he had eaten 'a cup of chocolate and the whites of six fresh eggs . . . in a salad dressed with Lucca oil and Four Thieves vinegar'. These egg whites, Casanova had been given to believe, would allow him to ejaculate forcefully five or six times. To ease his discomfort and test the aphrodisiac's efficacy his compliant muse offered to relieve him of his first 'egg white' with her able manual assistance. His more famous advice, from the same love affair, that no sauce better suits an oyster than the saliva of one's lover, was replayed in a number of his seductions, and as an element of his sex-education games with younger women. 'There is no more lascivious and voluptuous game . . . it is comic but the comedy does no harm.' They laughed, they ate, they kissed and they fell into his arms. The game, he explained, involved passing living molluscs from mouth to mouth, then eating them off breasts and other body parts. This is not to be tried in restaurants.

He recalled the first M.M., possibly his most adventurous and also most food-obsessed lover, enjoying a dish cooked by de Bernis's French chef. To please her he determined to learn how to cook it; 'The cook, who was called du Rosier, became my friend . . . the dish was called the Françiade,' he explained. He did not, frustratingly, tell us what the recipe was. In similar vein he makes note of the preference of Louis XV's queen for chicken fricassée – in an age when the French royal family were obliged to eat stiffly in public with the grandees of Versailles reduced to waiting staff. He does not explain what was so special about it.

Could Casanova cook? By the evidence of his own hand, only poorly and simply: he was more a man to direct a chef than be one. He did make an omelette for Giustiniana, but he was more likely to instruct an innkeeper or chef in what he wanted: a *chevalier* would not cook. He instructed an Italian on the making of English 'blancpudding' – blancmange possibly, or perhaps some form of 'white pudding' sausage – for young Betty from Hammersmith, a recipe he must have picked up in London in 1763. He believed in dressing and ordering a table before an important and planned seduction, and does this on a number of occasions, recalling the details of what was eaten as part of the foreplay in his mind's-eye. However, among his papers he left a seven-page collection of recipes, which he had assembled on his travels. In the style of the period, it mixes medical prescriptions, travellers' advice, astrology and chemistry with food – it even includes advice on how to clean paintings and a recipe for tooth-whitening. This item, with the note for a 'travelling stove, Italian seasoning and cooking pot', was a prerequisite for the road and gives an unexpectedly self-sufficient new-man image to Casanova the gadabout lover.

His little acknowledged position as a leading gourmet and also one of the eighteenth century's most varied sources as a social historian of food belies other vital truths. By framing almost every erotic and romantic encounter, and many that were merely sociable, in the context of food Casanova reveals himself as a dedicated sensualist with a need to reaffirm his own existence, and his memory of it, in the realm of tastes. His apparent sexual compulsion may be explained then less by appetite and opportunity as by a damaged or hungering psyche that found balm only in companionable sensuality.

ACT FIVE

IL TRAVIATO, THE WANDERER

1766–70

'These are the handsomest moments in my lifestory; these happy, unexpected, unforeseeable and purely fortuitous remeetings . . . and hence all the more precious.'

Casanova

He went on from Warsaw to Dresden to see his mother, then to Vienna and Augsburg. There he intended to lobby for a position with the Elector of Mannheim, through a friend he had made in Paris in 1757, Count Maximilian Lamberg, whose many letters to Casanova over the ensuing year survive in the Prague Archive. It would increasingly be Casanova's pattern to rely less on impressionable aristocratic women and the cabbala than on men like Lamberg who were literary enthusiasts and Freemasons. But his last years as a wanderer were in the almost operatic tradition of one who has lost his way: a traveller and lost soul, a *traviato*.

He travelled on to Cologne, Aix-la-Chapelle and Spa, where the watering season of 1767 saw him taking the cure from August until September. His own account of the season is matched by the souvenirs he seems to have kept for nostalgic reasons and are still in the Prague Archive: shop cards, lists of society names in town and calling cards. More than two thousand curistes visited Spa annually in the 1760s, drinking the waters rather than bathing in them. They were there as much to gamble and socialise as for their health, as they did in Baden Baden, Aix-les-Bains, Karlsbad, Teplice and Bath; the profits from the gambling went in part to the Prince Bishop of Liège, whose jurisdiction covered the town. Casanova knew many of the gamblers and promenaders, the shifting crowd who flitted between in Paris, Dresden, Rome and Spa.

A former acquaintance, the Marquis della Croce, was there, no longer with the Mademoiselle Crosin whom Casanova had once escorted south to Marseille and beyond, but another young mistress, Charlotte Lamotte. Croce lost all his money at the gaming tables, and even gambled away Charlotte's jewels, leaving her, penniless and pregnant, in the care of a man he had known before to befriend women in distress. Casanova took her back to Paris to have her child. Croce was right that he would look after her: he nursed her through her confinement, and was at her bedside when she died in childbirth.

After her funéral, which he attended alone, Casanova received bad news from Venice. Bragadin had died; his friend Dandolo sent his bequest of a thousand *écus*, but Casanova's long financial support was over.

Such things are known to come in threes. Possibly at the instigation of the family of the Marquise d'Urfé, but just as likely at the behest of his creditors, Casanova received a *lettre de cachet* signed by Louis XV. This amounted to temporary banishment from France, which had been Casanova's home for a decade. He was given forty-eight hours to leave Paris.

The Duc de Choiseul, long-time partner in financial affairs and a friend of de Bernis, arranged passage for Casanova across the Pyrenees to Spain, with letters of introduction from the Princess Lubomirska and the Marquis de Caraccioli to various Spanish government ministers.

Casanova travelled via Bordeaux, crossing the Pyrenees to Pamplona by mule. He had sufficient funds to travel with a great quantity of books, which he regretted at the border where they were confiscated. He arrived in Madrid via the Alcala gate and found lodgings on the Calle de la Cruz. He went almost immediately to the head of the Spanish government, the Conde d'Aranda, who bore him no ill will although he held legitimately the title that Casanova's ward Joseph Cornelys had used. Despite his lack of credentials, career, money or background, Casanova nevertheless suggested himself for employment with the Spanish government at the highest level. He was, understandably, rebuked by the Spanish prime minister and told he should address himself, if anywhere, to the Venetian embassy; he was rejected with the same reasonable response by the Spanish Duque de Lossada.

When he approached one Gaspar Soderini, secretary to the Venetian ambassador Mocenigo, Soderini, too, claimed to be aghast at Casanova's impudence – was he not a fugitive from Venetian justice? – and laughed in his face. Casanova pointed out coolly that he was not asking to be presented to the representative of the Venetian *Inquisition* but the Venetian *State*, with which he had no quarrel. Dandolo was working on his behalf in Venice, and won for him an admission a few weeks later that Venice had no further quarrel with him, even if the Inquisition did, and that he should be extended all courtesies while in Spain.

So began Casanova's Spanish sojourn and his entry into Madrid's social life, exotic for its blend of the erotically charged and the repressed. The Holy Office, or Inquisition, permeated all aspects of life. There was a thriving theatre scene, but the lower portions of the boxes had been removed so that the Inquisition's spies could keep an eye on everyone's legs. There was riotous music and opera, but actors and orchestra were obliged to fall to their knees if the shout '*Dios!*' went up, signifying the passing of a religious procession. And Spanish women, Casanova remembered, would cover religious images in their bedrooms with their veils before they took him to their beds.

On 17 January 1768, St Anthony's Day, Casanova attended a mass at the Church of the Soledad on the Calle Fuencarral and followed a girl home from the confessional to ask her father, who turned out to be a bootmaker, for permission to take her to a ball. This was the way to do things, Casanova explained in the *History*, in Madrid. Her name was Donna Ignazia, and she became the object of his attentions while he was in Spain. She and her father negotiated her terms as a courtesan through Casanova's Spanish page. However, Donna Ignazia was a truly pious Catholic who seemed to have little grasp, at least initially, of what was being asked of her by her father and the Venetian. At first she agreed to dance the fandango, new to Casanova, with her supposed lover, 'so voluptuously', Casanova wrote, 'that she could not have promised me everything more eloquently in words'. But for a long time she would go no further. She and Casanova developed a strong affection for each other, but it was an arduously fought affair that was never, to his way of thinking, properly consummated.

Waiting for royal favour, after he had courted diplomatic good grace, Casanova inevitably fell into financial difficulties. As ever he was living beyond his means in an increasingly ill-reasoned attempt to impress those in positions of power that he deserved to join them. Also he was found to have hidden pistols, which was against the law in Madrid. He fled to the home of the court painter Raphael Mengs, his brother's friend whom he had met in Rome seven years previously but was arrested on 20 February 1768.

Casanova spent only two days in the Buen Retiro prison, but he was shaken – by his memories of The Leads as much as the lack of any real charge against him. The Spanish government apologised and made financial amends, but he became ill – he claimed he had a fever, but it may have been a further attack of the syphilitic infection from London or elsewhere. He missed Easter Sunday mass, too ill in bed at Mengs's house to accept an invitation to join the court and diplomatic corps at Aranjuez; as a result his name was posted by the Inquisition as a likely atheist, and Mengs was obliged to ask him to leave.

Casanova was furious – not with the Inquisition but with Mengs. He got out of bed and made his way to Aranjuez church, confessed his sins publicly and proclaimed himself a Catholic. He never forgave the painter, but later, back in Rome, Mengs explained that he, too, had been under surveillance by the Spanish Inquisition, which suspected him of being a closet Protestant.

Ambassador Mocenigo offered Casanova introductions and invitations. Casanova ate at the Venetian embassy and there impressed Pablo Olivades that he might be the man to help the Spanish government with its plan to colonise the Spanish Sierra Morena with Catholic Swiss and Germans. He ended up loitering in Spain on the prospect of being part of this scheme, but it came to nothing. His entrepreneurial zeal seemed emboldened as the years passed, but less and less came to fruition. He continued to claim expertise in the silk industry, though his business in Paris had failed and the Venetians, like the Russians, had spurned his ideas on dyeing and on mulberry plantations. He proposed a tobacco factory in Madrid and had a soap factory in Warsaw, but nothing was backed with capital or application. Casanova sought to dazzle, which is only intermittently an ingredient in business success.

Through all of this, he was never out of contact with his literary friends and ambitions, which took up much of his time and energy. He and the court chapel master in Madrid collaborated on ideas for a new opera with an Italian libretto that Casanova eventually wrote. But he left Madrid under a cloud of gossip and indiscretion. He let slip that a young procurer of male prostitutes to the Venetian ambassador who called himself Conte Manuzzi was in fact the son of a lowly

Inquisition spy, Casanova's nemesis, Giovanni Manuzzi. Casanova earned the everlasting opprobrium of Manuzzi *fils* for this hypocritical and unnecessary indiscretion – neither was precisely what he purported to be – and left for Valencia, then Barcelona late in 1768.

Here, he got into deeper trouble. Set upon by two men, who may have been employed to rob or even murder him, Casanova drew his sword and killed one. He was imprisoned for forty-two days, during which letters seem to have been circulating, several of which have only recently come to light, that colluded to brand him a liar, fraudster and thief. In large part, the whispering campaign was orchestrated by Giacomo Passano, his former co-conspirator and secretary in the protracted d'Urfé affair. Passano had written to Teresa Cornelys in London, to the Marchese della Pietra in Genoa, to Count Ricla, captain general of Catalonia in Barcelona, and to Joseph Bono, Casanova's friend in Lyon, either to blacken his name or, in Pietra's case, to persuade him to instigate a law suit against Casanova. Passano's animus was extreme, and Casanova knew in part he was to blame. The mixed charges, however, of circulating invalid bills of exchange and failing to honour gambling debts, were damaging to an itinerant player like Casanova, and unlikely to be true: though Casanova had owed money for many years, he would not have been foolish enough to renege on a gambling debt in the small world of trans-European travellers.

Passano was animated by his bitter dislike of Casanova and the sense that he had been duped in the ostensibly profitable d'Urfé affair. In this he was right. Casanova had made many thousands of *livres* from the d'Urfé estate, while his co-conspirators had received what amounted to minor expenses. He tried for some months to leave Spain, needing a passport both from the new Venetian ambassador, Querini, and from the Spanish authorities, who issued such, as was the case in Russia, to prevent foreigners leaving the country with substantial debts.

His crime was judged justifiable in self-defence – one theory is that the attackers were in the pay of the Spanish or Barcelona authorities, not Passano's – and Casanova received the papers he needed to leave Spain.

They came, however, devoid of all mention of his real or supposed titles, without even the accord, from Venice, of 'Monsieur'. Rootless, stateless and without status, he travelled on to Perpignan, Narbonne, Béziers and Montpellier – where he met again a former lover Mademoiselle Blasin, now happily married – and went on to the sanctuary of the literary household of the Marquis d'Argens in Aix-en-Provence where he recuperated for four months.

In the first few months of 1769 Casanova seems to have suffered a second major breakdown akin to that in London. He stayed at an inn on the rue Quatre Dauphins, occasionally visiting or being visited by d'Argens, who loaned him books, and observing the comings and goings of clerics to the papal conclave: his old acquaintance Clement XIII, had died on 2 February and several cardinals passed through *en route* to the Vatican. Casanova's malaise may have been exhaustion or another recurrence of the syphilis that was slowly attacking his system – he refers to this period as his 'great illness' and the mercury treatment as 'the great cure'. It may instead have been a fever or pleurisy, as he wrote.

In his occasional delirium he was attended by a nurse. He assumed she had been summoned by the inn keeper but it turned out that Henriette had sent her. They had been aware of each other's presence in the little town – 'I constantly thought of Henriette, already knowing her real name, and I was always expecting to see her at some town gathering, at which I would have played towards her whatever role she wanted of me.'

Meanwhile he settled into the comfortable world of the little Aix boarding-house. D'Argens visited him as he recuperated – formerly the director of the Academy of Sciences in Berlin, and well known in Frederick the Great's household, he counselled Casanova about academic sinecures and writing.

It was only as Casanova was leaving Aix for Marseille that he decided to visit Henriette. He stopped at the Croix d'Or on the Aix–Marseille road, and found his way with his coachman back to the château where in 1763 he had been taken in after breaking down nearby with Marcolina. He knocked on the door. It was answered by the woman who had nursed him in Aix – Henriette's housekeeper. She said that her mistress, by coincidence, was in Aix at her townhouse, which told Casanova that she could have met him easily if she had so wished. Out of pride, or discretion, he decided not to chase her. He wrote to her, leaving the letter with the housekeeper, and an address in Marseille to which she might reply. When she wrote, it appeared that they had been in the same company in Aix, but Casanova, twenty years after they had last made love, had not recognised her:

Nothing my dear old friend is more from the pages of romance than that we should all but meet six years ago at my house and now [this] after twenty-two years and Geneva. We have both aged. Will you believe that, though I still love you, I am very glad that you did not recognise me? It is not that I have become ugly, but putting on weight has changed my face, I know. I am a widow, happy, and rich enough to offer to help you [if you need.] Do not come back to Aix . . . for your return might lead to gossip . . . If you would like to write, I shall do all I can to regularly reply . . . I promise [this] now that you have given me such strong proofs of your discretion . . . Farewell.

For several decades, Casanova claimed, they exchanged letters, which do not survive in the Prague Archive. Perhaps he did exactly as he had always done with Henriette and protected her name and reputation by destroying them before he died. At least with Henriette, Casanova was, as she had stated, 'the most honourable of men'. Alternatively, the letters had never existed.

At about this time, after fourteen years in exile, Casanova began to think increasingly of returning to Venice. According to the Inquisition files he had been courting official approval in Venice since at least the late 1750s. His industrial espionage had not impressed the authorities so he chose to conflate his literary and political ambitions by writing a polemic. He had already been working on the modern political history of Poland and a translation of *The Iliad*, but put them aside in favour of a treatise on Venetian government, much satirised at the time, and structured as a response to Amelot de la Houssaie's 1676 *Histoire du gouvernement de Venise*. This seems to have kept him busy as early as his imprisonment in Spain, and he discussed it with d'Argens in Aix and frequently, by letter, with a regular correspondent Gariba de la Perouse, who offered to subscribe in advance to fifty copies. He solicited more subscriptions – the expected route towards publication – and found some at the home of Sir William Lynch, the British consul in Turin, when he arrived there in the autumn of 1769 via Antibes, Nice and Piedmont. The issue began to press of where to print the *Confutazione*, as it became known, and Casanova and his sponsors settled on Lugano 'where there was a good press and no censorship'.

The memoirs – almost the handwriting itself – show that Casanova's spirits lifted with the prospect of publication. It was an ambitious work, and he took an interest in everything from paper to typeface. In three volumes, eventually, it sold out its first printing. 'My purpose in printing this work', Casanova was categoric, 'was to earn a pardon from the Venetian State Inquisitors. After travelling from one end of Europe to the other, I was so overcome by a longing to return to my native country that it seemed to me I could no longer live anywhere else.' Although, point by point, he argues in favour of the Venetian way of government, when Amelot had described it as medieval and obscurantist, this irony cannot have been lost on him. He sent a copy to Venice in December 1769 with Signor

Berlendis, the Venetian minister in Turin. The Venetian political establishment made no response.

Casanova was forced to look for more immediate financial prospects. From the British consul, Lynch, he garnered a letter of introduction to Sir John Dick, British consul at Livorno, and set off for the town in January 1770 hoping to work with Count Alexis Orlov. Orlov, a friend of Casanova's from St Petersburg, and brother of Catherine the Great's former lover, Prince Orlov, was there to amass a Russian fleet to attack the Ottomans in the Black Sea. Orlov remembered the intellectually adventurous Venetian from Petersburg's Summer Gardens. He offered to take Casanova east with the fleet, unpaid, as a writer and observer. Casanova declined the invitation. He could no longer afford adventure for its own sake. There was still no word from Venice.

He travelled on to Florence, where his presence was noted in the *Gazette*. He demanded a retraction from the editor of their statement that he was a Venetian nobleman, more evidence that he was frantic to solicit good favour in the Doge's palace: 'We described in the last *Gazzetta* [a certain] Sig Giacomo Casanova di S. Gallo [*sic*] a Venetian nobleman. We must state the person mentioned has come in person to tell us that he is Venetian but not noble, declaring that he had never attributed this quality to himself.'

He journeyed on through Pisa, Parma, Bologna, and Siena, seemingly with Rome as a final destination. He was several weeks in Siena, where, as was increasingly his habit, he sought out the local libraries and archives, and worked briefly with Abbé Chiacheri, librarian at Siena University. He spent time with the anatomist Tabarrini and they exchanged books, with the bluestocking Marchesa Chigi and a Conte Piccolomini, famous for not speaking during six months of the year to free his mind so that he could write. And he was entertained by two sisters famed for their ability to improvise classical verse. It was intellect in women that increasingly attracted him, far more than any physical attributes, but at the same time he noted ruefully that he had spent a long period without a lover.

Henriette was not the only person to note that Casanova, now in his mid-forties, had aged. The Conte de la Perouse in Turin and the Chevalier Raiberti had also told him so, as had Mademoiselle Crosin in Marseille. He had been a vain man, and a dandy in his time, and it hurt. His skin, commented upon throughout his life as dark by the fashions of the time, was becoming lined, he had not quite the vigour – sexual and otherwise – that had typified his earlier years and the decline in the former, which had been his one unshakeable solace in harsh times, became a major psychological blow as the years went by.

On the road to Rome in the early summer of 1770 that was briefly to change. As he wrote, travelling in a small vehicle over Europe's roads was a fast way to adventures of all varieties. The young woman with him was English. By coincidence, she had been at school in Hammersmith with Casanova's daughter, Sophie Cornelys, so he had news of Sophie while subtly omitting to explain why he wanted it. Betty, the English girl, was not the wife of the man she was travelling with, that much Casanova soon guessed, to he courted her all the way to Rome. They had Sophie in common, whom Betty had loved at school. Casanova claimed only distant kinship, saying the resemblance, between himself and the girl, which was startling, was a fluke. In Casanova's favour, too, was the bad behaviour of Betty's travelling beau, d'Étoiles, who left a trail of destruction in his wake, supposedly riding in front to assure them meals and accommodation but more often getting into fist-fights with inn staff. When Betty confessed that he was also violent with her, Casanova was won over – but still needed to convince her that d'Étoiles was worthless. He did this by offering him a wager that he would never let Casanova sleep with Betty. D'Étoiles accepted, then tried to convince Betty to sleep with Casanova. Betty was insulted and stayed in Casanova's room out of hurt pride. In the morning d'Étoiles had absconded with Casanova's valuable portfolio of travelling documents and bills of exchange.

Later Casanova won her, but the affair, satisfying though it was, taught him new lessons in the art of love on the road. He accepted with regret that he had to play the role of Betty's father in public for fear that others might assume he was her pimp. He does not refer directly to the clear generation gap and her association with his daughter, but Betty described her former protector in Livorno to Casanova as 'old – like you', which Casanova recalled with a flinch. He noted also that their one night in bed together was a reminder to him of his singular passion not for sex *per se* – he had had brief encounters earlier that year – but for *affairs*. Not since Ignazia in Spain had his heart and mind been engaged at the same time as his libido.

Casanova was reunited with his precious portfolio and Betty was reunited with her English baronet, Sir B. Miller – who forgave her indiscretion with d'Étoiles and was left in ignorance of her indiscretion with Casanova – and they travelled on together to Rome. Miller and Casanova had a mutual friend in Lord Baltimore, whom Casanova had not seen since London in 1763. Baltimore was in Rome *en route* to Naples, just as Miller, Betty and Casanova arrived. Casanova, always happy to accept an invitation and always happy to go to Naples, agreed to travel on south with the three Britons even though his affair with Betty had ended, and, unusually, he would be unable to dominate the conversation: despite his year in London, he had never bothered to learn English.

ACT V SCENE II

PAPAL KNIGHT AND OYSTER-EATER

1770–74

'I said I should be very sorry to suppress my desires . . . indeed I
cultivate them . . . Emelia said that anything so delicious must
be a sin, because the taste was so delicious . . . And our Lord
Pope does not forbid it?'

Casanova, of oysters, 1770

Neapolitan society had always been good to Casanova, and
rarely more so than in the summer of 1770. Half the
population of every salon he attended seem to have encountered
him elsewhere in Europe. Abate de Gama was there from Turin,
and Agathe, former mistress to Lord Hugh Percy but now
married to a Neapolitan lawyer. Ange Goudar was there, his
some time friend from London who, indeed, had later introduced Lord Baltimore to La Charpillon; he had enjoyed favours
denied to Casanova, favours by 1770 enjoyed instead by John
Wilkes.

Goudar had married Sarah, an Irish barmaid he had met in
London who now passed herself off as a cultivated musical
prodigy. In that, she and Casanova had something in common
and became friends. Casanova gambled a little with Goudar,
'who supported himself and his wife with gambling'; Casanova

seems to have won – he was able to pay twenty Neapolitan ducatis, or eighty French francs, back rent for a student singer called Agathe Carrara known as La Callimena, and her aunt. It was a typical Casanova gesture.

Meanwhile, through his many former London-based friends then in Naples he became briefly part of the British expatriate crowd. He dined often at the elegant table of Sir William Hamilton – not yet married to the more famous Emma – whose *soirées* included Casanova's friends from the past, among them Elizabeth Chudleigh the former Lady Hervey, now the Duchess of Kingston. They were invited to the King of Naples's property at the foot of Vesuvius by Michele Imperiali, Prince of Montena and Fancaville, who entertained them royally, in all the usual manners, with the added spectacle of a gaggle of royal pages persuaded to swim naked for the guests' delectation. The Duchess of Kingston was said to be thrilled. Not to be outdone, Casanova swam in the same pool when challenged; 'It nearly killed me,' he later wrote.

The last of Casanova's fortune – or the Marquise d'Urfé's – was dissipated in and around Naples in 1770, mainly on Agathe Carrara and her family. Unlike many of Casanova's previous 'dancers' and 'singers', she seems to have had real talent, which Casanova was keen to foster, though this cost her her virginity and him the settling of her entire family's debts. It was a classic arrangement of the time between a female performer and an aristocratic sponsor. Except Casanova was neither aristocratic nor rich. The jewels he had once given to another Agathe, one-time mistress of Lord Hugh Percy and now Signora Orcivolo, found their way back into his purse. She and her husband had realised his impecuniosity and she seems to have given him the impression that Casanova was her godfather. With these jewels, which amounted to over 15,000 *livres*' worth of transportable currency, Casanova started planning to go north to Rome. But not before he had visited his beloved Anna Maria and their daughter Leonilda.

In the years since he had last seen them, and made a play for Leonilda before he knew she was his daughter, Leonilda had prospered. She had married a marchese, and she and her mother lived in some style at a large country estate reminiscent in Casanova's mind of the gardens of Frascati where Leonilda had been conceived. When Anna Maria found that he was in Naples, she invited him to visit their daughter and her husband.

For the second time in her short life – she was still only twenty – Leonilda was with a man who was all but impotent. The old Marchese de C., as Casanova was obliged to title him (Anna Maria, Leonilda, and Leonilda's later son, another Marchese de C., were alive when he was writing in the late 1780s), was gout-ridden. He was unable to stand when his young wife introduced him to the Chevalier de Seingalt. Leonilda, Casanova noted, had grown several inches, but had lost none of her girlish impet-uousness – she ran into Casanova's arms. The marchese kissed him on the mouth, which surprised him only because, he wrote, Freemasonry was uncommon in that part of Italy among the nobility of that generation.

Casanova and Anna Maria reaffirmed their friendship, and discussed their concern for their daughter. Though Leonilda had married well, and Anna Maria had profited by it, she feared her daughter was unhappy: she wanted a child and a lover. The old marchese was a nervous occasional lover, so he would perhaps be persuaded to believe that child was his. Anna Maria and Casanova must have remembered a young woman in Frascati in similar circumstances.

They walked in the gardens, mother, daughter and Casanova. It was a hot day, but there were shady arbours and a cold spring that cooled the house. It was, indeed, much like Aldobrandim gardens of Frascati. All three seem to have been complicit in what happened next.

We went down to a grotto where, as soon as we were alone, we surrendered to the pleasures of calling each other 'father' and 'daughter' which gave us the right to pleasures, which, though imperfect, were sinful nonetheless . . . [Anna Maria] warned us to restrain ourselves and . . . not to be led into consummating our mutual crime but, so saying, went to another part of the garden . . . but her words, following her departure, had the opposite effect . . . Determined to consummate our so-called crime we came so close to it that an almost involuntary movement forced us to consummate it . . . completely . . . We remained motionless, looking at each other without changing our positions, both of us serious and silent, lost in reflection, astonished, as we told each afterwards, to feel neither guilty nor tormented by remorse.

It is one of the more astonishing episodes in the memoirs, and an almost unique confession of incest. It is given a specific contextual background: Leonilda's need for a child, Anna Maria's interest in finding her the most discreet lover, and mitigated, arguably, by contemporary values – the lack of seriousness attached to incest in some church circles, the lack of privacy in family life. But incest it remained. In the sad downward trajectory of the second half of Casanova's life, his affair with Leonilda stands out as a brief moment of erotic happiness, coloured, perhaps, by a desire to recapture his and Anna Maria's youth and to explore all bundaries of intimacy and of taste.

What began as merely shocking soon became farcical. Casanova, his sexual confidence rekindled in the most unorthodox manner, began a serious flirtation with Anna Maria's maid, Anastasia. It was a smokescreen. Everyone, including the old marchese, teased them about it, especially after Anastasia confided in Leonilda that their middle-aged guest was making passes at her. 'Appetite,' as Casanova pointed out 'grows with eating', and he found himself keeping Anastasia happy at night, and meeting Leonilda 'only two or three more times' in the garden. He was back to his old self, and everyone, briefly, was happy. Naturally it could not last. The old marchese was aware that Casanova's fortune was much depleted, that he was Leonilda's father, (the Duke of Matalona had told him so) and of the marriage portion Casanova had bestowed on her years earlier, through Anna Maria. He offered it back to Casanova, all five thousand ducats, and Casanova accepted. It was his cue to leave.

He travelled back to Rome via Monte Cassino in the blistering September of 1770. He had money in his pocket and a spring in his step, despite having to leave two women he loved.

A few weeks later, Leonilda discovered she was pregnant.

Setting up house in Rome across the Piazza di Spagna where he had lived in 1745 and stayed in 1760, 'in a pretty apartment with a view of the Spanish embassy', Casanova soon set about his conquest of local society. He was back on form. He achieved a rare and unusual seduction of his landlady's daughter, Margherita Poletti, by buying her a false eye from a British oculist in Rome, John Taylor, who had served George III. In late-night talks in Casanova's bedroom, she confessed to having lost her virginity to a young tailor, who lived nearby, in the presence of another teenage girl. It was a familiar tale to Casanova, who had had his first sexual experiences in similar circumstances. He set up rendezvous with Margherita, her girlfriend Virginia Buonaccorsi and their seducer, Marcuccio. He enjoyed the intrigue and, increasingly, he liked to watch. Aged forty-five, Casanova became entangled in a promiscuous *ménage à quatre* that he found exciting as much on account of young Marcuccio, and perhaps his memories of C.C. and M.M., Nanetta and Marta, as in any participation on his part: 'Loving both [girls]', he wrote, 'and feeling the greatest affection for the youth, I often arranged to have the pleasure of watching him performing amorous exploits.' But his eye remained a connoisseur's and arguably a deviant's. He needed extra stimulation to regain what had once come so easily: 'I was very glad to see that, instead of being jealous of his [Marcuccio's] enjoyment and his abilities, [I found that] he was so generously endowed by nature that, when I saw the object, I felt the beneficent influence to the point of [at last] sharing in the festivities with an increase of enjoyment that the sight of the youth . . . handsomer than Antinous, procured me.'

At about this time de Bernis came back into Casanova's life. Although there had been contact between the two men in Madame de Pompadour's Paris during the late 1750s, Rome now allowed a rekindling of the friendship and complicity in bad behaviour that dated to Venice and M.M. Cardinal de Bernis was now a leading figure in the Church, but he openly enjoyed the favours of a mistress, a well-known Roman socialite, the Principessa Santa Croce.

Casanova's portrait of Roman high society at this period matches those of other travellers. Santa Croce's friend the Principessa Borghese Agnese Colonna had became a tourist attraction at her fabulous *palazzo*: the British consul in Turin, Casanova's friend, sent young British aristocrats to her to be 'brushed up', and Lord Chesterfield punned that 'Nothing dresses a young fellow more than having been between Colonna's pillars.' Casanova solicited de Bernis's help in obtaining leave of absence from a convent of two young novices. He had met them through Marcuccio, who, although he was sleeping with Casanova's landlord's daughter and her friend, was in love with another. Her name was Emilia and she was sequestered in the Instituto di Santa Caterina de' Funari near the Porta San Paolo. His sister Armellina was there too. He and Casanova visited, and Casanova fell for Armellina – and for the prospect of helping the youngsters to circumvent convent rules. De Bernis officiated. It was like old times.

His tales of Rome in 1770 are a rich tapestry of church corruption, Jesuit politics and the sexual roundelay that always, for Casanova, seemed at its most orgiastic in Rome. Later Casanova became embroiled in a political argument with the church authorities over relaxing convent visiting rules so that girls might meet prospective husbands rather than having to chose between the veil or prostitution. He spent a great deal of time on this – and a great deal of money he could not afford – on and with his new young friends. He took them often to the theatre, and taught them his Venetian oyster-eating game, in which the molluscs are passed from mouth to mouth between lovers. The scene took the older Casanova several pages to describe. He was also happy to oblige, with Marcuccio, when the girls asked to be shown the differences between male and female bodies, and their purposes, and happy too to relate all this to the appreciative audience of Cardinal de Bernis and his royal mistress. Such was Casanova's later Rome: the coffee houses of the Condotti, the oyster taverns of the Spanish Steps and the beds of girls young enough to be his daughters.

He was introduced to two even younger girls, both his relatives. One, Guglielmina, was the daughter of his brother Giovanni from his time in Rome as an art student with Mengs. He had not married the mother, and was by this time in Dresden. The other girl had been christened Giacomina and was Giacomo's own daughter by Mariuccia, with whom he had had a brief affair in 1761.

Mariuccia had married a wigmaker, the match orchestrated by Casanova after their brief affair, but their first child, Giacomina, was undoubtedly Casanova's. She was now nearly ten and knew her cousin, Guglielmina, because Giovanni's former mistress was now Giacomina's music teacher. Mariuccia was keen to effect an unconventional family reunion, and took Casanova to meet the girls. They were asleep together in bed and Mariuccia showed Casanova their naked bodies, then made love to him herself in a scene both disquieting and dangerously prescient. The older he became, Casanova frankly admitted, the more he was attracted to young girls. This time, he had the sense or decency to refrain from contact with Giacomina, but with his niece, he was not so circumspect.

He continued contact with the families of the two young girls. He took them out in Rome and bought a series of lottery tickets after divining some winning numbers – a rare late example in the memoirs of his continuing interest in the cabbala. He made a great sum – equivalent to around six thousand pounds – for Mariuccia's husband, about half that for one of Guglielmina'a aunts and about twenty thousand for himself.

Little by little, he convinced himself that he was in love with his niece, Guglielmina, and she with him. On the one hand, she was of an age that had frequently attracted him, and he had her mother's compliance in their growing attachment – he considered writing to Giovanni in Dresden to congratulate him on his daughter, which is testimony to the lack of regard then given to romantic relations between uncles and nieces. What is as shocking to us, as it was to Casanova is the interest, frankly sexual that his small daughter took in him. Nothing happened in the physical sense, and her mother was aware of everything that was going on, but Casanova and Guglielmina made love on several occasions when Giacomina was in bed with them, taking a keen interest in the process. Her father told her she could watch, ask, but not touch.

Casanova spent ten months in Rome, from September 1770 to July 1771. His time there coincided with the demise of the Jesuit order in Europe. Pope Clement XIV had been elected with French and Spanish support on the understanding that he would act against the rich and powerful order. The papal bull that banned it was still a few years away, but Casanova was aware of the brewing storm and, as a Papal Knight of the Golden Spur, was expected to have an opinion on it. De Bernis was intimately involved with the anti-Jesuit camp but nevertheless managed to get Casanova accreditation to work at the Jesuit Library in Rome, where he continued his translation of *The Iliad*. His days were spent there, a papal knight among the Jesuits, while his nights were frittered with convent refugees and his niece. Rome's Academy of Arcadians granted him full honours, and his discourse there on Horace's *Scribendi recte sapere est principium et finis* was, according to one paper, 'greatly applauded'.

But he was beginning to feel directionless again. He had been a guest for some time at the Palazzo Santa Croce with the princess and the cardinal, he had amused himself with girls far too young for him, but in the end spent more and more time with Margherita, the landlord's daughter from the Piazza di Spagna – 'She alone made me laugh.' And he was thinking ahead. His plan had been to spend six months in Rome 'in quiet tranquillity', writing, keeping his head low and his name respectable. He had not quite managed it. 'I thought,' he wrote, 'I had grown old. Forty-six seemed a great age . . . I reflected seriously on myself, convinced me that I must seek a dignified retirement.'

He left Rome quietly. With some of the money he had won, some jewels and a coach he could sell, he headed for Florence, there to live and write quietly in the hope of an eventual pardon and a return to Venice. When he moved on to Trieste, it seems his presence there warranted a report by the Venetian Inquisition. They were indeed keeping a close eye on him: 'He is a man of high stature, of good and vigorous aspect, very brown of skin with a vivacious eye. He wears a short chestnut-coloured wig. From what I am told he is of bold and disdainful character, but especially, he is full of the gift of talking, and, as such, witty and learned.'

He diverted his energies to writing. He finished his history of Poland, or its recent troubles, based on his studies in 1765 and 1766. His *Istoria della turbolenza della Polonia*, in Italian rather than the French he preferred, so clearly for Venetian consumption, was published eventually in Gorizia in 1774. He wrote a theatre comedy, *La Forza della vera amicizia*, which was performed in Trieste in July 1773. He wrote poems, libretti, cantatas and hundreds of letters, pleading ever more assiduously, ever more carefully and with ever greater hope of success to be allowed home.

In September 1774 a letter arrived with the lion seals of Venice upon it. Nearly nineteen years after his escape from The Leads, he was granted pardon and permission to return to Venice.

Much as he might have wanted to believe that this late clemency was a result of his literary efforts and standing, it was other skills that had won his reprieve. For many months of his stay in Trieste, he was in the employ of the Venetian authorities on clandestine diplomatic missions. Imprisoned and exiled by the Venetian Inquisition for crimes it never explained, he found his route back into favour by turning inquisitor of sorts himself. He was nothing if not a pragmatist: 'I was not displeased to be in the employ of that same tribunal [the Inquisition] that had deprived me of my liberty and whose power I had challenged. It seemed to me a triumph, and I felt honour bound to be useful to it in every manner that did not violate natural laws or those of men.'

VENICE REVISITED

1774–82

'Casanova? What do you want to know?: he drinks, he eats, he
laughs, he tells extraordinary tales.'

Portrait of Casanova, Prince Belloselki

The History of My Life ends in 1774 when Casanova was
forty-nine. The last page finds Casanova, in a half-finished
sentence and halfway down an untidily written side, narrating
an inconsequential affair with an actress in Trieste. It looks as if
he was cut off mid-stream, by death even – as is sometimes
stated. It is unclear whether or not he intended to carry on
beyond his return to Venice in 1774: the years after that, he said,
became increasingly distressing rather than amusing to recall,
and the dramatist in him perhaps liked the symmetry of a return
to port. Real life was less structured.

His reception in Venice, on 14 September 1774 was warm. It
was, Casanova wrote to a friend, 'the happiest day of my life'.
Dandolo was still alive. Casanova saw Marcolina, Angela To-
selli, Madame Manzoni and Christine and her husband, whose
marriage he had helped arrange decades earlier. They loaned
Casanova money. He met up with Caterina Capretta, with whom
he had run around naked in the gardens of the Giudecca, now a
respectable matron. His friendship with Andrea Memmo was still

intact, though Memmo was now a grand patrician, and Casanova, one gets the impression, slightly embarrassed him; Giustiniana Wynne was a long time in his past.

The former ambassador, now procurator, Lorenzo Morosini, and Senator Pietro Zaguri had lobbied hard on Casanova's behalf for many years and were newly appointed to the Council of Ten so he still had friends in high places, but mainly they were those Venetians who understood the wider world of Europe, where Casanova's exile had seemed just one more example of Venice's Byzantine backwardness.

He found the city much changed. The Inquisition still held sway, but there was growing discontent among the middle classes. More specifically, there was a tumultuous, political and competitive publishing culture from which Casanova would profit and, ultimately, suffer.

He took a small house, in the Calle de la Balote near San Marco and set to writing his attempted masterwork: a modern translation of *The Iliad*. The first volume would be published in 1775, the next in 1776 and a third in 1778, but after that publication was abandoned through lack of subscribers. Worthy classical literature was not the vogue any more in Venice – and his 339 subscribers were drawn from his coterie of international friends, not the locals who might have supported him in the style he wished to adopt in Venice.

In 1776 he accepted a post working, again clandestinely, for the Inquisition, as part of its network of civil informers. This was quite another matter than foreign espionage: he was being asked to turn gamekeeper in a cruel twist of sporting rules, working the same patch, indeed, that Manuzzi had twenty years before. Casanova's files, under the name Antonio Pratolini in his unmistakable beautifully turned hand, exist to this day. The Inquisition paid him a monthly salary of fifteen ducats for the ignominious task of spying on his fellow citizens as they went about their business. But it afforded him with a regular income, with the small sum Dandolo still gave him. He sought to augment these stipends by joining the world of Venetian journalism. He started a monthly literary review, *Opuscoli Miscellanei* in January 1780, with a variety of articles, all written by himself. It lasted only a few months. Next he returned to the family trade as a theatre promoter, at which he had had some success in the past. He booked the Teatro Sant'Angelo and a cheap company of French actors with a more expensive star. He also founded a weekly magazine of dramatic criticism, to publicise the work at the Sant'Angelo. The journal was called *Le Messager de Thalie*, but it, too, did not last.

By his standards, his life was sedate and bourgeois. In the summer of 1779 he met a seamstress, Francesca Buschini, and they moved as a sort of a common-law couple, with her mother and brother, into a little house at 6673 Barberio della tolle which still stands, overlooking the Vivaldi high school in an area that was then all but naval dockyard. We know little about their life together, except that she wrote to him for seven years after he left her, tender, gossipy, concerned letters; she must have loved and understood him, and felt she could offer him the warm domesticity he had never really known and she thought he needed. They had lived together for several years as a respectable Venetian couple.

He made a few new friends, among them an up-and-coming writer with whom he had much in common. Lorenzo da Ponte, a Jew who had converted to Christianity, was secretary to Senator Zaguri, who had lobbied for Casanova's return to Venice, so they came across each other at the Palazzo Zaguri and in Venice's bustling theatres. His was a frequent name in the lists of those who argued with Casanova over coffee and *malvasie*: '[We would meet] sometimes at Zaguri's and sometimes at Memmo's,' da Ponte recalled, 'both of whom loved what was good in Casanova and forgave what was ill, and taught me to do the same. And even now . . . I do not know to which side the balance leant.' In some respects, Casanova had found the 'retirement' he had looked forward to, with old and new like-minded friends, discussing books, theatre, their lives and loves. But literary glory, not to mention financial security, still eluded him.

In eighteenth-century terms he was getting quite old and his life was punctuated now by others' deaths. His mother died in Dresden in 1780, she was sixty-eight, and Manon Balletti the same year, aged only thirty-six. Dozens of her love letters travelled with him when he left Venice a few years later – perhaps she had been right in believing she could only hold Casanova's heart by yielding to him nothing else. And Bettina Gozzi, who had first taught him about lust, if little about love, died in his arms.

Casanova was becoming cantankerous. For one thing, he felt Venice, and the wider world of French literature, owed him recognition, although the majority of his work was still unpublished. But in the antagonistic journalistic culture of late-eighteenth-century Venice, he began to find an outlet for his talent for bile. Aggressive polemical pamphlets were daily on sale in Venice and arguments invariably centred round particular factions usually headed by a patrician or locally famous writer. Casanova was seduced, willingly, into courting controversy. While taking the waters at Abano near Padua in the summer of 1779 he began work on a piece designed to shock: a direct attack on Voltaire, *Scrutinio del libro 'Eloges de M de Voltaire' par differens auteurs* was published in Venice in 1779 and Casanova, with the other writers he had involved, was briefly celebrated in the manner to which he aspired. It may have been his reputation as a 'man of no consequence', an international gadabout and player that prevented Venetians taking him as seriously as he wished or deserved, or the inescapable fact that he was the son of a comedy actress. His frustration at his exclusion was a vast burden to a man who had never found equanimity with his past, his reputation or with the apprehension of even the smallest slight. He became dangerously embittered.

In May 1782 when he was dining with the patrician Carlo Grimani, at the magnificent Palazzo Grimani di Santa Maria Formossa, he fell into conversation with one Carletti, who was owed money by Carlo Spinola, a Genoese diplomat for whom Casanova was doing menial secretarial work. Carletti asked Casanova to mention the debt to his employer. Casanova said he would do so, but grudgingly, 'compelled . . . by the present state of my affairs'. Grimani stood as witness to their agreement that Casanova would receive a percentage of the money, in effect as debt-collector. He went to Spinola, achieved his signature of intention to pay and returned.

Carletti refused at first to pay Casanova, except as a percentage of the periodic payments Spinola had agreed to. Grimani said nothing. Casanova objected. He accused Carletti of breaking his word. Carletti rained insults on him. At this juncture Grimani entered the argument. He told Casanova that he was in the wrong, and should sit down. He did so, and Carletti continued to abuse him.

Casanova was furious with Grimani, who had witnessed the agreement and had the rank to help. He sat down, and fumed. 'The secretary of Spinola became the object of general derision' around Venice it was said. This was not so much for what he had done – opinion was divided over the relative breaches of honour involved in the complicated debt arrangement – but in accepting a torrent of abuse he had undermined the glory he had won for fighting duels with aristocrats. He had been exposed as a time-server and a dupe. As da Ponte said of him, 'this singular man' hated nothing more than appearing 'to be in the wrong'.

What Casanova did next put the argument on a different footing. Using his journalistic contacts, he wrote and had published a biting satire, the sort of thing that was passed daily round Florian's coffee house, about the event. The row had been public enough, and the participants famous enough in Venice, for his masking of them as classical figures to fool no one. An accompanying play-list made his point still clearer. In his *Ne amori ne donne* – *Not for love or women* – Carletti was portrayed as a mad dog, 'owned by one Alcide, the bastard son of an aristocrat,' who represented Grimani. It was reference to an ancient slur on Grimani's background that few would miss. In the story Casanova, portraying himself as the innocent bystander Econeon, describes his unusual relationship with the Alcide/Grimani family: Econeon is exposed as the illegitimate son of Alcide's own supposed father by an actress. While his mother lived, Casanova might have avoided saying this aloud, but the truth had no nobility. He and Grimani were brothers of sorts, and Casanova had a twisted claim to nobility: *he* was the son of Grimani's supposed father, Michele, but doomed to walk on the wrong side of the road for having been born to an actress. Carlo Grimani, born in a *palazzo* to an adulterous mother, was no son of Michele. When it came to sex, and the secrets and lies by which we are procreated, there was an equality Casanova understood. Who knew who Carlo Grimani's father was? How dare he undermine Michele's true son? It was explosive stuff.

Lorenzo Morosini advised Casanova to leave town, if only temporarily. The Grimanis remained Venice's wealthiest and most powerful family, and that which had always alarmed the authorities about Giacomo Casanova, his disrespect for class boundaries, rankled again. Casanova regretted his rashness and despatched apologetic letters to his half-brother Carlo, as well as inventing or embroidering a ten-page genealogy of Gaetano Casanova in his memoirs to rewrite his confession about his mother and Michele Grimani. It was to no avail. He begged to loiter in Venice at least as long as it might take to write to his brother Francesco in Paris or to Giovanni, now head of the Academy of Arts, in Dresden, but it was not to be. He fled to Trieste, fearing imprisonment or official banishment. 'I am fifty-eight years old,' he wrote to Morosini, 'winter approaches . . . and if I think of becoming again an adventurer on the road, I begin to laugh at myself as soon as I see myself in the mirror.'

But the road was unavoidable.

He took his leave of Francesca on 17 January 1783. He was able to come back briefly on 16 June 1783 to collect some of his belongings – his letters, books, a few clothes – but did not set foot on a Venetian *fondamenta*, the canal quayside, for fear of arrest. He would never see Francesca – or Venice – again.

DON GIOVANNI

1783–7

'Love is like nourishment, I need women like I eat bread.'
Don Giovanni, Lorenzo da Ponte, 1787

'Oh seducing sex! Source of pain! Let a poor innocent go in
peace. I am no revolutionary, I would never offend you.'
Don Giovanni, Giacomo Casanova, 1787

From Venice to Trieste, then Vienna, Bolzano and Innsbruck,
Augsburg, Frankfurt, Aix-la-Chapelle, Spa, The Hague,
Rotterdam and Antwerp. He was in Paris by 20 September
1783 – and too old for this sort of thing.

In Paris he found refuge with Francesco, who was painting his
epic battle scenes at the Louvre and Fontainebleau for Louis
XVI. He was introduced there to the diplomatic representative
of the new American nation: Benjamin Franklin. Casanova kept
a record of their meeting on 23 November 1783, and the
subjects discussed: the recent ascent of the Montgolfier balloon
and the possibility of directing air flight. 'This thing is still in its
infancy,' Franklin had advised the Parisian Academy of Sciences,
with Casanova in the audience, 'so we must wait and see.'
Casanova was more than just an audience member, however: he

had been invited to attend by the 'celebrated American Franklin' as a result, it would seem, of some previous meeting and discussion on science. Later Casanova used some of the ideas in his science-fiction novel, *Icosaméron*, and the following year was considering practical experience of balloon flight in Vienna. He decided he was too old.

He needed a passport from Venice to leave France; it arrived in November at Fontainebleau. He and Francesco travelled from Paris together to Dresden to see their brother and his family and thence to Vienna. After his years in the studios of Simonetti and then in Paris, Francesco had found a long-term aristocratic sponsor in Vienna in the person of Prince Kaunitz. This had presumably been for him the purpose of the journey. For his elder brother, as ever, there was a less defined goal. He managed one brief rally of mischief-making, sneaking into a diplomatic bag that was being sent from Vienna to Venice a report that the Republic would be rocked by an earthquake on a date prefigured in the cabbala. There was panic in Venice. But only briefly. And it was a joke Casanova was not there to enjoy. Francesco stayed in Vienna, painting for Kaunitz, but Casanova travelled back to Dresden, then to Berlin and Prague. There, he received an invitation to work for the Venetian ambassador, based in Vienna, and in 1784 Sebastian Foscarini engaged him as his secretary. It was something of a come-down.

Another renegade Venetian was in Vienna at this period. Lorenzo da Ponte and Casanova understood each other well. They had both had multiple careers, after unorthodox beginnings in Venice, and had determined to live life without boundaries. They had been noted and enthusiastic libertines in their youth, despite their clerical careers, but it was their love of theatre that brought them together in the late 1780s. The article of main concern in this intriguing relationship was their collaboration on da Ponte's masterwork, the libretto for Mozart's *Don Giovanni*. The names of the Don and of Casanova have become almost interchangeable in the Western imagination. The specific textual connection, as well as Casanova's likely input in those conversations in Vienna's Graben promenade, is a story set also in Prague, and its Italian-theatre communities.

It is difficult to overemphasise the fashionability of Italian opera at this period. It made Casanova feel at home in almost every city he visited. After the overwhelming success of Mozart's *Marriage of Figaro* in Prague at the beginning of 1787, it was inevitable that he would be asked to write more for the audience of the Bohemian capital and their new Nostitz – later 'Estates' – Theatre. And as Casanova, with the Habsburg court and its embassies moved back and forth between Vienna and Prague, he came to know the Italian theatricals in both capitals. One of his friends, Pasquale Bondini, principal of the Graflich Nostitzsches National Theatre of Prague, commissioned Mozart to write a new opera for late in 1787.

Little is known about the subsequent development of the commission, *Don Giovanni*, except that Mozart and da Ponte immediately fell behind schedule in the planning of the new work. The date for the Prague première was set to coincide with the festivities marking the marriage of Prince Anton Clemens of Saxony. While the couple were travelling south from Dresden via Teplice, Mozart and da Ponte hurriedly submitted the first libretto for the court censors in Prague. It missed out key sequences, the closing moments of Don Giovanni's ball, where the whole company called for '*Liberta!*' is thought not to have been submitted to the censors at all, and scenes were added later, some, it seems, inspired and 'improved' by the old *roué* da Ponte knew could give a fresh spin to the story of the dissolute, punished. It was not until October, according to the latest watermark research on Mozart's manuscript, and in Prague, that *Don Giovanni* achieved the form now widely known. Later still more arias were added. But with only days to go before the première the opera still lacked its heart-stopping overture, half a dozen small scenes now taken as integral to it, a finale and happy resolution.

At about this time da Ponte arrived back in Prague and was obliged to change the libretto, risking court censure with a brave new take on several aspects of the drama by the company and Mozart. Into this mêlée stepped Casanova. His involvement with *Don Giovanni* is elusively documented, relying on two pages of notes, now in the Prague Archives in which he appears to have amended da Ponte's book, the words of Leporello and the Don in Act II, and on a story told by a Prague musician, A. Meissner. But several facts are clear: da Ponte was *not* in Prague for the last-minute additions to the opera, but Casanova was. He knew the company well, Mozart a little, and may have stepped into the breach.

He gatecrashed a gathering of the Italian opera company that worked at the Estates or Nostitz Theatre. The company included several Venetians – many known to Casanova – and was rehearsing, or trying to rehearse, the haphazardly prepared new opera arriving in pieces from the study of Herr Mozart. Exasperated, according to Meissner, they eventually locked Mozart into an upper room and told him he would not be allowed out till he had completed *Don Giovanni*. By the force of his rhetoric, charm, and perhaps his long experience of dealing with professional histrionics, Casanova persuaded the rebellious cast that Mozart would finish the opera and should be allowed out from his enforced solitary confinement. Mozart, duly grateful, wrote the overture that night, sampling the ominous chords from scene xv of Act III in the opening moments of the opera. Even so the première had to be delayed: on the appointed evening the theatre manager decided that Mozart's new opera was unfit to be seen, and the company put on their much-loved *Marriage of Figaro* instead. *Don Giovanni*, with Casanova expectantly in a box at the side of the Nostitz Theatre, finally met its audience on 29 October. The Prague and, later, Vienna audiences adored it. Goethe was among many who noted its appeal: 'It was given nightly for four weeks, the whole city being so excited by it that the merest shopkeeper had to perch in the stalls or a box with his whole extended family, and no one could bear to have missed seeing Don Juan roast in hell.'

Neglected for nearly two centuries, evidence in the Prague Archive supports Meissner's story that Casanova worked on *Don Giovanni*, either with and for da Ponte and the Italian opera company, or for his own amusement. Even if the latter is the case, the close interest and precise knowledge of the newly performed text argues in favour of him having been involved in its creation. In the Prague archive there are two variants of Act II scene x, in which the Don and his servant Leporello have been caught out with swapped costumes and identities, in Casanova's unmistakable hand. The dialogue is worked on quarto-folded expensive paper. These are more than notes: they read like a proposal or part of a longer draft.

What were these elegantly presented pages for? Did da Ponte see them, or only the company members struggling to tie together a work-in-progress in the absence of the original librettist and with a hopelessly overstretched composer? How much of *Don Giovanni* was and is Casanova? In simple textual terms, very little. Of the surviving Casanova notes, there is only a situational connection to the libretto as now performed and it is unknown if these suggestions were or were not incorporated by da Ponte into what was first performed at the Nostitz. Possibly he reworked this scene in his own words for later productions and dropped Casanova's 'original', or perhaps Casanova kept his notes because they were never incorporated. We do know, however, that Casanova attended the première at the Nostitz in 1787. Frustratingly, he writes nothing about it, beyond the notes for the libretto. Was he insulted that his ideas were not, ultimately, included? Was he jealous of the esteem heaped on his friend and occasional adversary in telling what Casanova must have thought of as 'his' story? Somewhere around the same time, Casanova began to conceive his own 'catalogue song'. It would never amount to anything as hyperbolic as Don Giovanni's eighteen hundred conquests, but it would be unashamed, unrepentant and, in its way, would rival and parallel the great da Ponte/Mozart opus he watched at the Nostitz.

THE CASTLE AT DUX
1787–98

'Have you sounded out this extraordinary man? . . . I know few persons who can equal him in the range of his knowledge and of intelligence and imagination.'

Count Lamberg to J. F. Opiz on Casanova, 1785

'There is another complete original [at Dux], the brother of the painter Casanova de Vienne, a man of letters; Poet, Philosopher, Astrologer, Diviner and Wizard – half mad.'

Count Clary on Casanova 1787

I n his capacity as secretary to the Venetian ambassador in Vienna, Casanova had attended, some time in February 1784, a dinner attended by Count Joseph Charles de Waldstein, the head of an illustrious Prague family with estates all over Bohemia. He was still in his twenties, unmarried – to the chagrin of his mother – chamberlain to Emperor Joseph II and owner of the demesne of Dux, or Duchcov, in north-east Bohemia. Dux was near the fashionable hot springs of Teplice and not very far from Dresden, so it is likely Casanova knew of it. He may not have known that the castle had a library, boasting, he claimed, forty thousand volumes – only twelve thousand, according to

Waldstein's brother, 'and most of those I would fling on the fire', but a collection which in 1784, was in want of a librarian.

Casanova often hit it off with boisterous young aristocrats, and Waldstein was one such. They had in common only their wide-ranging reading tastes, and some specific knowledge of the cabbala. Waldstein mentioned the Clavicles of Solomon the first time they met, and later that evening, in his bluff way, turned to the Venetian cabbalist and said, 'So, come to Bohemia with me. I am leaving tomorrow.'

The invitation was not immediately accepted, but when Foscarini died, on 23 April 1785, Casanova found himself unemployed and homeless. Again. He travelled to Karlsbad to see his old friend Princess Lubomirska, there taking the waters, then on to Teplice and Dux. He accepted Waldstein's appointment as castle librarian at an annual salary of a thousand florins, then about a hundred pounds; it was a respectable stipend, and would be ameliorated with family meals, guest status and regular trips to nearby Teplice. Although he was frequently in Prague – to supervise publication of his novel *Icosaméron* and the *Don Giovanni* and *Clemenza di Tito* premières, and more often in Teplice, he lived longer in the little Bohemian town than he had anywhere else. His move to Dux was to be his last.

His host, Count Waldstein, was frequently absent from Dux. Casanova doubtless envied the dash Waldstein cut across the frontiers of Europe: attempting to abduct to safety the French royal family, lauded in London and Vienna for his gallantry and bravery, Waldstein may well have been one of the models for the fictional Scarlet Pimpernel. His family seat and its librarian, however, he neglected.

The rooms Casanova was assigned in the castle open on to the main courtyard and the central square of Dux, then as now a bleakly provincial little town. The castle was relatively modern in parts, built in a classical Italian-baroque style so that it resembles an ecclesiastical institution and also a barracks. It was run as the latter, and as a hunting-lodge for the garrulous, sporting count; it stabled 120 horses – the area then was prime hunting forest, and known for its inclement weather, the long snowy winters, and an atmosphere heavy with the smell of surface-mined coal. The baroque obelisk by the castle gates rises ominously from the stone-carved fires of hell. When Casanova considered the fall of *Don Giovanni* into the trap-door of the Nostitz stage, he may have reflected that he was suffering his own version of the '*dissoluto punito*' – the punishment of a provincial hell – for having lived too widely and too well.

He was not the only unhappy inhabitant of the castle or the only one with ill-defined status. The castle chamberlain, a German called variously George Feldkirchner or Faulkircher, considered himself of greater import than the impoverished Italian librarian, and made Casanova's life miserable. Another castle official, Karl Viderol or Wiederholt similarly despised Casanova's pretensions to aristocracy and literary renown, but then again, Viderol could not read. Dux castle was described as a community of 'real eccentrics' by those who visited, 'there was a Jewish equerry, French coachmen, English horses – you didn't know what country you were in', which suited Casanova down to the ground. There was an elegant, frescoed baroque garden pavilion, or *hôpital*, to walk to across the formal gardens and a 900-metre English garden, in which horses were raced.

But the librarian necessarily had a somewhat tangential relationship with an establishment given over to racing, hunting and pheasant shooting. The noise and smell of horses dominated the grounds, and meals, in the absence of Waldstein, were in the reluctant company of Viderol and Feldkirchner and presented by a recalcitrant, untalented cook. Food was the one sensual joy left to Casanova, but there was little pleasure to be found on the table at Dux.

One advantage, however, of Dux from Casanova's point of view was its proximity to Teplice, briefly an epicentre for pleasure-seekers and *curistes* in a war-torn Continent. In 1787 Johann Nepumuk Clary-Aldringen had inherited the princedom with Teplice's large castle, a palace really, that still dominates the little town. He was married to the Belgian princess Christine de Ligne who, like her father, the Prince Charles Joseph de Ligne, was a refugee from the French Revolution by the time Casanova befriended them in Teplice. De Ligne was related to Waldstein through his wife and had known Casanova in Vienna and Prague. With the de Ligne château at Beloeil confiscated by revolutionaries, he spent increasing amounts of his time at his daughter's home in Teplice through the late 1780s and 1790s, in a grand suite of rooms overlooking the town square. He felt himself fortunate to find another refugee of sorts from pre-revolutionary high society, and Casanova became again with the Prince de Ligne the Chevalier de Seingalt; his last happy performance.

The revolution, and the horror of the Terror, appalled them; many of Casanova's friends and former lovers went to the guillotine along with de Ligne's. The voluble, witty, rich and sophisticated Clary-de Ligne family all but adopted the librarian from the château next door, and he became a fixture at Teplice events and in the little theatre at the castle: 'Put your wig on, we're going to Teplice – all the Clarys and de Lignes will rejoice to see you', enjoins de Ligne in his customary style of breezy, loving friendship. '*Mon cher* Casanova', as Casanova became to him, you are 'never old – not with your heart, your genius, and your stomach . . . Come and see us, we never stop speaking about you . . . My fleas are all but jumping with excitement at the prospect.'

It was to de Ligne, writer, great lover of women, and knowledgeable about the courts and customs of Europe from Versailles to St Petersburg, that Casanova first showed some early drafts of his memoirs. He said he could not read a single chapter without envy, amusement, astonishment or an erection. He was as fascinated by it as he was fascinated by Casanova. He was the perfect commentator, having lived a parallel life, opining, for instance, that Casanova's pen sketches of Tsarina Catherine II of Russia and Frederick the Great of Prussia were the clearest and most truthful he had seen. De Ligne's testimony, as world traveller and companion in old age, to the memoirs' essential credibility makes him perhaps the premier witness for the defence of Casanova. They fell into each other's arms, it was said, like refugees from a lost era, knowing the world outside was 'going to the devil'.

De Ligne left a sad portrait of his friend at Dux, whose unhappiness, however, he felt was self-inflicted:

A day did not go by that he did not have a quarrel, over his coffee, over his milk, his plate of macaroni on which he insisted. The cook had failed to give him polenta, the equerry had given him a bad coachman to come and see me, dogs had barked in the night; more guests than Waldstein had expected had led him to eat at a small table. A hunting horn had annoyed him by false or sharp notes. The priest had bothered him by trying to convert him . . . The count had not said good day to him at first . . . The count had lent a book without telling him . . . He grew angry, people laughed. He showed his French poems; people laughed. He gesticulated while reciting his Italian poems; people laughed. He made a bow, when entering as Marcel, the famous dancing master, had taught him to do sixty years ago; people laughed. He had performed at a castle ball the grave step of his minuet; they had laughed. He had dressed up with his . . . [old] suit of gold-embroidered silk . . . and his garters with spangled buckles and silk stockings, and they had laughed. [He called them] 'scum'.

On rare occasions Casanova ventured further afield than Teplice. He spent time in Prague in 1787, and again in 1791 for the coronation of the new Habsburg emperor, Leopold II. It was a chance to catch up with old friends. It was here, at the theatre and again at an embassy reception, that he came across a young Italian in the suite of the King of Naples. The Marchese de C. was Leonilda's son, and therefore probably Casanova's grandson. He was twenty-one. Casanova noted the strong resemblance he bore to his mother's husband, the late marchese, and chose to ignore the possibility that the young man was his son, as well as his grandson, from his incestuous encounter with Leonilda in 1770. He was, Casanova noted, a young man wise beyond his age.

These were the years of Casanova's manic writing. He spent hours in the hope of winning an economics prize and in convincing governments of his prowess with lottery management. He thought of writing again on Voltaire, on Russia . . . and he penned dozens of letters, but fewer to far-flung European literati than to local friends and the young women who came to dominate his last years: Cecile de Roggendorf and Elise von der Recke.

There is a world of detail on the life Casanova could share, though, at the castles in Teplice and at Dux, as a result of de Ligne's ebullient grandson, Prince Charles Clary, always known as Lolo. He wrote an extensive journal and many letters about the man he called 'Cas', and about Casanova's growing friendship with his own 'wicked' grandfather, the Prince de Ligne and with a soulful divorcée Elise von der Recke, who became close friends with both ageing roués. They were, the eighteen-year-old Lolo wrote, great fun when they were not talking about old times and their souls, and full of tender reminiscences of past times. 'Have I ever spoken of the pain of memories?' wrote de Ligne. 'The dinner bell at the château here? Oh God! God! God! . . . What is life? How few moments of real happiness there are? And how short they are?' For a few months each year, Casanova and he had at least the solace of each other, reminiscing in the pretty and sociable little spa town of Teplice with its cosmopolitan salons and the little theatre in its castle.

Casanova's notes from Dux include a number of memoranda for other members of the household: instructions on how to make soap for his linen, how to prepare polenta and Buranese biscuits, complaints about firewood and often about his fellow pensioner, Feldkirchner. He also composed dozens of letters to

Feldkirchner, vituperative, rancorous and scornful; few, if any, were ever sent. One, scribbled on the back of his notes on calendar reform, throws back at Feldkirchner his offer of coffee: 'I would not wish,' writes Casanova, 'to imbalance your system of economy.' It was not a happy retirement home.

He was not only rancorous, though: depression stalked him. As his world narrowed to his rooms above the castle courtyard it was Elise and Cecile who brightened his life, but only sufficiently for Casanova to recall how reduced his circumstances were, how 'feeble' his ability to find 'enjoyment in pleasures'. Elise appears to have talked to him about his depression because he left her a sad little treatise on euthanasia. That route was not for him.

Little of what he wrote was published; for that required subscriptions from his ever-dwindling and put-upon circle of friends. *Solique d'un penseur*, a philosophical work, was published in 1786, followed by *Histoire de ma fuite* in 1787, a tale already well known around Europe but lucidly told with only occasional factual lacunae. He then concentrated on *Icosaméron*, the English-set science-fiction novel that would be published in Prague in 1788. It ran to five volumes and is a tough read, even judged by the standards of the day, but Casanova was increasingly cursed by prolixity, in life and in his writing. As the visitors became fewer at Dux, the letters become longer, the prose and mathematical works more voluminous. Nevertheless, three pamphlets on the calculation of doubling cubes, which had occupied mathemeticians from ancient Egypt via Descartes and Newton, were published to suitable rarified and academic acclaim as *Solution du problème déliaque* in Dresden in 1790. But he did not win the university prize he sought, or 'solve' the problem. This and the fantasy *Icosaméron* had been the works, Casanova wrote confidently, that would assure him immortality – and stop the Dux servants laughing at him.

Casanova's disappointment at the lack of critical response to his novel in particular may have been what led him to write full-length memoirs, though it should not be assumed that he sought the immortality they brought him, or that he even considered, at first, full publication. What began as an extension of previous autobiographical essays – his *Histoire de ma fuite* and his account of his duel with Count Branicki – turned into a full-scale autobiography of unpublishable length. He became addicted to writing as he had once been to adventure, travel and sex.

In his declining years his writing alarmed not just the illiterate servants at Dux but his friends. He left, at his death in 1798, 1,703 letters, fifty drafts of dialogues, 150 memos, sixty-seven printed items, 390 poems as well nearly five hundred pages of uncategorised writings; more than three thousand manuscript pages of various works in progress, in addition to his memoirs, that ran to nearly four thousand folio pages, and existed, once, in multiple hand-copied versions. His energy, even redirected, was breathtaking. But his ambition, as so often in life, vaulted his talent. *Icosaméron* and the rest failed, and he was left looking a little more ridiculous in his pride and vanity. He seems not to have sought a publisher for his memoirs, but he never gave up hope of finding literary glory. His last work, *À Leonard Snetlage*, in response to a lexicographer and containing more personal reminiscences – on Samuel Johnson and Frederick the Great, for instance – hinted at the unpublished masterwork in progress. *Snetlage* came out just before he died.

As the years passed Casanova grew desperately unhappy at Dux, and threatened to leave several times. He went to Teplice whenever he had an excuse to do so, and stayed in Oberleutensdorf at another Waldstein residence when he couldn't stand the company at Dux any longer. On one occasion he was beaten up in the street near the market place; on another a semi-trained wolf was set upon his little dog. It was a mean little town in the absence of the count and his entourage, and Casanova rubbed people up the wrong way.

Yet whenever Waldstein was about, he felt obliged to show his face about the castle, where the count accepted him and his moods with equanimity and good humour, 'soothing his vanity by saying how honoured he was to have so famous and extra-ordinary a house-guest'.

Towards the end of November 1797 Casanova was contemplating a final visit to Venice 'to say a last goodbye to my unfortunate country', though whether he was pre-empting his death or that of the Republic is unclear. He asked Waldstein for permission to leave his library for a trip that would keep him away from the castle for a few months. Waldstein wrote back that he approved 'the zeal with all my heart', for he was well aware, even if Casanova was not, that his travelling days were at an end.

On 22 February 1798 his young friend Cecile de Roggendorff wrote from Vienna with a linseed poultice recipe for his 'obstinate illness' – a bladder infection, though he seems to have been suffering from an inflamed prostate that eventually turned septic. Cecile signed off that she was 'extremely worried'. He never alludes to it directly, but it was probably the syphilis, from which he had suffered since at least 1763 and probably before, making its inevitable impact on his system. His complaints about an arthritic soreness and the cold at Dux, his irritability and depression may have been symptoms. So, too, may have been his manic energy and raging against the world. Or perhaps they were symptoms of old age.

Casanova survived past his seventy-third birthday and all through the spring of 1798, his large frame slowly withering, relying on soup – in which he had always had faith – made of crab, which must have been difficult to come by in the Bohemian mountains – or fresh little mountain-water crayfish, which came back into season as he lay dying.

The death of the old librarian came unexpectedly in the château. Casanova had been his usual self: cantankerous, bilious and demanding. His little dog Finette, a levrette greyhound given him by Princess Lobkowitz, the last of three and on which he doted, was with him. He was sitting in his armchair – it remains at the castle, a large, winged, salon throne of a type fashionable earlier in the century, and here he died in the bright afternoon sunlight that spills from the castle's forecourt into the rooms that had been his haven and his prison. 'I have lived as a philosopher but die as a Christian.' De Ligne quoted these as his last words, but it seems more likely that this was some regular mantra that de Ligne had heard Casanova expound upon at dinner in Teplice. For them, 'philosopher' invariably meant also free-thinker, Enlightenment libertine, man of the world; *livres philosophiques* was their euphemism for erotica. It was their joke. He did not go down shouting his disdain for morality, like *Don Giovanni*, he went with a wry smile and a knowing joke as the curtain fell. In the grey little town of Dux, where he was laughed at and kicked in the street, he had already known the fate of *il dissoluto punito*. Always an excellent self-administering doctor, though, Casanova had sought therapy for his last long exile and, fortunately, the one he found was writing.

A year before, Venice had been overrun by Consul Bonaparte and the thousand-year-old Republic ceased to exist.

The old Venetian's unpublished memoirs lay beside him.

It was 4 June 1798.

END OF ACT V

CURTAIN CALL

THE HISTORY OF *THE HISTORY OF MY LIFE*

'Every man is three people; the man as he sees himself, the man as others see him, and the man as he really is.'

Carlo Goldoni

They took the body of the old Venetian across the town square and down the little market street to the cemetery of Santa Barbara, between the old town walls and the lake. Though de Ligne said Casanova had died in his arms, it is impossible. Casanova's nephew-in-law Carlo Angiolini, who worked backstage at the Italian opera in Dresden, was present at the castle and he made arrangements for the burial. Casanova was interred in a grave that has since been lost. The cemetery was dug over and landscaped in the 1920s when a tombstone was found with Casanova's name and dates, but his bones are believed to have been moved. No one knows where his body lies.

Dux soon forgot its truculent Italian librarian, and the letters, memos, books and artefacts he had left in his room and the library lay largely undisturbed among the Waldsteins' capacious shelves for the next two generations. They later made up the great treasure trove that came into the hands of the modern Czech state; the papers Waldstein had agreed to buy from Casanova. They were moved in the early twentieth century to another Waldstein castle, Mnichovo Hradiště, where Casanova's books remain. Some of the letters in the collection, now

348

kept outside Prague, are still being catalogued. The memoirs, however, took a different, slow route to posterity.

Carlo Angiolini took his heavy inheritance back to Dresden with him after the funeral and seemingly forgot about it. Whether he showed it to Casanova's niece, Manon, is unknown. But Angiolini was ignorant of the magnitude of the gift. He was an odd choice, perhaps, as literary executor and, as it turned out, an infelicitous one.

The story of its publication, which is to say its slow 'unveiling', between 1822 and the present day is the story of the creation of the legend of Casanova, then the gradual re-evaluation of his work from the nineteenth and into the twenty-first century. This separate literary life of Casanova began in 1820, a full twenty-two years after his death, when the publishers Brockhaus, in Leipzig, was offered a manuscript, written in French, bearing the title *Histoire de ma vie jusqu'à 1797* by the 'very famous' Casanova. The publishers may have been under the impression at first that the memoirs were the work of one or other of Casanova's artist brothers, Francesco or Giovanni, who might rightly have claimed a greater posthumous fame at that time than their elder sibling. Brockhaus agreed to terms and an abridged version came out in an ill-translated German edition between 1822 and 1828. No one thought to question the authenticity of what was written.

The first pirated French version, retranslated from the German in the days before copyright, came out shortly afterwards. This convinced Brockhaus to publish a French edition based on the original, and it appointed one Jean Laforgue to edit. However, Laforgue took it upon himself to rewrite whole passages and add an inelegant, at times lewd, flavour that was not Casanova's at all. This practice was followed by another editor, Philippe Busoni, who completed a fourth edition of the memoirs from a 'lost' and different original. As with the historiography of Shakespeare's plays, it turns out that there were various originals, some only to be glimpsed via the later translations or editions. For instance, Casanova had made other, subtly differing, copies, for friends or for his own amusement; 'Send me quickly,' writes the Prince de Ligne, 'the third volume of your memoirs, the Count of Salmour . . . has devoured them and hungers for more.' These went out to friends in Casanova's own lifetime, some later went to Laforgue; none has ever been seen again. Only one of the originals remains, having survived even the Second World War firebombing of Dresden. After the war it was conveyed by lorry to Wiesbaden where no less a person than Winston Churchill immediately enquired whether it was among surviving treasures from Saxony's cultured capital. And in subterranean vaults in Wiesbaden it remains. It is not available to scholars and is viewable only in facsimile, in the form of a unique copy held in the castle archive in Dux. However, these different versions, translations and retranslations that came into the public domain through the nineteenth century soon began to muddy Casanova's reputation as much as his literary style. Errors on dates, facts, places and people were magnified in the re-rendering of his work, and the man himself was obscured. Casanova the idle braggart and Casanova the unreliable memoirist were born.

Through the twentieth century Casanova's reputation as erotic fantasist, con-artist and serial dissembler has been fuelled by the dramatic and filmic representations of the man, and the response to works based more directly on the memoirs has often been critical. The English press especially was tellingly underwhelmed by J. Rives Childs's seminal research work after the entire *History of My Life* was finally accessible in the 1960s: 'The result is impressive even though the subject is trivial,' sniffed the *Times Literary Supplement*. 'My loathing of Casanova,' wrote Harold Nicolson, in the *Observer*, 'has not been diminished by this painstaking hagiography.' Elsewhere in the world, his name has fared much better – as historian, writer and thinker. But despite the generation of international academic work since the Second World War that has sought to re-examine his life and works, his former reputation in the English-speaking world as an irrelevant and mendacious playboy has stubbornly persisted.

One reason people take against him, justifiably enough, is that he led such a blithely amoral life. Those who record their doings in memoir or diary live a pleasure thrice-fold – once in the living of it, once in the writing of it, and once in the later reading of what they have written – and by such a tally Casanova was a much-pleasured man. He had led, on the whole, a very happy life, full of incident and laughter, adventures and the ever-changing chiaroscuro of the eighteenth century. He is particularly despised by those who believe history to be the chronicling of disasters and unhappiness, or the deeds of the great or good. On all these subjects, Casanova had little to say. The further reason for writing memoirs, that of setting the record straight for posterity, may never have been Casanova's intention. Even so, posterity *is* beginning to pay proper accord, as the works of Casanova, his *great* work in any event, *The History of My Life*, begins to take its place in the record of the making of now. This has been as much do to with the wider revision of thinking on the period – the work on the Grand Tourists, on Enlightenment thinking and on libertinism – as it is to do with new evidence *per se* on Casanova. The eighteenth century, with Cupid as its ubiquitous emblem and Casanova as its primary social commentator, openly made love and sex fashionable; it was the beginning of the assertion of sexuality in the European consciousness that has been one of the most eye-catching hues of modern Western thought. Casanova's love-life, presented in intimate though rarely explicit detail, can now hold its place as one of the key documents of the era and in the birth of modern ideas of how to record a love life, how to record a whole life and, for that matter, *why* one would choose to. This uniquely Casanovan ability to both live and enunciate the new sexual freedoms – his invention of sex for the modern world – echoes down the generations, through the emancipation, political and feminist, of the nineteenth century and the sexual revolution of the twentieth. It is the other part of his literary afterlife, the one for which he was once derided but now appears prescient. In this new testament for the modern world, Giacomo Casanova cast himself as messiah and lead actor, lover, sex-god and principal protagonist but also lead fall-guy, comedian, fraudster, grifter and dupe. The psychological scarring that seems to have obliged him to address every human encounter, and especially his sexual ones, as a performance and then a re-creation of a sensual universe, a redramatisation in memoir, is audacious, touching and, in its way, inspiring. His modernity is at its freshest in his ability to laugh at himself, and to dissect some difference between what he was and how he appeared to be. As a biographer, or autobiographer, one could not aspire higher.

Casanova's life and his recording of it are also a deathbed testament to the joys of life, written with the expectation all Venetians have that the sea is inexorably rising, and, during the French Revolution, about the century that had preceded it. He wrote as an old man, repining with the Prince de Ligne that the world had all 'gone to the devil'; his work and life are heavy with the shadow of looming disaster and ripped by an undertow to the tide of pleasure as sure as it was dangerous. It was part of what makes the period, like Venice, so dramatic – the sense of imminent collapse – and one reason, perhaps, why Casanova rode life's day at a gallop. It is also alarmingly modern. Venice's dance with death was and remains mesmeric; the city of *buffa* and *commedia* knew that laughter and happiness could break down all barriers, create out of nothing, make love a game and life a theatrepiece, but the city was not content then or now merely to draw the dying old world to its carnival. And though Casanova's life and *Life* take us to happy intimacies of human nature and profound insights to his times, he also offers himself anew as a voice from one age that speaks eloquently to our own. His style is of a man on a sandbank, laughing at the tide. Maybe we are all Venetians now.

ACKNOWLEDGEMENTS

Casanova's life story, and the evidence for it, is littered across Europe. Access to and choice of the material that informs this book has therefore partly been a picaresque adventure in the footsteps of Casanova's own, and partly a matter of personal interest and necessary editing: there are too many places to go, too many adventures to choose from. However, I have been fortunate in gaining access to many archives across Europe and in the spirit of Casanova this book as a result has mainly been penned 'on the road', from the large sections of it written in Venice's San Maurizio, a stone's throw from Casanova's birthplace, to the archive of the castle in Dux where Casanova himself wrote and died, via Russia, France, Italy, Germany, Holland and the UK. My travels, and thus my thanks, have largely been defined by the archives and libraries where the records of Casanova's extraordinary adventures now lie, but, as a librarian himself, he might want first thanks to go to them.

Archives and Libraries

The staff of the Archivio di Stato di Venezia dei Frari, the Biblioteca Museo Correr, San Marco, the Biblioteca Fondazione Scientifica Querini Stampalia and the Archivio di Casa Goldoni and Palazzo Mocenigo in Venice, the Vatican Library, the Paris Bibliothèque Nationale, the RGADA (Russian State Archive of Ancient Documents), Moscow and Bakhrushin Archive, Moscow, the RGIA (Russian State Historical Archive) in St Petersburg and The Hermitage Library and Print Room, St Petersburg, and the St Petersburg Alexandrinski Theatre archive.

Marie Tarantová, Martin Sovák and the staff of Prague's Czech State Archive, which holds most of what Casanova left when he died, were particularly helpful; as were the staff of Dux Castle and Museum, in particular Jiří Wolf and Petra Kofraňová and Jiří Bureš. Without them, this book would not have been possible. Back in London the staff of the British Library, especially the Rare Books and Manuscripts Rooms, the London Library and the Wellcome Institute deserve special thanks, as do the staff of Duke Humphrey's at the Bodleian Library Oxford, and the Newcastle Literary and Philosophical Society.

Travels

The extensive travel necessitated in the research and writing of this book was only made possible by the generous support of Christine Walker of the *Sunday Times* Travel Section and Michael Batterberry of *Food Arts Magazine*, New York, both of whom welcomed the idea of travel and food articles based on the works of this early travel writer – Casanova. Without them, and David Wickers of the *Sunday Times*, the unusual array of archives consulted would have been beyond my means.

For similar aid in terms of writing hideaways, I owe thanks beyond measure to Blanche and Andrew Sibbald, Jeremy Irons and Sinead Cusack, Rob, Susie and all at Hill Close House and Kilcoe Castle respectively, and to Lee Hall, Max Roberts, Bev Robertson and all the cast and crew of the play *The Pitmen Painters* in Newcastle, and Rina and Takis Anoussis, The Ideas Foundry, 59e59 Theaters, Ryan Early, Simon Green and all involved with Ron Hutchinson's *Beau Brummell* in New York, and to the cast and crew of the film *Admiral Kolchak* in Russia.

Venice

My host and friend Jeremy Magorian and my friend and translator Maximilian Tedeschi must have first thanks for opening

Venice and its archives to me, along with Michelle Lovric and John Berendt, Craig Raine, Annie la Gravanese, Robin Skye, Rose and Peter Lauritzen, Francesco and Jane da Mosto, Ludovico di Luigi, Frank Billaud and the Alliance Française in Venice, Cat Bauer, Dale Wesson, Mark Ashurst and Sara Yellich, Federica Centulani at the Museo Correr and Museo Mocenigo archives and Alessandra Bonetti Rubelli at the Guggenheim, to Joyce Fieldsend at Gran Teatro La Fenice for her advice on *Don Giovanni*, and Anna Barnabo at the Palazzo Malipiero

Rome

Sita de Vesci, Prince Oddone Colonna, the Caccia Club, Italian Journeys and the staff of the Hotel Bernini Bristol. Andrea di Robillant, and for his guidance with the letters of his ancestor Andrea Memmo and Guistiniana Wynne. The mayor and Tourist Board at Frascati.

Prague

All the staff of the Prague State Archives, Tomáš Staněk at the Estates Theatre and all involved with their 2007 production of *Don Giovanni* and Katerina Palitova and all the staff of the Mandarin Oriental Hotel, also Jacqueline Hyman ACR of the Textile Restoration Studio on Bohemian theatre materials.

Duchcov

Jiří Wolf, Petra Kofranňová, Jiří Bureš, Anna Šejvlová, Pavel Koukal and the Director and Staff of Dux Castle and Dux Museum and the Casanova Archive. The Pensione Casanova. Mirka Higgins for translation

St Petersburg

My friend Tobin Auber, Irina Kutova, Galya Stolyazova and the staff of the *St Petersburg Times* gave more help than they might realise, as did the hospitality and insights of Dimitri Ozerkov at The Hermitage, Yelena Fedosova and Yergenia Syzdaleva at the St Petersburg theatre archive, George Walden, Mario Corti – who kindly sent me details on his theory on the anagrammatic meaning of 'Seingalt' – and the staff of the Astoria Hotel.

Moscow

Galina Stepanova, my research assistant, the production team of *Admiral Kolchak* and also Constantin Habensky, Olga Kharichkina, Andrei Kravchuk, Varvara Kas'kova and Nicolai Mironov and Evklid Kyurdzidis.

Amsterdam, Utrecht and Dresden

I am especially indebted to Marco Leeflang not just for the invitation to drive the last catalogue entries for the Dux archive back to Dux Castle from Utrecht via Dresden, and for all I learned *en route*, but also for his permission to quote his find in the *Amsterdamse Courant* of 16 September 1758. It should also be acknowledged that every Casanoviste consulting the Dux archive is massively in Marco's debt for his indefatigable and invaluable work in cataloguing, at his own expense and with his own time, the entire body of literature held there and, by extension, accelerating reference and access to the originals held in Prague.

Monaco and Menton

Diana and Max Tedeschi and the staff of the Bibliothèque Louis Notari and Archives du Palais de Monaco.

Croatia

Sasha Damianovski, for notes on a distant land and help and encouragement always.

Provence

Lindsay Clay and Matthew White, and the staff of the Hotel and Restaurant du Parc, Lorgues.

Casanovistes

I have further found the international coterie of writers, academics and archivists with specialist interests in Casanova almost invariably welcoming, supportive, encouraging and helpful to the point in several instances of reading early drafts of this material and giving correction and guidance. In particular I would wish to thank Marco and Janna Leeflang, Helmut Watzlawick, Tom Vitelli, Furio Luccichenti, Anthony Badalamenti, Marie-Françoise Luna, Gianluca Simeoni, Sandro Pasqual and Alan Hooker. In similar vein I should aver here that, like any writer working on Casanova, my work is built on foundations laid by several generations of finer historians and archivists. Bernhard Marr of Dux, and in his wake J. Rives Childs, Guy Endore, Charles Samaran, Lydia Flem, Derek Parker, Judith Summers, John Masters and, in particular Jeremy Black have all, in their different ways, closely informed this book. Errors, of course, are my own.

I also owe boundless thanks for counsel and support to Ivan Mulcahy, a valued friend and agent, also my editor, publisher and friend at Hodder, Rupert Lancaster, and to Joel George Fotinos, Ken Siman, Kat Kimbal and Sarah Litt at Tarcher-Penguin USA. Hugo Wilkinson, Laura Macaulay and Josine Meijer, and again the invaluable close attention and skills of

Hazel Orme and Marcia Goldstein have corralled this book and its images into place. My dear friend Erica Wagner, Charlie Viney and Jonathan Conway, Janie Jenkins at Mike Leigh Associates, Carl Raymond, Julie Peakman, Natasha McEnroe, Hallie Rubenhold, Kate Chisholm, Kate Williams, Simon Chaplin at the Hunterian Institute, Fiona Ritchie, Freya Johnson and all those involved with the Dr Johnson Conference at Pembroke College, Oxford, 2007, Isabel Pollen, Selina Cadell, Victor Wynd and David Piper of the Last Tuesday Society also deserve special thanks. For medical and psychiatric advice on Casanova and others: Dr Larry Dumont, Dr Kate Gurney, Mr Andrew Kelly but, most of all, the close and invaluable psychological input, friendship, advice and encouragement of Dr Victoria Kortes-Papp.

Enviable as Casanova's odyssey might seem, as counterpoint I should say that quite a lot of this book was written in Hackney, north London, no nearer Venice than Stoke Newington's Venezia Café, juggling a house-build and two small children. The support of friends and family has thus been more than usually important, and I would like to thank, largely for childcare but also in helping to build a home: my parents and brothers, Rachelle Albicy, Julia Mankin and Liam O'Flaherty.

But those who really gave their all – or rather pretty much gave up all of me while I chased Giacomo Casanova – were my son Oscar, my wife Claire, and our baby daughter Cecelia, whose conception, birth and first steps I nearly missed, due to this book: that I didn't – quite – is what makes me, I know, a luckier man than Casanova.

BIBLIOGRAPHY

The primary sources for this biography include three imprints of Casanova's *Histoire de ma vie*, all based on the original in the Brockhaus bank, Wiesbaden: one a facsimile of the same now kept at Duchcov (Dux) Museum and Castle Archive. I am indebted both to the Brockhaus officials and Duchcov Museum for permission to quote from the original, and to Johns Hopkins University for permission to quote from the Willard Trask translation and edition of 1967, republished in paperback in 1997. Translations are my own in most instances, from the facsimile in Duchcov [Casanova *HV* Dux facs.] for instance or from the Bouquins, complete French edition, Plon (1960) [Casanova *HV* Bouquins], and credited here as such, and otherwise are from the Trask English language edition (1967). [Casanova *HL* Trask]

Casanova, Giacomo (Jacques Casanova, Chevalier de Seingalt), *Histoire de ma vie jusqu'à 1774*, 12 vols, facsimile manuscript of Brockhaus original, Duchcov Archive (see below) [Casanova *HV* Dux facs.]

Giacomo Casanova, Chevalier de Seingalt, Trask, Willard R., trans., *History of My Life*, Baltimore and London, 1967, republished 1997 [Casanova, *HL*, Trask]

Casanova, Jacques, Chevalier de Seingalt, Bouquins, Laffont, Robert ed., *Histoire de ma vie, suivie de texts inédits*, Plon, Paris, 1960 [Casanova *HV* Bouquins]

Other Cited Works by Casanova

Casanova Giacomo (Jacques Casanova, Chevalier de Seingalt)
——(trans.) Cahusac, *Zoroastro*, Dresden, 1752
——*Les Thessaliennes ou Arlequin au sabbat*, Prague, 1752
——*La Moluccheide*, a comedy, Dresden, 1753
——*Confutazione della Storia del Governo Veneto d'Amelot de la Houssaye*, Amsterdam and Lugano, 1769

——*Icosaméron*, Prague, 1788
——*Lana caprina, o Epistola di un licantropo*, Bologna, 1771
——*Istoria delle turbolenze della Polonia*, Gorizia, 1774
——*Dell'lliade di Omero (The Iliad) tradotto in ottavo rima*, Venice, 1775–8
——*Opuscoli miscellanei*, Venice, 1779
——*Scrutino del libro; 'Éloges de M. de Voltaire' par differens Auteurs*, Venice, 1779
——*Lettere della Nobil Donna Silvia Belegno*, Venice, 1780
——*Le Messager de Thalie*, Venice, October 1780 to January 1781
——*Di Aneddoti Viniziani e Amorosi Del Secolo Decimoquarto*, Venice, 1782
——*Ne Amori ne donne ovvero la stalla ripulita*, Venice, 1782
——*Lettre historico-critique sur un fait connu, dependant d'une cause peu connue*, Hamburg, 1784
——*Exposition raisonnée du différence qui subsiste entre les deux républiques de Venise et d'Hollande*, 1785
——*Histoire de ma fuite des prisons de la République de Venice qu'on appelle les plombs, écrit à Dux en Bohème en 1787*, 313 Paris. 1788
   À Leonard Snetlage, Geneva 1797
——*Examen des Études de la Nature*, Leeflang, Marco (ed.), Utrecht, 1985
——*The Duel*, trans. Nichols, J.G., Hesperus, London, 2003

Manuscripts and Archive Material

STÁTNÍ OBLASTNÍ ARCHIV V PRAZE-STATE ARCHIVES, PRAGUE [PSA]

The Marr Collection and reference system obtains to everything Bernhard Marr of Duchcov catalogued in the early twentieth century of the nearly three thousand items on nine thousand pieces of paper left in the castle in 1798, owned then by the Waldstein Estate. The collection is currently held in the Prague State Archives. The references are Marr's own and refer to papers including letters, but also Casanova's verses in several languages, plays, dialogues, advice, memos, aphorisms, codes, mathematical problems – particularly geometry and the duplication of cubic volume – chemistry, political treatises and many volumes of dialogue between a theologian and philosopher along with 'varia' including laundry lists, recipes and passports. Author is Casanova unless otherwise stated.

U1.1 *Della filosofia e de filosofi* 1780?; U1.4 *rêve dieu et moi*, 1792; U2.18 1780; U2.98 de Ligne, 1794; U2.102 de Ligne, *poème, Pourquoi parler sans Cesse de la Mort?*' 1794?; U2.135 de Ligne, letter, 1994?; U4.9 *récipe pour faire la lessive*, undated; U4.13 Casanova to Orlov, 1765; U4.59 address of Casanova in London, 1764?; U4.82 Sophie Cornelys to Casanova, London, 1764; U5.13 *passeport*, Russia, 1765; U6.17 Anglais et Venetien 1791?; U7.8 *Tetide et Peleo*, atto primo sc. 1–5, Casanova, 17??; U7.9 *Ulisse et Circe*, ballet pantomime, Casanova, 17??; U8.41 Wilkes to Casanova, 1757; U8.55 Charpillon to Casanova, 1763; U8.67 recipe, Semina Lini, 1798; U8.126–U8.161 Manon Balletti to Casanova, 1757–60; U8.162–U8.200 Francesca Buschini to Casanova, 1779–87; U8.209, London 1763; U8.210 Charpillon to Casanova, London 1764?; U8.211 Manon Balletti to Casanova, Paris, 1757; U8.214 Caterina Capretta Marsili to Casanova, 1779?; U9.35 *L'affaire 'Ne Amori ne donne'*, 1782?; U9.46 Notes for *mémoires*, 1791?; U9.48

'*Sur les Paradoxes de J.J. Rousseau*', 1769; U9.63 Notes *sur la réformation du calendrier*, 1792; U10D.1–U10D.18 Lorenzo de Ponte to Casanova, 1792–95; U12.59 Dr Peipers to Casanova, prescription, 1766; U16a.27 *poème* sur Angleterre, 1764; U16a.66 *poème*; '*Noblesse est un zéro*', 1796?; U16b.22 'In Praise of the French Language', 17??; U16c.12 varia laundry list, 1792?; U16.c.13 *poème*; '*La belle Valville*', 1765?; U16c.29 *poème*; '*Les Cinq Doigts*', 17??; U16c.36 *poème*: 'Praga' 1788?; U16d.2 varia, '*Recettes*' 17??; U16h.31 *Don Giovanni*, fragment, 1787; U16i.5 memo, list of friends to be asked for help, 1792?; U16i.8, *sur l'affaire Charpillon*, 1763; U16i.16 *Le mot Paradisum*, 1787; U16i.31 A prayer for understanding, 17??; U16i.33 *poème*, '*A Sophie* 1792?; U16i.34 On shame, modesty, 17??; U16i, '*Orgueil et Sottise*', 1791; U16k.2 varia List of Travel Necessities, 1793?; U16k.18 '*C'est des bisquits que je veux manger*', 1798; U16k.26 on Passion, 1789?; U16k.41 Note *pour les mémoires*, 1793; U16k.59 on dissimulation, 17??; U16k.63 On the female sex, 17??; U17a.12 *poème*, '*La langage des soupires*', 1790; U17a.42 *Introduction pour les Mémoires*, 1791?; U17a.54 Note *pour les mémoires, surtout* Vol. 4., 1789?; U17a.55-u17a.68 *Duplication du cubes et problèmes géometrique*, 1789–90; U18.29 Letter on Republic, 1793?; U19.4 '*Si l'homme ne parloit pas, penseroit-il?*, 1790?; U20.2 proposal for a lotto in Venice, 1782?; U20.5 '*Loterie grammaticale*', 17??; U20.8 on Jesus Christ and Lying, 17??; U21.1 *Précis de ma vie*, 1797; U21.4 *Histoire de mon éxistence*, 1791; U21.9 About Mulberries and silk production in Russia, 1765?; U25.1–U25.8 *Dell'Iliade d'Omero*, Cantos 1–18, 1765?; U29.1 '*Songe d'un quart d'heure, Dieu et moi*', 17??; U30.19 '*Pouvons nous être mécontent*', 1789; U31.35 Suicide, *courte réflexion d'un philosophe*, 1793; U31.37 '*Sur Voltaire*', 1794; U33.1 *Trésor Cabaistique (nombres heureux))* 1757; U33.2 Customs declaration for Count Farussi, 1764; U36.20 *Avis aux amateurs de l'histoire*, 1784

DUCHCOV CASTLE, CZECH REPUBLIC INCLUDING MANUSCRIPT FACSIMILES [DCM]

Casanova, Jacques, Chevalier de Seingalt, *Histoire de ma vie à 1797* (facsimile of Brockhaus original)

de la Houssaie, Amelot, *Histoire du Gouvernement de Venise*, Paris, 1685?

Casanova, G. *Esposizione Ragionata della Contestazione, che susiste tra'le due republiche di Venezia e di Olanda*, 1785

Rives Childs, J., ed., *Casanova Gleanings*, 21 vols, Paris and Geneva, 1958–78

Marr, Bernhard, *Pour le dossier de Miss XCV*

Marr 40 1–300, *Casanova archive extérieures à Dux* (collected Casanova references and letters, facsimiles and copies, not in Prague State Archive or Dux collection)

Leeflang, M. *Dux Ionnaire*, vols 1 and 2, Utrecht, 2005

Dossier de Dux (documents concernant Dux et Casanova), Utrecht, 1998

Les Archives de Dux, Utrecht, 2002

ARCHIVIO DI STATO DI FRARI, VENEZIA-FRARI STATE ARCHIVES, VENICE [ASV]

Letter e riferte dei confidante ex 137 199 bb 542–662

Inquisitori di Stato ex 197 Tome I–III

Appunti sul Giovan' Battista Manuzzi, 1750–59
Inquisitori di Stato referta del 22 marzo 1755
Inquisitorial documents on Giacomo Casanova, 11 Novembre 1754–24 Iuglio 1755
referta Casanova, Giacomo:
1773 29 genio e seg 181
1771 30 genio 159
1763–1782 565 confid riferte; Venezia, Londra, Trieste
1756 31 luglio–1 Octobre 962 V polizza di speca sel mantimento
1756 29 settembre condamnato anni 5 per co di religione
1769 27 genio 171 ma opera 'Confutazione d'amelot' lett. Torino
1774 3 settembre salvo condotte
1766–1768 922 Memmo, Nob. Andrea correspondanza col duca di Wirtemberg
   Memorie storiche degli ultimi cinquenta anni della repubblica di Venezia, Venice,
   1854

BIBLIOTECA MUSEO CORRER, VENEZIA-CORRER MUSEUM, VENICE

Gli Abiti de Veneziani di quasi ogni eta con diligenza racolti e dipinti nel secolo XVIII
   di Grevembroch

ARCHIVIO GIUSTINIAN RECANTI, VENEZIA

Prospetto schematico dei palchi del teatro di San Samuele.

ARCHIVIO CASA GOLDONI, VENEZIA-GOLDONI LIBRARY, VENICE

Catalogo Drammi per musica, Venezia, 1883
Teatro San Samuele, Volume Primo e secondo 163–4 1710–29, vol. V e VI 167–8;
   1742–51

ST PETERSBURG, ROSSIJISKIJ GOSUDARSTVENNYJ ISTORICHESKIJ ARXIC (R.G.I.A.)-RUSSIAN STATE ARCHIVE

Matveeva, Andreja Zapiski, *Russkij diplomat vo Francii*, 1705–6
Axonometric Plans of Saint Petersburg 1765–1773, F2/4, 146, L, M52
Sankt Peterburgskie Vedomosti (The *St Petersburg Gazette*), 1728–1765 *Primecha-niya k Vedomostyam* (Footnotes to the Gazette) 1728–42

MOSCOW, ROSSIJSKIJ GOSUDARSTRENNYJ ARXIV DREVNIX AKTOV (RGADA)-RUSSIAN STATE ARCHIVE OF ANCIENT DOCUMENTS

Sankt Peterburgskie Vedomosti (The *St Petersburg Gazette*,) 1728–65 *Primechaniya k Vedomostyam* (*Footnotes to the Gazette*) 1728 to 1742
Russlili Telegraf

MOSCOW, BAKHRUSHIN THEATRE ARCHIVE

Novikov, N., manuscript article, 'The experience of a historical dictionary maker on writers in Russia' on Volkov, Feodor, 1729–63
Volkov, Feodor, *Feasting Minerva*, court masquerade in honour of Catherine II, 1763

PUBLIC RECORDS OFFICE, KEW

Letters of Sarah Bentham, d. 1809, PRO 30/9/43

BODLEIAN LIBRARY, OXFORD

Ms. Add. A 366 fol. 60, Dodwell Tracy Letters
Ms. Eng. Misc. d. 213, Edmund Dewes, servant, on tour of Italy, 1776
Ms Douce 67, George Carpenter, 1695–1749

BRITISH MUSEUM

Add Man 351222, Burney, Charles, *Journal written during a Tour through France and Italy undertaken to collect material for a General History of Music*, 1770
Add Man Burney 002844853 519 b, *Gazetteer and London Daily Advertiser*, 1743–96
Add Man N R Burney 5465–18632, *Public Advertiser (London)*, 1728–94 (1763 and 1766)

Other Primary Material

Agrippa, Henry Cornelius of Nettesheim, *Three Books of Occult Philosophy*, London, 1651
Anonymous/'Abbé du Prat', attrib, Jean Barrin or François de Cavigny de la Brétonnière, *Venus dans le Cloitre ou la Réligieuse en Chemise*, Paris, 1737
Addison, J. *Remarks on Several Parts of Italy*, London, 1705
Baschet, A., '*Archives des affaires étrangeres, serie Holland* 1759, Paris 1851
Beckford, William, *The Travel Diaries of William Beckford of Fonthill*, London, 1781
Black, J., trans., *Memoirs of Goldoni written by himself*, 2 vols, London, 1814

Brady, F., and Pottle, A., (eds), Boswell, James, *Boswell on the Grand Tour; Italy, Corsica and France 1765–1766*, Yale University Press, New Haven and London, 1955

Brooke, N., *Observations on the Manners and Customs of Italy by a Gentleman*, Bath and London, 1798

Brosses, Charles de, *Lettres Familières écrites d'Italie en 1739 et 1740*, Paris, 1869

Burney, Charles, *The Present State of Music in France and Italy or the Journal of a tour through those countries, undertaken to collect Materials for a General History of Music*, London, 1771

Burney, Charles, *Music, Men and Manners in France and Italy, 1770 Being the Journal written by Charles Burney, MusD. During a Tour through those countries undertaken to collect material for a General History of Music*, Folio Society, London, 1974

Catherine II, Tsarina, *'Le Tracassier', composé par cette princesse, Théâtre de L'Hermitage de Catherine II*, Paris, 1799

Clary-Aldringen, Prince Charles Joseph (Lolo), *Le Journal*, Tome 1, 1795–98

Coyer, Abbé G. F., *Voyages d'Italie et de Hollande*, Paris, 1775

Créquy, Marquise de, *Souvenirs*, 8 vols, Paris, 1842

de Ponte, L. and Mozart, W. A., *Il dissoluto punito ossia il Don Giovanni, dramma giocoso in zwei akten text von Lorenzo da Ponte KV 527*, Vienna and Prague, 1787

D'Arcy Collyer, Adelaide (ed.), *The Despatches and Correspondence of John, Second Earl of Buckinghamshire, Ambassador to the Court of Catherine II of Russia 1762–65*, London, 1899

Dashkova (Daschkaw), Princess Elizabeth, *Memoirs of Princess Daschkaw, Lady of Honour to Catherine II Empress of All the Russias, written by Herself, comprising the letters of the Empress and other correspondence*, London, 1840

de Ligne, Prince [Charles], *'Amant Ridicule', Théâtre de L'Hermitage de Catherine II*, Paris, 1799

de Ligne, Charles, *Lettres et Pensées du Maréchal Prince de Ligne*, Paris, 1809

de Ligne, Charles, *Letters and Papers*, New York, 1899

de Ligne, Charles, *Annales Prince de Ligne*, 19 vols, Brussels, 1920–38

de Ligne, Charles, *Fragments de l'histoire de ma vie*, 2 vols, Paris, 1928

de Ligne, Prince, *Mémoires et mélanges historiques du prince de Ligne*, Paris, 1828 (Tome IV quoted as *Fragments sur Casanova*, in *Mémoires de Jacques Casanova de Seingalt suivi de Fragments des mémoires du Prince de Ligne*, 1921)

de Ligne, Charles, *Fragment sur Casanova, suivi de lettres à Casanova*, Paris, 1988

de Vries, Leonard, and Fyer, Peter (compilers), *Venus Unmasked or an Inquiry into the nature and Origin of the Passion of Love, interspersed with curious and entertaining Accounts of Several Modern Amours, 1705–93*, reprinted Arthur Baker Ltd, London, 1967

Dittersdorf, Carl Ditters von, The Elder, *Autobiography*, trans. A. D. Coleridge, London, 1896

Doran, John, *"Mann" and manners at the Court of Florence 1740–1786*, 2 vols, London, 1876

Goethe, J. W., *Travels in Italy*, trans. Rev. A. J. W. Morrison, London, 1849

Goldoni, Carlo, *Mémoires de M Goldoni pour server à l'histoire de sa vie et à celle de son théâtre*, 3 vols, Paris, 1787

Halsband, R. (ed), *The Complete Letters of Lady Mary Wortley Montagu*, Oxford, 1967

Hanbury-Williams, Charles, *Letters*, 92 vols, 1928

Hoare, R. C., *Hints to Travellers in Italy*, London, 1815

Kelly, Michael, *Reminiscences of Michael Kelly of the King's Theatre and Theatre Royal Drury Lane*, London, 1826

La Lande, J. de, *Voyage en Italie*, Geneva, 1790

Lamberg, Maximilian, *Memorial d'un mondain*, Paris, 1774

Macartney, George, Earl, *An Account of Russia addressed to the King*, London, 1768

Meissner, Alfred, *Rococobilder*, Gumtoinnin, Germany, 1871

Molmenti, Pompeo (ed.), *Letters*, Andrea Memmo to G. Casanova, *Epistolari veneziani del secolo XVIII*, Milan, 1914

Nugent, Thomas, *A Grand Tour through the Netherlands, Germany, France and Italy*, 4 vols, London, 1749

Parfait, *Dictionnaire des théâtres*, Paris, 1756

Pick, C. (ed.), Wortley Montagu, Lady, Mary *Embassy to Constantinople*, London, 1988

Pitton de Tournefort, Joseph, *A Voyage into the Levant*, London, 1718

Postel, Guillaume, de Barentonius, *De originibus seu de Hebraice linguae et gentis antiquitate*, Paris, 1538

Rava, Aldo (ed.), *Lettere di donne a Giacomo Casanova*, Milan, 1912

Rose, William Stewart, *Letters from the North of Italy addressed to Henry Hallam Esq., in two volumes*, London, 1819

Sharp, Samuel, *A View of the Customs, Manners, Drama &c of Italy as they are described in 'The Frusta Letteraria' and in The Account of Italy in English by Mr Barretti, compared to the Letters from Italy by Mr Sharp*, London, 1768

Shaw, Joseph, *Letters to a Nobleman*, London, 1709

Sidgewick, Owen, *The Universal Masquerade or The World Turn'd Inside Out*, London, 1742

Southwell, Edward, *The Hell-Fire Club: kept by a Society of Blasphemers – a Satyr*, London, 1721

Walpole, Horace, *Correspondence*, 3 vols, London, 1837

Wilkes, John (Pego Borewell), *An Essay on Woman*, London, 1763

Wolf, J. Christopher, *Bibliotheca Hebræa sive notitia tum auctorum hebr.*, Hamburg and Leipzig, 1715

OTHER PERIODICALS

Gentleman's Magazine, London, 1763–5

Lady's Magazine, London, 1773

Sankt Peterburgskie Vedomosti (*St Petersburg Gazette*) 1728–65, *Primechaniya k Vedomostyam* (Footnotes to the *Gazette*), 1728–42

Amsterdamse Courant, Amsterdam, 16 September 1758

Gazetta Urbana Veneta, Venice, 31 May 1788

Secondary Texts

Andrieux, Maurice, *Venise au temps de Casanova*, trans., Mary Fitton, Unwin, London, 1972

Andrieux, Maurice, *Venise au temps de Casanova*, Hachette, Paris, 1969

Aries, Philippe, *Centuries of Childhood*, trans. Baldick, R., Pimlico, London, 1996

Aries, Philippe, *L'Enfant et la familiale sous l'ancien regime*, Plon, Paris, 1962

Ashton, John, *A History of English Lotteries*, London, 1893

Auden, W. H., and Mayer, Elizabeth, trans. and eds., *J.W. Goethe; Italian Journey 1786–1788*, Penguin, London, 1962

Barbier, Patrick, *The World of the Castrati*, trans. Crosland, Margaret Souvenir, London, 1998

Bartolini, Elio, *Le Crépuscule de Casanova*, trans., Abrame-Battesti, Paris, Éditions Desjonquères, 1994

Benedict, Barbara M., *Eighteenth Century British Erotica*, 5 vols, Pickering and Chatto, London, 2002

Berelowitch, Wladimir, and Medvedkova, Olga, *Histoire de Saint-Pétersbourg*, Fayard, Paris, 1996

Black, Jeremy, *Italy and The Grand Tour*, Yale University Press, New Haven and London, 2003

Black, Jeremy, *The Grand Tour in the Eighteenth Century*, Sutton, London, 1992

Bleakley, Horace, *Casanova in England*, London, 1923

Bloom, Harold, *Kabbalah and Criticism*, Seabury, New York, 1975

Bond, Frederick Bligh and Simcox, Thomas, *A Preliminary Investigation of the Cabala contained in the Coptic Gnostic Books and of similar Gematria in the Greek text of the New Testament shewing the presence of a system of teaching by means of the doctrinal significance of numbers*, Oxford, 1917

Bowman, Horace Bushnell, *The Castrati Singers and their Music*, PhD thesis, Indiana University Library, 1951

Molmenti, P., *Venice; the Decadence*, trans. Brown, H. F., 2 vols from the original *La Storia di Venezia nella vita privata dalle origini alla caduta della repubblica*, London, 1908

Busetto, G., *Pietro Longhi Gabriel Bella, Scene di vita veneziana*, Bompiani, Venice, 1995

Cairns, Christopher (ed.), *The Commedia dell'Arte from the Renaissance to Dario Fo, The Italian Origins of European Theatre VI. The Papers of the conference of The Society for Italian Studies*, Edwin Mellen Press, Lewiston/Queenston/Lampeter, 1988

Comisso, Giovanni, *Agenti segreti veneziani nel '700 1705–1797*, Milan, 1941

Cusset, Catherine, (ed.), *Libertinage and Modernity*, Yale University Press, New Haven, 1998

Darnton, Robert, *The Forbidden Best-sellers of Pre-Revolutionary France*, New York, 1995

de Vries, Leonard, *Venus Unmasked*, Barker, London, 1967

di Robillant, Andrea, *A Venetian Affair*, Vintage, New York, 2005

Endore, Guy L., *Casanova, His Known and Unknown Life*, London, 1930

Erdogan, Sema Nilgun, *Sexual Life in Ottoman Society*, Dönence, Istanbul, 1996

Farrell, Joseph (ed.), *Carlo Goldoni and the Eighteenth Century Theatre*, Edwin Mellen Press, New York, 1997

Franzoi, Umberto, *Le Prigioni di Palazzo Ducale a Venezia*, Electa, Venice, 2005

Fraser, David, *Frederick the Great, King of Prussia*, Penguin, London, 2000

Gatrell, Vic, *City of Laughter – Sex and Satire in Eighteenth Century London*, Atlantic Books, London, 2006

Ginger, Andrew, Hobbs, John, Lewis, Huw (eds), *Selected Interdisciplinary Essays on the Representation of the Don Juan Archetype in Myth and Culture*, Edwin Mellen Press, New York and Lampeter, 2000

Ginsburg, Christian, *The Kabbalah – Its Doctrines, Development and Literature*, Routledge, London, 1920

Goldoni, Luca, *Casanova, romantica spia*, Venice, 1998

Grayling, A. C., 'The Age of Reason', in Rizzol, *RA magazine*, no. 93, winter 2006

Gregor, Joseph, *Casanova in Petersburg*, H. Bauer, Vienna, 1947

Günther, Pablo, *The Casanova Tour, A Handbook for the Use of the Private Travelling Carriage in 18th-Century Europe*, Lindau (printed by the author), 1999

Halevi, Z'ev ben Shimon, *Kabbalah, Tradition of Hidden Knowledge*, Thames & Hudson, London, 1979

Hallamish, Moshe, *An Introduction to the Kaballah*, trans. Ruth bar-Ilan and Ora Wiskind-Elper, State University of New York, New York, 1999

Heriot, Angus, *The Castrati in Opera*, Martin Secker & Warburg, London, 1956

Holme, Timothy, *A Servant of Many Masters, The Life and Times of Carlo Goldoni*, Jupiter, London, 1976

Hunter, Mary, *The Culture of Opera Buffa in Mozart's Vienna: A Poetics of Entertainment*, Princeton University Press, New Jersey, 1999

Jervis, Henry W., *The History of Corfu*, London, 1852

Kihli-Sagols, Didier, *La Comédie médicale de Giacomo Casanova*, Theles, Paris, 2005

King, C. W., *The Gnostics and their Remains, Ancient and Medieval*, London, 1887

Krondl, Michael, *The Taste of Conquest; the Rise and Fall of Three Great Cities of Spice*, Random House, New York, 2008

Labande, Leon-Honoré, *Histoire de la Principauté de Monaco*, 2e edition, Monaco, archives du Palais, 1934

Lauritzen, Peter, *Venice: a thousand years of culture and civilization*, Weidenfeld & Nicholson, London, 1978

Leppman, Wolfgang, *J.J. Winckelman*, Knopf, New York, 1970

Lovric, Michelle, *Venice, Tales of a City*, Abacus, London, 2003

Lowe, Alfonso, *La Serenissima, The Last Flowering of the Venetian Republic*, Cassell, London, 1974

Luna, Marie-Françoise, *Casanova, Fin de Siècle; Actes au colloque international*, Honoré Champion, Paris, 2002

Luna, Marie-Françoise, *Casanova Mémorialiste*, Honoré Campion, Paris, 1998

MacCarthy, Fiona, *Byron: Life and Legend*, John Murray, London, 2002

MacDonogh, Giles, *Frederick the Great*, Weidenfeld & Nicholson, London, 1999

Mamy, Sylvie, *Les Grands Castrats Napolitains à Venise au XVIIIe Siecle*, Mardaga, Liège, 1994

Mangini, Nicola, *I Teatri di Venezia*, Mursia, Milan, 1974

Mansel, H. L., *The Gnostic Heresies*, London, 1875

Mansel, Philip, *Prince of Europe, The Life of Charles-Joseph de Ligne 1735–1814*, Weidenfeld & Nicholson, London, 2003

Marr, Bernhard, and de Givry, G., 'La Kabbale de Jacques Casanova', *Sirène*, ed. III, p. ix–xxi; *Patrizi e avventurieri* Milan, 1930

Massi, E., *La vita, i temps, gli amici di Francesco Albergati*, Bologna, 1878

Masters, John, *Casanova*, Joseph Publishing, London, 1969

Maynial, Edouard, *Casanova and his Time*, trans. Ethel Colburn Mayne, London, 1911

McMahon, Darren M. *The Pursuit of Happiness*, Allen Lane/Penguin, New York, 2006

Molmenti, P., *Storia di Venezia nella vita privata dalle origini alla caduta della repubblica*, Bergamo, 1908

Monglond, A., *Revue d'histoire diplomatique*, Paris, 1938

Monnier, Philippe, *Venice in the Eighteenth Century*, London 1910

Mudge, Bradford K., (ed.), *When Flesh Becomes Word, An Anthology of Early 18th Century Libertine Literature*, Oxford University Press, Oxford, 2004

Neyremand, M., *Séjour en Alsace de quelques hommes célèbres*, Paris, 1861

Noat-Antoni, Olivia, *Vivre à Monaco aux XVIIe et XVIIIe siècles*, Nice, Serre Editeur, 2000

Norwich, John Julius, *A History of Venice*, Vintage, London, 1989

Norwich, John Julius, *Paradise of Cities – Venice and its Visitors*, Penguin, London, 2003

Ober, Willian B., *Boswell's Clap and other Essays*, Feffer and Simons, London, 1969

Olschki, Leo. S. (ed.), *Giacomo Casanova tra Venezia e l'Europa*, Comune di Venezia, Venice, 1999

Ozerkov, D., Padiyar, S., and Alexandrian, S. (eds), *The Triumph of Eros, Art and Seduction in 18th Century France*, Fontanka Press, St Petersburg and London, 2006

Parker, Derek, *Casanova*, Sutton, London, 2002

Pearson, Roger, *Voltaire Almighty*, Bloomsbury, London, 2005

Petráň, Josef, *Kalendář – aneb Čtení o Velkém plese korunovačním v pražském Nosticově divadle* 12. září 1791 v časech francouzské revoluce, trans. Mirka Higgins, Nakladetelství Lidové Noviny, Prague, 2004

Picard, Liza, *Dr Johnson's London*, Phoenix, London, 2000

Plath, Wolfgang, and Rehm, Wolfgang, Introductory notes to *Il dissoluto punito ossia il Don Giovanni, dramma giocoso in zwei akten text von Lorenzo da Ponte KV 527*, trans. Douglas Woodfull-Harris, Kassel, London, and Bärenreiter, Salzburg, 1977 and 1991

Porter, Roy, and Rousseau, G.S., *Exoticism in The Enlightenment*, Manchester University Press, New York, 1990

Porter, Roy, *Flesh in the Age of Reason*, Allen Lane, London, 2003

Porter, Roy, *The Enlightenment*, Palgrave, London, 2001

Porter, Roy, *The Creation of the Modern World*, Norton, New York and London, 2000

Pottle, F., and Brady, F. (eds), *Boswell on the Grand Tour, 1765–1100*, Yale University Press and William Heinemann, London, 1955

Purks Maccubbin, Robert (ed.,) *'Tis Nature's Fault – Unauthorized Sexuality during the Enlightenment*, Cambridge University Press, Cambridge & New York, 1987

Quennell, Peter, *Casanova in London and Other Essays*, Weidenfeld & Nicholson, London, 1970

Regnier, Henri de, *Casanova chez Voltaire*, Plon, Paris, 1929

Rives Childs, J., *Casanova: a New Perspective*, Paragon, New York, 1988

Roubinek, O., Cerny, J., Jerie, P., and Kral, J. (eds), *The Theatre of the Estates*

Rousseau, G.S., and Porter, R. (eds), *Sexual Underworlds of the Enlightenment*, Manchester University Press, Manchester, 1987

Saige, Gustave, *Monaco, Ses origines et son histoire d'après les documents originaux*, Imprimerie de Monaco, 1897

Sainsbury, J., *John Wilkes*, Ashgate, London, 2006

Samaran, Charles, *Jacques Casanova, vénitien, une vie d'aventurier au XVIII siecle*, Paris, 1914

Scholem, G., *Major Trends in Jewish Mysticism*, Thames & Hudson, London, 1955

Scholem, G., *Kaballah*, Dorset Press, New York, 1987

Scholz, Piotr O., *Eunuchs and Castrati*, Markus Weiner, Princeton, New Jersey, 1999

Selvatico, Riccardo, *Cento note per Casanova a Venezia, 1753–1756*, Neri Pozza, Vicenza, 1997

Sollers, Philippe, *Casanova l'admirable*, Plon, Paris, 1998

Spector, Sheila A., *Glorious Incomprehensible; the development of Blake's Kabbalistic Language*, Associated University Presses, London, 2001

Spector, Sheila A., *Wonders Divine; the Development of Blake's Kabbalistic Myth*, Associated University Presses, London, 2001

BIBLIOGRAPHY

Steptoe, A., *The Mozart-Da Ponte Operas*, Clarendon, Oxford, 1988
Straub, Kristina, *Sexual Suspects; Eighteenth Century Players and Sexual Ideology*, Princeton University Press, New Jersey, 1992
Summers, Judith, *Casanova's Women*, Bloomsbury, London, 2006
Taylor, G. Rattray, *Sex in History*, Thames & Hudson, London, 1968
Thomas, Chantal, *Casanova, un voyage libertin*, Denoël, Paris, 1985
Traverso, O., *The Church of San Samuele, Venice*, Marconi Arti Grafiche, Genoa, 2002
Urban, L., Romanelli, G., Gandolfi, F. (eds), *Venise en fête*, Chêne, Paris, 1992
Waite, A.E., *The Holy Kabbalah*, New York, 2003 (unabridged republication of the original, Williams & Norgate, London, 1929)
Weil, Taddeo, *Teatri Musicali Venezani dell Settecento*, Venice, 1897
Wilson, Frances (ed.), *Adventures of Casanova, Selection from The History of My Life by Giacomo Casanova*, Folio Society, London, 2007
Ze'evi, Dror, *Producing Desire; Changing Sexual Discourse in the Ottoman Middle East 1500–1900*, University of California Press, Berkeley, California, 2006.

NOTES ON SOURCES

Full bibliographical data for each of the cited works appears in
the Bibliography.

The following abbreviations have been used:

ASV   Archivio di Stato, Venezia
BM   British Museum
Casanova, *HV*, Dux facs. (Casanova, Giacomo; *Histoire de ma
                vie, Dux facsimile MS)
Casanova, *HL*, Trask (Casanova, Giacomo; *History of my
                Life*, trans. Trask, Willard, R.)
Casanova *HV*, Bouquins (Casanova, Giacomo, *Histoire de ma
                vie*, Bouquins, Robert Laffort, ed.)
DCM   Duchcov Castle Museum Archive, CR
PSA   Prague State Archive

Act I sc. i: The Calle Della Commedia

'A man born in Venice': Casanova, G., *The Duel* (1780), trans. Tim Parks, 2000, p. 3.
'Four days after Easter': Casanova was born on 2 April and baptised on 5 April.

Prelude: The Teatro Del Mundo

'In the first minute . . . dazzling lights': PSA, U1/1 XV, Casanova, *Songe d'un Quart
d'heure, 'Rêve Dieu et Moi'*, première minute, 1791/2.
'*Porcheria tedescha*': Roubinek, O., Cerny, J., Jerie, P., and Kral, J. (eds), *The Theatre
of the Estates*, p. 9.
'ells of Bohemian red linen': An ell of fabric is approximately a yard or metre in length.
The actual length of the ell varied from forty-five inches in England to fifty-four in
France and seemingly twenty-seven in Prague.
'Antonio Salieri . . . through the proscenium': Petran, Josef, *Kalendář – aneb Čtení o
Velkém plese korunovačním v pražském Nosticově divadle* 12. září 1791 v časech
francouzské revoluce, pp. 13ff.

'*mondi nouvi* – New Worlds': cf. Correr collection, Venice; also Urban, L., Romanelli, G., Gandolfi, F. (eds), *Venise en fêtes*, pp 89ff.

'eyeballs and noses . . . familiar to me': PSA, U1/1 XV.

Introduzione: The Opera Buffa Called Venice

'Casanova's memoirs . . . an era': Rives Childs, J., *Casanova: a New Perspective*, p. 2.

'The only remedy': Casanova, *HL*, Trask, vol. 1, p. 9.

'Notoriously unreliable': *Casanova*, starring Heath Ledger: *New York Times*, 26 June, 2004.

'perhaps he wrote too much': '*Casanova disse tutto, forse troppo e qualche volte it non vero*', *Lettre a Pananti*, Lorenzo da Ponte, in Samaran, *Jacques Casanova, véritien*, p. viii.

'Have courage to free yourself: Grayling, A.C., 'The Age of Reason', p. 43.

'You tell your story . . . sought after': Casanova, *HL*, Trask, vol. 3, p. 133.

'the very essence . . . its spirit': Ozerkov, D., Padïyar, S., and Alexandrian, S. *The Triumph of Eros, Art and Seduction*, p. 36.

'John Wilkes . . . Betsy Green': Pottle, F., and Brady, F. (eds), *Boswell on the Grand Tour*, p. 58n.

'prophylactic against melancholy': Casanova, in Kihli-Sagols, Didier, *La Comédie médicale de Giacome Casanova*, p. 129.

'to fence against the infirmities of ill health, and other evils of life – by mirth': Laurence Sterne, in Porter, R., *Flesh in the Age of Reason*, p. 287.

'in the middle of the sea . . . by art alone': Andrieux, M., *Venise*, 1972 p. xxx.

'The air was full . . . business': Molmenti, in Lowe, Alfonso, *La Serenissima. The Last Flowering of the Venetian Republic*, p. 31.

'The ghetto . . . their wares': Molmenti, P., *Storia di Venezia nella vita privata dalle origini alla caduta della repubblica*, vol. III, p. 206ff.

'The scripts . . . ceased to be God's': Porter, R., *Flesh in the Age of Reason*, p. 285.

'What was required . . . is to dazzle': Casanova, *HL*, Trask, vol. 3, p. 108.

'Rote . . . drawing the curtain': Rives, Childs, J., *Casanova Gleanings*, vol. XIX, p. 17.

'fear of being hissed': Casanova, *HL*, Trask, vol. 1, p. 35.

Easter fell on 1 April in 1725. Baptismal records from the parish of San Samuele now held at San Stefano and published in *Memorie storiche degli ultimi cinquanta anni della repubblica di Venezia*, Venice, 1854.

'The son of . . . Michele Grimani': Casanova, G., *Ne Amori ne donne*; GC alludes to his being the son of Michele Grimani; see also Casanova, *HL*, Trask, vol. 1, p. 326 n.

'Calle della commedia': now the Calle Malipiero.

'The house on the Calle': Calle della Commedia is now Malipiero, running behind the Palazzo Malipiero from the San Samuele church. The theatre occupied the site of the large school at the far end. The plaque marking Casanova's birth in 1725 rightly acknowledges that the actual house is unknown, though it is supposed to have been either 3082 or 3083, based on the later numbering system, and according to later descriptions of parties there.

'An area still marked': The carved cobblers' signs are most prominent still on the corners of the Salizada San Samuele and Crosera della Bottegue. See also Traverso, O. *The Church of San Samuele, Venice*, p. 17.

'Abomination': Casanova, *HL*, Trask, vol. 1, p. 43.

'The first memory that stuck . . . Queen of the Night': Ibid., pp. 44–5.
'Vegetating . . . incapable of thought': Ibid., p. 29.
'Then as now . . . glass' Nugent, T., *Grand Tour*, vol. III, p. 110.
'Venice in miniature': Goethe, *Travels in Italy*, p. 295.
'Two pounds of blood . . . like an idiot': Casanova, *HL*, Trask, vol. 1, p. 48.
'Like Noah's ark . . . as on board a ship': Burney, Charles, *Music, Men and Manners*, pp. 85–6.
'Sublime genius . . . lascivious manner': Casanova, *HL*, Trask, vol. 1, p. 49.
'Always reason logically': Ibid., p. 50.
'Got rid of me': Ibid., p. 51.

ACT 1 sc. ii: At School in Padua

'It was applause . . . happiness': Casanova, HL, Trask, vol. 1, p. 62.
'Plump, modest, polite': Ibid., p. 58.
'*Satyra sotadica de Arcanis Amoris et Venus:*' Titled *Aloysea Sigeia* and mentioned by GC simply as *Meursius*, ibid., p. 63. First published in Lyon in 1660, attributed to Luisa Sigeea but actually by Nicolas Chorier, 1609–92, translated into French 1730 as *l'Academie des dames de Meursius*, which seems to have been what the doctor had in his collection or GC was translating into French. It was more commonly available in Italy at this period as *Dialogues de Luisa Sigeia*.
'Marvellously beautiful . . . uncomfortable': Ibid., p. 58.
'*Discite Grammatici* . . . set me on the pinnacle of happiness': Ibid., pp. 60–62.
'Putting on stockings . . . dishonoured her': Ibid., p. 96.
'When I leave the table . . . other times': Ibid., p. 69.
'my first love': Ibid., p. 52.
'that he was not particularly intelligent . . . the departure': Ibid., p. 91.

ACT I sc. iii: I Become a Preacher

'He was handsome . . . twenty mistresses': Casanova, *HL*, Trask, vol. 1, p. 97.
'He had just come . . . Padua': Ibid., p. 96.
'six feet' or 1.86 metres. There has been controversy over GC's height due to mistranslation. 'Crébillon [the French tragedian] was a Colossus. He was six feet high, taller than me by three inches', leading some documents to place GC's height as five foot nine. The old foot referred to in *Histoire de ma vie* was a tenth longer than the modern foot. Cf Endore, Guy L., *Casanova, His Known and Unknown Life*, p. xxiv.
'her greatest comfort': Casanova, *HL*, Trask, vol. 1, p. 96.
'men of wit . . . gone the pace': Ibid., p. 97.
'pretty, wilful and a flirt': Ibid., p. 100.
'so great . . . tears': Ibid., p. 103.
'What do you say . . . astonishing things': Ibid., pp. 104–105.
'nearly fifty *zecchini* . . . when I was greatly in need of money . . . a preacher': Ibid., p. 107.
'a low murmur . . . in good earnest': Ibid., p. 109.

ACT 1 sc. iv: Enter Lucia, Nanetta and Marta

'they said . . . in bed together': Casanova, *HL*, Trask, vol. 1, p. 139.

'twin rocks eminently shaped': Ibid., p. 121.

'Nanetta and Marta Savorgnan': Casanova does not give the second name, Rives Childs, J., *Casanova Gleanings*, vol. III, p. 17.

'perfect dragon of virtue': Casanova, *HL*, Trask, vol. 1, p. 107.

'exasperated beyond measure': Ibid., p. 114.

'having a kind of virginity': Ibid., p. 114.

'devouring gnats': [August 11/12 1770]' Burney, Charles, *Music, Men and Manners*, p. 78.

'charged with . . . Africa': Rose, William Stuart, *Letters from Italy*, vol. 1, pp. 296–7.

'Unable to bear . . . redoubling the desire': Casanova, *HL*, Trask, vol. 1, p. 119.

'I had been proud . . . her misfortunes': Ibid., pp. 149–150.

'a fear . . . full enjoyment': Ibid., p. 123.

'bosom friends . . . all her secrets': Ibid., p. 123.

'*utroque jure*': Doctor's degree in civil and canon law. GC was enrolled at Padua University, aged twelve, on 28 November 1737, to obtain the *laurea*; studies had to be pursued for four consecutive years. Casanova, like many law students, spent part of his time in Venice, and part in Padua, obliged to return to Padua, to Dr Gozzi's, to fulfil the obligations for the degree. Ibid., pp. 135 and 329n.

'they had their backs . . . varied skirmishes': Ibid., pp. 141–2.

'repeatedly making love': Ibid., vol. 2, p. 60.

'this love . . . self-interest': Casanova, *HV*, Bouquins, vol. 1, p. 134.

'Giulietta Preati': Giulia Ursala Preati 1724–*c*.90, also known as La Cavamacchie, Countess Preati, Signora Querini, Signora Uccelli.

'Opera by Metastasio': Casanova, *HL*, Trask, vol. 1, p. 110.

'charms upon me': Ibid., p. 145.

'stained with the visible': It has been suggested that Casanova, as a young man and perhaps throughout his adult sexual life, 'suffered' from excessive seminal discharge during arousal, and before orgasm, as well as from premature ejaculation.

'ever a skilful swordsman won': Ibid., p. 153.

'you *know* why': Ibid., p. 155.

ACT 1 sc. v: Seminarian No More

'I eventually abandoned the church': Casanova, Giacomo, *Histoire de ma fuite des prisons*, p. 1.

'Bernardo de Bernadis': 1699–1758, made Bishop of Martorano 16 May 1743. Casanova, *HL*, Trask, vol. 1, pp. 156–7 and 334n.

'I see you at last a bishop': Ibid., p. 158.

'great and substantial': Ibid.

'both excited and alarmed him': For more discussion on the disputed chronology of Casanova in 1741 and 1745 in Corfu and Istanbul see Rives Childs, J., *Casanova Gleanings*, vol V, p. xxx.

'laughable': Casanova, *HL*, Trask, vol. 1, pp. 164–5.

'until his penis bled': Ibid., p. 166.

'road to the Papacy': Ibid., p. 162.

'handsome seminarian of fifteen': Ibid., p. 168.

'no seminarian got into bed with another': Ibid. p. 170.

'worry . . . abstinence': Ibid., p. 174.

'the Doge . . . wed the sea': Ibid., p. 175.

'*medicina spagirica*': dating from Paracelsus (1493–1541), alchemical compound used in treating venereal disease. It seems Casanova's infections were repeated doses of gonorrhoea, which was taken, incorrectly, as a variant of syphilis at the time and often treated also with mercury chemotherapy, which Casanova self-administered in later life.

'which greatly raised . . . regretting nothing': Casanova, *HL*, Trask, vol. 1, p. 201.

INTERMEZZO: Casanova and Travel

'I take pleasure . . . travelling': Casanova, *HL*, Trask, vol. 6, p. 225.

'It was the fourth sexual adventure': Casanova, *HV*, Dux facs., vol. 11, p. 003344.

'compact stove and pisspot': PSA, U16 k/2 main de Casanova note, 1793?.

'64,060 kilometres': Günther, P., *The Casanova Tour*, p. 2.

'In 1770 Charles Burney . . . fire aside': Burney, Charles, *Music, Men and Manners*, p. 23.

'the company . . . worth mentioning': Ibid., p. 24.

'a lewd poem': Poem to Valville, PSA, U16c/13

'twenty-seven different currencies and 471': Günther, *The Casanova Tour*, p. 225.

'every traveller ought': Hoare, R. C., *Hints to Travellers in Italy*, p. v.

ACT II sc. i: The Road to Rome and Naples

'the man fit to make . . . in London': Casanova, *Histoire de ma vie*, Leppman, W., *J. J. Winckelmann*, pp. 145–6.

'Friulian red wine': Casanova names it as Refosco. Casanova, *HL*, Trask, vol. 1, p. 207.

'splintery square five or six inches across': Ibid., p. 214.

'The harbour . . . is exceeding bad': Nugent, T., *A Grand Tour*, vol. III, pp. 196–7.

'sordid freak': Casanova, *HL*, Trask, vol. 1, p. 259.

'one hundred and fifty-six miles': Nugent, *Grand Tour*, vol. III, p. 185.

'naked and drunk . . . policeman in the Papal States': Casanova, *HL*, Trask vol. 1, p. 224.

'without love . . . a vile thing': Ibid., p. 227.

'San Francesco': Casanova states that he went to a Minimite monastery at Monte Magnanopoli, part of the Quirinal Hill, but the Minimite monastery was San Francesco di Paola. Ibid., p. 342n.

'What a poor present': Ibid., p. 238.

'always slept with my breeches on': Casanova, *HL*, Trask, vol. 1 p. 240.

'Vesuvian lava': Burney, Charles, *Music, Men and Manners*, p. 124.

'Queen Maria Amalia': Maria Amalia Walburga, Queen of Naples from 1739.

'what afflicts me . . . the affairs of others': Rives Childs, J., *Casanova: a New Perspective*, p. 31.

'Anna Maria d'Antoni': Ibid.

'pestilential Pomptine marshes . . . malaria': Hoare, R.C., *Hints to Travellers in Italy*, p. 33.

'The one man in Rome': Casanova, *HL*, Trask, vol. 1 p. 258.

'In Rome everyone wants to be an Abate': Ibid., p. 265.

'Standing face to face . . . love I thank thee': Ibid., p. 280.
'Alas for anyone . . . in perfect concord': Ibid., p. 271.
'Alas . . . you will never get over me': Ibid., p. 276.
'Benedict xiv . . . liked a joke': Ibid., p. 285.
'Rome is small': Ibid., p. 284.
'I give you . . . employment': Ibid., p. 317.

ACT II sc. ii: Love and Travesty

'Our word *Person* . . . an *Actor* is': Hobbes, in Porter, R., *Flesh in the Age of Reason*, p. 272.
'all the verve . . . playfulness': Casanova, *HL*, Trask, vol. 2, p. 6.
'ravishingly handsome': Ibid., p. 5.
'it was extacy[sic] . . . Enchantment!': Burney, Charles, *Music, Men and Manners*, pp. 205–8.
'made no resistance to the desires': Casanova, *HL*, Trask, vol. 2, p. 5.
'*première actrice*': Casanova, Giacomo, *Examen des Etudes de la Nature*, p. 57.
'white truffles, shellfish, Ximenes': Casanova, *HL*, Trask, vol. 2, p. 15.
'all we castrati . . . deformity': Ibid., p. 6.
'consent to the infamies': Ibid., p. 17.
'monstrous clitoris': Ibid., p. 18.
'to make her . . . same situation': Ibid., p. 32.
'Artemisia Lanti or Angiola Calori': Summers, Judith, *Casanova's Women*, pp. 120–22.
'by refusing . . . our happiness': Casanova, *HL*, Trask, vol. 2, p. 25.
'my own master . . . such a man': Ibid., p. 32.
'neither woman nor men . . . dressed as a man': Casanova, *Examen des Etudes*, p. 57.
'Rimini opera calendar . . . 1745': Rives Childs, J., *Casanova: a New Perspective*, p. 25.
'corroborative evidence': Ibid., pp. 23–6.
'Sharing her lot . . . silenced my heart': Casanova, *HL*, Bouquins, vol. 1, p. 85.
'Casanova . . . none of your business': Casanova, *HL*, Trask, vol. 2, pp. 46–7.

ACT II sc. iii: Constantinople

'Never in my life . . . my nature': Casanova, *HL*, Trask, vol. 2, pp. 94ff.
'garrison of 200 Slavonians': Ibid., p. 60.
'You communicated . . . fresh start': Ibid., p. 63.
'Earl Marischal Lord Keith': Ibid., pp. 100 and 314n.
'it sprawled up to thirty-five miles': Pitton de Tournefort, Joseph, *A Voyage into the Levant*, vol. 1, p. 348.
'its situation [being] most agreeable': Ibid., p. 348.
'The Seraglio' . . . gilt-roofed': Ibid., pp. 351 and 362.
'did not know the Koran': Casanova, *HL*, Trask, vol. 2, p. 70.
'I am a complete man . . . absolve us': Ibid., p. 84.
'was not of that persuasion': Ibid., p. 83.
'recent research on Ottoman': Ze'evi, Dror, *Producing Desire*; see chapter 'The view from without – Ottoman sexuality in Travel Accounts', pp. 149ff.
'most often gypsies': Pick, C. (ed.), *Embassy to Constantinople*, p. 115.

'entire liberty of following their inclinations': Ibid., p. 111

'You may easily imagine': Ibid., p. 111.

'One French writer': Pitton de Tournefort, Joseph, *A Voyage into the Levant*, vol. 2, pp. 47ff.

'Like him I found myself . . . in my nature': Casanova, *HL*, Trask, vol. 2 pp. 94ff.

'Wortley Montagu . . . Baron de Tott': Ze'evi, *Producing Desire*, pp. 153ff.

'25 November': Following his separate chronology for these years, J. Rives Childs dates Casanova's return to Venice as March 1746; Rives Childs, J., *Casanova*, p. 40

ACT II sc. iv: Palazzo Bragadin

'I felt ashamed . . . I let my ambition sleep': Casanova, *HL*, Trask, vol. 2, pp. 182–5.

'two musical comedies . . . by Bertoni': Weil, Taddeo, *Teatri Musicali Venezani dell Settecento*, Venice, 1897, in 1746.

'after the defrocking . . . respect for religion': ASV, Inquisitori di Stato, Manuzzi Gio Battista, busta 612, 22 March 1755 (trans: author's own with Dottore Maximilian Tedeschi).

'war memorial . . . Campo Sant'Angelo': This was a marble table, clearly seen in Bella's *Bear Baiting in the Campo Sant'Angelo*, c. 1780– so the tabletop was evidently repaired or restored. It no longer exists. Busetto, G., *Pietro Longhi Gabriel Bella, Scene di vita veneziana*, p. 204 and opposite.

'The close attachment . . . quite deliberately': Casanova, G., *Histoire de ma fuite*, (trans. author's own), p. 5.

'one Casanova scholar': Masters, John, *Casanova*, pp. 255ff

'the association with Bragadin . . . sold theirs': Ibid., p. 226.

'the affection and esteem of men of position': Casanova, *HL*, Trask, vol. 10. p. 119.

'Those he is acquainted . . . in every sense: '*che lui ha molte conoscenze co' forestieri e con il fior della gioventù che practica in case di moltissime figlie, maritate e signore e donne d'altro genere che lui procura divertirsi in ogni guisa*', ASV, Inquisitori di Stato, Manuzzi, Gio Battista, busta 612, 17 July 1755 (Author's italics.)

'[Casanova] is trying to elevate himself: Ibid.

'Calle Bernardo, *before* his "heart-attack" ': There are several Calles Bernardo in Venice, but the bridge Casanova mentions appears to be the one north of the Palazzo Soranzo. He may have misremembered, and even Venetians get lost in Venice. It is also possible at such a large gathering that gondolas were waiting all around the area in prearranged spots. I am indebted to John Masters for beginning to raise suspicions about Casanova's behaviour here, and to Max Tedeschi for an extensive tour of the back canals of San Polo.

'they were middle-aged': In 1746 Matteo Bragadin was fifty-seven, Marco Dandalo forty-two and Marco Barbaro fifty-eight.

'I took the most creditable . . . better than I': Casanova, *HL*, Trask, vol. 2, p. 199.

'the magnanimous Bragadin . . . did not live to see it so': Casanova, G., *Histoire de ma fuite*, (trans. author's own), p. 5.

'Bragadin was always giving me . . . money': Ibid., p. 6.

'though far from . . . Dr Gozzi's': Gozzi had left Padua for a rural parish near Chioggia, and his sister Bettina, whose marriage had failed, lived with him there.

'Under an obligation . . . numerous acquaintances': ASV, Inquisitori di Stato, Manuzzi, Gio Battista, busta 612, 22 March 1755.

'left Venice in January 1748': Casanova accounts this as 1748; J. Rives Childs is

convinced it must have been 1749. Rives Childs, J., *Casanova: a New Perspective*, pp. 42 and 294.
'no one paid any attention to me': Casanova, *HL*, Trask, vol. 2. p. 276.
'and you can believe him for he is my pimp': Ibid., pp. 276–7.
'well set up for for love . . . handsome': Ibid., p. 284ff.

ACT II sc. v: You Will Also Forget Henriette

'They who believe . . . extent of my happiness': Casanova, *HL*, Trask, vol. 3, pp 49–50.
'The ardour with which . . . in such a fashion': Ibid., p. 15.
'Not only do I feel . . . has no such power': Ibid., p. 35.
'elder by almost a decade': If Henriette was Jeanne-Marie d'Albert de St Hippolyte she was in her early thirties in 1749; Summers, Judith, *Casanova's Women*, pp. 161ff.
'Let me laugh . . . this instant': Casanova, *HL*, Trask, vol. 3, p. 36.
'Be sure that I love you . . . in a rage': Ibid., p. 37.
'I swore that I would never . . . won her heart': Ibid., p. 38.
'gloves, fans, earrings': Ibid., p. 49.
'The new Duke of Parma . . . his new subjects': Doran, John, *'Mann' and manners at the Court of Florence 1740–1786*, vol. 1, p. 293.
'for Henriette . . . was representing': Casanova, *HL*, Trask, vol. 3, p. 52.
'seemed always as if it were for the first time': Ibid., p. 53.
'Those who say that one can . . . end': Ibid., p. 59.
'It is I, my only love . . . Adieu': Ibid., p. 78.
'During the last . . . ever meet her [again]': Ibid., p. 76.
'When I consider . . . time I remember': Ibid., p. 77.

INTERMEZZO: Sex in the Eighteenth Century

'Madame, I am a libertine': Casanova, *HL*, Trask, vol. 10, p. 5.
'When it comes to vice': '*Sur la dissimulation . . . En qualité de vice la dissimulation doit être aussi ancienne que l'homme*', PSA, Marr U16k/59.
'For what it is worth . . . an entire lifetime': Byron to Count Giuseppino Albrizzi, 5 January 1819, 'and twice as many to boot' = 90 + 30, 'also 'around two hundred'; see MacCarthy, F., *Byron*, pp. 340ff; and Sainsbury, J., *John Wilkes*, pp. 81ff; Ober, W.B., *Boswell's Clap and Other Essays*, pp. 1–39 and pp. 40–2n.
'indefatigable Lord Lincoln': Henry Fiennes-Clinton, 1720–94, Earl of Lincoln, was said to have slept with hundreds of women throughout Europe. An Ode to his Grand Tour ran '*Four times each Night some amorous Fair/He swives throughout the circling year/This Course of Joy pursuing./Of Feats like these what Annals speak;/'Tis eight-and-twenty times a week,/And, faith, that's glorious doing.*' etc. Hanbury Williams, *Letters*, NRA 22338 Lewis Walpole Library, vol. 69, pp. 80–81.
'nice big omelette of infants': Padiyar, Satish, quoting Diderot in 1767, in Ozerkov, D., Padiyar, S., *et al.*, *The Triumph of Eros*, p. 21.
'From Casanova's point of view . . . come to higher: Private collection, Brockhaus (uncatalogued as of February 2006, intended for DCM [Marr], in possession of Leeflang, M.).

'an air of theatricality': Darnton, Robert, *The Forbidden Best-sellers of Pre-Revolutionary France*, pp. 72–3.

'render happiness . . . enveloped in a skin': Kihli-Sagols, Didier, *La Coméde médicale, de Giacono Casanova*, pp. 126ff.

'fatal plumpness': Ibid.

'English riding-coats . . . peace to one's heart': Ibid.

'I took from my wallet . . . unclear': A *pouce*, or thumb, is sometimes taken to mean a measure one-tenth longer than a modern imperial inch, so the condom in question measured about nine inches. See also Hunterian Institute Collection, Royal College of Surgeons, London.

'unfurled and inelastic . . . with abandon': Casanova, *HL*, Trask, vol. 7, pp. 12ff.

'the only preservative. . . [sword thus shielded]' Taylor, G. Rattray, *Sex in History*, p. 187.

'extraordinary fine thin substance': Mudge, Bradford K., (ed.), *When Flesh Becomes Word*, p. 264.

'of different sizes . . . met with': Ibid., p. 276.

'Unknown big belly . . . well made Cundum': Ibid., p. 318n.

'small golden ball . . . fell out of position': Kihli-Sagols, *La Comede médicole*, pp. 126ff.

'Why do you . . . Bellino was a girl?': De Ligne, *Fragment sur Casanova, suivi de lettres à Casanova*, p. 68.

ACT III sc. i: The Road to France

'Every young man . . . Freemasonry': Casanova, *HL*, Trask, vol. 3, p. 116.

'Next in Turin . . . I think of it': Ibid., p. 113.

ACT III sc. ii: Madame De Pompadour's Paris

'At the beginning of my stay': Casanova, *HL*, Trask, vol. 1, p. 119.

'Paris . . . influence of fashion': Ibid., p. 203.

'providing an education d'amour': Ozerkov, D., Padiyar, S., and Alexandrian, S., *The Triumph of Eros*, p. 35.

'but for Sylvia would never . . . balls': Casanova, *HL*, Trask, vol. 3, pp. 134–5.

'You are in France . . . make the most of it': Ibid., pp. 143–4.

'She has ugly legs . . . are her legs': Ibid., pp. 154–5.

'Jacobite Lord Keith': Ibid., p. 155, and n. NB Some of the evidence for Casanova's visit, or visits, to Turkey earlier in his life is his correct verification of Keith's presence there too, although, as has been noted, he may have discovered details about the east elsewhere, including with Keith in Paris in 1750.

'a perfect beauty . . . which beheld her': Ibid., p. 199.

'Pleasure is immediate . . . pleasures': Ibid., p. 195.

'She was adorable . . . in conversation': Ibid., p. 208.

'loving pleasure . . . on her lips': Ibid., p. 208.

'I was madly in love . . . beyond me': Ibid., p. 213.

'whenever she felt the need . . . benefit of the nation': Ibid., pp. 175–7.

'slashed it twenty times with his sword': Ibid., p. 215.

'They were the first oratorios performed': The *abbé*'s oratorios were not premièred until after Casanova's later visits to Paris, on 14 March 1758; Rives Childs, J., *Casanova: a New Perspective*, p. 49ff.

ACT III sc. iii: Lust in Cloisters

'I returned to Venice . . . entirely happy': Casanova, G. *Histoire de ma fuite*, p. 2.
'The day fades, dying of love': Anon. 'Abbé du Prat', attrib . . Jean Barrin or François
  de Cavigny de la Bretonnière, *Venus dans le Cloitre ou la Religieuse en Chemise*.
'Pietro Antonio Capretta': Rives Childs, J., *Casanova: a New Perspective*, p. 64.
'neither as honest man nor libertine': Casanova, *HL*, Trask, vol. III, pp. 243ff
'sick with love . . . could not continue': Ibid., p. 250.
'The more innocent . . . to possess her': Ibid., p. 257.
'dark circles . . . into a [woman]': Casanova, *HV*, Bouquins, vol. 1, p. 679.
'The letter was white . . . have business': Casanova, *HL*, Trask, vol. 4, pp. 11–12.
'an infidelity of a kind': Ibid., p. 19.
'six wide ribbons . . . deserved her mercy': Ibid., p. 44.
'New Year's Eve . . . chamber of love': Ibid., pp. 69–70.
'And de Bernis . . . dine at my house': de Bernis to Comtesse des Alleurs, Constantinople, 1 September 1754, in Monglond, A., *Revue d'Histoire Diplomatique*,
  1938, pp. 22–4.
'an adventure that he had with a nun': De Ligne, *Letters and Papers*, vol. 1, New York,
  1899, p. 146.
'played havoc with . . . we performed': Casanova, *HL*, Trask, vol. 4, p. 120.
'made a splendid present . . . for you': Ibid., p. 122.
'two notes found': PSA, U8 214.
'a man with a tendency . . . to cheat': ASV Appunti sul Manuzzi, Giovan Battista,
  1750–59, ASV Inquisitori di Stato referta del 22 marzo 1755, trans. author's own.
'He is a dandy . . . makes himself ridiculous': Abate Pietro Chiari's heroine in *La
  Commediante in Fortuna*, a novel on 'Casanova'; in Andrieux, Maurice, *Venise au
  temps de Casanova*, 1972, p. 218.

ACT III sc. iv: Prison and Escape

'a man shut up . . . to despair': Casanova, *HV*, Bouquins, vol. 1 (trans. author's own),
  p. 868.
'a question of religion': ASV Inquisitori di Stato, Casanova, G., *condamnate anni 5
  per co di religione* 1756, 29 settembre.

ACT III sc. v: Comédie Française

'I am going to respond . . . distress you': PSA, Balletti to Casanova, 1757, U8/139.
'I saw that to accomplish . . . chameleon': Casanova, *HL*, Trask, vol. 5, p. 19.
'[Casanova] has a carriage . . . he recounts admirably': Giustiniana Wynne to Andrea
  Memmo, in private collection, quoted from di Robillant, *Andrea, A Venetian
  Affair*, p. 169.
'medically inviolable at the time': Quite separately Casanova claimed that there was
  blood in his semen if he attempted more than five orgasms in one night. This was a
  widespread fear; see also *The Pleasures of Conjugal Love*, London, 1740, in *Venus
  Unmasked*, 1967, pp. 57ff.
'signing off with kisses': PSA, Manon to Casanova, 1757?, U8/158.
'oh how I wish this absence': PSA, Manon to Casanova in Amsterdam, 1760, U8/126.

'If only you knew . . . not succeed': PSA, U8/145.
'I enjoy myself . . . always of you': PSA, Manon to Casanova, U8/139.
'Always love me . . . Burn all our letters': PSA, U8 139 and U8/161.
'Your love has lessened . . . one discovers them': PSA U8/150.
'Falling in love with Manon . . . I was aiming': Casanova, HL, Trask, vol. 4, p. 83.
'You go and enjoy yourself . . . dinner à deux': PSA, Marr, U8/128.
'cher mari': PSA, Marr, 'adieu cher mari', U8/127.
'surrendering now to love . . . both at once': Casanova, HL, Trask, vol. 4, p. 99.
'with all the grace . . . of the Regency': Ibid., p. 108.

ACT III sc. vi: The Marquise d'Urfé

'The Marquise . . . an immortal being': Souvenirs de la Marquise Créquy, vol. 3, chapter 1.
'a genuine adept under the mask': Casanova, HV, Bouquins, vol. II, p. 95.
'virgin comtesse . . . thirteenth birthday': Ibid., pp. 731–2.
'at the age of thirty-eight . . . fatal misfortune': Ibid., p. 42.
'write to Teresa Imer in London': DCM, Marr, 40/130.

Intermezzo: Casanova and Cabbala

'Those who possess this . . . down': PSA, U22.1s 41.
'The doctrines of mathematics . . . in vain': Agrippa, Henry Cornelius, of Nettesheim, Three Books of Occult Philosophy, London, 1651, p. 167.
'top spies on his tail': ASV, Appunti sul Giovan' Battista Mannuzzi 1750–59, busta 612–4, especially 612, 17 July 1755.
'dating to Abraham': According to tradition, 'Melchizedek, the King of Righteousness and of Salem . . . initiated Abraham into the knowledge of the esoteric Teaching, which concerns man, the universe and God': Halevi, Z'ev ben Shimon, Kabbalah, 1978, p. 32.
'Casanova had read this': Casanova, HL, Trask, vols 1–2, p. 320, n. 18.
'and as Casanova drew out': PSA, U20/5c.
'trésor cabalistique': PSA, U33/a.
'drew out in old age': PSA, U20/5a.b.c.d.
'the famous Kircher Tree': The Kircher Tree in Athanasius Kircher, 1652 depiction of the Tree of Life, is based on a 1625 version by Philippe d'Aquin. This is still the most common arrangement of the Tree in Hermetic Cabbala.
'the ultimate sacrament is the sexual act': Waite, A.E., The Holy Kabbalah, p. ix.
'out of Venice in the sixteenth and seventeenth centuries': Leo the Hebrew, published in Rome, 1535, and reprinted in Venice, 1541; trans. into Latin and printed 1564, Vienna, and as Artis Cabalisticae Scriptores, Basle, 1587; see ibid., pp. 428ff
'such copulative felicity . . . fragile body': Leo the Hebrew, see ibid., p. 431.
'The creation of Golem . . . Book of Genesis': Scholem, G., Major Trends in Jewish Mysticism, p. 99.
'Paradise means . . Persian': PSA, U16/i16 1786/1787.
'dream-notes featuring cavorting sex organs': PSA, U1.
'It may be an anagram of genitale . . . plays on paracelsus': I am indebted for this theory to the work of the Russo-Italian Casanoviste Mario Corti, Russkii Telegraf, Moscow, 16 March 1998.

'turned again to the joys of pure maths': PSA, U16 K/11, U33 1 varia, U20/2, U20/5, U31/15, U33/, U20/5.a.b.c.d.

'I am infinitely happy': Casanova, *HL*, Trask, vol. 2 pp. 14–15.

'cabbala's *Book of Zohar*': See Waite, A.E., *The Holy Kabbalah*, pp. 428ff.

ACT IV sc. i: Conversations with Voltaire

'On Thursday 7 September . . . asked': A parcel marked ESBZ (Emmanuel Symons Benjamin Zoon), *Amsterdamse Courant*, Saturday, 16 September 1758, in the Stadsarchief, Amsterdam: I am indebted here to the 2007 archival researches of Marco Leeflang.

'Casanova estimated he had been a millionaire': Rives Childs, J., *Casanova: a New Perspective*, p. 99.

'My research, my travels . . . 50% reduction': ASV, Inquisitori di Stato, Casanova, Giacomo, busta 565 1, London, June 1763 (trans. author's own with Dottore Maximilian Tedeschi).

'he appeared most indiscreet': Baschet, A. *Archives des affaires etrangères, serie Holland*, 1759, p. 22.

'You wish me to speak . . . I trust you': Letter sold at auction in Paris at Maison Drouot 12 October 1999. Quoted with permission of current owner, wishing to remain anonymous, in di Robillant, Andrea, *A Venetian Affair*, p. 185.

'like a surgeon . . . blew out the candle': Casanova, *HL*, Trask, vol. 5, p. 206.

'I cannot remember . . . about so much': Anonymous letter to Andrea Memmo, 10 July 1759, James Rives Childs Collection, quoted in di Robillant, *A Venetian Affair*, pp. 195 and 297n.

'27 May 1759 . . . abbess of Conflans': Alexandre Fortier, notaire au coin de la rue de Richelieu et de la rue Neuve des Petits Champs, Archives Nationales, Minutier Centrale, Étude XXXI, quoted in Marr, Bernhard, *Pour le Dossier de Miss XCV*, (DCM) p. 24.

'princess': Casanova, *HL*, Trask, vol. 5, p. 215.

'Venetian Pope': Ibid., p. 221. Carlo Rezzonico, whose palace in Venice is now the city's museum of the eighteenth century, was elected pope as Clement XIII in 1758. He died in 1796. De Bernis was made a cardinal in 1758, and exiled from France the same year. He remained French ambassador in Rome from 1769 to 1791.

'People paid him . . . made his living': Ibid., p. 223.

'not a man at that time': PSA, 'Sur Voltaire', U31/37.

'Honour me with another twenty': Casanova, *HL*, Trask, vol. 6, p. 225.

'at least as far as salon wit was concerned': Letter from Voltaire, July 1760; see Ibid., p. 311, n. 39.

'you should . . . humanity as it is': Rives Childs, J., *Casanova: a New Perspective*, pp 124ff.

'encounter with Voltaire . . . his most famous': Zottoli on Voltaire, and Maynial on Voltaire and Casanova, in ibid., p. 127.

'what horrified me was that I did not have the same vigour': Casanova, *HL*, Trask, vol. 6, p. 220.

'as further evidenced by two notarial acts': I am indebted to the renowned Casanoviste Marco Leeflang for his research in the Amsterdam archives and for the reference to the *Amsterdamse Courant* of 16 September 1758 and notarial acts.

'anagram of "genitales" ': See Intermezzo on cabbala p. 219.

'the majority [of Venetians] . . . foreign orders': Rose, Aldo (ed.), *Letters from the North of Italy*, vol 2. p. 113 and n.

'read or so much as touch . . . Dutch officers': Rives Childs, J., *Casanova*, pp. 111 ff.

'We have here in Berne . . . dressed or equipped': Ibid., p. 120.

ACT IV sc. ii: Chevalier de Seingalt

'I think nothing of those who attach importance . . . sell them': de Ligne, Charles, *Lettres et Pensées du Maréchal Prince de Ligne*, p. 287.

'arriving in Antibes . . . keep quiet': Piazza, Antonio on Luigi Gritti, in *Gazetta Urbana Veneta*, 31 May 1788.

'The most honest man of my acquaintance': Casanova, *HV*, Dux facs., vol. 8, p. 002486.

ACT IV sc. iii: London

'A Single Lady . . . Pall Mall': *Gazetteer and London Daily Advertiser*, 5 July 1763, no. 10,705, p. 2; BML MSS, Burney, 519b.

'they all think they are superior': Casanova, *HL*, Trask, vol. 9, p. 161.

'one letter from London dated 1763': 'My research, my travels, my studies have allowed me to be a master of the secret [silk dyeing] which I am offering to my country. I can offer the dye for real cotton more beautiful than that of the orient and which I can sell at 50% reduction . . .' ASV Inquisitori di Stato, Casanova, Giacomo, busta 565 1, London, June 1763 (trans. author's own with Dottove. Maximilian Tedeschi).

'I give twelve suppers . . . every year': Bleakley, Horace., *Casanova in England*, p. 30.

'London Public Advertiser': BM, Add, Man. N. R. Burney, 5465–18632, *Public Advertiser (London)*, 1728–1794, 18 May and 1 December, 1763.

'The expense is enormous': Casanova, *HL*, Trask, vol. 9, p. 171.

'Lord Fermor': Casanova seems to have conflated dates and figures and may have been alluding to Teresa's former lover, John Fermor; see Summers, J., *Empress of Pleasure*, pp. 76ff.

'An allegory she had not understood': PSA, U4/83, 16 fevrier 1764.

'of the highest nobility . . . claiming acquaintance': Casanova, *HL*, Trask, vol. 9, p. 191.

'Garrick sisters': No relation to the famous actor, but both mentioned in 'The Meritriciade', 1761, and 'The Courtesan', 1765 – lists of contemporary courtesans.

'the moon indeed was full': Bleakley, *Casanova in England*, p. 99.

'her mother, grandmother . . . father': PSA, Charpillon to Casanova, U8/55, and Casanova U16i/8, 1763.

'more than four thousand French livres': PSA, U16 i/8, 1763.

'notes in mispelled French': PSA, U8/210.

'in the Tudor maze': Casanova, *HL*, Trask, vol. 9, p. 311.

'everything made him sure that she was to be': Ibid., p. 312.

'the beast with two backs': Ibid., p. 313 – *Othello*, Act 1 sc i.

'I have too much respect . . . frightful crime': PSA, U16 i/8, Casanova, 1763, Londres.

'great treatment': Casanova, *HL*, Trask, vol. 10, p. 21.

'Having proposed to write . . . the least understood': Wilkes, J., *An Essay on Woman*, p. 5.

ACT IV sc. iv: Frederick the Great

'Diminishing their ages . . . are old': Casanova, *HL*, Trask, vol. 10, p. 74.

'which must have been awkward': Ibid., p. 79.

'who had astonished Europe . . . not be opposed': James Boswell, quoted in MacDonogh, Giles, *Frederick the Great*, p. 331.

'hydraulician': Casanova, *HL*, Trask, vol. 10, p. 69.

'I consider it a swindle . . . fallacious confidence': Ibid., pp. 69–70.

'unnatural tastes': Fraser, David, *Frederick the Great, King of Prussia*, p. 41.

'[we] dined at Rufin's . . . and of everything else': James Boswell, *Travels*, 1 September 1764, in Pottle, F., and Brady, F., *Boswell on the Grand Tour*, p. 76.

'and a score of books on mathematics': Casanova, *HL*, Trask, vol. 10, p. 80.

ACT IV sc. v: St Petersburg

'Of course one thing . . . you might': '*Un tiens vaut toujours mieux que deux tu auras*', Catherine the Great, *Le Tracassier*, 1768

'In Russia only men . . . this is right': Casanova, *HL*, Trask, vol. 10, p. 138.

'several months before': Ibid., p. 345n.

'Empress and Autocratrix etc': Macartney, George, Earl, *An Account of Russia addressed to the King*, p. 87.

'28 Millionnaya': The numbering system is thought to have changed; '28' appears to be a St Petersburg tradition. Casanova only wrote that he had lodgings 'opposite' the new 'temple' being built on Morskaya. Casanova, *HL*, Trask, vol. 10, p. 131. In the 1740s the street received its present name after the nickname given to the palace of Prince A.M. Cherkassky (building 19), which since 1743 came to be known as the Sheremetiev's Million House, hence the Million Street, where the Million House stood.

'known to everyone . . . with difficulty': Ibid., p. 101.

'half-million Russian aristocrats': Macartney's estimates are based on what he was told in Russia, and on this, as on almost everything he says, he may be in error beyond his immediate experience of St Petersburg and Moscow. Macartney, George, Earl *An Account of Russia addressed to the King*, p. 8.

'a city built . . . in haste': Casanova, *HL*, Trask, vol. 10, p. 126.

'fish factories and rhubarb': Rhubarb was a major export, worth 21,000 roubles in 1763, as was fish-produced isinglass, used in most eighteenth-century dessert recipes, and the sixth largest single item on St Petersburg's exports to Britain: Appendix to Note C to page 227, D'Arcy Collyer, Adelaide A (ed.), *The Despatches of John, Second Earl of Buckinghamshire, Russia 1762–1765*, pp. 255–6.

'a handsome young man . . . the English impertinence': Casanova, *HL*, Trask, vol. 10, p. 107.

'Locatelli's . . . for a rouble a head, without wine': Ibid., p. 108.

'British envoy Macartney': Robins, E., *Our First Ambassador in China*, London, p. 21.

'She once courted . . . whilst dressed as a man': Princess Dolgorukiy, Келлер Е.Э. Праздничная культура Петербурга: Очерки истории. СПб., 2001, pp. 90–94, 126–7.

'upon which there were . . . hot meats': Ibid.

'bestrewn with diamonds . . . several rows': Pylyaev, M., *Staryi Petrburg*, Moscow, 1991, trans. Irina Kutova, p. 194.

'I am convinced of it . . . recognise her': Casanova, *HL*, Trask, vol. 10, p. 101.

'not worth ten kopecks': Ibid., p. 101.

'In Celebration of Minerva': Moscow, Bakhrushkin archive, 1763 court masquerade, written in honour of Catherine II by Feodor Volkov.

'beergardens at Krasni-Kabak': A tavern located on the seventh *verst* of Petergofskaya Road. Named after Krasnenkaya Road, it was located at the building constructed for Tsar Peter I in the early eighteenth century as a rest stop on his way to Peterhof. It was arranged 'according to the model of German public houses, and to sell vodka and tobacco there'. Пыляев М. И. Забытое прошлое окрестностей Петербурга. СПб., 1996. С. 115–19.

'ill temper, tears and fits': Casanova, *HL*. Trask, vol. 10, p. 118.

'buggers . . . whore': Casanova writes 'b . . .' for *bougres* and 'p . . .' for *putain*.

'sins against nature': Casanova, *HL*, Trask, vol. 10, p. 120.

'500 Italian miles': An eighteenth-century Italian mile was 1.86 kilometres

'He was there as a tourist . . . famous [Kremlin] bell': Casanova, *HL*, Trask, vol. 10, p. 130.

'particularly in the evening . . . midnight': Matveeva, Andreja Zapiski, *Russkij diplomat vo Francii*, p. 67–8.

'especially to Voltaire': Pylyaev, M., *Staryi Petrburg*, Moscow, 1991, p. 190.

'music produced the same impression . . . noise': Ibid., pp. 190–91.

'Reveries sur la mesure moyenne . . . Gregorienne': Owned still by Brockhaus and unpublished.

'just a few years before he died': PSA, U9/63.

'This great lady . . . from moderation': Casanova, *HL*, Trask, vol. 10, p. 149.

'I wish to enter into a liaison . . . for you': Ibid., p. 150.

ACT IV sc. vi: Polish Duels

'My Lord . . . will satisfy you': Casanova, *HV*, Dux facs. vol. 10 p. 002953.

'It is pleasant for a Venetian . . . butterfly': Rives Childs, J., *Casanova: a New Perspective*, p. 212.

'Countess Catherine . . . Christianpol': Rives-Childs, J., *Casanova Gleanings*, vol. VIII, pp. 16–21.

'*History of the Polish Troubles*': Casanova, G., *Istoria delle turbolenze della Polonia*.

'I read . . . system of Poland': Casanova, *HL*, Trask, vol. 10, p. 164.

'Venetian poltroon': Giacomo, *The Duel*, trans., Parks, Tim, (from the Italian, *Il duello*, 1780) Hesperus, London, 2003 p. 10

'as far away as London': *London Public Advertiser*, 3 September 1766.

'For M. Casanova . . . Moszysnki': PSA, U 11/C5.

'having received . . . 1766': DCM, Marr, 40–12.

'a man known . . . knowledge': Lamberg, Maximilian, *Memorial d'un mondain*, p. 4.

'It is a pity . . . state of a worm': Massi, E., *La vita, i temps, gli amici di Francesco Albergati*, p. 197.

Intermezzo: Casanova – Food-Writer

'He carries three . . . desires': ASV, Inquisitori di Stato, Manuzzi, Gio Battista, busta 612, 21 July 1755 (trans. author's own, with Dottore Maximilian Tedeschi).

'I am insatiable . . . intolerable': Casanova, *HL*, Trask, vol. 3, p. 134.

'these are the biscuits . . . lot of sugar . . .': PSA, U16k/18.

'For men . . . unique experience': '*En mangeant les differens ragoûts il [l'homme] a toujours senti un plaisir différent. Il en est de même dans la jouissance amoureuse. Chaque femme est un ragoût different de l'autre. Le fait est la même mais on ne lo voit bien qu'après . . .*' PSA, U16k/63.

'The sense of smell . . . of Venus': Casanova, *HL*, Trask, vol. 3, p. 114.

'a roast hare . . . finger food': lepre arrosto, PSA, U16/k2.

'cinnamon and sugar': Krondl, Michael, *The Taste of Conquest; the Rise and Fall of Three Great Cities of Spice*, p. 32.

'ratafia . . . and kirsch': Casanova, *HL*, Trask vol. 3, p. 128.

'notes the cane chairs': Ibid., p. 127.

'Everything is delicious . . . imagined': Ibid., vol. 11, p. 284.

'I have always found . . . become visible': Wilson, Frances (ed.), *Adventures of Casanova*, p. xiii.

'I commented to her . . . rum not arrack': Casanova, *HL*, Trask, vol. 4, p. 60.

'a cup of chocolate . . . vinegar': Ibid., p. 66.

'There is no more lascivious . . . does no harm': Ibid., p. 68.

'the cook . . . Franciade': *À Leonard Snetlage*, pp. 82–3.

'medical prescriptions . . . tooth-whitening': PSA U16d/2a.b. [recettes].

ACT V sc i: Il Traviato

'These are the handsomest . . . precious': Casanova, *HV*, Dux facs., vol, 11, p. 003312.

'in the Prague Archive': due to be published or the first time in the original language in 2008, edited by Marie-Françoise Luna.

'inn on the rue Quatre Dauphins': Casanova says the Three Dolphins Inn, but Shakespeare, among others, makes the same slip. The road is now the rue du Quatre Settembre.

'I constantly thought . . . wanted of me': Casanova, *HV*, Dux facs., vol 11, p. 003301.

'Nothing my dear . . . Farewell': Casanova, *HV*, Dux facs., vol. 11, pp. 003306ff.

'twenty-two years': twenty years; Henriette was in error, and the letter appears not to have been corrected by Casanova.

'where there was a good press': Casanova, *HL*, Trask, vol. 11, p. 184.

'My purpose in printing . . . anywhere else': Casanova, *HV*, Dux facs., vol. 11, p. 003332.

'He sent a copy to Venice in December 1769': ASV, ma opera '*Confutazione d'amelot*' lett. Torino, 1769 27 genio 171

'We described in the last *Gazzetta* . . . himself': Rives Childs, J., *Casanova: a New Perspective*, p. 242.

ACT V sc. ii: Papal Knight and Oyster-Eater

'I said I should be . . . not forbid it?' Casanova, *HV*, Dux facs., vol. 12, pp. 003506–7.

'who supported himself . . . gambling': Casanova, *HL*, Trask vol. 11, p. 263.

'twenty Neapolitan ducati or 80 French francs': Ibid., p. 274.

'We went down to a grotto . . . tormented by remorse': Casanova, *HV*, Dux facs., vol. 11, pp. 003435ff.

'in a pretty apartment . . . Spanish embassy': Ibid., vol 12, p. 003453.

'Loving both . . . Antinous, procured me': Casanova, *HL*, Trask, vol. 12, pp 19–20.

'brushed up . . . between Colonna's pillars': Black, Jeremy, *The Grand Tour in the Eighteenth Century*, p. 211.

'greatly applauded': Rives Childs, J., *Casanova: a New Perspective*, p. 254.

'in quiet tranquillity . . . a dignified retirement': Casanova, *HV*, Dux facs., vol. 12, p. 003453.

'He is a man . . . witty and learned': ASV, *Relazion del Segretario* busta 208, 1715–1782.

ACT V sc. iii: Venice Revisited

'Casanova? . . . he tells extraordinary tales': Portrait de Casanova, 1788, in Kihli-Sagols, Didier, *La Comédie médicale de Giacomo Casanova*, p. 7.

'an untidily written side . . . an actress in Trieste': Casanova, *HV*, Dux facs., vol. 12, p. 003670.

'beyond his return . . . in 1774': The Brockhaus original, however, has clearly written on the first page 'Histoire de ma vie . . . à 1797'. Ibid., vol. 1, p. 000001.

'The happiest day of my life': PSA U21/1 Casanova to Cecile Roggendorff, 1797.

'under the name Antonio Pratolini': ASV, Busta Pratolini, 1775.

'She wrote to him for seven years': PSA, U8, Bruschini letters, 1779–87.

'This singular man . . . in the wrong': 'Da Ponte memoirs, quoted in Rives Childs, J. *Casanova: a New Perspective*, p. 283.

ACT V sc. iv: Don Giovanni

'It was not until October . . . happy resolution': Plath, Wolfgang, and Rehm, Wolfgang, *Il dissoluto punito ossia it Don Giovanni*, Preface, p. i.

'His involvement with Don Giovanni': PSA, U16h/31.

'a story told by a Prague musician': See Meissner, A., quoting his grandfather, G. A. Meissner (1753–1807), in *Rococobilder*, p. xxx.

'It was given nightly . . . roast in hell' Ginger, A., Hobbs, J., and Lewis, H. (eds), *Representation of the Don Juan*, p. 61.

'There are two variants of Act II . . . longer draft': PSA, U16H/31.

ACT V sc. v: The Castle at Dux

'There is another . . . half mad': DCM, Marr, 2 juillet 1787, U 40–131.

'and most of those I would fling on the fire': DCM, Franz Adam Waldstein, Marr, 40/137.

'140 servants': Ruso, Alexandra, and Jancarel, Petr, *Dux 1240–1990* (English summary), Teplice, 1990, p. 10.

'Viderol could not read': PSA, U39–1.

'real eccentrics': DCM, Marr, 40–131.

'There was a Jewish equerry . . . country you were in': DCM, Marr, 40–131.

'put your wig on . . . rejoice to see you': PSA, U2–103.

'*Mon cher* Casanova . . . at the prospect': PSA, U2/103.

'fell into each other's arms . . . going to the devil': De Ligne, *Fragment sur Casanova, suivi de Lettres à Casanova*, p. 52.

'A day did not go by . . . scum': Ibid., pp. 71ff.

'wrote an extensive journal': Clary-Aldringen, Prince Charles Joseph (Lolo), *Le Journal*, 1795–8.

'old times and their souls': DCM, *Nouvelles Annales Prince de Ligne*, pp. 133ff.

'reminiscences of past times': Clary, vendredi, 31 juillet 1795, p. 43.

'how short they are': De Ligne, Fragments 1, 15, quoted in Mansell, Philip, *Prince of Europe*, pp. 196–7.

'feeble . . . enjoyment in pleasures': PSA, U31/35.

'1703 letters . . . over 3000 manuscript pages': DCM, Leeflang, M. *Dux Ionnaire*, vol. 1, 2005, p. 108.

'soothing his vanity . . . extraordinary a house-guest': Lolo Clary, 1795, DCM, Leeflang, M., *Dossier de Dux*, p. 6.

'the zeal with all my heart': DCM, Leeflang, M., *Les Archives de Dux*, Marr, 14M36 and note.

'obstinate illness . . . extremely worried': PSA, U8/67.

'I have lived as a philosopher . . . die as a Christian.' Neyremand, M., *Séjour en Alsace de quelques hommes célèbres*, p. 96.

'Always an excellent . . . his memoirs': '*Toujours excellent médecine de soi-même, il cherche une thérapie contre ces maladies et a notre grand plaisir il la trouve dans l'écriture de ses mémoires*', Watzlawick, Helmut, in Olschki, *tra Venezia e l'Europe*, 1999, p. 343.

Curtain Call: The History of The History of My Life

p. 'Casanova's nephew . . . burial': DCM, Marr, 40/22.

p. 'still to this day being catalogued': The last of the Casanova/Feldkircher letters, catalogued by Marco Leeflang for DCM, 2007.

p. 'very famous': Endore, Guy L., *Casanova, His Known and Unknown Life*, p. xii.

p. 'The Prince de Ligne': Ibid., p. xvii.

p. 'Winston Churchill': Rives Childs, J., *Casanova Gleanings*, vol. XIX, p. 5.

p. '*TLS . . . Observer*': Ibid., vol. VI, p. 42.

p. 'gone to the devil': De Ligne, *Fragment sur Casanova, suivi des Lettres à Casanova*, p. 52.

PICTURE
ACKNOWLEDGEMENTS

Plate sections: pages 1–16

Art Archive: 7 above (Correr Museum, Venice). Bridgeman Art Library: 2-3 (Louvre, Paris), 4 above (Fondazione Querini Stampalia, Venice), 4 centre and below (Ca' Rezzonico – Museo del Settecento, Venice), 7 below (National Gallery of Scotland, Edinburgh), 10 above (Wallraf-Richartz-Museum, Cologne), 10 below (Private Collection), 12 below (Museum of London), 13 above (Musée du Grand Orient de France), 13 below (Private Collection), 14 above (State Russian Museum, St Petersburg), 14 below (Hermitage, St Petersburg). Correr Museum, Venice: 5, 6 below. Duchcov Museum Archive, Czech Republic: 15 below. Getty Images: 15 above (Roger-Viollet). Historical Museum, Moscow: 1. Hunterian Museum at The Royal College of Surgeons of England: 11 below. Lebrecht Music and Arts: 8 (Leemage), 11 above (Interfoto). © National Gallery London: 9. State Regional Archive, Prague (photo: © M. Klimeš): 6 above, 12 above, 16.

Illustrations for chapter openers taken from: Vittoria, Eugenio, *Il Gondoliere e la sua gondola* (Venice: Editrice EVI, 1979) and Thrupp, George A, *History of Coachbuilding* (London, 1877), with the exception of page 274: Bridgeman Art Library

INDEX